QuarkXPress
Tips&Tricks

QuarkXPress
Tips
&
Tricks

Industrial-Strength Techniques

Second Edition

By
David Blatner
Phillip Gaskill
Eric Taub

Edited by
Stephen F. Roth

An Open House Book   **Peachpit Press**

QUARKXPRESS TIPS AND TRICKS, 2ND EDITION

By David Blatner, Phillip Gaskill, and Eric Taub
Edited by Stephen F. Roth

PEACHPIT PRESS

2414 Sixth Street
Berkeley, CA 94710
510/548-4393
510/548-5991 (fax)

Copyright ©1994 by David Blatner, Phillip Gaskill, and Eric Taub
Editor: Stephen F. Roth
Cover design: Lee Sylvester/Art Direction
Cover photograph: © Luis Veiga/ImageBank
Interior design and production: Glenn Fleishman
CD-ROM design: David Blatner
CD-ROM source art: Clement Mok Studio's CMCD series

ISBN 1-56609-137-3

9 8 7 6 5 4 3 2 1

 Printed on Recycled Paper

Printed and bound in the United States of America

table TOC OF CONTENTS

CHAPTER 1

QuarkXPress Basics

CHAPTER 2

Document Construction

CHAPTER 3

Word Processing

CHAPTER 4

Type & Typography

Pictures

CHAPTER 7

Color

CHAPTER 8

Printing

CHAPTER 9

Problems and Solutions

CHAPTER 10

Macros and Scripts

CHAPTER 11

XTensions

CHAPTER 12

Version 3.0/1 and System 6

CHAPTER 13

Windows and QuarkXPress

APPENDIX A

XPress Tags

APPENDIX B

Resources

note

A Word to Windows Users

One of the coolest "features" of QuarkXPress for Windows is that it's so similar to its Macintosh counterpart. So, while the tips in this book are clearly focused on the Macintosh version of Quark-XPress, almost every technique detailed here is identical in XPress for Windows. You can just use them right out of the box. Also, check out Chapter 13, *Windows and QuarkXPress*, in which we discuss working in a mixed-platform environment.

Of course, the keystrokes for the Windows version of XPress are different from the Mac keystrokes (the Command key often translates to the Control key; Option often translates to Alt), but the underlying concepts and tricks are mostly identical. You'll find a tear-out chart of all the Windows keyboard shortcuts for XPress in a book David co-authored with Bob Weibel: *The QuarkXPress Book* (Second Edition for Windows).

preface

"Quark? What kind of program is that?"

Eight years ago, we weren't the only ones asking this question. We each read (on our respective sides of the United States) about a new desktop-publishing program with a funny name that could actually wrap text around pictures. Too cool for words, we thought, as we pestered our bosses to get us copies of it. Little did we know at the time that we were beginning a love/hate relationship that would, at times, dominate our every waking moment.

Many of those waking moments (and some dreaming ones, come to think of it) were spent trying to figure out ways to get this beast to do things faster, better, easier. In those bygone days, our objective was usually to persuade QuarkXPress to perform tricks that it would have just as soon not performed. Remember parent-child boxes? Remember not being able to move stuff from box to box, let alone page to page?

No, there was none of this easy click and drag from page to page for us budding *Quarkistas.* No sir! No ma'am! If we had to move things, we deleted them on the first page, and did them all over from scratch on the second. We didn't need no stinking shortcuts. And we *liked* it!

Why We Wrote This Book

Several years ago, David wrote a book called *The QuarkXPress Book* (actually, he also got help from Eric Taub, who—for some reason—didn't get cover credit). The comments he got back about that book have been flattering (to say the least), but the one thing he kept hearing from readers was that they wanted even more tips like the ones in the book. So, after all those years of using XPress, and talking to other people who've had similar experiences, we put together a collection of the best tips, tricks, and industrial-strength techniques for getting exactly what we want out of the program.

We began by including almost all the tips from *The QuarkXPress Book, Fourth Edition for Macintosh.* They're among the best tips we know, and we wouldn't want to force purchasers of this book to also run out and get *The QuarkXPress Book* for more tips. (On the other hand, we think that it's a great book, and complements this book well).

Then we scoured the online services, attended meetings and conferences, and talked to scores of real-world QuarkXPress users, culling the best tips we could find from the general boasting and complaining that QuarkXPress users sometimes seem prone to.

The result of our labors is that much more than half of these tips are new, never before seen in print. Our goal was to include tips that will be of use to everyone from first-timers putting out a four-page newsletter on their LaserWriters to old pros tossing off six-color, 300-lpi jobs on Heidelbergs. Everyone—even an old pro—can learn new tricks, and if these tricks make your life just one tad bit easier or speed up the production of your work, then we can sleep better knowing that we've done our job.

How the Book Is Organized

If you're familiar with *The QuarkXPress Book,* you're already familiar with the basic chapter layout of this book, too. We start by looking at the basic structure and interface of the program—QuarkXPress Basics, then move along to Document Layout, Word Processing, Type and Typography, and then Copy Flow (that somewhat arcane and certainly confusing business of getting text in and out of QuarkXPress with formatting and styles intact). Moving right along, we enter the realm of Pictures—including the curious world of text wrap—Color, Printing, and Problems and Solutions (of course, we can't imagine anyone ever running into *problems* while using XPress!). Next we take a look at Macros and Scripts—the clever user's way to make a great program even greater—and an in-depth discussion of some of our favorite XTensions. Finally, if you use either XPress for Windows or an older version of the program, we haven't left you out: the last two chapters cover those issues. Two appendices give a comprehensive listing of XPress Tags and software, hardware, and other resources.

We don't believe in idle chitchat, so we've kept the chapters lean and mean. Just the tips, ma'am nothing but the tips. (OK, the truth is we *love* idle chitchat, but we've saved it all for this preface. The rest of the book is dead serious. Well, mostly serious.)

How to Read This Book

As you've no doubt noticed, this book is enormous. It's filled with so much information that it's overwhelming to many folks. But before you get into a tizzy, remember that there are three great ways to find the tips you need. David's favorite way to read it is to put it in the bathroom (or any other room you sit around in occasionally), pick it up every now and again, and read a few tips out of it. Phil typically uses the index to find all the tips on a particular subject. Eric, however, likes the table of contents: he usually knows what tip he's looking for, and he knows what chapter it's in.

Acknowledgments

Before we jump into the tips, we'd like to roll the credits and thank the people without whom this book would be dog meat.

First we must thank the folks at Quark who created and support that program we've come to know and love: Tim Gill, Fred Ebrahimi, Kristen Kollath-Harris, Mark Niemann-Ross, Alf Kober, Peter Warren, Margie Levinson, and Paul Tower, among others (*many* others).

Next we must thank the QuarkXPress users we've been in contact with directly or indirectly. These folks have given an enormous amount of their time to helping others get the most out of their QuarkXPress systems, often while on electronic bulletin board systems such as CompuServe and America Online. A necessarily abbreviated list includes Mike Arst, Sal Soghoian (who also wrote many of the tips in the XTensions chapter), Dave Shaver, Ralph Risch, Ole Kvern, Carlos Sosa, Shane Stanley, Chris Ryland, Greg Swann, Kathleen Tinkel, and the inestimable Brad Walrod.

Also, a big thanks to the folks at the XChange, especially William "Buck" Buckingham, Jim Wiegand, and Robin Riley. If you have questions about XTensions, don't call us; call them!

Steve Roth, our incredible editor, and Open House's managing editor, Glenn "POPCO" Fleishman, made this book as good as it is. Thank you both.

And now a few words from us, individually.

Phil: "Thanks to all the Steves (Jobs, Wozniak, Roth, Broback), all the Gills (Eric, Tim), and all the Jeffs (Cheney, Harmon), for their various contributions to my life and therefore to the contents of this book. To Ole Kvern, the Grand Poobah of Thunderlizardry, who taught me most (if not all) of what I know. To David, of course, for asking me to co-author this book with him, and for all his encouragement. And to Ange, for putting up with my vicissitudes and vagaries while I tried to be an author in my spare time — and for helping test some of the tips and tricks that are in this book."

Eric: "I'd like to thank our editor, Steve Roth, who 'discovered' me back in his days as editor of *Personal Publishing*. My family, for putting up with my ridiculous schedule while working on this book. Tim Gill, for answering the phone, and giving us this fun toy to play with. David Biedny, for setting a good example (and where's that book you owe me?). Dan Brogan, for *still* answering the phone. From America Online, Mike Fischer for keeping the DTP forum moving along, Bob Martin for his ubiquitous comments, Gene Steinberg, and all the other AOL tin gods. And, of course, the Japanese company that makes coffee-in-a-can, without which I'd never have gotten this finished."

David: "A grand round of appreciative applause to Barbara Blatner, Richard Fikes, and Fay Fisher, who have not only helped to provide me with Macintosh computers over the past seven years, but also refrained from calling me crazy when I said I was going to write computer books. Also, my thanks to Adam, Allee, and Alisa Blatner, for their enduring support from afar.

"Thanks to Debbie Carlson, Mike McKay, Doug Peltonen, Greg Vander Houwen, Ole Kvern, Steve Broback, Bill Woodruff, Jeff McCord, Gary Marshall, for their support, technical expertise, and friendship."

David Blatner
Phil Gaskill
Eric Taub

quarkxpress
BASICS

Don't be fooled by the title of this chapter: QuarkXPress Basics doesn't just mean basic tips. It means power tips and techniques that relate to the very core of this program. We know people who've used XPress for years and who consider themselves power users who have found plenty of useful tips in here. From using the tools to customizing XPress to the way you work, there's a tip in here for everyone.

INSTALLATION
Installing with an Upgrader

Installing QuarkXPress 3.3 is done with one of three tools, depending on whether you're buying a new, shrinkwrapped copy or already own a version of XPress. There's an installer, an upgrader, and an updater.

▶ The 3.3 installer is a full set of installation disks that you get when you buy a new copy of the program.

▶ The 3.3 upgrader—also a whole set of disks—is shipped directly from Quark to people who purchase upgrades from versions 3.0 or 3.1.

Can't Update EfiColor

When you update your version of XPress to 3.3 (or perhaps you already did), you may find that the EfiColor XTension won't update properly. When you run the XTension updater program, XPress often says that your version of EfiColor is not an updatable version.

The problem is probably that you've set the EfiColor Preferences at one time or another. When XPress sees that you've set a preference, it thinks that it's not the version of the XTension that it's looking for (strange, but true, according to Quark). The solution is to delete your own copy of the EfiColor XTension from your hard drive and drag a new copy over from your original 3.2 disks. Now you can update this "clean" copy with no problem.

Turnkey QuarkXPress

If you want XPress to start automatically whenever you start up your Macintosh, put a blank XPress document or an alias of the XPress program in the Startup Items folder in the System Folder. As soon as you boot up, the Mac starts XPress and opens that file. The few times you don't want QuarkXPress to start like this, hold down the Shift key as soon as you see the hard drive icons showing on your desktop (after startup). Keep holding it down until you're sure XPress isn't going to start.

▶ The 3.3 updater only updates version 3.2 to version 3.3 (it's a single disk).

Both the updater and the upgrader require that you have a copy of the older version present on your hard disk in order to install 3.3.

But what if you've used the upgrader and you need to re-install the latest version at some point due to a hard disk failure, file corruption, or some other obscure reason? Do you need to reinstall version 3.2 and then upgrade it? No. Just hold down the Option key while you click the OK button in the first flash screen of the upgrader (see Figure 1-1). This installs a copy without an older version having to be around.

This doesn't work with the version 3.2-to-3.3 updater. Because the move from 3.2 to 3.3 was so slight, Quark didn't want to put a lot of money into sending out a whole set of expensive disks. So this updater can't reinstall—it can only update.

Starting Clean

Note that Quark recommends that you turn off all your system extensions and control-panel devices before you install Quark-XPress. (This is excellent advice when installing almost any application, not just XPress.) You can do this by holding down the Shift key while restarting your Macintosh. (Hold it down until you see the message "Extensions Off" in the Welcome to Macintosh startup box.) This is an important step and helps avoid system damage or corruption of the application you're installing if you use any sort of automatic virus-detection utility.

Quark also recommends that you reinstall XPress after you update your system software. We don't know why; we just figure they must know what they're talking about! On the other hand, we've made several minor upgrades since we upgraded to System 7—from 7.0 to 7.0.1 to 7.1—and we haven't reinstalled XPress once. Perhaps their advice is primarily for major upgrades. (As we go to press, we're preparing to upgrade to system 7.5; we'll probably reinstall XPress after that.)

Figure 1-1
The multi-disk version 3.3 upgrader (for any version) and the one-disk 3.2-to-3.3 updater

Hold down Option while clicking OK in the upgrader (3.0 or 3.1 to 3.3) to reinstall a full copy of QuarkXPress without the original application.

The 3.2-to-3.3 updater must have a copy of 3.2 to update.

XTENSIONS

Updating XTensions

Remember that some XTensions that worked fine with older versions of QuarkXPress don't work well or at all with newer versions. There's no way to tell in advance whether or not this will be true of any particular XTension. If there's no information on the topic in the "ReadMe" file or in the printed documentation, you can try to run XPress with the XTension loaded; if it's not compatible, you typically get a message to that effect. XPress might also bomb a lot when you run it with that XTension (see Chapter 9, *Problems and Solutions*).

It's unlikely that you can actually harm anything (i.e., the program itself or your document) by trying this, especially if you quit immediately upon getting an incompatibility message. Also, see Chapter 11, *XTensions*, for information on which XTensions that Quark provides are current and which are not.

Don't Be a Pack Rat

QuarkXPress comes with about a zillion files, many of which you'll probably never need. Since every hard disk is too small, you don't want to tie up your valuable disk-based real estate with files you're never going to use. You'd probably never miss the Frame Editor, so ditch it and its Help file (or chuck them *after* you've created a custom Crop Marks frame, as described in "Creating a Crop Marks Frame," in Chapter 2, *Document Construction*). If Microsoft Word is your main word processor, you won't need all the other word-processor filters included with XPress, so get rid of them. You can always copy them off the original disks later if you find you really need them.

Even if you're a pack rat and absolutely must keep everything from Quark on your hard drive, put the filters you don't use in a folder, such as the Other Filters folder. Every filter and XTension that's either loose in your QuarkXPress folder or in the XTension folder (Version 3.3 and later) makes the application take that much longer to launch and take up more of your available memory. Plus, they all count as open files, making it that much easier for you to bump up against your Mac's maximum open files limit (see "Too Many Open Files," in Chapter 9, *Problems and Solutions*).

Who Owns "Your" Copy of QuarkXPress?

In case it's ever important to know who "owns" the copy of XPress you're using, here's Quark's answer: the owner is the company name, if any, that was entered in the registration procedure. That's the name that shows up in the opening splash screen when you launch the program. If no company name is present, then the copy is owned by the person's name.

If you purchase an upgrade or Multi-Pak directly from Quark and the business name that appears on XPress's splash (startup) screen is wrong, call Quark customer service and have them send you a new disk. Also make sure they have your correct information in their database.

If You Sell Out

Why you'd ever want to sell your copy of QuarkXPress is beyond us. However, in case you do, you'd better know Quark's rules about such things. First of all, you have to notify Quark that you want to sell their product. (The closest thing to this that we've encountered in real life is someone telling their parents that they want to buy birth control pills.) Quark's customer service will send you a Transfer Request form and a license agreement for the person to whom you're selling. After both of you sign the forms and you return them with the $25 "transfer fee," Quark updates its database and the deed is done. The only reason we even bring this up is that we've heard of people getting into weird situations—not getting free updates for free, for instance—because they didn't follow the rules. So now you know.

XTension and PDF Folders

In every version of QuarkXPress up to 3.2, most Printer Description Files (PDFs) were included in the application itself, and XTensions were kept loose in the QuarkXPress folder. With 3.3, the times they are a-changin'. Quark has reorganized the contents of the QuarkXPress folder by adding a PDF folder that includes all the PDFs and an XTension folder to hold all of your active filters and XTensions (see Figure 1-2). If you want to turn off an XTension or remove a PDF, you can move it to another folder (which you can name, for example, "Other XTensions") and Quark-XPress won't load it. If you don't use a DuPont 4Cast printer (few people do), you just move that PDF someplace else and it won't show up in the popup menu in the Page Setup dialog box.

We like this new setup because it makes it easier for us to customize and organize our system. However, note that if you change the name of the folders even by a letter, QuarkXPress can't find them at all.

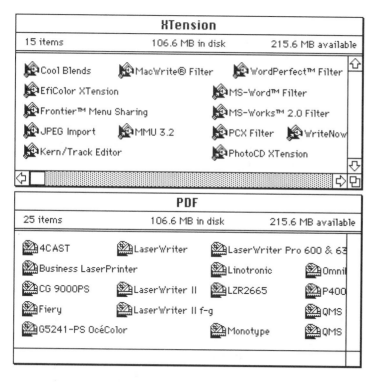

Figure 1-2
Some of the items in the XTension and PDF folders

Cleaning Floppies

The Desktop file is an invisible file on all Macintosh disks which can take up well over 100K of space even on a supposedly blank floppy disk (hard drives have a different scheme). It shouldn't, but if the disk has had a lot of files on it at one time or another, it can be big because the Desktop file stores the index of all file names—

Closing Up Shop

If you want to quickly close all open documents, you can either press Command-Option-W or Option-click the close box.

Launching QuarkXPress

When you launch XPress (double-click on the QuarkXPress icon), the program performs all sorts of operations while it's loading. For example, it figures out which fonts are in the system and which XTensions are available for its use. While it's doing all this, you don't see too much happening on the screen.

When XPress loads certain XTensions, it scrolls a little image of the XTensions in the splash screen; some XTensions don't have animated icons, so they don't appear. If the icon is scrolling across too quickly, you can hold down the mouse button to slow it down. Conversely, if you want to speed up a slow one, holding down the mouse button speeds it across. One particular roadblock at launch time is the NetworkConnection XTension, which looks out over your network for other QuarkXPress users; it's a fun XTension, but slows down the launch considerably.

Finally, you know that the computer is ready to go when you see XPress's menu bar across the top of the screen, the Tool and Measurements palettes appear, and all the appropriate menu names are solid.

and even after files have been deleted and the trash emptied, the system doesn't do a very good job of keeping the Desktop file cleaned out.

There are two ways to clean up your floppy's Desktop file.

▶ Hold down the Command and Option keys before inserting the floppy and keep them held down until the system asks you if you really want to rebuild the desktop; if it's a full floppy it can take a couple of minutes. Typically, however, it's a fast process. (You won't get this message if it's a locked disk, of course; eject the floppy, unlock it, and try again.)

▶ Delete the Desktop file. Because this is an invisible file, you have to use a separate utility to make it visible before you delete it. We usually use PrarieSoft's DiskTop to do this. After selecting the Desktop file in DiskTop, you can uncheck the Invisible box in DiskTop's Get Info dialog box. Now you can go back to the Finder and drag the now-visible Desktop file to the trash. Next, eject and reinsert the disk. When you reinsert the floppy, the Mac sees that a Desktop file isn't present and it automatically builds it from scratch. Finally, empty the trash to get rid of the original Desktop file.

Though it takes a little extra time, deleting the desktop file is significantly more effective, and you end up with a minimal Desktop file, the same size you'd have after a full initialization of the disk (about 768 bytes). But of course, this is much faster than initializing a disk.

No Such Thing as Too Much RAM

Although QuarkXPress ships with a Quark-suggested RAM allocation of 3,000K, you should really allocate significantly more RAM if you commonly open files larger than 500K—at least 5,000K, if not more. You can easily give more RAM to QuarkXPress (or to any application, for that matter) by selecting the application's icon in the Finder when the program isn't running, and selecting Get Info from the File menu. (see Figure 1-3). Enter the new RAM allocation in the Current Size field (System 7.0) or the Preferred Size field (System 7.1 or later) in the lower-right corner.

We usually bump this value up to 5,000K; you can make do with less if you're running an earlier version of XPress. That's a burden if you don't have a lot of RAM in your machine, but it's worth buying the extra RAM if you're going to work with complex or large files. You can also consider Connectix's RAM Doubler, which uses some tricks to let you run more applications with more apparent memory than you actually have.

One power user, Greg Swann, says he "never ever crashes" when he gives XPress eight megs. Of course, your Mac needs at least 10 or 12 Mb before you can allocate any one program this much.

Note that the Environment dialog box in QuarkXPress (see "Your Environment" in Chapter 9, *Problems and Solutions*) shows you the amount of memory allocated to the application and how much is free when you bring up the dialog box. These are the two values listed after "Memory."

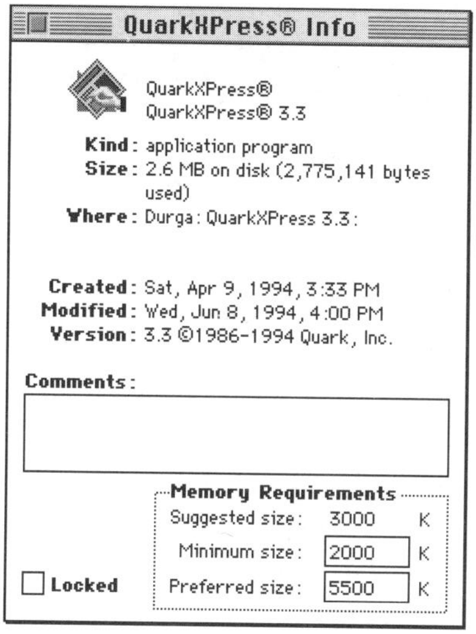

Figure 1-3
The Get Info dialog box

Precise RAM Requirements

In the last tip we gave you a blanket statement about how much RAM QuarkXPress needs. However, the proper amount for your system depends on what you're doing.

Here are a few things that use up RAM in huge chunks.

▶ Large rotated color images—especially PICTs

▶ Large numbers of linked text boxes on a page

▶ Long text chains

If you want to get precise about it, you can experiment to figure out how much RAM to assign. Time an operation that takes a long time. Then start raising the RAM allocation; start at perhaps 500K more than the suggested minimum. Time your event again. Is it faster? Then raise the allocation again and again in 250K increments, until the times stop getting faster. You've just arrived at the optimum amount of RAM for that document.

Another method we've heard about how to calculate how much RAM you'll need is the following formula.

(Largest file size you'll open × 2) + 1 megabyte

MEMORY

Upping XTension RAM

XTensions use a little part of the memory allotted to QuarkXPress in the Finder; so when you run several XTensions at the same time, be sure to raise XPress's RAM allocation (see "No Such Thing as Too Much RAM," above).

You can tell whether you need to increase the RAM allocation when XTensions simply won't load past a certain point. In other words, if you think six XTensions should be loading but only two of them are, then you probably need to allocate more memory to QuarkXPress.

Because each XTension takes up RAM, you shouldn't keep XTensions in your XPress or XTensions folder if you don't plan to use them (remember that import/-export filters and PDFs take up resources just like XTensions).

Memory Management

Everything you do in QuarkXPress takes up a little more memory. If you import a picture, XPress has to save that picture in its memory; if you move the picture within the picture box, it takes up a little more memory; if you cut or delete a group of items from the page, it takes up a little more memory.

That memory comes first from the amount of RAM you have allocated to XPress in the Get Info dialog box (from the File menu on the desktop). And when XPress runs out of memory, it starts using its own virtual memory. That means it starts saving stuff on your hard drive (the same drive as the program is on).

The curious thing about the way XPress handles memory is once it starts using hard drive space, it rarely seems to let it go until you quit the program. Its temporary files get stored in a folder called "Temporary Items," which it creates on your startup volume (the volume that has your active System Folder on it).

In other words, to be getting the most out of XPress, you should do three things. First, make sure you have XPress running on a fast hard drive. Second, quit and re-launch the program every now and again. Third, make sure you have enough RAM in your system (and a large enough chunk of it allocated to XPress) so that XPress has to do very little writing to disk.

Where to Put All Those Files

Just a quick digression on the topic of hard-disk management. Apparently, one of the most difficult techniques for Macintosh users to understand and control is the effective management of files on their hard disks. Now, we know that *you* wouldn't do something like this, but there are those who just toss their files and applications all over their hard disks, sometimes into folders and sometimes not. They are making life hard for themselves.

The Macintosh's folder system is designed to make life easy for you (see Figure 1-4). We like to keep one folder called "Quark-XPress 3.3 Folder" that contains the actual QuarkXPress application and all the filters and supplemental files we need. We have a folder inside of that one for keeping extra add-on modules and filters that we sometimes need but don't want around most of the time. Then, in a different folder from the XPress folder, we keep our QuarkXPress documents (usually a specific folder for each project we're working on).

If you aren't familiar with folders and how they work, we heartily suggest you look into the matter. You may not self-actualize from using folders well, but your life is sure to be the better for it.

Updating Older Documents

If you've updated or upgraded to a newer version of QuarkXPress (and who hasn't?), you may have had trouble on the desktop. That is, when you try to double-click on one of your older files, it either opens an older version of XPress, if you still have one loaded, or gives you the dread, "Application that opens this document can't be found."

All you have to do to convert a document made with an older version of QuarkXPress to a newer one is to open it once in the newer version (using the Open command or by dragging the document onto QuarkXPress's icon), make some kind of change, and save it. Then go to the Finder's desktop and close the document's folder (if it was open) and reopen it. From now on your troubles should be gone.

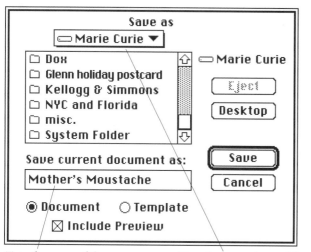

Figure 1-4
The Save As dialog box

Type the name of the file here.

Your document is saved in whatever folder is listed here

Apple added the Macintosh Easy Open control panel to the system software in System 7.5 (it also ships with Aldus Fetch and some other applications). When you click on a document created in an older version of XPress with the control panel installed, you'll be prompted to select an application to open it with. You can also set this as a permanent choice, so that the next old document you click on automatically launches the correct version of XPress.

TEMPLATES

Preview When Opening

One of the neat things about saving a document as a template (see "Saving over a Template," later in the chapter) is the handy preview of the document's first page that you see whenever you select the template in QuarkXPress's file-opening dialog box. As it turns out, any document that you create in QuarkXPress version 3.2 or later can have a first-page preview attached to it by checking Include Preview in the Save As dialog box. Note that QuarkXPress can't preview documents saved in earlier versions of the program. You have to open them and use Save As first. Adding a preview to a document only adds about five or 10K to the file's total size.

For power users only: You can use ResEdit to copy and paste previews between documents, or even use Photoshop to create your own thumbnails. This could come in handy if you want your company logo (or some other picture) to appear in the Open

SAFETY

It Never Hurts to Save As

As you work on an XPress document, constant edits and revisions can cause the file to grow a little and increase the risk that an unforeseen disaster (cosmic rays? dust-sucking CPU fans?) could corrupt the file. You can guard against this file bloat by occasionally using the Save As command. You can save with the same name or a different one; either way, the file usually shrinks a little to its proper size because all the "garbage" has been swept away. Note that if you have Auto Save turned on, XPress is performing this Save As feature for you behind the scenes, so you don't have to worry about it.

RESEDIT

Things ResEdit Can't Do

Just in case you were planning on trying this, we thought we'd let you know that you can seldom, if ever, use ResEdit to change things in XPress such as the status of checkboxes or radio buttons, or the positions of windows. These things are usually hard-coded (that is, written directly into the code itself rather than being contained in easy-to-get-at interface resources). Oh well.

DESKTOP FILES

Fill 'Er Up with Backups

After working with Auto Backup for a couple of weeks, you may find your hard drive mysteriously filling up. Remember, those backup files (as many per file as you specified under Application Preferences) don't go away by themselves; only the oldest backup file gets deleted each time you save. You need to delete them when you're done with them. One suggestion: Set your Auto Backup to save to a special backup folder on a seldom-used drive, then occasionally take a peek in that folder to see what you want or don't want to keep.

Another problem is that when you rename a file, all of its current backup files are orphaned. If you have "Wedding invitation 1st draft" with an Auto Backup setting of five differently named files, and go through five or six drafts, you could have 30 backup files left over from this one document's few iterations.

dialog box's Preview window on a number of different documents. In ResEdit, copy the PICT resource from one XPress document to another. Documents that don't have previews don't have a resource fork; click Yes when ResEdit asks you if you want to create one for the document to which you're copying the preview.

RESEDIT

Using ResEdit on QuarkXPress

Some of the tips in this book involve using ResEdit on your copy of QuarkXPress. We sincerely advise you to use extreme caution when using ResEdit on *anything* (in addition to mandating that you always work on a copy, not on your original).

Another thing to watch out for is the distinct possibility that QuarkXPress might think it's been invaded by a computer virus if you make any changes to it with ResEdit.

In addition, of course, there's Quark's license agreement, which states that you are not allowed to modify the program in any way.

We'll still include the tips in the book, but you need to be aware of these caveats before you use them.

TEMPLATES

Saving Over a Template

You've probably noticed that when you open a template, the window name is "Untitled", not the document name. Then, when you select Save from the File menu, it shows you the Save As dialog box. That's the way it's supposed to work; you're forced to use the template as the basis for a new document, leaving the original template unchanged. But what if you actually *want* to change a template. What to do? To update (replace) an existing template, simply use the Save As dialog box to save the modified file to the same location, with exactly the same name (don't forget to select the Template option). The system will prompt you with two buttons: Replace and Cancel. Click Replace.

Backing Up Your Documents

The first rule of computers is: Save Every Five Minutes. The second rule is: Make Backups. If you can make backups of your documents on a separate disk, it's all the better. There are two ways to make these incremental backups: manually and automatically.

Manually. One person we know of uses this method: every once in a while she quits QuarkXPress, selects the file she's working on (let's say it's called "July-News"), and duplicates it (Command-D). That file is automatically called "JulyNews copy". If she wants more than one copy around, she duplicates a copy and changes the name to "Old JulyNews copy", or something like that.

David does something similar. Every now and again, especially at big turning points in a job, he'll use Save As to create a new document with a suffix such as ".1" or ".2" or whatever. This way, he doesn't need to quit QuarkXPress, and he can easily discern older versions.

Automatically. XPress 3.2 and later have an Auto Backup feature, found in the Application Preferences dialog box (under the Edit menu, or type Command-Option-Shift-Y;

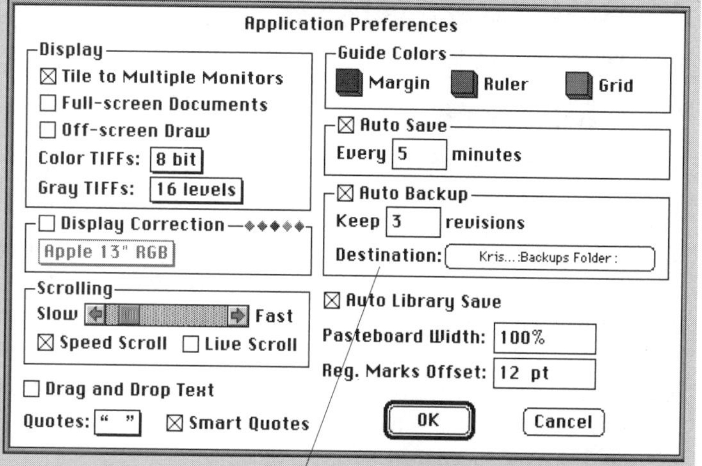

Auto Backup lets you easily save backup versions of your document.

Figure 1-5
Automatic backups

see Figure 1-5). When this is turned on, QuarkXPress saves a backup every time you save your document. You can tell the program where to save it (the default is in the same folder as the document itself, but we usually change this to a special backup folder on a different hard drive) and how many backups to keep (the default of five seems high to us; we typically reduce it to two or three). Each new backup file XPress saves has the next higher number appended to its name. The oldest backup file is then deleted.

However you do backups, we highly recommend keeping *another* backup of your documents someplace else, too. For instance, in David's offices, they use a DAT drive that backs up all of our computers every night. Those tapes are stored in a special fireproof vault when not in use. Remember, our livelihoods are based on all those ones and zeros.

Locking Documents

In addition to making a template, there are two other ways to create QuarkXPress documents that cannot be easily changed: locked files and stationery files. Both of these methods access the file-locking feature of the Macintosh system that prevents changes in the file from being saved.

Revert to Last Minisave

XPress's Auto Save feature goes by another name, too: PageMaker calls these things minisaves. Sometimes you want to use a minisave as something other than crash insurance. In version 3.3, you can actually revert to the last autosave instead of going back all the way to the last full save. For instance, if you saved 10 minutes ago, and XPress autosaved five minutes ago, you can revert back to that autosaved version. Just hold down the Option key when you select Revert from the File menu.

You can lock a file in the Finder if you select the document, choose Get Info from the File menu (Command-I), and click the Locked checkbox. You can also lock a file is by using one of a number of utilities, such as PrairieSoft's DiskTop. This is handy for locking documents on the fly. In Greg Swann's utility Shane the Plane (version 2.0 or later) open the file and turn on the Locked flag under Change Finder Flags.

If you open a locked QuarkXPress document by double-clicking on it, you are told that this is a locked file and that you won't be able to save your changes. If you open the locked file from within QuarkXPress and later try to save it, you get a nasty, "Can't Write to Disk" error. The only way to save a locked file is to perform a Save As under a different name.

Adding Your Own Keystrokes

This is *not* a paid political announcement. We love QuicKeys. To be fair, there are other macromakers around, but we know QuicKeys the best and we're continually amazed at what it helps us do (see Figure 1-6). For those who don't know what making macros is all about, let us elucidate. Macros are miniprograms that you can build that tell the computer to do a set of actions: type a key, pull down a menu, hide an application, and so on.

For example, if you use the Show or Hide Guides feature from the View menu often (we do), you may want to create a macro that selects it for you in a keystroke rather than having to pull

Figure 1-6
QuicKey 3.0's main window

Menu item

Alias keystroke

Sequence

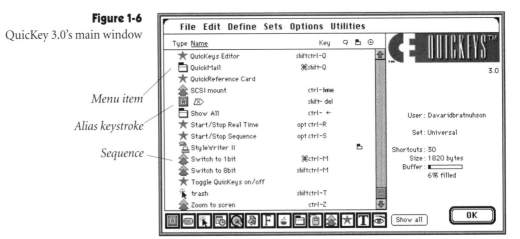

down a menu yourself. We have one of these: Command-Shift-G. This saves more time than you can imagine.

Macros don't have to be as simple as just selecting a menu item, though. For example, one macro we have selects a paragraph, applies a style, puts an extra rule above the paragraph, and places a special character after the paragraph's last word. One keystroke sets the macro off and running.

Anytime you find yourself doing the same sequence of events repeatedly, you should think to yourself, "I could write a QuicKey to do this." For more on macros and scripting, take a look at Chapter 10, *Macros and Scripts*.

KEYSTROKES

Pushing Your Buttons

Many buttons in XPress's dialog boxes can be activated with a keystroke. The keystroke is usually the Command key plus the first letter in the button's name. For example, if a dialog box has Yes and No buttons, you can select them by pressing Command-Y and Command-N. When you're checking the spelling of a story, you can select the Skip button by pressing Command-S.

DESKTOP FILES

Making Stationery

System 7 introduced the concept of Stationery, which hasn't caught on even after its third anniversary. Instead of saving a file as a document or as a template, you save it as a document or a stationery pad. QuarkXPress doesn't implement this, but you can use the Finder's Get Info command on a document and then check the Stationery Pad box. Then, when you open that file, it automatically opens it as an "Untitled" document. Stationery isn't only for XPress documents; any Macintosh document can be made into a template using this Get Info feature. In some programs—mainly Claris applications—this has replaced the Template option in Save As.

KEYSTROKES

Keyboard Palettes

You can access and select items on either the Tool or Measurements palette using keystrokes (see at left). We find this significantly faster than moving the cursor all over tarnation to select tools or fields.

Keystroke	Action
F8	Show/Hide Tool palette
Command-Tab or Option-F8	Select next tool down
Command-Shift-Tab or Shift-Option-F8	Select next tool up
Shift-F8	Toggle between Item and Content tool
F9	Show/Hide Measurements palette
Command-Option-M	Jump to first item of Measurements palette
Command-Option-Shift-M	Jump to Font field
Tab	Jump to next item in Measurements palette
Shift-Tab	Jump to previous item in Measurements palette

Table 1-1
Keystrokes to keep in mind

CHANGES
Continuous Apply

You probably know that the Apply button temporarily applies the changes you've just made in a dialog box. You can then decide whether you want to actually make those changes by pressing OK, revert by pressing Command-Z, or cancel the operation and any changes you've made entirely by pressing Command-period.

Although if you press Command-A, it speeds up the process somewhat, we often find it helpful to be in a continuous Apply mode by pressing Command-Option-A or Option-clicking on the Apply button. This highlights the button (turns it black), as if you were holding the button down continuously—not only in the dialog box you're in, but in every other dialog box that has an Apply button. Now every change you make in the dialog box is immediately applied to your page item (however, if you make a change to a field, you typically have to press Tab or click in another field before XPress knows you're ready for the change to be applied). Press Command-Option-A or Option-click the Apply button to turn continuous Apply off again.

Note that any button that is highlighted (has a thicker border than a normal button) can be selected by pressing Enter or Return. You can press Command-Z to undo the last change in a dialog box or Command-period to cancel the dialog box.

SPEED
Speeding Up Onscreen Operations

Getting tired of how long it takes your screen to draw everything? Here are some things you can do to make screen redraw faster.

- ▶ Set Greek Below to a fairly large size in Typographic Preferences (press Command-Option-Y).

- ▶ Check Greek Pictures in General Preferences (press Command-Y).

- ▶ Set your monitor to one-bit color or grayscale.

- ▶ Work in as small a window as possible.

- ▶ For Find/Change, make your document window as small as possible, so it accommodates only one word, or the largest phrase you're searching for.

WINDOWS
Windows Menu Shortcut

The Windows submenu sure is useful, but getting to its hierarchical commands is a pain in the mouse, especially since Quark has placed it right in the middle of the View menu. Fortunately, there's an easy and eminently logical shortcut. Hold down the Shift key and drag on the title bar of your active document window; up pops an exact replica of the Windows menu, from which you can select any window or stack or tile them all (see Figure 1-7). What better place for a Windows menu than in a window itself?

TILING WINDOWS
Quick-Tiled Thumbnails

Quark, being the progressive company it is, tries to help you streamline your work whenever possible. When they can shave off

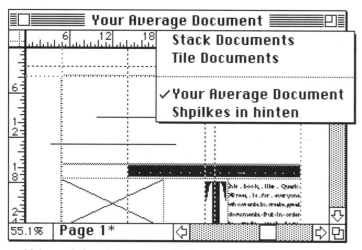

Hold down Shift and drag on the title bar.

Figure 1-7
Popup menu from the title bar of a
document window

a step or two from a process, they like to oblige. The two-step process of tiling your windows (select Tile Documents from the Windows submenu) and then switching to Thumbnails mode can be squished into one step: Hold down the Option key while selecting Tile Documents. All windows open are automatically switched to Thumbnails mode for you. Using Command changes all documents to Fit in Window; Command and Option switches to Fit in Pasteboard (this doesn't appear on any menu); and Control sets all documents to Actual Size. Note that if you have master pages displayed on a document, it'll tile but not resize.

PREFERENCES
Tiling to Multiple Monitors

Our associate Glenn runs QuarkXPress from his Macintosh Duo, and when he's in the office he uses both the Duo screen and an additional monitor. It turns out that if you have more than one monitor attached to your Mac, you can have QuarkXPress tile documents so that the tiling spreads across all your available monitors. So if you have two monitors and four open documents, two documents will appear in each monitor (on some systems, XPress seems to place three on one monitor and one on the other . . . we don't know why). You can turn on this feature by checking the Tile to Multiple Monitors box in the Application Preferences dialog box. If you leave this box unchecked, QuarkXPress tiles all the open documents within your main monitor only (the one that's displaying the menu bar).

LITTLE GEM
Interruptible Screen Redraw

Late into the evening, the night before the deadline, while you're working at a furious pace and QuarkXPress isn't redrawing the 58 items on your page fast enough, you're sure to wish for interruptible screen redraw. Both Photoshop and PageMaker have a dynamic interruptible redraw that lets you stop the redraw of the page at any time by performing any action. XPress (3.2 and later) has a manual or forced interrupt version of this: when you press Command-period, it stops drawing as soon as it finishes drawing the current object. After the drawing stops, you can perform any action you want—you can even select an "invisible" object (one that XPress hadn't gotten around to drawing yet) if you know where it is on the page. Then, when you want a fresh screen, you can click the zoom box (in the upper right corner of the document window).

Controlling Order of Tiling

If you have multiple monitors and want to control which document appears on the main screen, Quark tiles the active window first, followed by the windows in the order they're stacked on the screen. So if you're working on a main document with other subsidiary docs, you can bring your main document to the front before selecting Tile Documents.

If you want to switch which of two or more windows is on the main monitor, you just bring it to top, then Shift-drag on the title bar and select Tile Documents. If you have just two windows open it swaps them instantly. Pretty cool!

NUMBERS
Specifying Measurements

Unless you raise horses and measure everything in hands, chances are that QuarkXPress and you share a common measurement system. QuarkXPress understands measurements in points, picas, inches, ciceros, centimeters, and millimeters. It even understands Q measurements (one Q is a quarter of a millimeter; this is used in some Asian countries). You can use these measurement units at any time, no matter what the default setting is. Table 1-2 shows how to specify a value for each system.

You also can specify measurements as simple equations using one or more measurement units. For example, if a measurement were set to 10 picas, and you wanted to add four centimeters, you could type "10p+4cm". Similarly, if you wanted to subtract one pica and two points (ever since calculators, our math skills have degenerated horribly), we could type "10p-1p2". This is actually one of the coolest features of QuarkXPress, as it makes it very easy to move or resize objects by a specific amount, without having to perform tedious arithmetic to arrive at their new locations or dimensions (after all, what are computers for?).

Similarly, you can use * (the asterisk) for multiplication and / (the forward slash) for division in any field (if you're working with version 3.1, you'll need the Son of Bob XTension to make this work). If you have a text box that measures 4.323 inches, and you want to make it two-thirds as wide, just add "*2/3" to the right of the inch mark. Or, if you want to make a picture box 120 percent of its current size, just type "*1.2" after the width measurement. Remember that you can mix and match all the measurements, too; so even "3p+24mm/3*9" is valid (though we can't think of why you'd need it).

MEASUREMENTS
Changing Points Per inch

Attention traditionalists! Changing the Points Per Inch setting in the General Preferences dialog box can lead to some bizarre side-effects. Yes, the traditional typesetter's point is 72.27 to the inch; but even the authors of this book—who include some traditional "old-style" typesetters—say "Who cares any more? Let's just use what works."

You can spec . . .	By typing . . .	Examples
points	pt or p	6pt or p6
picas	p	10p or 2p6 (2 picas, 6 points)
inches (decimal)	"	6" or 6.5" or 6.888832"
ciceros	c	2c or 6c3 (6 ciceros, 3 points)
centimeters	cm	3cm
millimeters	mm	210mm
Q (Japanese unit)	Q	4Q

Table 1-2
Measurement systems

In other words, there's nothing inherently wrong with 72 points to the inch. For one thing, it simply works out better (mathematically). And there's nothing sacred about the 72.27 measurement either; it's only been around for about a hundred years (which might seem like a long time, until you remember that type has been around for about 550 years), and "standard" for less than that, and standard only in the United States.

Anyway, if you switch back and forth between one number of points per inch and another, your existing settings (for example, point size, leadings, and indents in existing style sheets) at the time of the switch will all have very funny-looking values afterwards; 12 points becomes 12.045 points, et cetera.

And then the big rub is that XPress Tags *always* converts to PostScript points (72 to the inch) no matter what you've done, so you can easily have two different sets of values.

It's better just to not mess with that Preference setting in the first place, believe us. If it were important to change it, we'd be the first to tell you, but it's not.

NUMBERS

Fractions in Arithmetic

In the last tip, we mentioned that you can use multiplication and division to perform some impressive feats with XPress. Let's look at two ways we use this all the time: fractions and placing items on a preset grid.

To get an eighth of a pica, you can type "1p/8" (one eighth of a pica is, of course, the same as one pica divided by eight). To place a text box at 3⅞ inches from the left side of the page, place it at "3"+7"/8" (XPress does the division or multiplication in an

PREFERENCES
Full-Screen Documents

You've probably noticed that whenever you open a document or make a new one, the document window sizes itself nicely to the size of your screen, except that it leaves some room at the left and bottom edges for the default locations of the Tool and Measurements palettes and at the right edge for your disk icons and trash can. Even if you click the window's zoom box, the document expands but leaves the palette areas untouched.

However, you can choose how you want QuarkXPress to behave when you zoom a window. In the Application Preferences dialog box, under the Display section, there's a Full-Screen Documents checkbox. Check the box (the default is unchecked), and whenever you open or create a new document, or zoom a document window, it'll fill your entire screen. Leave it unchecked, and zooming respects the default locations of the Tool and Measurements palette.

NUMBERS
Even Measurements

David knows someone who actually specs measurements in multiples of .014 inches (approximately one point). Because we can't do this, we use pica/point measurements for everything except basic page size. This is the standard among designers and printers and allows precision without having to deal with numbers like .08334 inches (which is six points, or half a pica). It also makes it easier for you to think of picas and points in dealing with your document's type, since that's how type is specified.

NUMBERS
Accurate Rulers

One of the minor irritations in XPress 3.0 was that unless you were at preset magnifications, like 50, 100, or 200 percent, the tick marks on the rulers wouldn't be accurate. You could drag an object so that the gray line in the ruler aligned to the two-inch mark, but, if you were at an odd magnification, you might really be at 1.987 inches, or 2.003. Since version 3.1, however, if the gray line is at a tick mark, the object you're dragging will be aligned exactly to that measurement, regardless of the magnification.

equation first, then the addition or subtraction). To make a line 25 percent longer (125 percent of the current width), multiply the current length by 1.25 (to make a percentage into a real number, move the decimal point to the left two spaces). To cut a box in half, multiply its height or width by .5 (or divide by two).

Similarly, let's say you're using a strict leading grid and you want to put a picture box exactly 20 lines down. If the leading grid is based on 13-point leading, you can set the vertical origin of the box to "13pt*20" (leading value times the number of lines down the page).

NUMBERS
QuarkXPress as a Calculator

If for some obscure reason you don't have a calculator around (remember that there's the Calculator under the Apple menu) and you still have nightmares about math class, you can use QuarkXPress to figure out the conversion described in the last tip.

1. Change your measurements in the General Preferences dialog box to Points, Inches, or Centimeters.

2. Draw a line on your page or pasteboard and set the line mode to Left Point in the Measurements palette.

3. Type the equation into the length field of the line's Measurements palette.

4. When you press Enter or Return, the length of the line shown in the Measurements palette is the percentage value you want.

5. Delete the line.

We know that this is a really twisted way to get this number (you could just pop up a calculator utility on screen, or pull one out of your desk drawer), but sometimes you really have to stretch to get your work done!

The Item and Content Tools

There is almost no error we make more frequently than using the wrong tool for what we're trying to do. Trying to select text with the Item tool, for example, or trying to move a picture box with the Content tool. Of course, the former makes the computer beep at you; the latter moves the picture rather than the box. This should be the first thing you think about when QuarkXPress does something unexpected.

Remember that you can move from one tool to the next using Command-Tab and Command-Shift-Tab (or the F8 key, along with various modifier keys). Also note that you can temporarily use the Item tool by holding down the Command key. (Keep in mind, however, that you can't select multiple items with this temporary Item tool.)

QUIRK

Where Did the Rest of My Page Go?

QuarkXPress novices, and even experienced users, often get a rude shock when working on complicated page layouts because of a curious side effect of the Content tool. Whenever you select a text or picture box, that box hides all page elements it overlaps. This feature can be useful because it lets you edit the contents of a box free of any distractions caused by other page elements (see Figure 1-8). However, the sudden disappearance of many or most of the elements on a page can make even the most experienced users momentarily confused.

Of course, these "vanished" elements return to view if you deselect the box you're editing (click someplace else) or switch to the Item tool. (Remember, you can quickly switch from the Content tool to the Item tool by pressing Command-Shift-Tab or Option-Shift-F8, and back again with Command-Tab or Option-F8.)

NUMBERS

Round Numbers

Try to use round numbers for most of your measurements. Creating a box while at the Fit in Window size often gives you measurements that have coordinates out to the thousandth of a point, such as "6p3.462". This is because whenever you move an object in QuarkXPress, it moves pixel by pixel. At 100-percent view—Actual Size—on a 72-dot-per-inch Mac screen, every pixel maps to a point (which, not coincidentally, is defined as 72 of them to an inch).

At odd magnifications, however, pixels don't equal points, but some fraction of a point. Nevertheless, QuarkXPress still drags things pixel by pixel; so, instead of moving objects point by point, you're moving them fraction by fraction. Hence the three-places-after-the-decimal-point measurements.

It might seem like a picky detail, but, in the long run, it can come in handy to either create your boxes at Actual Size and then resize them if needed, or, if you must work at a reduced or enlarged view, go into the Measurements palette or the Item Specifications dialog box (double-click on the object with the Item tool or press Command-M) and change all the measurements to round numbers (see the next tip). If that's too difficult, at least make sure your magnification is a round multiple of 100 percent (200, 50, and so on). That way you'll at least be dragging objects at simple fractions or multiples of a point.

Figure 1-8
Opaque text boxes

*Using the
Content tool*

*Using the
Item tool*

Viewing Changes as You Make Them

It's often a hassle to move, resize, or rotate a picture or text box because while you're doing it QuarkXPress only shows you the outline of the box rather than the contents. Or does it?

If you hold the mouse button down on a picture-box handle for about half a second before dragging it, you can see the picture crop (or scale, if you have the Command key held down, too) as you move the handle. Similarly, if you move or rotate the box, you can see the text or picture rotate while dragging if you simply pause for half a second before starting to drag. No, you don't have to count out half a second; just wait until you see the object flash quickly before you start dragging.

TOOLS

Rotate Around a Single Point

Let's say you want to rotate 10 objects around a particular point. If the point is the middle of the 10 objects, you've got no problem: select them all and type the rotation value into the Measurements palette. But what if the point isn't in the middle of the group of objects? Here are two ways to do it.

▶ You can use the Rotation tool. This is, in fact, the only time we ever use this tool. Select the objects, select the tool, click the point around which you want to rotate, and drag the mouse around until you get the angle you want. This is perfectly good if you don't need a specific angle, but trying to rotate a bunch of objects to exactly 30 degrees like this is nearly impossible.

▶ David likes this method: Draw a big picture box that surrounds all the objects you want to rotate. Make sure the center of the box is where you want to rotate from (when Show Guides is turned on, you can see the center point; it's where the diagonal lines join). Select all the objects you want to rotate, along with the picture box. Then type the rotation value into the Measurements palette. XPress rotates around the center of the biggest box that surrounds all the objects.

SHORTCUT

That Ol' Specifications Dialog Box

As handy as the Measurements palette can be, it's the Specifications dialog box that gives you the most options for modifying an object. So it's really handy that QuarkXPress has three—count 'em, three—different ways of accessing a Specifications dialog box for any page element.

▶ Double-click on the page element using the Item tool (remember, you can hold down the Command key to temporarily work with the Item tool).

▶ Select the item with either the Content or the Item tool and press Command-M.

▶ Select the item with either the Content or the Item tool and choose Modify from the Item menu.

Once you're in the dialog box, you can tab through the fields to get to the value you want to change. After a while, you start to memorize how many tabs it takes to get to a field, and you can press Command-M, Tab, Tab, Tab, Tab, Tab, enter the value, press Return, and be out of there before QuarkXPress has time to catch up with you. (Don't forget that Shift-Tab backs up a field!)

LITTLE GEM

Keeping Your Tools Around

After you use a tool like the Text or Picture Box tool, the Tool palette automatically reverts back to either the Content or the Item tool, depending on which of the two you last used. This becomes a hassle if you want to use the same tool again. Instead, you can hold down the Option key as you select a tool. Then that tool remains selected until you choose another one.

KEYSTROKE

Deselecting 'En Masse'

Starting in version 3.3, you can deselect every selected item in one stroke by pressing Tab when the Item tool is selected. We find this really helpful when we're zoomed in on the page and can't tell what's selected and what isn't. Note that this is the same keystroke as in FreeHand. Also, remember that the Tab key means something different with the Content tool: it makes a tab (if your cursor is in a text box, that is).

KEYSTROKE
Grab Down Deep

There are plenty of times we need to reach through one or more objects on our page and grab a picture or text box that's been covered up. Moving everything on top is a real hassle. Instead, you can select through page items to get hold of objects that are behind them. Hold down the Command-Option-Shift keys while clicking with either the Item or Content tool to select the object one layer down. The second click selects the object on the next layer down, and so on. With the Item tool and an object selected, we've occasionally been unable to grab down deep without first deselecting the object.

Once you have the object selected, you can move it out from under the other objects by changing its horizontal or vertical origin in the Measurements palette. For instance, you could add three inches to the horizontal origin to move it over. When you're finished making your changes to the object, you can move it back three inches by subtracting the same value from the origin. The item stays at the same layer it was at before.

NUMBERS
Moving an Item's Origin

PageMaker lets you set the origin of a page element from any of its corners or its center, rather than just the upper-left corner. Until QuarkXPress does the same, we can only offer a somewhat weak workaround for specifying alternate origins: use the built-in math functions. If you want the right side of a 12-pica-wide picture box to be set at the 2.75-inch mark, type "2.75"-12p" into the x-origin field of the Measurements palette. That is, simply subtract the width of the box from the right point. Or, if you want the center of a 16-pica-wide text box to be at the 18-centimeter mark, you can type "18cm-16p/2" (see Figure 1-9).

NUMBERS
Proportional Resizing by the Numbers

If you know that the one-by-two-inch box (two inches tall) that you have on a page should be five inches wide, you can type "5"" into the width box. But what do you put in the height box? If you want to keep the aspect ratio, you can let the program do a little math for you: type "*newwidth/oldwidth" after the height value. In this example, you'd type "*5/2" after the height. This multiplies the value by the percentage change in width (if you divide five by two, you get a 250-percent change, or 2.5 times the value).

Figure 1-9
Figuring out the origin values

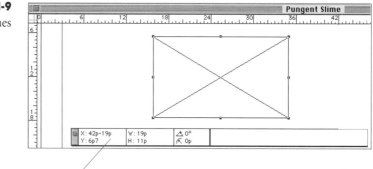

The left edge of this box is set so that the right origin sits at 42 picas.

Locked Items

There are certain features that some people never seem to use, even though they're very useful. The locking feature is one of them. When you lock a page item, you can't accidentally move it or change it with the mouse. This is especially great for items on a master page.

Unfortunately, locking items is far from perfect. For example, a locked item will move if it needs to when you use Space/Align on it. Another way you can move a locked item is by changing its Origin Across and Origin Down settings in the Item Specifications dialog box or in the Measurements palette. Look at it this way: you're trying to keep the object from being *accidentally* moved; if you've gone so far as to type new values into the Measurements palette, the program has to assume that you *want* to move the object. Granted, once you know these "limitations," you can actually use them to your benefit when necessary.

SHORTCUT

Snapping to the Point

If you want to place an object at an exact place on the page, you have several options. First, you could use ruler guides. Once you place a ruler guide, anything that comes within a certain number of pixels (the default is six; it's defined in the General Preferences dialog box) snaps right to it as long as Snap to Guides is turned on. You can use an XTension such as Grids&Guides to place these guides quickly and precisely, or you can just follow the values in the Measurements palette while dragging out the guide.

The second method is to drag the object to where you want it. In early versions of QuarkXPress, you could never quite be sure where a page item was unless you looked in the Item Specifications dialog box. However, now QuarkXPress does reflect ruler markings properly, so when an object looks like it's at the two-inch mark, it really is (instead of 2.019 inches, or some other strange number).

The third way is probably the easiest: while the object is selected, type the x and y coordinates into the origin fields in the Measurements palette or the Item Specifications dialog box.

LITTLE GEM

Maintain the Ratios

In order to maintain an item's width and height ratio while stretching it, you can hold down the Option and Shift keys while dragging. If you want to constrain the box into a square or circle, hold down just the Shift key while dragging. (If the object is a rectangle or oval, it snaps into a square or a circle.)

GUIDES

When Snapping Is Annoying

You know that little feature in XPress that snaps objects to all sorts of guides on the page? It can be pretty annoying sometimes, especially when you're trying to position something by hand. Don't forget that you can turn it off in the View menu (that's one of those obvious tips that almost everyone forgets some days).

Also, some people choose to leave it on, but reduce the Snap amount in the General Preferences dialog box (Command-Y). To some, snapping at two pixels is reasonable, while six (the default value) is just too much.

Figure 1-10
Bounding boxes

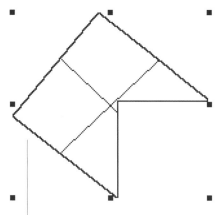

*Even polygons
have rectangular
bounding boxes*

Picture Boxes Are Always Rectangles

Even though QuarkXPress can create rounded-corner, oval, or polygonal boxes, the program thinks of them as rectangles. That's why there's a rectangular bounding box around them when Reshape Polygon is turned off (see Figure 1-10). The important thing about these rectangles is that they have origins, widths, and heights that can be manipulated in the program.

For example, sometimes we find that we want to make a circle with a specific radius or diameter. To do this, all we need to do is create any oval, then set both the width and the height to the desired diameter (twice the radius).

Mixing Corners on Picture Boxes

In a few rare circumstances, you might want to have mixed corner types on the same picture box. For instance, you could have two round corners and two square corners. Here's how you do it.

1. Use the Rounded-Corner Picture Box tool to create a box. To specify a corner radius different from the quarter-inch radius XPress gives you automatically, enter a number in the Measurements palette or the Picture Box Specifications dialog box (Command-M).

2. Create guidelines that align with the box edges. Turn on Snap to Guides, which will help you both here and later.

3. Choose the Polygon picture box shape in the Box Shape submenu under the Item menu.

4. Choose Reshape Polygon from the Item menu.

5. For each corner you want to be square, delete all handles but one (by holding down the Command key and clicking on the handle; see Figure 1-11).

Grabbing Difficult Polygon Handles

One of the troubles with adjusting polygons (when Reshape Polygon is turned on in the Item menu) or text runaround polygons (when Manual is selected in the Runaround Specifications dialog box) is that sometimes points get overlaid on other points or on other objects and it's difficult to select them. In times of stress, remember that you don't have to grab a point itself to move it. You can drag a whole line segment, too, by clicking and dragging it someplace (this moves the points on both ends of the segment).

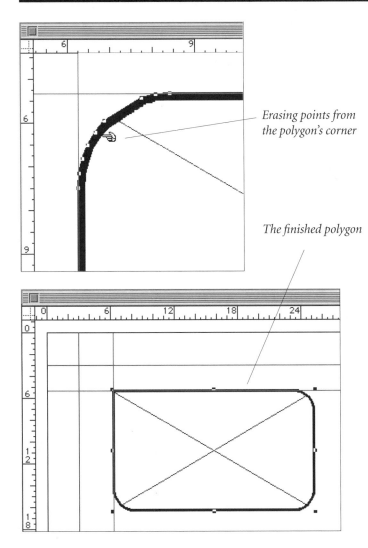

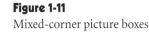

Figure 1-11
Mixed-corner picture boxes

Erasing points from the polygon's corner

The finished polygon

6. Drag the remaining handle to the intersecting guidelines. Remember, you've previously turned on Snap to Guides.

7. Apply your frame as usual.

You might want to save your custom box in a library for future use so that you don't have to recreate it each time. Note that you cannot rescale this sort of picture box either proportionally or disproportionately while Reshape Polygon is checked. Rather, when you turn Reshape Polygon off, you can scale by dragging the bounding box handles.

WARNING
Oval Picture Boxes

Use oval and polygonal picture boxes advisedly: they can really slow you down. Placing pictures in a rectangular or square box can cut your printing time in half or even to a third of what it takes when you use ovals. Drawing the oval is not what takes the time, but rather having the PostScript interpreter trim the picture down to that shape. An oval or polygon without a picture (that is, just the frame) prints very quickly, though.

Constraining Lines to Rotated Space

If you want a set of lines to always be at 20 degrees, you can draw them using the Orthogonal Line tool (that's the one that only lets you draw vertical and horizontal lines). Then—and here's the trick—rotate them to the angle you want using the Measurements palette. Now, even if you stretch them, they remain at that angle.

How Thick is a Hairline Rule?

When you specify the thickness of a line in XPress, you can choose Hairline (or type zero; it does the same thing). However, the result depends on what version of XPress you have. In version 3.0, a hairline was defined as a quarter of a point thick. In version 3.1 and later, it's defined as an eighth of a point (.125 points). On screen, though, all rules are always at least one pixel thick so they're visible.

Note that our preference is not to use Hairline at all. It's too ambiguous for our tastes. Better to spec the thickness to exactly what you want.

The Polygon Blues

David recently conducted a seminar in Texas in which a woman proclaimed that she had a desperate problem. "If you can answer this one question, it'll be worth the cost of the whole seminar," she said. Her problem, it seemed, was that she'd often make very complicated polygons—so complicated, in fact, that she sometimes couldn't find the beginning point of the polygon. This became frustrating to her because without clicking on the first point of the polygon, she couldn't figure out how to stop adding points and move on to something else. Her solution? Reboot the computer.

"There's got to be a better way," she said. The key techniques that she was missing were simple ones.

▶ To cancel a polygon at any time: Command-period.

▶ To automatically close a polygon: Double-click.

The look of relief on her face when she realized she could stop rebooting her computer was worth more than the admission price, we think.

Onscreen Display of Frames

For some reason, XPress treats frames differently than rules (rules are another word for "lines" and should not be confused with ruler guides) in deciding whether to display them at all on screen.

▶ Rules are always display at a minimum of one screen pixel; no matter how far out you zoom, a line won't disappear.

▶ Frames, however, are calculated so that they display only if their screen width rounds up to at least one pixel. If, for example, your box frame is .25 point thick, it'll only display on-screen at 200% view or higher. (Remember that your screen is 72 dots to the inch, and a point is $1/72$ of an inch, so a pixel at Actual Size is the same as a point.) Yes, this is a crazy way to do it. No, we don't know why they don't change it.

LINES
Extending Lines, Part I

You probably already know that you can constrain the line to a 45- or 90-degree angle by holding down the Shift key. In the same vein, if you want to extend a line by dragging it while retaining its angle, you can hold down the Option and Shift keys while dragging one of the endpoint handles of the line.

LINES
Extending Lines, Part II

Extending a line by dragging its endpoint is all well and good, but if you want to extend it by a particular amount (let's say, two inches), then you're in for some troubles. Fortunately, line modes come to your rescue. One of the most ignored features of lines, line modes lets you spec a line in either Endpoint, Midpoint, Left Point, or Right Point mode; and you can change what mode you're in at any time (see Figure 1-12).

First, set the line mode to reflect the end of the line that you want to stay stationary. For instance, if you want the left point to stay where it is and the right point to extend by four centimeters, set the line to Left Point mode. Then, in the Length field of the Measurements palette or the Line Specifications dialog box—after the value that's there now—type "+4cm".

LINES
Making Line Joins Join

We're putting a bid in here for a line tool that can draw more than one segment at a time (like a polygon that doesn't have to be closed). Until then, however, we are forced to use single-segment lines, carefully joining them at their corners. Note that if you place two lines' endpoints together, they won't necessarily join properly. That is, if two lines come together at a 90-degree angle, and their endpoints are specified as exactly the same, the corner joint looks chiseled out (see Figure 1-13).

You can fill this missing piece in two ways. First, you can move the endpoint of one of the lines half the line thickness of the other. For example, if you are using 12-point lines, one of the lines

LINES
Rotating Lines by Modes

We learned at left about how to extend lines, particularly noting the usefulness of line modes. Rotation is the same deal. You can rotate a line from either its left-, right-, or mid-point by selecting the mode and changing the rotation angle in either the Measurements palette or the Line Specifications dialog box.

However, QuarkXPress has a hidden feature that may help or hinder you in your work. When you set a specific angle using this method, the program resets that line's "zero degree" to the new angle. Let's say you draw a line, then change its angle (in any of the three modes) to 20 degrees. Of course, you can extend the line in any direction as usual, simply by dragging an end point. However, when you hold down the Shift key while you drag, you'd expect it to snap to zero, 45, or 90 degrees. It does not; rather, it snaps to 20, 65, and 110 degrees. The "zero-degree" angle has been reset to 20 degrees.

Figure 1-12
Line modes

| X1 : 7p5 | ⊿ 270° | Left Point | W : ▶ 18 pt |
| Y1 : 7p9 | L : 5p1 | | |

| X1 : 7p5 | X2 : 7p5 | Endpoints | W : ▶ 18 pt |
| Y1 : 7p9 | Y2 : 12p10 | | |

| XC : 7p5 | ⊿ 270° | Midpoint | W : ▶ 18 pt |
| YC : 10p3.5 | L : 5p1 | | |

You can change the line mode popup menu in the Measurements palette

The lines don't join

Top line extended by six points

Figure 1-13
Joining lines

should be extended six points. Remember, you can adjust the line mode and specify an endpoint coordinate as an equation (for example, "45p3.6+6pt").

The next method is probably easier: use Space/Align from the Item menu. If you align the left edges of the two lines, the notch disappears. Nonperpendicular lines cause all sorts of other problems; sometimes you can join them using Space/Align, but other times (depending on their angle), it's best just to manually tweak them at 400-percent view.

LINES

Where's the Edge?

When you draw or select a line on a page, the coordinates and values in the Measurements palette and Line Specifications dialog box show the location of the center points of the line. However, if you select the line along with another object, or group a line with other objects, the Measurements palette and Group Specifications dialog box take the entire thickness of the line into account.

For instance, if you draw a 12-point vertical line and place it two inches from the left margin, the center of the line is at the two-inch mark. However, if you select the line and an object that's to the right of the line, then set the origin of the group to sit at two inches, the left side of the line aligns with the two-inch mark.

The same thing happens when you align objects. If you set a line and a box to align on the left edges, QuarkXPress sets the left edge of the line at the location of the left edge of the box. However, if you set the horizontal origins of the line and the box to the same value, they won't align.

GROUPS

Watch What You Select

We love the ability to drag a marquee out with the Item tool in order to select multiple objects. It's fast, it's effective, and it picks up everything in its path. The entire object doesn't have to be surrounded by the marquee; the marquee just has to touch any part of the object. Sometimes it even picks up things you don't want.

For example, let's say you have an automatic text box on your page and then place some picture boxes on it. If you drag a marquee across the page to select the picture boxes, chances are you'll select the text box, too. You may not notice this at first, but if you start dragging the group off into a library or someplace else, you'll be dragging the text box along for the ride. This spells havoc (so press Command-Z quick to undo the last action).

A quick lesson from people who've been there: watch out for what you select and group. And if you do select more than you want, remember that you can deselect items by holding down the Shift key and clicking on them (the same technique works for adding more items to a selection).

GROUPS

Modifying Groups

If you've ever sat in front of your computer for an hour selecting boxes one at a time to change their frame or background specifications, you're going to feel pretty stupid reading this. When you select any grouped objects (or multiple-selected objects, which—by their nature—act as temporarily grouped objects) that don't contain any other grouped objects, you can modify each and every frame in the group at one time by selecting Frames from the Item menu (or pressing Command-B). You can change the background color by selecting Modify (or pressing Command-M, or double-clicking on one of the objects with the Item tool). You can even turn Suppress Printout on for all the objects using this method.

KEYSTROKES

Resizing Type and Lines Quickly

If you're the kind of person who likes to memorize as many keystrokes as possible (we think you should; it's the best way to be superefficient in XPress), note that the keystrokes that change type size are the same as those that change line sizes. Pressing Command-Shift-period/comma raises/lowers the point size by a preset amount. Add the Option key to resize rules in one-point increments. If you know just what point size you want, type Command-Shift-\ to bring up the Font Size or the Line Width dialog box.

GROUPS

Multilevel Grouping

Not only can you group multiple objects, but you can group multiple groups, or you can group groups and objects. This means that you can build levels of grouped objects. For example, on a catalog page you may have six picture boxes, each with a caption in a text box. You can group each caption box with its picture box, then select these six grouped objects and group them together. Later, if you ungroup the six objects, each picture box is still grouped with its caption box.

Multiple and Excessive Grouping

Here's a little tip to keep in the back of your mind while you work: only group when you need to. Grouping is a wonderful feature. But like all good things, it can be overused. In some earlier versions of QuarkXPress, grouping groups of objects can cause some problems (we haven't seen any problems since version 3.2 came out). Also, if you have too many groups on a page, it can slow XPress down.

Selecting a Single Object Within a Group

Don't forget that the Content tool lets you select a single object within a group, without having to ungroup it. This can be very handy if you want to quickly modify a single object, from moving and rotating it to editing the text in a text box. You can move it by either changing the x and y coordinates of its origin in the Measurements palette, or by holding down the Command key (which gives you the Item tool).

Moving Objects to Other Documents

QuarkXPress's ability to drag objects around the page (or from one page to another) doesn't stop at the boundaries of the document window. You can use the Item tool to drag an object or group of objects to another document. You need to have both documents open and visible on the screen—we often use the Tile Documents command in the Windows submenu under the View menu to move the document windows into place quickly (see "Windows Menu Shortcut," earlier in this chapter).

Copy and Paste Between Documents

Moving objects to different pages or different documents is relatively easy; you can either copy and paste the boxes or lines, or you can just drag them with the Item tool. However, there's a gremlin just waiting to pop out here: different open documents can have different current tools. That means that if you copy a text box with the Item tool and switch to a different document, the Item tool may not be selected any more. When you try to paste the box, XPress just beeps at you—or maybe it pastes the box as an anchored box in some text, if you currently have an insertion point in text.

Similarly, let's say you've selected five objects using the Item tool in your first document, and you drag them over to the second document. If the second document's "current" tool is the Content tool, then the objects are copied successfully, but they no longer remain selected. This isn't usually a big problem, but it's something to watch out for so as not to get confused.

Transparent Boxes

If you don't need a box to be transparent (background color of "None"), then don't make it transparent. Transparent backgrounds force XPress to take longer to redraw the screen (it has to think harder) and can sometimes have disastrous effects on graphics (see "Making Grayscale Pictures 'Transparent'" in Chapter 6, *Pictures*).

The corollary to this tip is: If you want a box to have a background color, just give it one instead of making it transparent and putting it over a different colored box (unless you need to for some other effect). These seem like really simple tips, but you'd be surprised at how many people get screwed up because they don't think of them.

Making Rectangles

If you're going to make a lot of tinted or colored rectangles on your pages, use picture boxes rather than text boxes. It's not a big deal either way, but picture boxes do take up slightly less memory.

DELETING

Repeat Delete

Here's something that either you already know ("ho-hum" territory) or that you'll think is the neatest thing since sliced bread.

If you have a bunch of objects to delete, but don't want to take the time to Shift-select them and then hit the Delete key (or Command-K) for each item, try keeping the Delete key held down while individually clicking, in turn, on each item you want deleted. You don't have to preselect anything at all.

This technique requires that you use the Item tool rather than the Content tool. Note that your Mac beeps at you like crazy while you're doing this; just ignore the noise and keep clicking on items.

By the way, this isn't actually a QuarkXPress function at all; rather, it's a little-known function of the System software.

WARNING

Keep Things Simple

We know you'd never do this, but just in case your mother does: Never try to delete objects by covering them up with some other object. Just because you can't see it, doesn't mean it's not really there and that QuarkXPress doesn't have to think about it. In fact, even if you have a few miscellaneous empty boxes floating around your page, we suggest you go through your document before printing it and weed them out. As someone at Quark tech support once said, "Out of sight, out of mind, may be true for some things, but it's not true of QuarkXPress documents."

DELETING

Alien Deletions

Macintosh software has a long history of Easter Eggs: wacky little useless features that programmers include late at night after too many hours of staring at the screen. QuarkXPress has its fair share of Easter eggs. One is the little Martian that walks out on your screen and kills an object on your page (see Figure 1-14). You can call this little fella' up from the depths by selecting an item and pressing Command-Option-Shift-K (in version 3.2, you only have to press Command-Option-K); or you can hold down the modifiers while selecting Delete from the Item menu.

Figure 1-14
The Martian

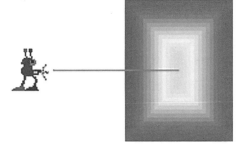

NAVIGATION
Doing It to the End

QuarkXPress is smarter than the average computer program. In fact, it's slowly learning plain English. For example, if you want to delete from one page to the end of the document, but you don't know what the last page number is, you can type "end" in the Thru field of the Delete dialog box. This also works in the Move dialog box. For instance, you can move all pages from page 15 to the end of the document by typing "15" and "end" in the appropriate fields. (Yes, it works in the Go To dialog box, too, but isn't it easier just to press Command-End?)

DELETING
Dangerous Multiple-Item Deletions

The ability to undo a multiple-item deletion is new in version 3.3, and it's about time, in our humble opinion. However, it's not a perfect system yet. Here's two problems you can run into when you delete a group of objects and then try to undo it.

▶ If the group you deleted includes one or more text boxes that are linked to other text boxes in a chain (that is, if you didn't delete *all* the boxes in that text chain at once), the text links are irrevocably broken. You'll have to link them together after undoing.

▶ All layering information is lost when you delete a group of objects. If you undo the deletion, all the objects get brought to the top. Well, actually not quite the top: they're stacked up underneath the topmost object that you deleted (see Figure 1-15).

Figure 1-15
Undoing multiple deletions messes up layering

Before deleting

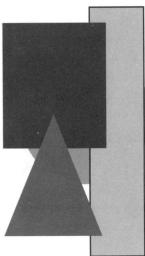

After deleting three objects and then selecting Undo

NAVIGATION
Moving Around Documents

There are many ways to get from Point A to Point B in a Quark-XPress document. You can always page around a page or through a document by clicking in the scrollbar (see "Live Scrolling," below), but you can save time with the keyboard shortcuts shown in Table 1-3. Note that some of these shortcuts use the Control key (though they all have non-Control-key equivalents). Other than zooming, these are the only instances in which QuarkXPress uses the Control key.

Also, note that the Home and End keys on extended keyboards take you to the beginning or end of a document; they're equivalent to dragging the scroll box to the top or bottom of the scrollbar. This means that you may end up looking at part of the pasteboard rather than the actual first or last page. To go to the first or last page in a document, press Shift-Home or Shift-End, respectively (Command-Home and Command-End also give the same results).

To move to . . .	Press . . .	Extended keyboard . . .
One screen up	Control-K	Page Up
One screen down	Control-L	Page Down
Start of document	Control-A	Home
End of document	Control-D	End
First page	Control-Shift-A	Shift-Home
Last page	Control-Shift-D	Shift-End
Next page	Control-Shift-L	Shift-Page Down
Previous page	Control-Shift-K	Shift-Page Up

Table 1-3
Moving around your document

NAVIGATION
Live Scrolling

When you drag the little rectangular box along the vertical or horizontal scrollbar, it's often difficult to tell how far on the page you've gone. This is because the vertical scrollbar represents the entire length of your document and the horizontal scrollbar represents the full length of the pasteboard. If you have multiple-page spreads in your document, the pasteboard can be very large.

But if you hold down the Option key while you drag the scrollbar box, the screen scrolls "with you," so you can see how far you're going (this is called live scrolling). You can also use the Application Preferences dialog box (accessed from the Edit menu) to make live scrolling the default; this way, you'll always get live scrolling, unless you Option-drag the scroll box to temporarily deactivate live scrolling.

NAVIGATION
Story Scrolling

Of course, you may want to jump to the beginning or end of a text story rather than the beginning or end of your document. Using the Content tool, select any point in any linked box belonging to the story. Press Command-Option-Up Arrow and the insertion point jumps to the beginning of the first text box of the current story. Press Command-Option-Down Arrow and it jumps to the end of the story.

If you hold down the Shift key when you do this, you select from the current insertion point to the beginning or end of the story. This is a great way to select all the text that is overset past the bounds of a text box.

NAVIGATION
Scroll Speed

If you use the scrollbar arrows to get around, you definitely want to examine the Scroll Speed feature in the Application Preferences dialog box. This feature lets you control how far each click on a scrollbar arrow takes you. For example, if you have the Scroll Speed set to Fast, then clicking an arrow may move you an entire screen or more. If you have it set to Slow, a click may only move the screen one or two pixels.

Don't confuse Scroll Speed with Speed Scroll; the latter tells QuarkXPress to temporarily greek pictures while you're scrolling (this is a great thing and should always be left on).

Figure 1-16
View Percentage field

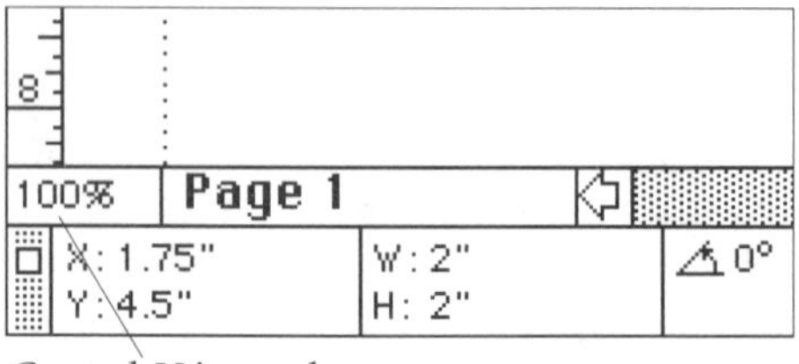

Control-V jumps here

NAVIGATION
Use the Grabber Hand

The Grabber Hand is arguably the most important tool in Quark-XPress. (Some think this is PageMaker's greatest contribution to desktop publishing.) The problem with the scrollbars is that you can only scroll in one direction at a time. It's a hassle: down a little, over to the left, down a little more, now to the right, and so on. But if you hold down the Option key at any time, the cursor turns into the Grabber Hand, and when you click and drag, the page moves where you move the Grabber Hand. Try it! We think it's one of the greatest methods for getting around the page.

In earlier versions of QuarkXPress, you could turn this feature off entirely; since 3.2, it's always on. However, you can temporarily disable it by turning on Caps Lock. This turns Option-click into a zoom toggle between Fit in Window and Actual Size.

NAVIGATION
200% Toggle Zoom

The only problem with the previous tip is that because the Grabber Hand keystroke (Option-click and drag) was used in earlier versions to zoom between Actual Size and Fit in Window views, Quark decided to change the game so that this zooming control only works when the Caps Lock key is down. However, you can still zoom between 200% and Actual Size views by pressing Command-Option-click. (If you install the free Scaling Clicks XTension, found on the disc bound in this book, you can toggle between the old and new Grabber Hand defaults.)

NAVIGATION
Manual-Entry Zoom

One of our favorite methods for zooming in and out is by adjusting the View Percent field in the lower-left corner of the document window (see Figure 1-16). Note that when you're in Actual Size view, this field displays "100%". Whenever you zoom in or out, this field changes. Well, you can change it yourself by clicking in the field, typing a scaling percentage, and pressing Enter or Return.

But don't bother manually clicking in the field; instead, press Control-V to jump there quickly (this is one of the few Control-key keystrokes in QuarkXPress).

NAVIGATION
Center Zooming

QuarkXPress centers any selected page item whenever you change your view percentage (either through the View menu or the View Percentage field). This works if any part of the page that contains the item is visible in your document window, or—if the item is on the pasteboard—if any part of that item is shown in the document window.

For example, if you select a short rule on a page while at Fit in Window view, and then select Actual Size, QuarkXPress zooms in and centers that rule on your screen. If the selected item is a text box and you have the Content tool selected, then QuarkXPress centers on where the cursor is or on whatever text is highlighted. This makes zooming in and out on a page much easier: if you're editing some text, you can use the Fit in Window view to see the "big picture," then select Actual Size view (or 200%, or whatever) to zoom back to where your cursor is in the text.

KEYSTROKES
Fit More in Your Window

If you select Fit in Window from the View menu or press Command-zero, QuarkXPress fits the current page to the window. However, if you hold down the Option key while selecting Fit in Window, it zooms to fit the entire width of the pasteboard into the window. Back in version 3.1, Quark didn't let you use Command-Option-zero to get this view because Apple apparently reserved this keystroke for the Open dialog box. However, Quark now ignores Apple's guideline and includes the keystroke.

LITTLE GEM
Fit Spread in Window

If you work with facing-page spreads a lot, you'll find yourself wondering why QuarkXPress doesn't have a "Fit Spread in Window" command. Fortunately, you can make one yourself. When

NAVIGATION
Magdrag Zoom

Our favorite zooming technique is to hold down the Control key (to get the Zoom tool) and drag a marquee around a specific area. When you let go of the mouse button, QuarkXPress zooms in to that area at the precise percentage necessary to fit it in your window. (Our editor likes to call it "magdrag" for magnification-drag.) That is, if you're at Actual Size view and drag a marquee around one word, Quark-XPress zooms in to 400 percent (as close as it can zoom) and centers that word on your screen. You can use this method to zoom out, too, by dragging a marquee that's larger than your screen (the screen scrolls along as you drag the marquee), but we don't find this as useful as using a keystroke or Control-Option-clicking.

NAVIGATION
Accidental Zooming

You've probably had it happen to you: you select Fit in Window from the View field (or press Command-zero), and suddenly you jump to a different page. It's really not as strange as it seems. Fit in Window always fits the current page in the window. But what's the current page? It's the page that is in the upper-left corner of the document window. If just a tiny bit of the previous page is showing at the top or left of the window, that's the one that will get centered (see also, "Fitting More in Your Window").

Quick Screen Redraw

Every now and then, QuarkXPress won't refresh its screen display properly, and you have to manually force it to redraw the image of a page. A common way to do this is to simply scroll down the length of your screen, then scroll back up. But you can force a redraw even more simply by clicking on your document's zoom box. If this resizes the window in an undesirable way, click the zoom box again, and the window will return to its previous size.

When Going to Thumbnails

Often, if you have very complex pages—and especially if you have text or picture greeking turned off—when you jump to a small zoom percentage it can take a *long* time to redraw all those pages (at a small percentage, you might have 10 pages on one screen!). Instead, *first* make your window very small, just big enough to accommodate one or two pages in Thumbnails view. This way, you won't have to wait a year and a half for your screen to draw 85 thumbnails.

you hold down Option while selecting Fit in Window, XPress shows you the entire pasteboard width. If you change the Pasteboard Width setting in Application Preferences to 10 or 20 percent, then doing this acts just like fitting the spread in the window.

Zoom Adjusting for Bitmaps

Let's say you have a 72-dpi bitmapped image (like a screen shot) scaled to 38 percent. At the low resolution of the computer screen (72 dots per inch), it's difficult to see the bitmap accurately. And if you zoom in to a random percentage, the bitmapped image still looks odd because the resolution of the bitmapped image does not have an integral relationship with the resolution of the screen.

You can make sure you get a proper match and have your bitmapped image look normal by zooming in using the correct percentage. You can figure this percentage out by dividing the scaling percentage you used into 10,000. In the example used above, the bitmapped image was scaled to 38 percent. Divide that into 10,000, to find that you should zoom in to 263.2 percent. If you try to do this by hand, you'll take all day. Instead, press Control-V and type the equation into the View Percentage field. For instance, you can type "10000/38" in the field and press Enter, and XPress figures out the number for you.

Again, this tip only applies to 72-dpi images, such as screen shots. For more on scaling bitmapped images so their resolution has an integral relationship to a given device, see "The Right Way to Resize Bitmaps," in Chapter 6, *Pictures*.

When a Windoid Is the Active Window

David likes to call the floating Library palette a *windoid*—a mini-window that always floats over a document window, even when the document window is being actively edited. Like other Quark-XPress palettes, the Library palette is always visible above the document window. Yet, sometimes the Library palette or other window can become the active window for QuarkXPress, and this can lead to some confusion.

For example, if you click in the Library palette, and then subsequently hit the Page Up or Page Down keys, the window that will be paged through *isn't* the document window, but rather the library, because the library was the last window in which you actually clicked, making it active. Clicking inside the document window will make it active again, and you'll be able to use the keyboard to navigate through your document as before.

MANIPULATING PAGES

Moving and Deleting Multiple Pages

It's easy to select more than one page at a time while in Thumbnails mode or delete or move pages while in the Document Layout palette. If the pages are consecutive (from page four through nine, for example), hold down the Shift key while you select each page or click on the first page in the range, hold down the Shift key, and click on the last page in the range. Every page is then selected between the two (this is just like selecting text).

You can select noncontiguous pages—such as pages one, three, and nine—while in Thumbnails mode or in the Document Layout palette by holding down the Command key while clicking on each page.

TEXT LINKING

Dragging Linked Pages in Thumbnails

If you need to do a thumbnail drag on multiple pages that have linked text boxes, you need to select all pages in the text chain. Hold down the Command key while you select each page; or, if the pages are contiguous, you can merely select the first page, then hold down Shift while selecting the last page. Then drag the whole clump of pages simultaneously to the other document.

If you drag the pages separately, you'll get the entire story repeated on each page. Probably not what you need.

TEXT LINKING

Adding a Box to the Middle of a Chain

We're not sure why, but linking text boxes together often appears daunting to new QuarkXPress users. It shouldn't be. One task which confuses some is adding a text box in between two other boxes in a chain. The trick? Just do it. If you want to add a box (let's call it "A" just for the sake of clarity) between box "1" and box "2", click on box "1" with the Linking tool, then click on box "A." The box is added into the chain. Simple as that.

MANIPULATING PAGES

Thumbnail Drag and Facing Pages

Remember that if you want facing pages to drag correctly to a new document, the new document must be in facing-pages mode too. Otherwise, your facing pages will drag okay, but they'll all be right-hand (i.e., nonfacing) pages.

TEXT LINKING

Adding a New First Text Box

You can't just draw a new text box and make it the first one in a chain. Instead, you draw a text box and insert it in the chain between the current first and second boxes (select the Linking tool, click on the first box and then on your new box). Next, click on the new box and then back on the first box, and your new box has become the first box in the chain.

Getting Rid of the Flashes

Many people get flustered when they select a text box with the Linking tool and then decide they don't want to link the box to anything after all. The text box is just sitting there flashing, seeming to call for some special action. Nope, no special action required. You can either click someplace where there's no text box, or just switch tools, and the flashing stops.

Unlinking from the Middle of a Chain

If you unlink a text box from the middle of a chain by clicking on the arrowhead or tail feathers with the Unlinking tool, the entire text chain is broken at that point. Instead, you can tell XPress to remove a text box from the text chain without breaking the rest of the flow by selecting the Unlinking tool, then holding down the Shift key while clicking anywhere on the box you want to remove.

Moving Background Windows

If you're working on a small screen and you need to resize and move your document windows in order to drag across page items or even full pages, you might find it helpful to know that you can move a window without actually selecting it.

Normally, if you click on a window, that window is brought to the front and becomes active. You can move a window without bringing it to the front by holding down the Command key while you click and drag the bar at its top. Note that this isn't only a QuarkXPress tip; it works in most other Mac applications, too (including the Finder's desktop).

Moving Guides

When you have your guides set to show in front of objects on your page (in the General Preferences dialog box), you can select them and move them with the Item tool. However, sometimes it's tricky to move them when you have the Content tool selected because the Content tool won't let you select a guide when it's over an object. Instead of going through the trouble of selecting the Item tool, use a shortcut: hold down the Command key. That gives you a temporary Item tool, which you can use to move the guide (or the object, if you want). When you let go of the Command key, you get the Content tool back.

Page Versus Pasteboard Guides

It turns out that there are two sorts of guides in QuarkXPress: page guides and pasteboard guides. If you drag a guide from a ruler and release it while the mouse pointer is on the page itself, it runs the length of the page from top to bottom or from side to side. It doesn't cross over a spread or onto the pasteboard or anywhere beyond the page. This is called a *page guide*. If you let the guide go while the mouse pointer is on the pasteboard, however, the guide runs the length of the whole spread and all the way across the pasteboard. This is called a *pasteboard guide*.

You can also turn a page guide into a pasteboard guide by dragging it onto the pasteboard. However, you can't change a pasteboard guide into a page guide. Note that pasteboard guides show up on master pages, but not on document pages based on that master page (however, page guides on master pages *do* show up on document pages).

GUIDES
Moving Guides Deselects Objects

You may or may not have noticed that when you have two or more objects selected and you go and move a guide, the objects are automatically deselected. What a pain! If you only have one object selected, it works just fine. Here's a quick workaround developed by Kristen Kollath-Harris, one of Quark's great tech support people: hold down the Shift key while you move the guide. That way XPress won't deselect the objects.

GUIDES
Getting Rid of Ruler Guides

No matter how easy it is to move guides around, it's always a hassle to add 20 guides to a page and then remove them individually. So take a shortcut: Hold down Option while clicking the horizontal ruler once, and all the horizontal guides disappear. Option-clicking the vertical ruler has the same effect on vertical guides.

Actually, getting rid of those guides is a little more complicated than that. If your document page is "touching" the ruler that you Option-click, only the page guides disappear (see "Page Guides Versus Pasteboard Guides," above). If the pasteboard is "touching" the ruler, then only the pasteboard guides disappear, and the page guides are left alone.

GUIDES
Dashed Guides

If you change XPress's ruler guides to black in the Application Preferences dialog box, the guides become dashed lines. Some people like 'em that way, it turns out. For solid black guides, set the color to 99-percent black.

GUIDES
Making Guides View-Dependent

Apparently some programmer threw this feature in without telling anyone, because we found out that it's not even documented internally at Quark. If you hold down the Shift key when dragging a ruler guide out on the page or spread, it becomes magnification dependent. That is, if you pull it out at Actual Size view (100 percent), you'll only be able to see it at Actual Size view or higher (more zoomed in) magnification. If you zoom out (let's say to Fit in Window view), it disappears. This is great for those times when you want to see a thumbnail of the page with some guides but not others.

GUIDES

Deleting Guides One by One

You don't have to pull a horizontal guide into the top ruler to delete it, or a vertical guide into the left ruler. In fact, you can drag a guide off the page in any direction. Just grab it and drag it out of the top, bottom, left, or right of the window. When you let go of the mouse button, the guide is gone. (Don't feel ashamed, it took us three years of dragging guides back to their original rulers before we figured out this shortcut!)

SPACE/ALIGN

Space/Aligning Groups

The Space/Align feature is one of the coolest and most underused tools in XPress. You can use it to set up all sorts of relationships between items on your pages. For instance, you can tell two objects to be exactly two picas apart; or to place an equal amount of space horizontally between four pictures; or to align 50 different lines along their left edges.

One of the lesser-known features within the Space/Align function, however, is how it deals with groups. If you select three lines and set them to vertically center, then each line gets centered. However, if you group two of those lines first, then XPress centers the loose line with the group of lines (see Figure 1-17).

Here's an example of how this can be useful. In "Coupon Boxes," at the end of this chapter, we discuss, using the automatic dashed line frame to create boxes with proper corners. You can also create these using either line tool in XPress.

1. Draw one horizontal and one vertical line in XPress and set them to be dashed (in the Measurements palette, the Style menu, or select Modify from the Item menu).

2. Duplicate both of these, so you have four total lines, and set them up so that they're somewhat close to looking like a box.

3. Select the two horizontal and one of the vertical lines and use Space/Align (from the Item menu or press Command-comma) to horizontally align the right edges with a space of zero, and vertically align the Items with zero space between them.

4. Select these three objects and group them (from the Item menu).

5. Select the group of lines and the fourth line (the other vertical one).

6. Align the group of lines and the vertical line horizontally with zero space between their left edges, and vertically with zero space between their centers.

If you didn't group the first three lines, then step six would mess up the box totally.

Figure 1-17
Coupon boxes by
aligning groups

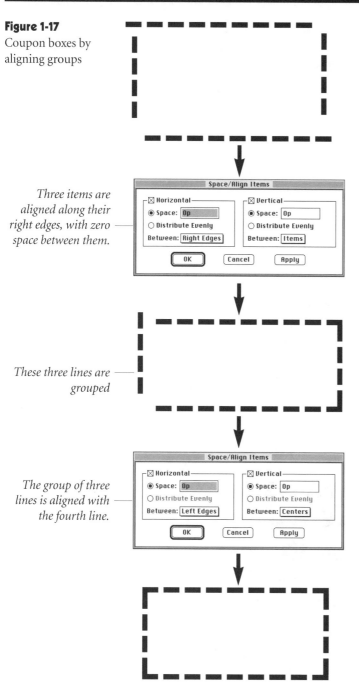

*Three items are
aligned along their
right edges, with zero
space between them.*

*These three lines are
grouped*

*The group of three
lines is aligned with
the fourth line.*

Spacing with Percentages

You don't have to type an absolute value into the Space field of the Space/Align dialog box. You can type a percentage, too. For instance, if you want two objects to be twice as far apart as they already are, you can type "200%" and click OK. When you're working in percentages, the Apply button has an additional function: it lets you apply that percentage more than once. If you type "150%" and click Apply, the objects are spaced one-and-a-half times their existing distance. Then, if you click Apply again, they're moved one-and-a-half times the new distance, and so on.

Measuring from Picture Box to First Baseline

We worked on a job not so long ago where the art director insisted that the first baseline of each caption under an illustration sit exactly two picas from the bottom of the picture. This is exactly the kind of thing that can drive you nutty trying to figure out, and it's exactly the kind of thing that QuarkXPress can do for you somewhat automatically (saving you from a life of frustration and mental anxiety). Instead of measuring each and every caption and picture box, try this method.

1. Use Space/Align to align the text (caption) and picture (illustration) boxes with no space between them. That means set the Vertical Space field to zero space between Items. You can also set the horizontal alignment, if that's required (we usually center them, for instance).

2. Set the first baseline of the caption's text box to the value you're looking for. In this case, it'd be two picas.

Voilá! The baseline of the caption is sitting two picas from the top of the text box, which is the same as the bottom of the picture box (see Figure 1-18).

Centering an Object on the Page

There are three ways we use to center an object on a page. The first uses the Measurements palette.

1. Select the object, and in the x-origin field of the Measurements palette, type the page width minus the object width. If the object was four inches wide on an 8.5-inch page, you'd type "8.5"-4"".

2. Type the page height minus the object height in the y-origin of the palette.

3. Go back to the x- and y-origin fields and divide those values by two (type "/2" or "*.5" after what's there already).

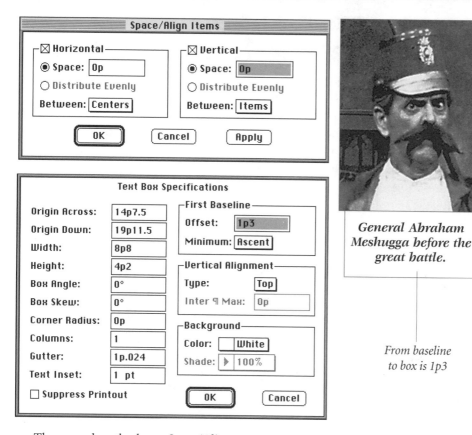

Space/Align Items

☒ **Horizontal**
- ◉ Space: `0p`
- ○ Distribute Evenly
- Between: `Centers`

☒ **Vertical**
- ◉ Space: `0p`
- ○ Distribute Evenly
- Between: `Items`

[OK]   (Cancel)   (Apply)

Text Box Specifications

Origin Across:	`14p7.5`	
Origin Down:	`19p11.5`	
Width:	`8p8`	
Height:	`4p2`	
Box Angle:	`0°`	
Box Skew:	`0°`	
Corner Radius:	`0p`	
Columns:	`1`	
Gutter:	`1p.024`	
Text Inset:	`1 pt`	

First Baseline
- Offset: `1p3`
- Minimum: `Ascent`

Vertical Alignment
- Type: `Top`
- Inter ¶ Max: `0p`

Background
- Color: `White`
- Shade: ▶ `100%`

☐ Suppress Printout   [OK]   (Cancel)

Figure 1-18
First baseline
to bottom of
picture box

*General Abraham
Meshugga before the
great battle.*

*From baseline
to box is 1p3*

The second method uses Space/Align.

1. Draw a box the same size as the page. We usually draw any ol' sized box, type zeros into the x- and y-origin of the Measurements palette, and the page size into the height and width fields.

2. Send this box to the back (don't forget the shortcut: Shift-F5).

3. Shift-select the object or group of objects you want to center (so that they're selected along with the background box).

4. Use Space/Align to align the centers of all the objects, vertically and horizontally.

5. Delete the page-sized box you drew.

If the objects you're centering are all grouped together, the whole group will be centered on the page. Otherwise, each individual object gets centered (they'll all overlap).

The third method is the simplest: use the Align to Page feature in the Kitchen Sink XTension (see Chapter 11, *XTensions*).

LIBRARIES
Libraries from Different Versions

Remember that a library is just an XPress document with a thumbnail preview; if you open an older-version library in a newer version of XPress, you'll no longer be able to open the library in the older version of the program. We speak from sad experience on this one, by the way. Yes, it can happen to *you*.

PAGE ITEMS
Neat 'n' Tidy Pasteboards

The pasteboard is a great resource; you can keep all sorts of page elements on it, just waiting to be placed on a page at a moment's notice. However, the more of these objects you have sitting around, the larger your document gets. For the sake of elegance and your sanity (rumor has it that the larger the file, the higher the chance of corruption or general weirdness), it might behoove you to keep extra page elements in a library rather than just loose on the pasteboard.

LIBRARIES
Labeling Library Items

You can group library items together (this isn't the same as grouping items on the page). You do this by giving them the same label. For example, if you have a group of lines that you use a lot for one magazine, you might label them all "Mag Lines". Then, when you need one, you simply pull down the Library palette's popup menu and select that label (see Figure 1-19).

However, if each one of the item's labels isn't exactly the same, QuarkXPress won't know to group them together. Instead of typing the same label over and over again for each item, you can just type it once. Then use the popup menu in the Library Entry dialog box to choose that item each time you want to assign it to an item within the library. This is faster and you avoid typos.

Figure 1-19
Labeled library items

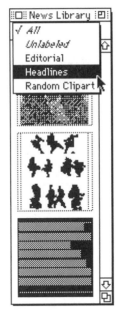

LIBRARIES
Send Libraries, Not Pictures

If you're preparing templates and picture libraries so that someone else can do the actual page-layout work, remember that you might not need to send them the picture files on disk. QuarkXPress captures a low-resolution preview image for each picture when you import it into a picture box, and that's saved within the library.

If you send just the library file, the person making pages can place, see, and print the screen representations. When the document file comes back to you, XPress remembers the locations of all the original graphics files on your disks and uses those for printing.

This is especially efficient if you're exchanging documents with someone via a modem or the Internet—or even by floppy.

Note that you can use the AutoLib XTension to automatically create a library from a folder full of graphics.

PREFERENCES

Document Versus Program

There's an important difference between changing your default preferences with a document open, and with no documents open. In most cases, if you have a document open when you change a preference, that change is specific to that document. Even if you have other documents open at the same time, the change is made to only the one that is active.

If no documents are open when you set a default preference, then you are setting new defaults for the whole program and that change is made to every new document you create from then on. These changes are stored in the XPress Preferences file and are used when creating new documents.

For example, if you set the increments on the Zoom tool (in the Tool Preferences dialog box; see below) to 100 percent while a document is open, the preference is logged for that document only. If you set it while no documents are open, that setting is made for every new document you create. However, documents that were created using the original setting keep their defaults.

You can also change the default settings of things like the "Normal" style sheet, the "Standard" H&J setting, and the tool preferences for things like runarounds or rule thicknesses to settings you use commonly. It saves you a lot of time when you don't have to continually change these settings every time you create a new document.

PREFERENCES

Fast Tool Preferences

We do almost anything to avoid actually making a selection from a menu. We just find other methods are faster for us, and they should be for you, too. For example, you can jump to the Tool Preferences dialog box by double-clicking a tool in the Tool palette. This automatically highlights the tool you chose, and

PREFERENCES

Save Those Preferences

XPress only saves its default preferences when you quit the program. That means if you set the program up the way you want it and then the system crashes, your customization work is lost (including placement of palettes on the screen). If you want to customize QuarkXPress, do it, then quit and relaunch the program. Then you're sure your changes will be saved. (Also, see "New XPress Preferences file," below.)

PREFERENCES

Customize for How You Work

If 90 percent of the picture boxes you create should be transparent, then adjust your Picture Box tool default to transparent boxes (see previous tip). If you almost always work in picas and points, then set up your general preferences to that measurement. If you don't want EfiColor on for any of your documents, turn it off once while no documents are open rather than repeatedly each time you open a new document. It might seem like such a small thing, but like so many subtle tips in this book, it can save you an enormous amount of time in the long run.

Converting XPress Data

Do you have one of those old XPress 3.0 XPress Data files that you need to convert to a new XPress Preferences file? It's simple. Take the current XPress Preferences file out of your QuarkXPress folder. Put the old XPress Data file in. Launch XPress. The XPress Data file is magically transformed into an XPress Preferences file!

you're ready to make your change. Unfortunately, this is one dialog box in which you can't use the keyboard to "push" buttons.

PREFERENCES

New XPress Preferences file

If you're replacing your old XPress Preferences file with a brand-new one for any reason (normally the only time you'd do this is for troubleshooting purposes; see Chapter 9, *Problems and Solutions*), you have two choices of how to do it.

▶ You can delete your old XPress Preferences file or move it someplace out of your QuarkXPress folder. When you launch XPress again, the program automatically creates a new one.

▶ You can drag in a new XPress Preferences file from your installation disks.

The only difference between these two choices is that when XPress creates a brand-new pristine copy of the preferences file, it doesn't include the fancy bitmap frames (which you probably shouldn't be using anyway). You do get all those frames if you drag the file from the installation disks.

Note that this tip has another implication. If you want a whole bunch of versions of QuarkXPress to have the same preferences, and so on, you can copy the XPress Preferences file from one machine to the others. This is a good way to maintain consistency *and* keep backups.

GRAPHICS

Creating Arrowheads

You can create arrowheads in a number of ways, though the easiest is by either drawing an arrowhead-shaped polygon or by drawing a very short line with just an arrow endcap. However, if the line is too short or too long, the arrowhead looks very strange indeed. If you draw a line with an arrow endcap, but just want the arrowhead, the "end" of the line should be just about where the end of the arrow endcap is (see Figure 1-20). Note that if you draw the line too short, it may look all right on the screen, but it prints strangely.

As they appear on screen   As they appear in output

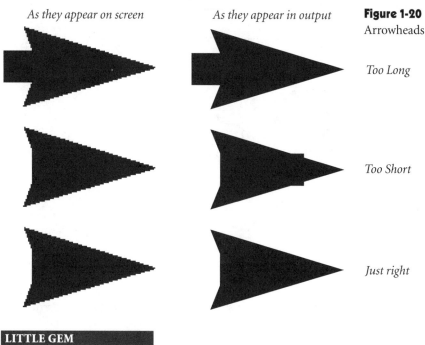

Figure 1-20
Arrowheads

Too Long

Too Short

Just right

Post-it Notes

If your QuarkXPress documents need to move from one person to another, you may want to add comments to certain objects or areas of a page. By taking advantage of QuarkXPress's ability to suppress the printout of any item, you can easily create noticeable, but nonprinting, electronic "Post-it" notes, to contain comments and suggestions about an individual document (see Figure 1-21).

Create a text box and enter the text of the note. Give the box a background of 100-percent yellow, a runaround of None, and turn on Suppress Printout in the Text Box Specifications dialog box (so as not to affect the printing of the document).

WindowShade Control Panel

David insists he can find every document on the desk in his office, even though there must be a couple of hundred of them lying about (if challenged about this, of course, he'll just change the

Figure 1-21
Post-it notes

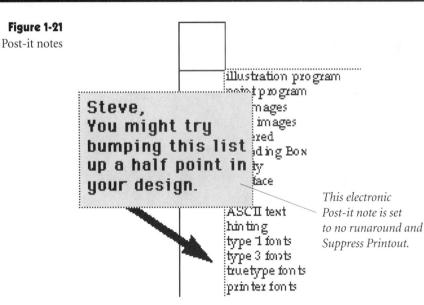

*This electronic
Post-it note is set
to no runaround and
Suppress Printout.*

subject). The logic is simple: you want documents open in front of you or else you may forget about them; however, the more you have open, the harder it is to get any work done.

The virtual Macintosh desktop, or QuarkXPress's workspace, are no different. But because screen space is even smaller than (real) desk space, your challenge is harder. Enter WindowShade, stage left. WindowShade is a free control panel device that is available from online services, and is on the disc that comes with the book. Apple's also included WindowShade in the release of System 7.5. Its job is simple: It rolls up open windows and windoids, both on the Finder's desktop and in applications like Quark-XPress (see Figure 1-22).

To roll a window up or down (after installing WindowShade in your Control Panels folder and restarting your machine, of course), you can double-click on the title bar of any window or palette to make it roll up into its own title bar. (David has his version set up so that you have to Option-double-click for it to roll up or down.)

WindowShade doesn't work well with horizontally oriented windows (with a vertical title bar), however, so don't expect to use it on your XPress Measurements palette. (If you do, your Measurements palette becomes a single pixel tall; to recover it, you have to select Hide Measurements from the View menu, and then display it again.)

WindowShade seems to be fully compatible with all current versions of the System software. As is so often the case with

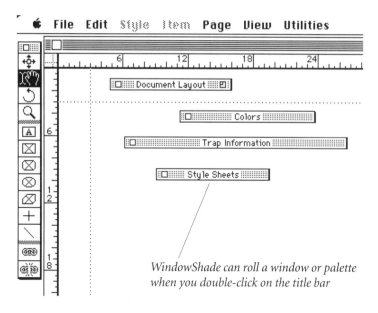

Figure 1-22
WindowShade

*WindowShade can roll a window or palette
when you double-click on the title bar*

utilities that modify the way the System works, one of us (Phil) has lots of trouble with it, but most people (including David) use it all the time with no problem.

LITTLE GEM

Postal Bar Codes

If you've ever sat around waiting to get a postal bar code from the USPS to paste on to your business reply card artwork, you should get wise and create them yourself (see Figure 1-23). Azalea Software has a great barcoding software package that is relatively inexpensive and can create many different types of bar codes (it even comes as an XTension, so you can make bar codes quickly within XPress; see Chapter 11, *XTensions*). However, if you can't justify that kind of expense, you might want to try creating one in QuarkXPress. Here's how to make a nine-digit postal bar code.

1. Draw a vertical line .02-inch thick and .125-inch tall (you may want to do this at a 200- or 400-percent view).

2. Step and repeat this line (Command-Option-D) 51 times with a .0475-inch horizontal offset and no vertical offset.

3. Now, here's the obscure part. You've got 52 tiny lines. These are broken down into 10 sections of five lines each, plus one tall line on each end. Each of these sections will

Figure 1-23
Postal bar codes

‖‖ıı‖ıı‖‖ıı‖ıı‖‖‖ıı‖ı‖ı‖ııı‖ı‖ı‖ı‖ı‖

Table 1-4

Postal bar codes

Number	Code
0	tall tall short short short
1	short short short tall tall
2	short short tall short tall
3	short short tall tall short
4	short tall short short tall
5	short tall short tall short
6	short tall tall short short
7	tall short short short tall
8	tall short short tall short
9	tall short tall short short

contain tall lines and short lines. The lines you've created so far are all tall lines.

4. Look at Table 1-4, which shows that each of the nine digits in the zip code corresponds to a pattern of tall and short lines. Go through the 52 bars and match tall and short patterns to the lines in your document. Each short line should be .05 inch tall (select the line, change to either Left Point or Right Point line mode and type ".05"" for the line length in the Measurements palette).

5. The last of the 10 sections is a checksum number (don't worry if you don't know what that means; it's not important). Add up the nine digits and subtract the second digit of the resulting number from 10. For example, if the numbers all add up to 36, subtract six from 10. The result is the number you should use for this tenth section.

We suggest grouping all the lines together for easy manipulation. You still need to use FIM codes (the ones that go at the top of an envelope or card) supplied from the USPS (unless you can figure out how to create your own; they're pretty easy). However, there are only five different types of these, so you can keep them on hand pretty easily.

Coupon Boxes

Trying to create coupon boxes (boxes that have a dashed-line border) is like trying to juggle chickens. If you make the box in an illustration program, those little dashed lines can keep moving around so that you don't get even corners. And, as it turns out, XPress may or may not let you make dashed frames.

The trick is that the XPress Preferences file that ships with QuarkXPress *does* have a dashed line frame built in to it. But many people have thrown their copy of this file away so that XPress builds them a fresh, new one. If you want XPress's own dashed line frame back, you can replace your XPress Preferences file with the one from your original disks. (Of course, all the other stuff that's saved in your Preferences file gets lost.)

Another choice is to buy an Electronic Border Tape product from Shade Tree Marketing (see Appendix B, *Resources*). Included in every package is the FrameMover utility, which can copy frames

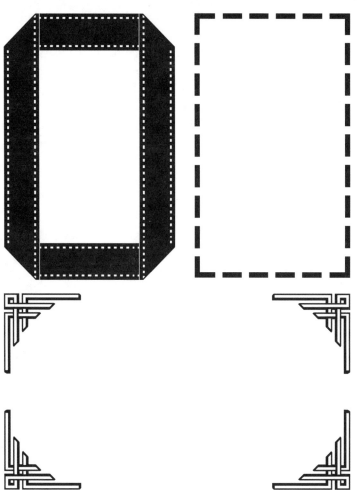

Figure 1-24
Coupon box and other borders

from one XPress Preferences file to another. The interface is simple; much like the Font/DA Mover utility from earlier Macintosh days. Of course, if you buy Electronic Border Tape, you also receive a number of weird and interesting borders (see Figure 1-24).

Also, "Space/Aligning Groups," earlier in this chapter, demonstrates how you can make coupon boxes using lines within XPress.

CONCLUSION
Use QuarkXPress for What It's Good At

What's amazing to us is the tenacity of some of the people who come to us with questions. They've got QuarkXPress files containing amazing shapes and pictures on their pages, plus scans of text doing the strangest things!

Hey. It's really okay to use programs other than QuarkXPress for some things. In fact, we recommend it. If you want a funky looking line or illustration, build it in FreeHand, Illustrator, or some other application and import it. If you want to doctor bitmapped images, use Adobe Photoshop. QuarkXPress can do some of these things (especially with XTensions), but other programs do it better, easier, and more efficiently. It's what they were built for.

document
CONSTRUCTION

Creating a document is, in many ways, much like constructing a building. No matter what kind of structure you make—skyscraper or apartment building or shack in the backyard—there's one rule that doesn't change: you want it to be built strong enough to last as long as possible. In this chapter we'll explore ways in which you can build and modify documents that last and that are flexible enough to be modified easily. You won't have to use a jackhammer, but you'll need every other tool in XPress.

Check That New Document Dialog Box

QuarkXPress remembers what you selected in the New Document dialog box for the last document and gives you those same specifications the next time you create a new document. This can be helpful or it can be a drag. At one office where Eric works, he had to track down and threaten bodily harm to someone who kept creating new documents with margins of .25 inch or less on communally used machines. Every time someone else came and created a new document, they'd get absurdly small margins! The

SETUP

Don't Make Documents Too Long

It's a good idea not to make documents longer than about 60 or 70 pages. Extra-long documents increase the chances that you may run into the dreaded "Bad File Format" message that can mean a terminally corrupted file. If you must make a 1,000-page book, break it down into smaller segments! Remember: never make a file longer than you'd care to recreate if you had to.

lesson? Verify each dialog box as you create a new document; don't just assume that you want every default setting.

SETUP

Page Size Is Not Paper Size

Page Size in the New Document and Document Setup dialog boxes refers to the size of the pages you want as your finished output—not to the size of the paper going through your printer. These may or may not be the same. In the Page Size area, type in the page dimensions of the actual piece you want to produce. For example, if you want to create a book page of seven by nine inches, enter these values in the Width and Height fields, even if you're printing to a laser printer capable of printing only letter-size (8.5-by-11-inch) pages (see Figure 2-1).

Figure 2-1
The New dialog box

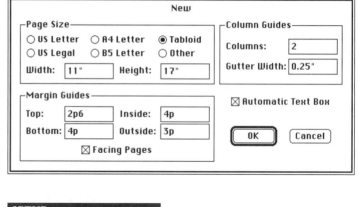

SETUP

Figuring Live Page Area

When you create a new page or adjust a page's margins, you can't change anything other than where the margins sit on the page. It might be nice to type in a live area width and let QuarkXPress handle where the margins should be. With XPress's math features, this is easy. Here are a bunch of simple equations to keep in mind:

live area width = page width − left margin − right margin

live area height = page height − top margin − bottom margin

left margin = page width − live area width − right margin

top margin = page height − live area height − bottom margin

For example, if you want the text column on your seven-inch wide page to be 24 picas wide, and you know you want an outside margin of one inch, you can make a new document that has an inside margin of "7"-24p-1"".

Here's an even more complex equation that helps you figure out the left or right margin if you know the other:

page width − (total # of columns × desired column width) − total space occupied by gutters between columns − the one margin you've specified

For example, with a letter-size page with three two-inch columns and two picas between columns, if you know you want a three-pica outer margin, you could type "8.5"-6"-4p-3p". (The six inches equals three columns at two inches each; the four picas equals two gutters between columns at two picas each.)

It's not superintuitive, but try it once and you'll find yourself using it a lot.

Figuring Text-Column Width

In the last tip, we saw how to figure various margin sizes on a page to create a live area of certain sizes. You can perform some similar math to tell QuarkXPress to make columns of a text box a specific size (see Figure 2-2). The formula is as follows.

gutter space = (box width) ÷ (number of columns − 1) − (number of columns/number of columns − 1) × column width

While that looks pretty ugly, it's pretty easy to plug numbers into. For instance, if you have a five-inch wide text box, and you want it to contain three eight-pica wide text columns, you can figure the gutter space (in the Text Box Specifications dialog box) as "5"/2-3/2*8p".

Facing- to Single-Sided Pages

You can make a facing-page document into a single-sided document by turning off Facing Pages in the Document Setup dialog box (from the File menu, or press Command-Option-Shift-P). But XPress won't let you do this if you have any facing-page master pages in your document. But as soon as you delete the facing-page master pages, you'll have no problem. Note that deleting master pages may delete items from any document pages based on those master pages.

Changing Page Size

When you change the page size of your document (by selecting Document Setup from the File menu or pressing Command-Option-Shift-P), any text box that reaches to the margin guides resizes itself to the new margin guides. Every other object, though, has to be resized or repositioned manually.

Figure 2-2
Finding gutter size
when you know
what column size
you want

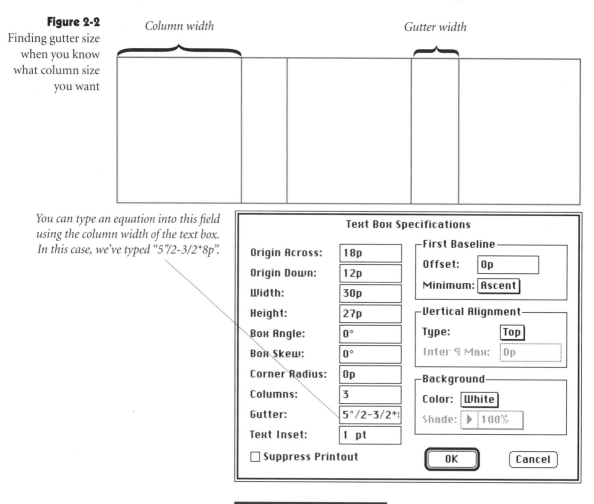

Column width

Gutter width

*You can type an equation into this field
using the column width of the text box.
In this case, we've typed "5"/2-3/2*8p".*

Text Box Specifications

Origin Across: 18p
Origin Down: 12p
Width: 30p
Height: 27p
Box Angle: 0°
Box Skew: 0°
Corner Radius: 0p
Columns: 3
Gutter: 5"/2-3/2*
Text Inset: 1 pt
☐ Suppress Printout

First Baseline
Offset: 0p
Minimum: Ascent

Vertical Alignment
Type: Top
Inter ¶ Max: 0p

Background
Color: White
Shade: ▶ 100%

OK   Cancel

PAGE SIZE

Exceeding Maximum Page Size

The maximum page size in XPress is 48 by 48 inches. If you need to exceed it, though, it's easy enough to do; it only requires a little arithmetic. Figure out the ratio of your required size to XPress's maximum, create your document at 48 by 48 (or 48 by whatever), and then type your ratio in the Reduce or Enlarge field in the Page Setup dialog box. Of course, you'll also have to use the inverse of your ratio on your desired point sizes and all other measurements, since they'll be printing larger than you've specced them.

For example, suppose you need a page size of 72 by 30 inches. Set up your page for 48 by 20 inches, type "150" in the Reduce or

PREFERENCES

Default Font

Tired of Helvetica being the font that's chosen by default when you create a new text box and type in it? The font you type in is defined in the "Normal" style sheet. To change the default font (or leading, or color, or any other paragraph or character formatting), modify your "Normal" style sheet. Simple as that. You can even change it when no documents are open to affect all subsequent files.

Enlarge field in Page Setup, and spec all your measurements, point sizes, and so on as two-thirds of your final, desired measurements.

Copying Page Geometry

Remember, there's no need to recreate boxes and graphic elements for the right side of a master page if you've already created the left side. Select each item and use the Duplicate or Step and Repeat features (under the Item menu) to create copies. A Step and Repeat with a vertical offset of zero ensures that the copies are at precisely the same vertical position on a page as the original (see Figure 2-3).

You can hold down the Shift key as you drag to constrain movement horizontally or vertically. After you move the items, change the text content and the character and paragraph formatting, as is appropriate to your right-master formatting plans.

PAGE ITEMS

Remembering Offsets

Remember that the Duplicate command uses the offsets you last used in Step and Repeat. So if you want to duplicate something right on top of itself (this is called "cloning" in many other programs), first go into Step and Repeat and set the two offset values to zero. You'll actually perform the cloning when you click OK;

TEXT BOXES

Formatting an Empty Text Box

Although you cannot enter text in an automatic text-link box while viewing master pages, you can assign character formatting to the box. Select the text box with the Content tool and specify the font, size, style, and so on—you can even apply a style sheet. Then, when you return to the document page, the text you type in that box appears in the font, size, and style that you chose. Text that is imported into that box does not necessarily appear in that font, however.

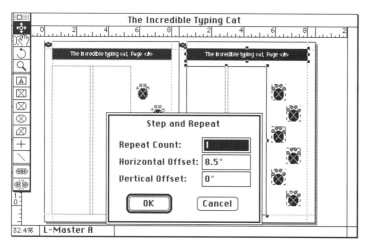

Figure 2-3
The Step and Repeat dialog box

Retrieving Document Layout Deletions

If you've deleted a master page from the Document Layout palette, the only way to get it back is by selecting Revert to Saved from the File menu. This, of course, only works if you've saved your document recently. Bear in mind that this method wipes out all changes you've made since your last save, so pause a moment and reflect before you jump into this last resort. (In version 3.3, you can also revert to your last minisave—if you had Auto Save turned on in Application Preferences—by holding down Option and selecting the Revert to Saved menu item.) We recommend doing Save or Save As before deleting pages for this very reason.

but then if you later (during the same XPress session) want to clone something else, you can press Command-D and you'll know where the copy will go.

David has a QuicKey set up for cloning items. It opens the Step and Repeat dialog box, types "1", presses Tab, "0", Tab, "0", and presses Return. He's assigned the Command-equals keystroke to it—the same as the Clone command in FreeHand.

Copying and Pasting Measurements

A very handy and often overlooked feature of QuarkXPress is that you can copy and paste numbers in the Measurements palette. This is extremely handy if you want to copy attributes such as origin (x,y coordinates), dimensions, rotation—just about anything that can be entered in the Measurements palette, from one item to another.

Let's say you want to make certain two items have exactly the same height.

1. Select the first item.

2. Press Command-Option-M, then press Tab and another Tab, to select the number in the Height (H) field of the Measurements palette.

3. Press Command-C to copy the number to the Clipboard.

4. Select the second item.

5. Press Command-Option-M, Tab, Tab, again.

6. Press Command-V to paste the number into the field.

7. Click outside of the palette, or press Return.

The second item is now the same height as the first.

This feature is particularly handy if you want to make sure items on different pages are in identical positions; other than the PowerPaste AppleScript on the disc, this is about as close as you can get in QuarkXPress to the "paste in position" feature of other desktop-publishing programs.

Basing One Master Page on Another

If you need a new master page but don't want to format it from scratch, you can base it on another that carries at least some formatting that you wish to retain. There are two ways to do this.

▶ Create a new master page as described above. Then select the icon of the particular master page whose formatting you wish to copy, and drag it over the icon of the newly created master page, releasing the mouse button when that icon is highlighted.

▶ Select the master page you want to duplicate, and click the Duplicate button in the Document Layout palette.

Master-Page Naming Conventions

Note that although you can name a master page anything you like, QuarkXPress displays page icons in the Document Layout palette with only the prefix rather than a whole name. Before version 3.2, you could only type one letter as a prefix; now you can type up to three. Therefore, we find it helpful to name master pages with the same letter as a prefix. For example, if "A-Master A" is a master page for the table of contents, we might label it "TOC-Table of Contents". Our next master page may be called "FM-Front Matter", indexes could be called "Ind-Index", and so on.

There's a failed correspondence between these prefixes and what shows up in the page popup menu in the lower-left corner of the document screen. (You only get this if you have the Features-Plus or Thing-a-ma-bob XTension installed.) The page popup menu shows the name as "Master A" or "A", depending on the XTension, instead of the names you chose. Also, if you reorder the master pages in the Document Layout palette, this new order doesn't show up in the popup pages either.

Copying Master Pages Between Documents

Have you ever wanted to copy a master page from one document to another? Kinda' difficult, isn't it? Well, no, not really. Put both documents into Thumbnails view and drag a page from the first document into the second. The master page that was assigned to that page comes over along with the page itself. Then you can delete the page, and the master page stays in the second document.

Printing Master Pages

It's simple enough, but people often can't figure out how to print master pages. The trick is that you have to have the master page you want to print showing when you select Print from the File menu. This prints both left and right pages if the document has facing pages (you can't print only the left or the right alone). Unfortunately, if you have 12 different master pages and you want them all printed, you have to print them one spread at a time.

Figure 2-4

Listing all master pages in a document

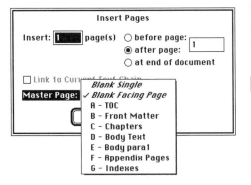

To get a listing of all the master pages' names, select Insert Page from the Page menu, then click the Master Page popup menu and—while holding down the mouse button—create a screen dump (press Command-Shift-3). You can then print this screen dump as a reference (see Figure 2-4).

DOCUMENT LAYOUT

Unintentional Multipage Spreads

There are problems in moving pages around in spreads that are just waiting to unfurl. If you insert the pages you're moving to the right or left of an existing page, you may unknowingly create a multipage spread instead of adding pages to the page flow. The trick is to be careful about what tiny icons you see when you're dropping the page. If you see a page icon, you'll get a spread; if you see a black arrow icon, you'll add pages to the document flow.

DOCUMENT LAYOUT

Making Facing Pages Display Separately

You can lay out the pages in your document any way you'd like. For instance, if you have a facing-page document but you want to scroll through it as though it were a single-page document (without seeing spreads), you can move pages around in thumbnails or in the Document Layout palette so that they appear that way. First, move page three straight down above page five, so that you see the black down-arrow (see Figure 2-5). Next, do the same thing with page five, and so on. It's not a fast method, but it works.

If you want all the pages on one side (so that they're directly "on top" of each other, like single pages are), you can drag the left-hand pages over to the right side in the Document Layout palette. However, note that all the pages are reassigned right-hand master page formatting when you take this extra step, which might screw up your design.

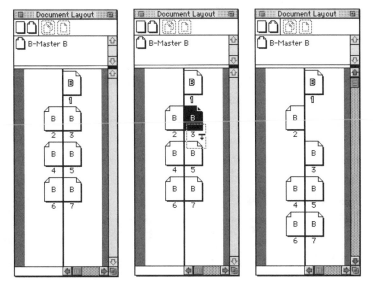

Figure 2-5
Making facing pages appear single sided

DOCUMENT LAYOUT

Starting on the Left

Do you want the first page of your document to be a left-hand page? If you've tried to simply delete page one, you've already found that page two jumps up to the right-hand page one spot. The problem is that left-hand pages are always numbered evenly in QuarkXPress. If you want page one to be on the left, use the Section dialog box (under the Page menu) to change its number to something even, like two. (Sorry, zero doesn't work!)

The problem is that only page one moves over to the left side; following pages don't follow along, and there's a blank spot where the second page should be (see Figure 2-6). Instead, first assign page two to be the section start, and then delete page one.

MASTER PAGES

Delete Changes Versus Keep Changes

The Delete Changes and Keep Changes options on the Master Page Items popup menu in the General Preferences dialog box are constant sources of confusion. Let's try to explain them once and for all. When you apply a new master page to a document page on which you've made changes, any modified master-page items on

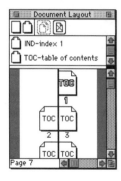

Figure 2-6
Making page one
a left-hand page

*Select the page
and click the page
number field.*

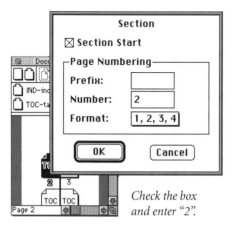

*Check the box
and enter "2".*

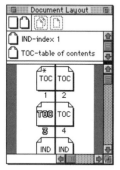

*The new layout
has the first page
on the left.*

the document page are affected by the way this option is set (see the next tip for more info on this).

Choose Keep Changes when you want to keep locally modified master items on a document page. Choose Delete Changes if you want *all* the old master-page items—both modified and unmodified—to be deleted from a document page and fresh master-page items applied when you apply a new master page to it.

Our feeling is that, unless you really know what you're doing, you should leave this option set to Keep Changes.

When Master Pages Are Reapplied

One of the most frustrating occurrences to both beginner and experienced XPress users is the seemingly random way XPress reapplies master pages to your document pages. However, there's really nothing random about it. Simply put, XPress automatically reapplies a master page every time a page switches sides in a facing-pages layout.

If you add one page before page four, then page four becomes page five, flipping from a left to a right page in the spread. In this case, QuarkXPress automatically reapplies the master page. If you added two pages before page four, then QuarkXPress doesn't reapply the master page at all. This is one reason that adding pages in even increments is so important in QuarkXPress when working with facing pages.

Master-Page Usage

Master pages appear to be part of your document, but they are distinct in many ways. For instance, when you perform a document-wide Find/Change, XPress won't find any instances on the master pages until you do the Find/Change while a master page is displayed. Similarly, when you open the Font Usage or Picture Usage dialog boxes, what you see reflects only the document pages *or* the master pages, depending on which you're displaying. If you have fonts or pictures on your master pages that don't appear in the document pages, you won't see them in the usage dialog boxes.

GUIDES

Make Separate Columns with Snap to Guides

It's often helpful to draw separate text boxes for each column rather than use one large text box separated into columns. The master page's column and margin guides make this process easy. If you have Snap to Guides turned on (under the View menu, or press Shift-F7), you can quickly draw a text box that fills one column. This text box can be duplicated, then positioned in the next column, and so on, until each column is created.

GUIDES

Quick Grids

Ever wish that QuarkXPress let you create automatic layout grids? If you don't have either the Grids&Guides or the GridLayout XTension (both of which do the job admirably), and don't feel like using one of the guide scripts on the disc in the back of the book, you're almost out of luck. Almost. Here's a way to quickly create evenly spaced guides by using a transitory text box.

1. In Preferences, set guides to draw in front of page items, and make sure you've selected Show Guides under the View menu.

2. Draw a text box across the area through which you want to space the guides. This could be an entire page, or just a section of a page.

3. Set the number of columns in this text box to equal the number of areas you want the guides to delimit (you can do this in the Measurements palette or the Text Box Specifications dialog box).

4. Set the Gutter between the columns to three points.

5. Drag guides from the vertical ruler to the box, aligning them by eye with the edges of the box and the gutters of the columns you've just created. Since QuarkXPress always evenly spaces columns, your guides will also be evenly spaced (see Figure 2-7).

DOCUMENT LAYOUT

Avoiding Alerts

We don't know about you, but we often spout spontaneous invectives when our computer alerts us to a dangerous procedure. Because we've used the program for so long, we *know* that what we're doing can't be undone or is potentially life-threatening to our document. One example is the "Are you sure you want to delete these pages?" prompt when you click the Delete button in the Document Layout palette. QuarkXPress is trying to be helpful, because you can't reverse this action. But it just typically annoys us. However, if you Option-click the Delete button, the pages are deleted without a prompt. Hoorah for progress.

Figure 2-7
Evenly spacing guides

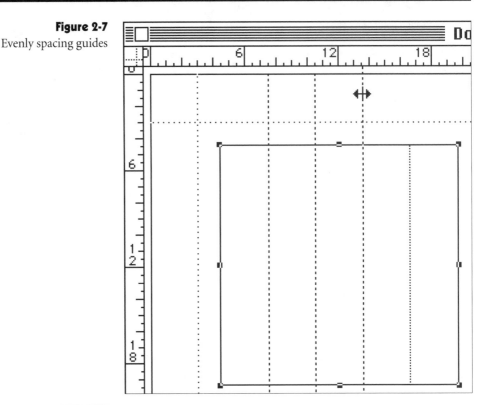

Figure 2-7
Evenly spacing guides

Figure 2-8
Frame Grids

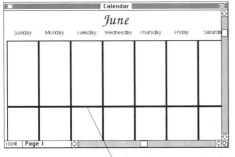

*These lines are twice the
thickness they should be.*

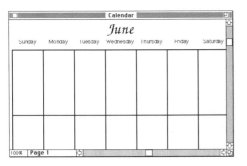

To create an evenly spaced grid, rotate the box 90 degrees, and drag guides from the horizontal ruler to the column gutters.

Of course, to make the most of these guides, create them on a master page.

FRAMES

Frame Grids

You can create a grid quickly by using Step and Repeat with framed text or picture boxes. For example, if you draw a one-by-two-inch text box and give it a two-point frame, you can step and repeat it six times horizontally, then select all those boxes and step and repeat them four times vertically. You end up with something that looks suspiciously like a calendar.

However, you have to be careful of what measurement you use to step and repeat with. To ensure equally thick lines, you should step and repeat vertically by the box height minus the frame thickness and horizontally by the box width minus the frame thickness (see Figure 2-8). In the example above, you would step

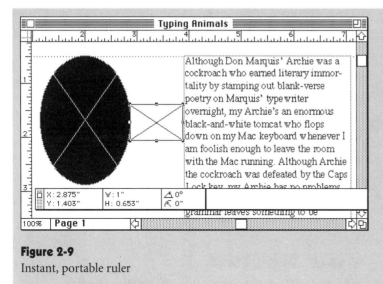

Figure 2-9
Instant, portable ruler

LITTLE GEM
The Portable Ruler

Sometimes, you need to verify that two objects are a precise distance apart. A quick way to do this is to make a picture or text box with the runaround set to None. Then use the Measurements palette to make the box's height or width the distance you want to check. Move the box over to the page objects, and compare their spacing to the box size (see Figure 2-9). Then just delete or move away your temporary measurement box. Of course, if you want to align two page items so that they are a certain distance apart, you'd probably want to use Space/Align instead.

and repeat the box horizontally two inches minus two points (remember that you can simply type "2"-2pt"). However, if your frames are set to Outside in the General Preferences dialog box, the width and height of the box may not be what you expect.

PAGE NUMBERS
Big Page Numbers

The problem with checking thumbnails on screen is that you can hardly ever figure out what page number is what. One reader tells us that she sometimes adds big automatic page numbers (Command-3) that hang off the edge of the pages onto the pasteboard for the left and right master pages (see Figure 2-10). You can set these text boxes to have no runaround and turn Suppress Printout on, and QuarkXPress acts as if they aren't even there. However, even at tiny sizes, you can see them attached to each page.

PAGE NUMBERS
Get to That Section Quickly

There's another way to get to the Section dialog box other than selecting Section from the Page menu, but the method depends on which version of QuarkXPress you're using.

PAGE NUMBERS
Page Numbers on Document Pages

We often find people forgetting that the automatic page-number characters (Command-2 for " previous page in the chain," Command-3 for "current page number," and Command-4 for "next page in the chain") don't function only on master pages: they also work perfectly well when used on document pages. For instance, you can use them for jump lines ("continued on page <#>") or even inside regular text paragraphs ("When we continue this story, on page <#>, we tell you . . . ").

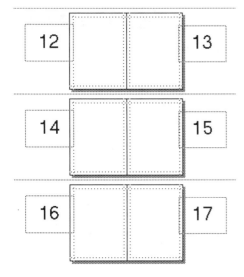

Figure 2-10
Thumbnail page numbers

▶ In 3.1, you get there by clicking a page icon and then clicking the master-page name area in the Document Layout palette.

▶ In version 3.2, first you have to select the correct page by clicking on it once in the Document Layout palette; then you click the page number below the icon.

▶ In version 3.3, they've changed it again: click on the page to select it, then click the page number field in the lower-left corner of the palette.

Any way you do it, it brings the Section dialog box up faster than having to reach for a menu.

DOCUMENT LAYOUT

Bleeding over Spreads

Bleeding an object off a page is easy: you just place it off the edge of the page on to the pasteboard. But when you're working with a document in facing-page mode, you can't bleed an object off the right side of a left-hand page or the left side of a right-hand page because there's another page in the way. However, you can get around this obstacle by using the Document Layout palette (this is similar to the process used in "Making Facing Pages Display Separately," earlier in this chapter).

Let's say you want to bleed an object off the right side of page two (a left hand page).

1. Open the Document Layout palette (press F10 or select it from the View menu) or go into Thumbnails view.

2. Drag page three straight down until it's almost over page five, and let go when you see the small black arrow point downward.

The following pages should be pushed out of the way, but should properly retain their spread settings and page numbers.

MASTER PAGES

Master Spreads Caution

If the only elements that extend across spreads on a master page are in front of every other element on each page, you're in great shape. However, if you create a master-page element that extends across a spread and that sits behind elements on one or both pages (such as a picture box containing artwork as the background for both pages of a spread), then you can run into problems.

The problem stems from how QuarkXPress manipulates pages internally. When QuarkXPress repaginates or adds pages, it doesn't build each spread as a whole. Rather, it creates the right page first and *then* the left page, so that the bottommost item on the left page is above the topmost item on the right page. Since an object which spans a spread "belongs" to the left-hand page, a box that spreads across the two pages appears behind everything on the left page and in front of everything on the right page (see Figure 2-11).

There are three solutions to this problem (we'll describe one here and one in the next tip). First, if you first create every page that you need in a document and *then* add page items that cross the master-page spreads, everything should be fine (as long as the cross-page item is sent to the back on the master page, and you want it to be behind all the right-page items).

Another solution to this problem can come in handy when master page items have already become screwed up.

1. Go to the master page that contains the problem spread.

2. Select the item or items that extend across the spread and bring them to the front.

3. Go back to the document pages. The items should be in front on both the left and right pages.

4. Once again, go to the master page in question, but this time, move the two-page items to the back.

Now when you go to the document pages the item is once again in the background of both pages, and the problem is fixed (at least for the time being).

Spreads in Two Pieces

Another solution to the spread problem in the tip to the left is to break the offending object into two pieces (or three, if you're working with a three-page spread). For example, on the master page, select the element that you're having problems with and clone it (see "Cloning an Object," in Chapter 10, *Macros and Scripts*, and "Remembering Offsets," earlier in this chapter). Then crop the two identical items back so that one is only on the left page and the other is only on the right page. This gives the appearance of an element extending across a spread, when in fact no element actually does (there are two elements, one on each page). You can then add and move pages freely without worrying about your layering getting messed up.

Working on Rotated Pages

It's no fun actually doing the layout work on a page where everything is rotated (either 90 or 180 degrees, or whatever degree the design calls for). But here's an easy way to "flip" an entire page, filled with any number of graphic and text elements, back and forth between rotated and unrotated status.

Figure 2-11

When page items fall behind other page items on a master page (A), unexpected layering problems can crop up (B). Don't worry, this can be fixed (C).

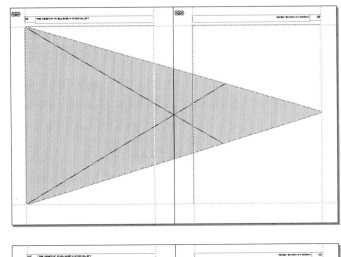

A

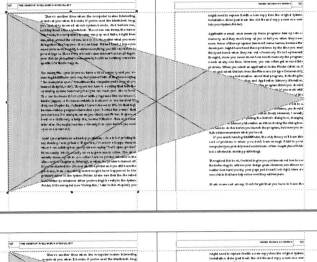

B

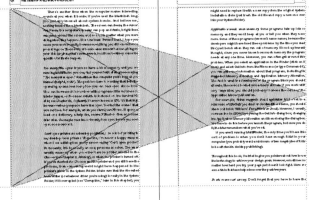

C

1. Draw a picture box the same size as the page itself (or one that extends the exact same amount past all four edges of your page). Make sure it totally encloses all other page elements.

2. Send that picture box to the back. (Optional: Group all the page elements together, including the new picture box.)

3. Press Command-A with the Item tool selected to select all the objects on the page (including the large picture box).

4. Rotate everything to the degree you want.

This works because XPress rotates multiple items, whether grouped or selected, around the center of the bounding box of the items. When you make the full-page object that encloses all the other objects, XPress rotates around the center of *that* object, which is the same as the center of the page (see Figure 2-12).

After you're done working on the job, you can delete the surrounding picture box.

THUMBNAILS

Editable Thumbnails

Although the Thumbnails view is quite useful for many operations (such as moving pages from one document to another), it annoys us terribly that you can't actually edit any page items while in the Thumbnails view. Or can you?

You can make an editable Thumbnails view by specifying an extremely reduced magnification, such as 15 percent. This gives you the appearance of Thumbnails view, but you can select, move, edit, or delete individual page items.

This reduced view is particularly handy for checking and troubleshooting document-wide text links, since you can see links on many pages at once (see Figure 2-13). Just click on a linked text box with the Linking or Unlinking tool, and you'll see the linking arrow for several pages in a single screen, rather than just one or two. If you've screwed up your links, this reduced view makes it easier to relink your document.

Figure 2-12
Rotating around the
center of a page

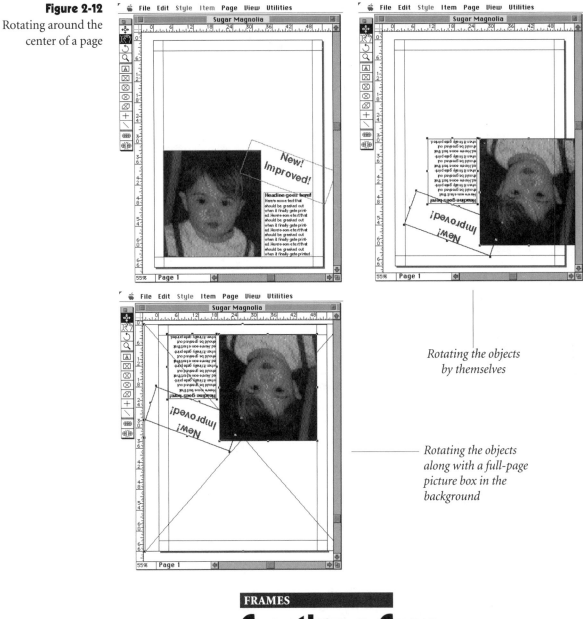

Rotating the objects
by themselves

Rotating the objects
along with a full-page
picture box in the
background

Creating a Crop Marks Frame

Since Quark's Frame Editor only creates bitmap frames, it's not terribly useful for high-quality design work—with one exception: you can use it to create frames for crop marks. This is handy if you want to create a page containing several objects to be cropped, such as business cards.

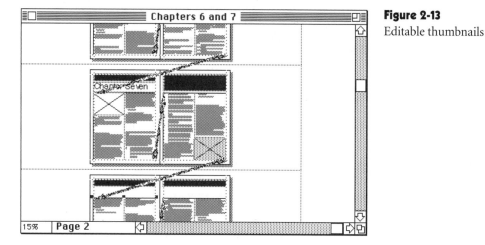

Figure 2-13
Editable thumbnails

In the Frame Editor, set the corner grids so you'll have enough room for both the crop marks and the space you want to offset them from your page. For instance, if you want a 12-point crop mark, offset six points from the trim, create 18-by-18-point corner grids, and apply the frame by setting its border to 18 points, so one grid unit equals one point (see Figure 2-14).

You can create quarter-point crop marks by *quadrupling* these grid dimensions. For this example, you'd make a 72-by-72-pixel corner grid, then specify the frame for an 18-point width. Each grid unit will translate to a quarter point, so if you've drawn your crop marks one unit in thickness at each corner, they'll translate to lines with a quarter-point weight when applied to your box. David wrote a script to make trim marks automatically; you'll find it on the disc at the end of the book.

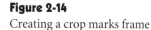
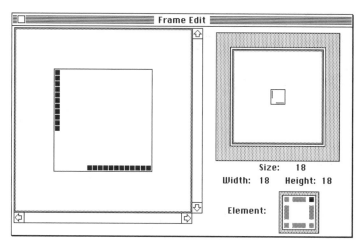

Figure 2-14
Creating a crop marks frame

Fancy Borders

Okay, we admit that we're graphics snobs, but we just don't like the bitmapped frames that Frame Editor creates (with a few exceptions: see "Creating a Crop Marks Frame," above). In fact, we just tell the QuarkXPress installer not to install the Frame Editor and Frame Editor Help at all.

If we want a nice border, we build it in an illustration program such as FreeHand or Illustrator, use one of the frames supplied in Adobe's Collector's Edition Pack, or use a typographic frame. This last one is pretty obscure, but you can make some really great frames with it. For example, you can create a nice border using characters from an ornamental typeface such as Adobe Caslon Ornaments (see Figure 2-15).

Figure 2-15
Typographic borders

TABLES

Shading Polygons for Tables

Many tables benefit from a little highlighting to communicate important information or to point out particulars of the table. One way to do this is to create a polygon or rectangular picture box that perfectly fits the area of the table, shade it, then send it to the back. (Make sure the background of the table's text box is None so that you can see through the boxes to the shaded area; see Figure 2-16.)

0	0	0	9	4	1	0	11
0	0	0	6	0	23	3	42
0	0	62	1	4	3	7	52
0	0	3	2	7	3	20	53
0	52	1	4	5	0	24	28
0	24	26	0	17	6	54	20
660	63	29	0	43	28	31	40
10	45	0	0	35	43	0	41
2	3	0	0	18	13	0	28
10	73	19	0	18	0	0	12
5	43	13	0	3	0	0	34
5	43	1	36	0	0	0	39
9	2	0	34	0	0	0	28

Figure 2-16
Shading polygons for tables

0	0	0	9	4	1	0	11
0	0	0	6	0	23	3	42
0	0	62	1	4	3	7	52
0	0	3	2	7	3	20	53
0	52	1	4	5	0	24	28
0	24	26	0	17	6	54	20
660	63	29	0	43	28	31	40
10	45	0	0	35	43	0	41
2	3	0	0	18	13	0	28
10	73	19	0	18	0	0	12
5	43	13	0	3	0	0	34
5	43	1	36	0	0	0	39
9	2	0	34	0	0	0	28

*Adding shaded polygons to this table can make
it easier to point out particular sets of data.*

PAGE ITEMS

Self-Centering Boxes

It's often helpful to know where the center point of a box is. Here's
one method for making a text box with a crosshair center point.

1. Make a text box.

2. In the Text Box Specifications dialog box, set Vertical
   Alignment to Centered and set Text Inset to zero.

3. Click in the text and bring up the Paragraph Formats dialog box. Set alignment to Centered and indents to zero.

4. Type a six-point semicolon in the Zapf Dingbats font. (Remember that you can press Command-Shift-Z to automatically make the next character you type Zapf Dingbats.)
   Don't type a return after it.

5. Select the one character you just typed, and baseline-shift
   it -1.2 points.

The result is a crosshair in the middle of the text box. Unfortunately, the cross hair prints out.

Here's one other method: draw a tiny picture box and use Space/Align to center it within another, larger box (either a text or picture box). Then turn on Suppress Printout for the picture box, set runaround to None, and group it with the larger box. This is now a center point that doesn't print, doesn't affect text runaround, and moves with the larger box.

FRAMES

Moving Frames

Suppose you've designed a custom crop marks frame (as described in "Creating a Crop Marks Frame," above). How do you get it from one copy of QuarkXPress to another? True, if you apply that frame to a box in an individual document you'll always be able to use that frame within that document, no matter what frames may or may not be residing in the XPress Preferences file of the copy of QuarkXPress you use to open it.

But if you elect to use custom information contained in a document when XPress asks you if you want to use the document's or XPress's preferences, you can't access custom information in your XPress Preferences file. So how do you get frames from one Preferences file to another?

You can't, unless you have help from a handy little utility called FrameMover, from Shade Tree Marketing (see Appendix B, *Resources*). Sold as part of their Electronic Border Tape collection of predefined frames, FrameMover lets you open up two copies of XPress Preferences and move frames between them. Written back in 1989, this program seems to work fine with newer versions.

word PROCESSING

3

If Shakespeare were alive today, would Hamlet replace "words, words, words" with "word processing"? Though on the surface word processing is somewhat mundane and unglamorous, there's no doubt that it is the centerpiece of much of the work people do these days.

We've split our discussion of text into three chapters. In the next chapter we detour into transforming text into typography; and in Chapter 5, *Copy Flow*, we discuss how to manipulate text with powerful tools such as Style Sheets and XPress Tags. All of these are important, but you won't get far unless you start with the basics: text-based issues such as editing and navigating through text, and search and replace. That's what we discuss in this chapter.

SELECTION
Multiple-Click Mouse Selection

Mac programs let you select an entire word by double-clicking on it. QuarkXPress adds triple, quadruple, and quintuple clicks, for making ever-larger selections (see Table 3-1).

Table 3-1
Effects of multiple clicks

To Select . . .	Click . . .
A word and contiguous punctuation or space	Twice
A line	Three times
A paragraph	Four times
An entire story	Five times

If you continue to hold down the mouse button after your final click, you can extend your selection by dragging. If you've selected a word by double-clicking, you can drag to select more text, word by word. If you've selected a paragraph with four clicks, you can similarly drag to increase your selection paragraph by paragraph.

SELECTION

Quick Text Selecting via Master Pages

Master pages are probably even more powerful than you think. Here's a little-known tip that uses text boxes on master pages.

Let's say you have to change a block of text on every page of your document; each page is different, so you have to do it by hand. To change the text block, you click on the text box, then carefully select the text you want to change, then change it . . . over and over and over again.

However, it turns out that if you select some text in an unlinked text box on a master page then switch to the document page, it remains selected on the document page, too. For example, you can put a folio number text box on the master page and select the text within the box. Now, when you move to the document pages, you only need to click on the box with the Content tool and the number is selected automatically (because you selected it on the master page). When you're finished making changes, you can return to the master page and delete that text box (because all the text boxes have local changes, they won't get deleted on the document pages).

Unfortunately, the master-page text selection doesn't get saved with the document, so it's gone as soon as you close it. (To get it back, just go to the master page and select it again.)

SELECTION

Select All

Sometimes the easiest way to spec all the type for a box is with the Select All command (Command-A). This instantly selects all the text in the box, plus any text that's in boxes linked to the one you're in, whether it's displayed or not. Quintuple-clicking (that's five times!) will also select all the text in the current chain. Either of these shortcuts is quicker and more fool-proof than dragging over all the text in the box, which can easily result in missing a character.

Use a Separate Utility

Veteran QuarkXPress users have discovered that while characters may be lost when typing at high speeds (especially when the text has to flow around pictures or other page items), type pasted in from the Clipboard never gets lost or damaged. One way to get text into the Clipboard quickly is to type it in a simple text-editing utility, and then copy and paste it into QuarkXPress. There are many such programs on the market. You could even make do with Apple's bare-bones Note Pad or McSink (on the disc in the back of the book). Then there are the excellent applications Vantage and MockWrite (part of PrairieSoft's MockPackage). No matter how fast you type, you'll almost never lose a letter or a word in one of these streamlined text editors.

The disadvantage of using text-editing utilities is that whatever text you create in them can be only pure text. You must apply any formatting attributes after you've pasted the text into QuarkXPress. Instead, it might behoove you to get enough RAM in your machine to run a full word processor alongside QuarkXPress.

Faster Editing

Give a proofreader an inch and they'll take a meter. If you have to enter 200 pages worth of changes that your boss or editor has made on a document, start from the end of the document or story, rather than the beginning. If you start at the beginning, then each change you make has the potential to reflow all the text that comes after it. By the time you're on page 10, your printed draft page (with markups) and your document on the screen don't look anything alike, so it's hard to find the areas where changes are needed.

If you make the changes from the last page, moving earlier in the text, the text doesn't reflow anything that you haven't worked on yet.

Using a Dummy Document

If you must make many changes to a story, you might find it easier to make a new document with a simple page layout, copy the entire story to be edited over to the dummy document, make all your changes there, then copy the story back to your original document. This is because text that flows in complicated columns—or around pictures or other page items—can often take longer to reflow than in a simple one-column document.

There's one caveat to observe with this technique: you have to be careful with your styles. Applying the "Normal" style in the dummy document, for example, can mess you up (see "Why to Avoid 'Normal,'" in Chapter 5, *Copy Flow*).

The simplest way to avoid headaches is to remember not to apply or change styles when you're editing text in a dummy document. If you must work with styles, then at least be sure that you know your style sheets well and that you avoid the "Normal" style (unless you really know what you're doing).

FORMATTING
Setting Text in All Caps

Never type two spaces after a period. Never type five spaces for an indent. Never cross the road without looking both ways. These are rules to live by, and if you follow them, they'll rarely steer you wrong. Here's another one: never type text in all capital letters in QuarkXPress. It's much more versatile to select any text you want capped and apply the All Caps type style (Command-Shift-K). Then, later, if you change your mind, you can countermand the style rather than having to retype all the text.

Of course, to every one of these rules there are exceptions. The exception to this one is when you're exporting the text as either ASCII text or another format that doesn't support the All Caps type style.

NAVIGATION
The Easy Way to Follow a Text Chain

QuarkXPress has a simple feature that can help if you need to follow a story through your document, but you don't remember the page to which or from which the text chain jumps. All you have to do is position the insertion point at the beginning or end of the story's text box on the current page. If you're at the beginning of the text box, use the Up Arrow key to move the insertion out of the current box to the previous box in the chain. If you're at the end of the box, use the Down Arrow key to jump the insertion point to the next box in the text chain. You can also use the Left Arrow and Right Arrow keys, if you're at the beginning of the first line or the end of the last line.

As soon as you move the insertion point out of the current box, QuarkXPress follows it, scrolling automatically to the page containing the text box to which you've moved the insertion point. If possible, QuarkXPress centers the box in the document window.

NAVIGATION
Moving Around Through (Hidden) Text

You don't have to see text to edit and manipulate it. No, this isn't a dare to create your next newsletter blindfolded. Rather, it comes in handy when you've got text that's overset, kerned outside of a box, or hidden behind some other page object. Remember that you can simply select all the text in a story by pressing Command-A (or clicking five times). Then you can change all the text's formatting at once.

You can also navigate through text that is hidden. For example, you can select all the text from where your cursor is to the end of the story, even when the end of the story is hidden or overset, by pressing Command-Option-Shift-Down Arrow. Table 3-2 shows various keystrokes for moving around through text.

To move to the . . .	Press . . .
Previous character	Left Arrow
Next character	Right Arrow
Previous line	Up Arrow
Next line	Down Arrow
Previous word	Command-Left Arrow
Next word	Command-Right Arrow
Start of line	Command-Option-Left Arrow
End of line	Command-Option-Right Arrow
Start of story	Command-Option-Up Arrow
End of story	Command-Option-Down Arrow

Table 3-2
Keyboard text editing

Add the Shift key to select the text.

FIND/CHANGE

Miniaturizing the Find/ Change Dialog Box

If you've got a small-screen Macintosh, you'll find that the Find/ Change dialog box fills the entire screen when you are searching or replacing attributes. Even with a larger screen, this dialog box takes up way too much room. Thus, when you click on Find Next, you usually can't see what the program found. However, you can reduce the size of the dialog box considerably by clicking its zoom box (see Figure 3-1). The reduced view shows only the buttons you need to navigate and change what you've specified. Clicking the zoom box again takes you back to the larger dialog box.

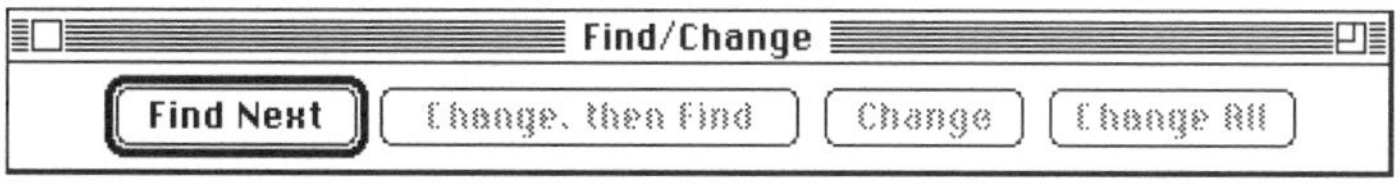

FIND/CHANGE

Searching the Entire Document

In earlier versions of XPress (pre-3.2), you had to ensure that no text boxes were selected when you wanted to search your entire document for text. However, that's no longer the case. Just make sure you've checked Document in the Find/Change dialog box.

Figure 3-1
Shrinking the Find/Change dialog box

FIND/CHANGE

Searching for Invisible Characters

Don't forget that the search-and-replace functions work with invisible characters, such as hard and soft returns, tabs, and new

FIND/CHANGE
Quick Finding by Formatting

If you're using Find/Change to find particular formatting, remember that if you uncheck Ignore Attributes in the Find/Change dialog box, XPress picks up the formatting from the current cursor location. For instance, if you select some 18-point Zapf Dingbats text, when you uncheck Ignore Attributes, XPress is all set to search for 18-point Zapf Dingbats. (Of course, you can change this setting; this is just the way it first comes up in the dialog box.)

SPELLING
One-Letter Misspellings

How many years have we used XPress's spelling checker before we finally figured out that it ignores one-letter words? That means if you're typing quickly and press the wrong key—for instance, you type "s boat is docked" rather than "a boat is docked"—XPress won't catch the word as misspelled. We suppose there's nothing like a final once-over for catching these little mistakes.

column or new box characters. There are three ways to search for an invisible character.

▶ Copy one of these characters from the text and paste it into the appropriate field in the Find/Change dialog box

▶ Type the code for that character. For example, you can search for a tab by typing "\t" in the Find What field.

▶ Hold down the Command key while typing the character. For instance, to search for a Return character, you can press Command-Return in the Find What field.

FIND/CHANGE
Searching for the Unsearchable

Earlier, we gave you some hints on how to look for invisible characters. However, there are some characters XPress doesn't let you search for. For instance, you can't enter the indent here, the non-breaking space, or the right-margin tab (Option-Tab) characters.

If you have some heavy duty search and replace to do with any of these characters, you can always export your story in XPress Tags format and search for the characters there.

We cover XPress Tags more in Chapter 5, *Copy Flow*, but let's just say the indent here character is coded with "<\i>", the right-margin tab is "<\t>", and the nonbreaking space is "<\!s>". Note that if you're doing the search and replace in XPress itself (if you've exported as XPress Tags and reimported the tags as ASCII text, *without* curling the quotes), you have to type two backslashes for every character code instead of one (for instance, type "<\\i>").

SPELLING
Editing Dictionaries with a Word Processor

QuarkXPress dictionaries are simply text files, with one word per paragraph. They have a type of "TEXT" and a creator of "XPR3" (you can view a file's type and creator with DiskTop, ResEdit, Shane the Plane, and several other programs). Because it's a text file, you can edit a QuarkXPress auxiliary dictionary with any word processor. But when you're done, remember to sort the file alphabetically, remove any empty lines, and save as text only. If your word processor changes the file creator (Microsoft Word does), you have to use one of the utilities noted above (the shareware ones are found on the disc in the back of the book) to change the creator back to "XPR3" so that QuarkXPress can "see" it. (In QuarkXPress 3.0, the creator code is "XPRS".)

SPELLING

Adding Your Microsoft Word Dictionary

The user dictionaries that Microsoft Word creates are text files as well, and like QuarkXPress dictionaries, they have one word per paragraph. They're usually called something like "User 1". Because Word's dictionaries are of type "DICT", you have to use Word's Open Any File command (Shift-F6) to open them. Once it's open, you can copy the contents and paste them into your QuarkXPress auxiliary dictionary.

Be aware that if you edit a Word dictionary and save it, you have to sort it in Word's special order (alphabetically in each of three groups: all caps, all initial caps, then all lowercase), save it as text only, and then change the file type back to "DICT" before Word will recognize it as a dictionary.

SPELLING

No Diacritical Marks in Dictionaries

When you're defining or editing an auxiliary dictionary for QuarkXPress, you can't put in any words that use diacritical marks, such as *cliché*, *mañana*, *Übermensch*, and so on. Quark-XPress doesn't like them, and you'll probably end up rendering the entire custom dictionary unusable. We wish we could tell you of a workaround; unfortunately, the only one we can think of means purchasing Quark's expensive multiple foreign-language version of QuarkXPress, which is called Passport.

SPELLING

Speed Spelling Check

If you've ever tried to check the spelling in an enormous document, you've probably found yourself waiting for the screen to redraw. Only after the redraw can you decide to move on to the next word. Bob Martin points out that the process goes more quickly if you first reduce the document window size considerably and then zoom in to 400 percent. QuarkXPress has very little to redraw on the screen each time. Plus, the found text is almost always more visible in the small window.

SPELLING

Lost Auxiliary Dictionaries

Similarly to graphics files, QuarkXPress can lose track of an auxiliary dictionary if you move or rename the dictionary or reinstall XPress. Help the program find the dictionary when it tells you it can't find it. It'll remember in the future.

SPELLING

Thunder 7 as an Alternative Dictionary

You might want to consider Thunder 7, from Baseline Publishing, as an alternative spelling checker. Thunder can check spelling interactively as you type, or check a selected word or text block (this last feature doesn't work that well with XPress, but Baseline Publishing is trying to fix it). It works with just about every Macintosh application, so if you use it religiously, you can trash all the other dictionary files that clutter your hard drive. You can use its neat Glossary feature to have one set of characters automatically replace others, so if you frequently misspell "the" as "teh," it automatically replaces the latter with the former. Or you could have "XPress" or "QXP" be automatically expanded to "QuarkXPress" whenever you type it.

And, yes, Virginia, you can enter diacritical marks in Thunder 7's custom dictionaries.

TABS

Don't Use Spaces for Tabs

Have you ever tried to align multiple columns using spaces? If you have, you have probably known frustration like no other frustration known to desktop publishers. We call it the "it-works-on-a-typewriter" syndrome. It's true; you can line up columns on a typewriter using spaces. But you shouldn't in desktop publishing. The reason has to do with fonts.

On most standard typewriters, the font you're using is a monospaced font. That means every character in the font is the same width. However, most typefaces on the Macintosh are not monospaced. Therefore, you cannot rely on an equal number of characters always being an equal distance. Figure 3-2 shows this phenomenon clearly. So, don't use multiple spaces when you're trying to align columns. In fact, don't use multiple spaces ever. Use tabs. Tabs have three distinct advantages. They always take you to a specific point in the row of text. They can be easily adjusted throughout a bunch of text. And you can add, change, or remove leaders quickly.

UNDERSCORES

Making Rules in Forms

The only thing harder than filling out a stack of forms is designing and producing the forms themselves. Fortunately, there are ways to make this process go by a little faster. For example, lines for "user reply" can be made in one of three ways, explained in this and the next two tips.

Figure 3-2
Using spaces for alignment

Title	Price	Code	
Tempest	129.95	SHK-322	
Merchant	31.95	SHK-335	*Aligned with spaces (bad)*
Survival Kit	22.95	BLA-001	
Virginia Woolf	14.95	ALB-113	

Title	Price	Code	
Tempest	129.95	SHK-322	
Merchant	31.95	SHK-335	*Aligned with tabs (good)*
Survival Kit	22.95	BLA-001	
Virginia Woolf	14.95	ALB-113	

The first way is the limited way. It's the way that we probably all started with: type out 30 or so underscores (Shift-Hyphen) in a row. But typing multiple underscores in a row is like typing multiple spaces to line up a column of text; it never really works right because they don't line up at the ends of the line. However, they often work fine in the middle of sentences (see Figure 3-3).

Hereto and forthwith, all references to _____ shall

be fully stricken from the _____ and the

_____, notwithstanding.

Name_____

Address_____

Telephone number_____

Figure 3-3
Using the underscore character

These characters had to be tracked together.

Multiple underscores never line up correctly.

UNDERSCORES

Underlined Tabs

Our favorite way of creating user reply lines that have to align is to specify tab stops with fill characters. For example, if you have the word "Name" followed by a line that extends to the right margin, just type a tab after the word. Then set a tab stop at the right margin and give it an underscore for a fill character (or—because version 3.3 lets you type two characters—type *two* underscores or you'll end up with a dashed line). As long as each tab stop is set to the same place, every line that has this tab in it reaches to the tab stop. However, there are two things to watch for. First, in some typefaces at some sizes, the underscores may not touch each other, resulting in a broken dashed line (see Figure 3-4). You can often fix this by selecting the tab character and applying -20 tracking. The other potential problem with this method is that you cannot precisely specify the thickness or the position of the line (you can, however, change the point size of the tab character, and hence the underscores, which changes position and thickness).

Also, if you want the tab stop to be all the way to the right margin, try using a right-aligned tab by pressing Option-Tab. Then add a tab stop anywhere and give it the desired Fill Character. You need to do this because the right-aligned tab picks up the fill character from the last tab stop.

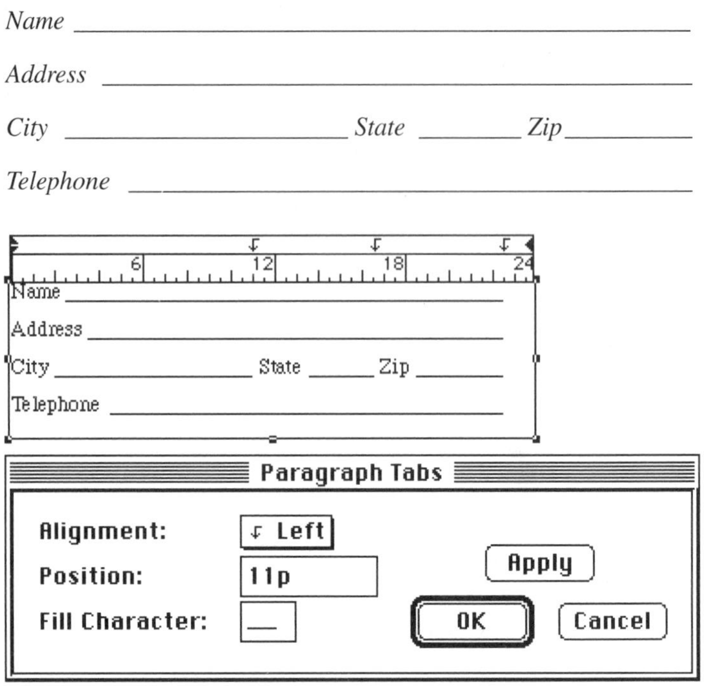
Name
Address
City
State
Zip
Telephone
6
12
18
24
Name
Address
City
State
Zip
Telephone
Paragraph Tabs
Alignment:
Left
Position:
11p
Fill Character:
Apply
OK
Cancel

Figure 3-4
Using tabs with Fill Characters

UNDERSCORES

Anchored Rule Below

A third method of creating underscores is slightly more tricky, but ultimately more powerful: applying a rule below the paragraph. Rule Below (Command-Shift-N) can be set to almost any offset and thickness. However, unless you're rather clever, you can't have more than one underline per line (like in Figure 3-5).

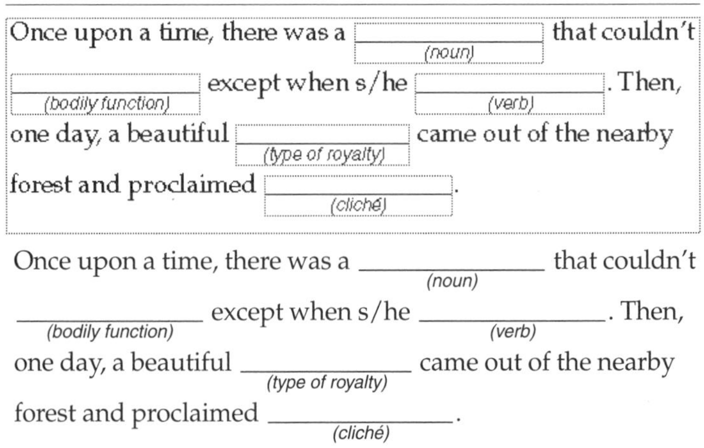
Once upon a time, there was a
(noun)
that couldn't
(bodily function)
except when s/he
(verb)
. Then,
one day, a beautiful
(type of royalty)
came out of the nearby
forest and proclaimed
(cliché)
Once upon a time, there was a
(noun)
that couldn't
(bodily function)
except when s/he
(verb)
. Then,
one day, a beautiful
(type of royalty)
came out of the nearby
forest and proclaimed
(cliché)

Figure 3-5
Anchored Underscores

IMPORTING

Fast Saves from Word

This tip is really directed more at Microsoft Word, but because so many QuarkXPress users bring files in from Word (we do), we thought this was relevant: Never use Fast Save in Microsoft Word. Fast Save is a feature that saves time in saving documents, but increases trouble down the line (both in Word and in XPress). For instance, text can get "lost" from one save to another, and sometimes text doesn't import correctly into QuarkXPress when the file was fast saved.

To get around Fast Save, go to the Preferences dialog box in Microsoft Word 5.0 and later and turn off the Allow Fast Saves checkbox (see Figure 3-6). (Other word processors might also have this capability; turn it off there, too.)

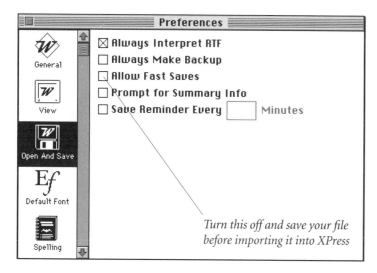

Turn this off and save your file before importing it into XPress

Figure 3-6
Fast Saves in Microsoft Word

TEXT

Saving as RTF

The title of this tip implies that you actually *can* save text out of QuarkXPress in RTF (Rich Text Format). We didn't quite lie, but the truth is you can't (at least not at the time of this writing). Sorry. If you really need RTF text, we suggest saving the file as a Microsoft Word file, then opening it in Word and saving it as RTF. If you know of an easier way, let us know! (Windows XPress supports RTF import and export; that the Mac doesn't is a mystery.)

CLIPBOARD

Copy and Paste Commonly Used Characters

Typing bullets at the beginning of each line in a long list can drive anybody absolutely bonkers. The same thing goes with any commonly repeated character, especially if the character is in a different font or requires a hard-to-remember modifier key. Instead, just copy one of them and paste them wherever you need them. Yes, the Command-V for pasting is also a keystroke, but it's easier than some keystrokes and certainly easier than changing the font, color, etc., all the time.

Footnotes

If you use a lot of footnotes in your text, you'll be happy to note (no pun intended) that QuarkXPress can import footnotes from Microsoft Word. However, it doesn't drop them at the bottom of each page. Rather, it places them at the end of the text flow. Plus, the numbers (or other reference marks) are maintained and set to the Superior style.

type 4
& TYPOGRAPHY

While QuarkXPress has recently been most applauded for its control of color, most of us remember the earlier days when the program was known far and wide as *the* program for professional typography controls. Certainly, its type features have not lessened any. In fact, XPress has added even more complex features. Of course, alongside those features are a large number of tips and tricks for getting the most out of them. Let's delve, shall we?

Use the Content Tool

The very first thing you need to know about the control of type in QuarkXPress is that you must have two things selected: the Content tool and the text you want to change. If you want to make a character-based change, you must have those characters you want to alter selected. If you want to make a paragraph-based change, you can select the paragraph (four mouse clicks) or any portion of the paragraph. You can even just have the cursor located anywhere within the paragraph, or have a portion of your selection extending into the paragraph. Just remember: if you want to change the *contents* of a text box, use the Content tool.

Jump to Font Field

If you've ever wondered how the Research and Development department at Quark decides what features to put into Quark-XPress, this might amuse you. Tim Gill, founder and senior vice-president for R&D at Quark, attended the first annual Quark Users' International Conference in New York City back in 1991. In the middle of a question-and-answer session, someone stood up and asked if there was a way to change quickly from one font to another.

He thought about it for a few moments and replied, "How about a keystroke that places you in the font field of the Measurements palette?" After a round of applause, he said, "Okay, it'll be in the next version." That keystroke, we're proud to report, is Command-Shift-Option-M (the same as jumping to the Measurements palette, but adding the Shift key).

Missing Fonts

People have come up with all sorts of ways to keep track of which fonts are in which documents, including typing the font names in the Get Info dialog box in the Finder or keeping elaborate lists lying about their desks (one look at our desks and you'll know why we don't even bother with this option). However, no matter what you do, you're likely to come up against that dreaded, "Fonts not installed" message.

Fortunately, you don't have to leave the program to load a new font if you're using a program like MasterJuggler or Suitcase. (And if you're not using one of these: Shame on you! Buy MasterJuggler or Suitcase immediately.) However, if the document came from someplace else, you may not even have the font. This is a job for that little super-feature: font substitution!

You can substitute fonts in two ways. First, when you first open the document and it tells you that one or more fonts are missing, you can bring up the Missing Fonts dialog box (see Figure 4-1). You can select fonts to substitute for the missing fonts and then click Replace.

The second technique is to select Font Usage from the Utilities menu once the document is open. Then select the missing typeface from the Font popup menu on the left side of the dialog box (see Figure 4-2) and select the typeface you want to replace it with on the right side.

Note that once you've substituted one font for another, your document's text is almost sure to reflow, so line breaks won't be the same and some text may be lost to overset. Nonetheless, it's better than the fonts coming out bitmapped or in Chicago.

Figure 4-1
Missing font dialog box

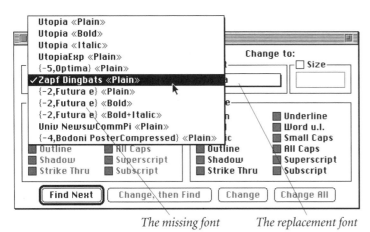

Figure 4-2
Font Usage dialog box

The missing font   *The replacement font*

Using TrueType Fonts

Once upon a time, there was a wise old guru sitting on a Himalayan mountain top, quietly contemplating the harmonious connection between her navel and the universal Om. She had studied the masters—the Bible, the Gita, the Koran, *The Wall Street Journal*—and she had meditated on the meaning of life and desktop publishing. One day, a young man appeared. Weary after months of climbing and struggling, he stumbled up to the guru and asked, "O wise one, I have traveled over oceans and through valleys to find you. Can you please tell me the secret to happiness?"

The guru looked at the young one with compassion. For she had once been there, too. Slowly, carefully, she uttered these words: "Don't use TrueType fonts."*

The Color of Type

When designers and typesetters talk about the color of a page or the color of type, they probably aren't talking red, green, or blue. They're referring to the degree of darkness or lightness (the grayness) that the text projects. The color of text is directly related to the typeface, the letterspacing, wordspacing, and leading. You can

---

* *Later, over a cup of espresso, she clarified her position: "TrueType is fine unless you're trying to do quality graphic design work, are working with other people, or are working with a service bureau. If you're serious about desktop publishing, use PostScript fonts."*

Jumping Forward in the Menu

If your font and style menus are really long and you want to jump to a certain point in the menu, you can use the two methods of selecting a font in the Measurements palette together. For example, if you're looking for Zapf Dingbats but can't remember how "Zapf" is spelled, you can type "Z" in the font field of the Measurements palette (remember you can get there quickly by pressing Command-Option-Shift-M), then clicking on the popup list. You are transported directly to the end of the list (well, the beginning of the "Z" section) as opposed to the beginning.

talk about the color of a word, a line of type, a paragraph, or even a whole page. It's usually a good practice to maintain a balanced color, unless you're trying to pull the viewer's eye to one area or another (see Figure 4-3).

One way to see the color of a page or a block of type is to look at the printed page at a distance. Some designers like to place the page on a table and then stand on a chair to look straight down at it. You can also turn the page over and hold it up to light, so you can see the text blocks without being distracted by the text itself. Or even flip the page top-to-bottom so that you're still looking at the page from the front but upside-down so you can't easily read it. Then things like general color—as well as bad H&J, kerning, tracking, and so on—really stick out.

Precision Font Sizing

If you want to change the size of all the type in a selection, simply use QuarkXPress's keyboard commands. Command-Shift-period

Figure 4-3
The color of text blocks

Eduardus ursus, amicis suis agnomine "Winnie ille Pu"—aut breviter "Pu"—notus, die quodam canticum semihiantibus labellis superbe eliquans

Helvetica 10/12

Eduardus ursus, amicis suis agnomine "Winnie ille Pu"—aut breviter "Pu"—notus, die quodam canticum semihiantibus labellis

Helvetica bold 10/9

Eduardus ursus, amicis suis agnomine "Winnie ille Pu"—aut breviter "Pu"—notus, die quodam canticum semihiantibus labellis superbe eliquans

Helvetica bold with -6 tracking

Eduardus ursus, amicis suis agnomine "Winnie ille Pu"—aut breviter "Pu"—notus, die quodam canticum semihiantibus labellis superbe eliquans

Palatino 10/12

Eduardus ursus, amicis suis agnomine "Winnie ille Pu"—aut breviter "Pu"—notus, die quodam canticum semihiantibus labellis superbe eliquans

Palatino italic 10/12

Eduardus ursus, amicis suis agnomine "Winnie ille Pu"—aut breviter "Pu"—notus, die quodam canticum semihiantibus

Palatino bold 10/15

Eduardus ursus, amicis suis agnomine "Winnie ille Pu"—aut breviter "Pu"—notus, die quodam canticum semihiantibus labellis superbe eliquans

Minion Black 10/12

Eduardus ursus, amicis suis agnomine "Winnie ille Pu"—aut breviter "Pu"—notus, die quodam canticum semihiantibus labellis superbe eliquans

Minion Black 10/9

Eduardus ursus, amicis suis agnomine "Winnie ille Pu"—aut breviter "Pu"—notus, die quodam canticum semihiantibus labellis superbe eliquans

Minion Expert 10/12

increases every character to the next highest of QuarkXPress's pre-set sizes (the familiar 9, 10, 12, 14, 18, and so on). Add the Option key and every character will be enlarged a point at a time. Similarly, pressing Command-Shift-comma and Command-Option-Shift-comma reduces every character by pre-defined sizes or a point at a time, respectively.

These commands are particularly useful when you're working with a range of text with characters of varying sizes. With a single keyboard command, you can quickly bump up or bump down the sizes of every character, while retaining (more or less) the relative differences in size between characters.

If you aren't satisfied with the preset font sizes or if you want all the characters in a selection to be changed to the same type size, you can type in your own—in .001-point increments—in the Font Size dialog box (see Figure 4-4). The slow way to get there is through the Style menu. The fast way to get there is by pressing Command-Shift-\. You could also just type the value in the point size field of the Measurements palette.

Figure 4-4
The Font Size dialog box

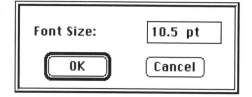

SMALL GEM
Finding Your 'x' Height

There are all sorts of generalizations for how big the x-height (the size of the lowercase characters) of a font should be. For instance, x-height is usually about half the size of the type size, and cap size (the size of a capital letter) is usually about two-thirds the type size. But if you want to know the exact size, here's a way to figure it out.

1. In a text box, type the lowercase letter "x", then press Return, then type "x" again.

2. Select the text. Set it to the size and font you're going to use.

3. Then adjust the leading of the two lines until the baseline of the first "x" hits the top of the second "x" (we like to use the Command-Shift-semicolon and straight quote keystrokes to get close, then add the Option key to fine-tune the leading). That leading value is the x-height (see Figure 4-5). Do this at 400-percent view to get a more accurate reading.

This also works for getting the height of capitals or symbols.

Figure 4-5
Finding the height of a lower-case "x"

Xephrox
Xephrox

type size: 34 points
leading: 34 points

Xephrox
Xephrox

type size: 34 points
leading (x-height): 15.3 points

RESEDIT

Adding a New Point Size to a Menu

Maybe you're the kind of person who always uses 26-point type. Maybe you're also tired of always having to select 26 from the Other Size dialog box (Command-Shift-\). Charlie Downs showed us how you can actually add that point size to the Size submenu in the Style menu and in the Measurements palette.

Note that you have to use ResEdit for this tip, so it's not for the faint of heart. Remember that when you're working in ResEdit, always work on a copy of the file so you don't accidentally destroy your original application.

1. Launch ResEdit and open a copy of QuarkXPress.

2. Double-click on the "MENU" resource (you can type "M" to jump to it).

3. Locate "MENU" resource number 35 and double-click on it (see Figure 4-6).

4. Select New Item from ResEdit's Resource menu.

Figure 4-6
Adding a point size in ResEdit

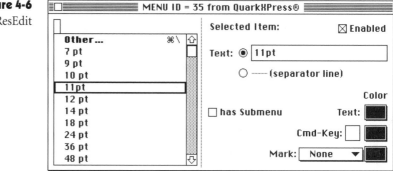

5. Type the point size you want to add in the Title box (you have to click in the field first).

6. Drag the new point size to where you want it in the list.

7. Repeat the process for each new point size you want to add.

8. Save your work and quit ResEdit.

When you launch this new copy of QuarkXPress, you can see the new point size(s) in the menu. You can even add a Command-keystroke to that number with QuicKeys or in ResEdit (see "ResEdit Keystrokes" in Chapter 10, *Macros and Scripts*).

FONTS

Fonts That Don't Change

There are many fonts that were never designed to be set in italic, bold, or bold italic. Among the most common are the Symbol, Zapf Dingbats, and Zapf Chancery fonts that come on many LaserWriters. Although you can make these fonts appear italic or bold on the screen, they don't print correctly on a PostScript laser printer.

When you italicize a face that doesn't have an italic, it either it comes out slanted about 10 or 15 degrees to the right (skewed along the X-axis), or it appears in the regular roman face. If you select bold for a font without a bold, it sometimes looks like it was double-struck on a typewriter (remember those?), or it might print in the regular face.

Other than just printing out tests to see what fonts can be italicized (assuming you know your typefaces well enough to know the difference), the best way you can tell whether there's a printer font or not is to look for a corresponding printer font for each screen font you're using. You can browse the folders where your fonts are stored on your hard disk, or you can do this quickly via a function in the Suitcase utility. Choose Show Resources from the Suitcase menu, click on the font name in the scrolling list, click Show, check Italic (or Bold or Bold Italic), and read the printer font name (Figure 4-7). If the name changes when you check one of the styles, you've just proved that there is a corresponding printer font. If the name doesn't change, then there's no printer font in that particular font family (at least Suitcase can't find one).

FORMATTING

Don't Make Text Plain Unless You Mean It

If there's a style attribute you want to remove from a range of text, or if you want to turn off a particular attribute as you're typing, be sure to turn off only that attribute. If you're too quick to click P for plain text in the Measurements palette, or press Command-Shift-P, you may find that you've removed not only the attribute you wanted to be rid of, but also other formatting you may have wanted to keep. It's far better to simply toggle off the specific attribute you want off.

For example, if you're typing in italic and want to switch back to roman, click I in the Measurements palette, or press Command-Shift-I to turn italic off. To remove italic from a range of text, select the text first. If *every* character in the selection is italic, the italic—and only the italic—will be removed. Bold, super- and subscripts, and so forth, will remain. If there are any characters in the selection that aren't italic, the attribute will be applied to the entire selection; if this happens, pressing Command-Shift-I again will remove the italic from the selection.

Figure 4-7
Suitcase 2's Resources display

You can also use Collect for Output for find out whether a separate font exists for the type style you've chosen. See Chapter 8, *Printing*, for how to use that feature. Look through the font list that the command generates and if you see the outline font in the rightmost column listed more than once, that means that font doesn't exist for at least one of the specified type styles.

FORMATTING

Reversed Type

There is no specific command in QuarkXPress for reversed type—typically white type on a background of any other color— as there is in PageMaker. But that doesn't mean you can't achieve that effect. Simply select the text and choose "White" from the Color submenu (in the Style menu), from the Color popup menu in the Character Attributes dialog box (Command-Shift-D), or in the Colors palette. If you want the reversed type on a black background, either place a black box behind it, or color the text box's background in the Text Box Specifications dialog box (Command-M with the box selected, or double-click on the text box with the Item tool).

RULE ABOVE

Reversed Type in Rules

You can anchor reversed type to text by assigning a thick rule above or below a paragraph and setting the type in the paragraph to white (see Figure 4-8). You need to specify a vertical positioning for the rule so that it "overlaps" its own line. Out of habit, we use a Rule Above sized about four or five points larger than the text size, and specify an offset (vertical position) of -2 or -3 points. You can use this same technique to create multiple-tinted tables.

Figure 4-8
Type in a rule

National	
Abraham	3421
Gosset	6662
Nash	8923
Casteneda	1221

— *Rule Above with an offset of -3 points*

Alternating Tint Stripes

It's a common technique when making tables to add a background of alternating tints so that it's easier to read the rows of text (see Figure 4-9). Our favorite method of making these tinted bars is to use the Rule Above feature.

1. Create a text box and put several paragraphs of dummy text in it. Some paragraphs should be one line only, others could be two or three lines deep.

2. Give the first paragraph a Rule Above with an absolute vertical offset of zero (either zero picas or zero inches, or whatever).

3. Set the thickness of the rule to the leading of the text (you should always use absolute leading when making these sorts of tables).

4. Set the color and the tint of the rule to whatever you'd like.

5. When you've finished making the Rule Above, go to the Style Sheets dialog box (Command-click on a style in the Style Sheets palette or select Style Sheets from the Edit menu) and click the New button. Give the style sheet a name and save it.

Now, whenever you apply this style sheet to a paragraph, the background tint is applied automatically. You can create more than one tint style sheet, and even a multiline style (multiply the number of lines you want tinted by the leading value).

Negative Text Rules

It's easy to use Rule Above or Rule Below to make a rule that only runs under text: just set the Length popup menu in the Paragraph Rules dialog box to Text. Here's how to make just the opposite: a rule that only prints where the text *isn't* (see Figure 4-10).

1. Apply a Rule Above to the paragraph in the size, color, and position that you want the reverse rule to be. For instance, in Figure 4-10, there's a one-point black rule at zero picas down (flush with the baseline). Make sure that the Length popup menu is set to Indent.

Tinted Boxes Behind Paragraphs

Highlighting a whole paragraph with a tint or color behind it can be tricky, especially if you need the highlight to flow along with the text. Try this.

1. Set the left and right indents of the paragraph (or the whole text box) to six points.

2. Give the previous paragraph an enormous Rule Below, with left and right offsets set to -6 points (the same offset as you used in step one). The vertical offset of the rule should be about half the leading of the text. The thickness of the rule should be the leading value multiplied by the number of lines in the highlighted paragraph. For instance, if you're highlighting a paragraph with six lines and the leading is 13 points, then the vertical offset should be about six points and the thickness should be 78 points.

3. You'll probably have to adjust the thickness and offsets of the rule so that it fits the paragraph better.

Figure 4-9
Alternating tints in a table

Type	Page	X-ref
Ephesians	325	✓
Philippians	402	
Colossians	488	
Thessalonians	561	✓
Leary	566	✓

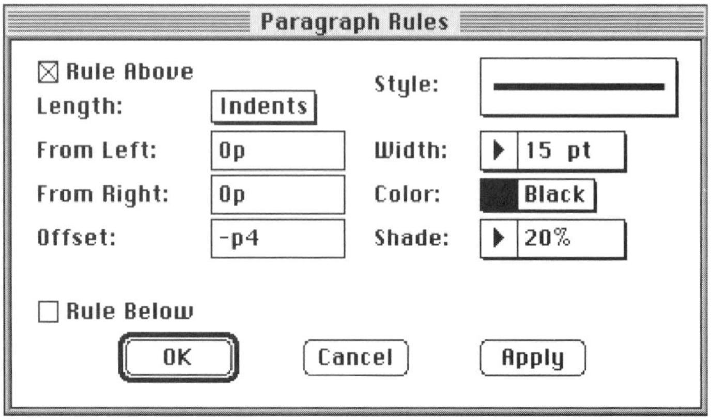

Paragraph Rules

☒ **Rule Above**
Length: [Indents]   **Style:** [—————]
From Left: [0p]   **Width:** ▶ [15 pt]
From Right: [0p]   **Color:** [Black]
Offset: [-p4]   **Shade:** ▶ [20%]

☐ **Rule Below**
[OK]   [Cancel]   [Apply]

2. Apply a Rule Below to the paragraph, and set the Length popup menu for it to Text. Make this rule thicker than the Rule Above, and set it slightly below the Rule Above. For instance, if the Rule Above is set to one point thick at zero offset, set this one to -3 points down and six points thick. Make this rule "White", or whatever other color that blends in to the background of the text box.

Because the Rule Below is white and only covers the text portion of the rule above, the Rule Above "sticks out" only where the text isn't, giving the illusion of a negative space rule.

DESIGN

Tips on Scaling Fonts Horizontally

There's no doubt that desktop publishing has encouraged some of the worst typography ever created. We can't teach you how to set better type, but we do want to throw in a few tidbits on design here and there, just to steer you in the right direction. Here are a few tips on working with horizontal scaling.

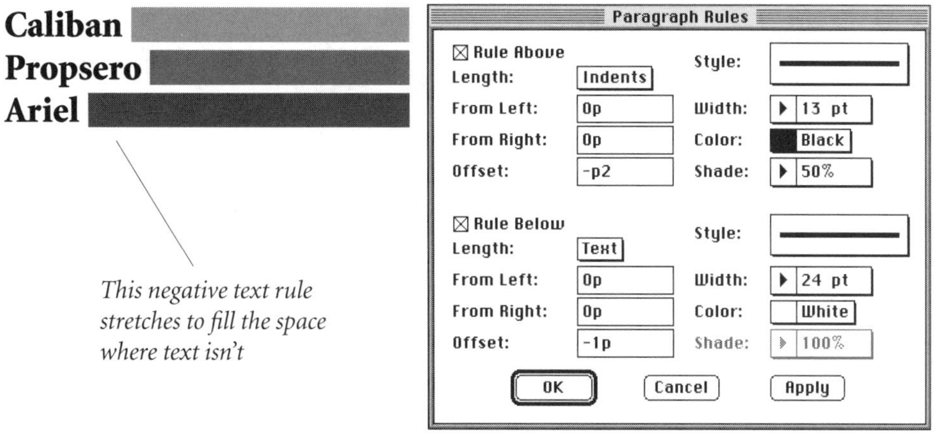

Caliban

Propsero

Ariel

This negative text rule stretches to fill the space where text isn't

Paragraph Rules

☒ **Rule Above**
Length: [Indents]   Style: [————]
From Left: [0p]   Width: ▶ [13 pt]
From Right: [0p]   Color: [■ Black]
Offset: [-p2]   Shade: ▶ [50%]

☒ **Rule Below**
Length: [Text]   Style: [————]
From Left: [0p]   Width: ▶ [24 pt]
From Right: [0p]   Color: [White]
Offset: [-1p]   Shade: ▷ [100%]

(OK)   (Cancel)   (Apply)

Figure 4-10
Rules in the space
before or after text

▶ If you can, avoid stretching type horizontally or vertically. Most graphic designers trained by Europeans say you should never scale a font disproportionately. Although we're more in tune with the American design attitude—which says that legibility is overrated—we still discourage the overuse of this feature.

▶ If you're going to use horizontal scaling, think carefully about the sort of typeface you're using. When you scale a font horizontally, the vertical strokes get thicker or thinner—depending on which way you're scaling—and the horizontal ones stay the same width. A typeface that has thick vertical strokes and thin horizontals (such as Bodoni) can become very odd-looking with just a little scaling. Faces that have only a little change in the weight of strokes throughout horizontals and verticals often handle scaling the best.

▶ Perhaps the worst sort of typefaces to horizontally scale are script faces such as Berthold Script or Park Avenue. These are very delicate, and stretching them makes them look horrible and reduces their marginal legibility even further.

▶ Faces that are more square in nature, especially those with serifs, can handle being compressed somewhat with elegance. ITC Garamond, Cheltenham, and New Century Schoolbook, for instance, don't distort too badly until you drop below 90 percent or above 110 percent.

RULE ABOVE/BELOW
Rules Between Paragraphs

To get a rule between every paragraph—say, in a column of classified ads—remember these tips.

▶ You only need a rule above *or* below, not both (except for the top or bottom of the column).

▶ Try specifying the offset as 50 percent, especially if you're using vertical justification.

▶ If you're using a percentage offset, remember that tops and bottoms of columns are a special case where you'll need to specify your offset in absolute values rather than percentages.

Inflexible Flex Spaces

Unfortunately, QuarkXPress doesn't have a specific command to type an em space. The workaround? The flex space (Option-Shift-spacebar). The "flex" in flex space derives from the ability to change its width to your specification. However, once you set the Flex Space Width in the Typographic Preferences dialog box, the space remains fixed in the document at that size (unless you change its value). Thus, the flex space is actually QuarkXPress's fixed space. It's a document preference (which means that you can also make it an application preference).

The flex space width is set as a percentage of an en space. The default value, 50 percent, equals a half-en space, which some people call a punctuation space or a thin space. To create a flex space that equals an em space, change the percentage to 200 percent. Then press Option-Shift-spacebar whenever you want an em space.

Know Your Ems and Ens

Many typographic controls are specified using units of measure called *ems* and *ens*. (Some people call the en a *nut* to distinguish it aurally from an em.) These are not nearly as confusing as some people make them out to be. The default for the em in Quark-XPress is the width of two zeros side by side in the font and size you're working in. If that sounds weird, it's because it is. We can't figure out why they did it that way, but that's just the way it is. An en space is half of the em space width—the width of one zero.

Because this is so weird and unreasonable, Quark has added a checkbox in the Typographic Preferences dialog box (Command-Option-Y) labeled Standard Em Space. This sets the width of an em space to the same width every other piece of software uses: the size of the typeface you're using. So if you're using 14-point Times with the Standard Em Space checked, the em space is 14 points wide. For consistency and a sense of doing the right thing, we recommend that you set this as your default (by changing the preference with no documents open).

If you're typing along and change point size, then the size of the em and en units changes as well. This can be a great aid. For example, if you change the size of a word after painstakingly kerning it, your kerning does not get lost or jumbled. The kerning was specified in ems, and therefore is scaled along with the type.

Em spaces and em dashes are not always equal in width. Often they are (especially when Standard Em Space is turned on), but (in the case of the em dash) it really depends on what the typeface designer decided.

Option-Spacebar Character

The Option-spacebar character is the only "fixed" space in a Mac font. However, although it is defined in the font as a specific width—usually equal to the spaceband character—different programs actually use it in different ways.

▶ Microsoft Word treats it as a nonbreaking fixed space and makes it the size of the current regular space character.

▶ XPress changes it to the width of a digit in the current font, which is how it defines an en space.

▶ PageMaker, just in case you were curious, treats it the same as Word does.

▶ Torquemada substitutes an Option-K for visibility on screen (it doesn't actually translate it to that character).

All of these ignore, when necessary, the width assigned by the font's designer.

KEYSTROKES

Fast Kerning

Don't even think about dragging that mouse all the way up to the Style menu to assign kerning or tracking! Instead, use that big ol' Measurements palette or the equivalent keystrokes. Command-Shift-] and Command-Shift-[increase and decrease kerning or tracking by 10 units each. If you add the Option key to these, QuarkXPress adjusts by a single unit, instead. Holding down lots of keys takes a little extra time; you can streamline the process even further by creating QuicKey aliases that press all those keys for you whenever you press F9 and F10, or whatever makes sense to you.

Note that these keystrokes exhibit an odd quirk: if you add 13 units of kerning, then press Command-Shift-] to add another 10, you won't get 23 units. Rather, XPress jumps to the next highest multiple of 10; in this case, 20.

KERNING

Kerning the Kerned

What shows up as the kern value when you click between a pair of characters that is kerned because of automatic pair kerning? Nothing. You'll still find a zero in the Kern Amount field. Quark-XPress regards the values applied in automatic kerning as the norm, so you don't have to worry about them.

However, if you manually kern a pair with automatic kerning switched one way, then later you switch it the other way, your kerning values may be way off. For example, if automatic kerning is turned off and you kern a headline so that it looks perfect, then turn automatic kerning on in the Typographic Preferences dialog box, the headline will probably look like crud. Then again, there are almost no reasons to turn automatic kerning off.

CHARACTERS

Punctuation Space Versus Spaceband

Here's some typographic trivia that may clear up some confusion for you. Shift-spacebar gives you a punctuation space in XPress, which is typically the same width as the normal punctuation (comma, period, etc.) in that typeface. However, in some faces the punctuation space looks like it's just the same width as the good old spaceband (the character you get when you hit the spacebar). That's 'cause it probably *is* the same.

They're the same because many font designers make both the spaceband (which is a character and has an assigned width in every font) and all the punctuation exactly half the width of their digits. Therefore, in many fonts, the two characters are the same width.

MEASUREMENTS

What's 7/200 of an Em?

Even though we define kerning and other type-spacing values in ems, don't feel you have to *think* in ems, unless you want to live and breathe typography. The important thing to remember is how the type looks, not all the numbers that get you there. When we're working in Quark-XPress, we almost never think, "Oh, we're going to change the kerning 1/20 of an em." We just say, "Oh, let's see how adding some kerning here would look." Focus on the results, and you'll get the feel for it pretty quickly.

Automatic Page Numbers Don't Kern

If you or the font designer has set up automatic kerning pairs for pairs of numerals, these pairs will *not* be kerned when they appear as automatic page numbers. QuarkXPress considers all automatic page numbers as single characters, even when they are comprised of multiple characters. Sadly, there's no ready fix for this one, except to use a typeface for page numbers in which the lack of automatic kerning won't cause an aesthetic headache.

Thin Spaces Before Punctuation

Sometimes people use (or are required to use) a typographic style that calls for small spaces (a specified percentage of the em) before colons, semicolons, question marks, etc. (This was the standard some years ago, and still is in some European countries.)

There are essentially two different ways of going about this:

▶ Use a fixed space. The ideal character to use in Quark-XPress is the flex space, since you can define it to be any width you want. (Remember, the number you type into the dialog box is the percentage of an en, which is either the width of a zero in the font or half a standard em.)

▶ If you want several different sizes of these thin spaces, you should use kerning instead because you can't spec the flex space to be multiple widths.

If your art director is asking for a percentage of an em—let's say a fifth—before punctuation, you can figure out how many units of Quark's kerning you need pretty easily. Because one unit of kerning is $\frac{1}{200}$ of an em, you want to add 40 units of kerning ($200 \div 5 = 40$).

Un-Kerning Your Numbers

This tip puts a spin on what we think is a bug: applying the small caps style to numbers makes XPress ignore any kerning information you set up in XPress's internal kerning tables for those numbers. On the positive side: If you kerned your digits using the Kern/Track Editor, and now you want to use that font in a tabular setting where you don't want the digits kerned after all, apply the Small Caps style to the digits. The characters stay the same, but the kerning goes away!

Note that this trick doesn't work if you've used another method (a commercial font-editing program) to kern your font.

Converting Kern Values

Note: If you don't know what a "FOND" kern value is, you simply don't need this tip.

Confused because you thought the "FOND" metric values (which includes the kern-pair values) were ¹⁄₁₀₀₀ of the point size and XPress's values were ¹⁄₂₀₀ of the point size, so you assumed you could simply multiply or divide by five to convert from one to the other? And it doesn't work out exactly?

The problem is that QuarkXPress's values are *not necessarily* ¹⁄₂₀₀ of the point size. Unless you have turned Standard Em Space on in the Typographic Preferences dialog box, they're ¹⁄₂₀₀ of the width of two zeroes in that particular font.

Here's the rub: In some fonts, the zero *is* exactly half the width of the point size; in most other fonts, it's somewhere fairly near that; but then in some other fonts, it's not at all close.

You can determine the kern-pair values, and the width of the zero, in any font by examining the AFM file (which comes with all fonts from Adobe and many other — but not all — font vendors) with a word processor, or by looking at the zero in a font-editing program like Fontographer.

Anyway, here's the conversion formula that works: divide the "FOND" value by the zero's width, moving the decimal to where it makes sense (you're probably going to see the zero's width expressed as a three-digit integer—like 500—in which case you'll need to move the decimal two places to the left, or as a three-digit decimal fraction—like .500—in which case move the decimal one place to the right). The answer is the value in QuarkXPress units.

For example: The AFM tells us that the width of the font's zero is 440 (so we move the decimal two places to the left) and that the FOND kern-pair value is 22. Divide 22 by 4.4, which gives you the QuarkXPress kern value, five.

The best solution, however, is simply to turn Standard Em Space on in the Typographic Preferences dialog box (if you're using version 3.2 or later). Then all this is made much simpler: a unit really *is* ¹⁄₂₀₀ of an em.

Removing Manual Kerning

Have you ever been handed a file in which someone had spent many hours laboriously kerning type by clicking between characters and adjusting the setting? What if you want to remove all that kerning before starting over? If you have Quark's free FeaturesPlus or Thing-a-ma-bob XTension installed (the former for versions 3.1 and 3.2, and the latter for version 3.3), you'll see a feature in the Utilities menu called Remove Manual Kerning. Just select the range of text you want to affect, then select Remove Manual Kerning from the menu. *Voilà!* All gone.

Document-Specific Kern Values

You'd like to have different kern-pair values attached to different documents? That's a legitimate thing to do. For example, different customers might use the same font but have different preferences about such things.

Choosing Kerning Table Edit from the Utilities menu (when the Kern/Track Editor is in the QuarkXPress or XTension folder) lets you change kerning pairs in QuarkXPress (it doesn't change the font itself, so you don't have to worry about your kerning messing up other programs). The kerning pair information that you add gets saved in both the XPress Preferences file and the document you're working on. That means that after you change the kerning pair (while in a document), that same kerning pair is applied to every new document you create from then on.

If you want the kerning pair to be for that document only, reset the kerning pairs with no documents open.

Later, when you open the changed document, XPress asks you whether you want to use the XPress Preferences or the document's preferences. Click Keep Document Settings to keep the kerning changes you made (if you accidentally click Use XPress Preferences, you'll lose your kerning work; to get it back, or choose Revert from the File menu).

Remember that you can create a template from your document. That way, every time you want to use those kerning pairs, you can simply open that template and start working.

Adding Kern Pairs to Your Fonts

It's possible to add a huge number of automatic kern pairs to your fonts by using either the XPress Kerning Table Edit command or a commercial product like KernEdit, MacKern, or LetrTuck.

If you do add pairs to your fonts using one of the commercial editors just listed, the most important thing for you to remember is that you will now have to send a copy of the applicable screen fonts (not the outline fonts, just the bitmap fonts) to anyone and everyone to whom you ever send the QuarkXPress document. The bitmap suitcase file is where the kern pairs are stored; if you send your file to someone for output without the modified bitmap font, then your kern pairs won't show up in the output job. You can get around this, of course, by sending a PostScript dump of the file instead of the file itself.

If you add pairs using only QuarkXPress's Kern/Track Editor, then the applicable pairs are stored in your document itself (in versions 3.1 and later; in 3.0, they're stored in your XPress Data file, which you have to send), so you don't need to send your bitmap fonts along with your jobs. This is a good argument for making your kerning pairs using this method.

There are two good arguments against using the Kerning Table Editor in XPress.

▶ At least one commercial kern editor (KernEdit) is far superior to work with.

▶ Fonts kerned with one of the commercial editors will still have custom kern pairs when you use the fonts in another program, such as PageMaker, Illustrator, or FreeHand).

Kerning the Spaceband

Many fonts include kern pairs that included the spaceband, such as "W" plus the spaceband. Let's be frank (you can be someone else): Every version of XPress until 3.3 totally ignored kerning pairs that included the spaceband . Sure, you could manually kern between a character and a spaceband, but the program wouldn't read any automatic kerning for character pairs that included a space (and it wouldn't let you create your own using the Kerning Table Editor).

If you're using a version earlier than 3.3 and care about how your type looks, you might consider the AgencyFit XTension from Monotype. It also includes very tight custom kern sets for 65 popular typefaces.

However, if you've upgraded to 3.3, you don't need to worry about any of this. Except for one thing: If you're opening document from older versions of XPress, QuarkXPress might reflow some of the text (see "Lost Kerning Tables" in Chapter 9, *Problems and Solutions*).

TABS

Spaced-Out Leaders

Even though XPress, starting in version 3.3, allows you to enter a two-character leader, such as a period followed by a spaceband, in its tab leader field, there are still times that you need to adjust the spacing between the dots in the tab leader (see Figure 4-11). Here's how.

1. Create a tab that uses a period for its fill character.

2. Select the tab character itself—the entire tab area will become highlighted.

3. Drop the size by a couple of points (one goal here is to simulate "en leaders" like those you can create on a typesetting machine; the point size change helps accomplish that).

4. With the tab still selected, set the tracking to some high number—try 50 for starters. Or do what the truly cool people do: press Command-Shift-] five times.

TRACKING

Adjusting Wordspacing

You know you can kern and you know you can manually track (which is, in some respects, really just kerning over a range of text). Both of these adjust letterspacing—the space between each character is increased or decreased. But what about wordspacing? Most typographers would agree that it's better to adjust the spacing

TRACKING
Stop Tracking Before It's Too Late

Tracking actually adds or subtracts space to the right of each selected character. If you want to track a single word and don't want the space after the last character adjusted, you should select not the whole word, but only the characters up to the last letter. For example, if you want to apply a -10 unit track to the word "obfuscation," without changing the space after the "n," you would only select the letters "obfuscatio" and apply tracking.

Period used as leader character (18 point; same as other type on the line).

Chapter 4.....................................47

Truly, madly . . . . deeply!

The character selected; reduced to 10 point; tracking value of 80 applied.

It droppeth-----------as the purple rain from ⓇⓇⓇⓇⓇⓇⓇⓇⓇHollywood

Other characters used as tab leaders. In the second line, the point size of the tab itself was reduced to 10 points.

Figure 4-12
Word spacing

Ye elves of hills, brooks, standing lakes, and groves, and ye that on the sands with printless foot do chase the ebbing Neptune, and do fly him when he comes back; you demi-puppets that by moonshine do the green, sour ringlets make, whereof the ewe not bites; and you whose pastime is to make midnight mushrumps, that rejoice to hear the solemn curfew, by whose aid

No added wordspacing

Ye elves of hills, brooks, standing lakes, and groves, and ye that on the sands with print-less foot do chase the ebbing Neptune, and do fly him when he comes back; you demi-puppets that by moonshine do the green, sour ringlets make, whereof the ewe not bites; and you whose pastime is to make midnight mushrumps, that rejoice to hear

Wordspacing of 60

between words than between characters, but most people don't realize that you can't do this in XPress in any way other than kerning each spaceband by hand. (Note that you *can* change the word spacing for an entire paragraph by changing its H&J definition.)

If you have either the FeaturesPlus or Thing-a-ma-bob XTension (they're on the disc at the end of this book), you can control wordspacing in a selected range of text using keystrokes: Command-Control-Shift-[and] (those are square brackets). Each time you press these keys, the wordspacing increases or decreases by 10 units (see Figure 4-12). If you add the Option key to the lineup, it changes wordspacing by one unit at a time.

Note that what XPress is really doing is pretty simple: it's adding kerning between each space band and the character that follows it. If you click after any space, the kern value appears in the Measurements palette. Therefore, the only way to take away all the "wordspacing" is to get rid of the kerning. We suggest using the Remove Manual Kerning feature, which also appears in the Utilities menu when one of these XTensions is loaded.

TABS

Insert Space

At least one traditional typesetting system has a feature called insert space, which sets some type flush left and the rest of the line flush right. You can do this easily enough in QuarkXPress in one of two ways (remember, we're only talking two columns of text with one big space between them).

The first method is to set the alignment of the paragraph to flush right. At the point where you want to insert space, press the

Tab key. If there are no tab stops assigned in the paragraph, the paragraph gets split into two: one part flush left and the other part flush right.

The second method is to use the right-aligned tab. Keep the paragraph flush left, and insert a right-aligned tab (Option-Tab) where you want the space. This is probably the preferred method.

There's also a technique using H&Js that lets you space out several words. See "Multicolumn Insert Space," later in this chapter.

FORCE JUSTIFY

Spacing a Line Out

Another quick-and-dirty way to space out a line of text is to make a new paragraph for just that line, and set the alignment to either Forced (Command-Option-Shift-J) or Justify (Command-Shift-J). If you select Forced justification, you have to insert a return after the line (in other words, you can't have this one line be the last line in the text box). If you select Justify, then put a line break (Shift-Return) at the end of the line. This spaces out the line of text you entered to fill the entire width of its text column (Figure 4-13). The type will be spaced out according to the H&J setting applied to the paragraph.

A refinement on this trick: if you want to enter more than one word on lines justified in this way, create a special H&J setting for such lines, with the intercharacter spacing set to zero. Put regular spaces between characters you want to be spaced out, and non-breaking spaces between characters that you don't want to be spread out (Figure 4-24 also shows this technique).

Figure 4-13
Justifying a single line

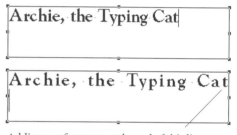

Adding a soft return at the end of this line causes the entire line to be spread out.

DESIGN

Tracking Tips

Ah, we hear the reader sighing, "But what about some real-world tips?" Okay, let's throw some rules out for you.

▶ If you're setting text in all capitals or in true small capitals from an Expert Set font, add between five and 10 units of space by tracking the word. Remember that you may not want to add tracking to the last character of the word (see "Stop Tracking Before It's Too Late," above).

BASELINE SHIFT
When To Avoid Baseline Shift

Please, please, please don't use Baseline Shift to align baselines among columns. Move the whole box or use First Baseline offset, or almost any other technique. In fact, you shouldn't apply baseline shift to more than a couple of characters at a time, unless you're ready for the consequences (like the text block looking totally wrong when text reflows, or any one of a number of other horrible problems). Remember: don't use character formatting to try to achieve anything other than character formatting.

BASELINE SHIFT
Maximum Limit of Baseline Shift

Is there a limit as to how much baseline shift you can apply? Yes; you can shift the text's baseline up to three times the text point size. Should you ever need to do this? Probably not.

▶ Printing white text on a black background often requires a little extra tracking, too. That's because the negative (black) background makes the white characters seem closer together.

▶ Larger type needs to be tracked tighter (negative tracking values). Often, the larger the tighter, though there are aesthetic limits to this rule. Advertising headline copy will often be tracked until the characters just "kiss." You can automate this feature by setting up dynamic tracking tables, which we'll discuss later in this chapter.

▶ A condensed typeface, such as Futura Condensed, can usually do with a little tighter tracking. Sometimes we'll apply a setting as small as -1 to a text block to make it hold together better.

▶ When you're setting justified text and you get bad line breaks, or if you have an extra word by itself at the end of a paragraph, you can track the whole paragraph plus or minus one or two units without it being apparent. Sometimes that's just enough to fix these problems.

Remember, however, that no matter how solid a rule, you are often obliged to break it if the finished design will be better.

BASELINE SHIFT
Point Size and Baseline Shift

If you change the point size of text you've previously applied a baseline shift to, you might notice that the amount of the baseline shift changes. If you had applied a baseline shift of -1 point to some 10-point text, and later changed the type to 12-point, the baseline shift gets changed to 1.2 points.

QuarkXPress is simply keeping the amount of shift proportional to the point size. This is typically what you want it to do, but it's likely to catch you at the worst possible moment. If you don't want the baseline shift to change, you have to respecify your baseline shifts one at a time by hand (or write a script to do it; see Chapter 10, *Macros and Scripts*).

The wonderful Xstyle XTension, from Em Software, has a palette very similar to the QuarkXPress Measurements palette that displays, among other useful formatting attributes, the amount of baseline shift. This is useful in this situation.

BASELINE SHIFT

Using Type Styles to Shift

The truth of the matter is that you can and will use the superior, superscript, or subscript type styles for almost every instance of raising or lowering a character. So what's the advantage of having a separate baseline shift control? Figure 4-14 shows several examples of how you might use these styles in your text.

Figure 4-14
Baseline shift

I DON'T NEED NO BASELINE SHIFT.

I FEEL A NEED FOR A SUPERSCRIPT.

ME, I'D RATHER BE A SUPERIOR CHARACTER.

OY. I'M FEELIN' KINDA UNSTABLE, WHAT WITH ALL THIS BASELINE SHIFTING GOING ON.

ALIGNMENT

Centering Text Horizontally

Specifying either horizontal or vertical center alignment may not result in your text looking perfectly centered. Why? Because the mathematical horizontal centering of text may not look as "right" as an optical centering, especially if you have punctuation before or after the text. To shift text for proper optical alignment, you can use invisible characters colored the same as whatever they're on top of; for example, white on top of a white background. Or, you can use altered indentation (see "Hanging Indents," below) to change the way the text looks (see Figure 4-15). Remember, what looks right is often more "right" than what the computer says.

ALIGNMENT

Centering Blocks of Text

Someone asked us recently about how to center a block of text (an address) in the lower-left part of a business card. She wanted to

SELECTION

Selecting Paragraphs

We often look over people's shoulders when they work, and what we see could scare a moose. One such scare is the technique of selecting a paragraph so that you can apply some paragraph formatting to it (leading, space before, or whatever). People think that they have to select the whole paragraph first. Not true! When changing paragraph formatting, you only have to have the cursor in the paragraph you want to change. That means you can have one word selected, or three sentences, or half of one paragraph and half of another, or just an insertion point (with nothing selected), or whatever.

Figure 4-15
When centering is not centered

"Take your little brother swimming with a brick."

This is not visually centered.

"Take your little brother swimming with a brick."

This is adjusted by placing invisible punctuation on each line.

HELL'S BELLS

Vertically centered

HELL'S BELLS

Vertically centered with baseline shift

ALIGNMENT
Centering Text Vertically

In the case of vertical centering, text in all capitals or text in fonts such as Zapf Dingbats may not appear to be centered in the box. This is because QuarkXPress does not actually find the center of the characters you've typed. Rather, it uses the full height of the font, including ascent (of the tallest character in the font, whether you're using that character or not) and descent, to calculate proper placement. We suggest using baseline shift to move the characters around until they look the way you'd like them to (see Figure 4-15).

Note that when we say you should baseline shift the text, we're only talking about a line or two of text. If you're dealing with a whole paragraph, you should change the First Baseline Offset value or use some other technique to move the text down. Otherwise, if you baseline shift a lot of text, you're bound to get yourself in trouble later.

avoid breaking it into a separate text box because she had to do a *lot* of these, and that'd take too long. We suggested setting the text to Centered alignment, and then making an enormous right indent (see Figure 4-16). Of course, you could do the same thing to center something on the right side. Make this a style sheet so you can apply it quickly!

Here's one other method: place a tab before each line and place a center tab stop where you want the lines to align. If you don't mind adding tabs to the text, this is probably the more flexible technique.

PREFERENCES
Watch the Text Inset

The default text inset for text boxes when you first run QuarkXPress is one point, so your text will be indented one point from each side of the box automatically. Make sure to change the value in the Text Box Specifications dialog box (Command-M) if you don't want the one-point indent for a specific box.

The best way to avoid this default problem is to close all documents, and double-click the Text Box tool. This brings up the Tool Preferences dialog box, where you can click the Modify button to change the Text Inset to zero. Of course, a text inset of zero sometimes makes the text a little hard to read on screen, because it bounces up against the side of the box.

Note that some XTensions, including SetInset and Kitchen Sink, let you set Text Inset separately for each side of the box.

Hanging Indents

You can use Left Indent and First Line (in the Paragraph Formats dialog box) to create hanging indents (used for bullet lists and the like) by typing a negative number as the first line indent. We often enter "1p6" (one and a half picas) for a left indent and "-1p6" for a first-line indent. Then, we type a bullet character, a tab, and the rest of our paragraph. The bullet is placed at the zero mark, and the subsequent lines return to the "1p6" mark (see Figure 4-17). The tabbed text after the bullet skips over to the "1p6" mark whether or not we have explicitly set a tab stop there (as long as there aren't any other explicit tab stops earlier on the line).

Tabs and Hanging Indents

Sometimes people think their tabs aren't working correctly at the beginning of a paragraph. It's a common misunderstanding and one—for once—we can give a simple answer to: a tab at the beginning of a line jumps to either the Left Indent position *or* to the first defined tab stop, whichever is closer to the left margin (see Figure 4-18).

If you place a tab stop to the right of the Left Indent position, the decimal tab won't seem to work; it doesn't jump far enough to the right. However, it's actually just doing its job.

More Hanging Tabs

There's a subtle feature in the decimal tab function that you'll love if you ever create balance sheets. The decimal tab doesn't just line up decimals. Rather, QuarkXPress thinks of any non-number that falls after a number to be a decimal point, and aligns to it. For example, if you press Tab and type "94c2.4" on a line with a decimal tab, QuarkXPress aligns to the "c" rather than the period.

We thought this was a bug, until we realized how handy it could be. For example, if you are lining up numbers in a column, the negative-balance parentheses hang outside of the column. You can even create hanging footnotes, as long as they're not numbers (see unit cost column in Figure 4-19).

Joey Fleishman
Technologist
National Insecurity Council
1400 Pennsylvania Ave
Washington, DC 10014
(201) 123-9876

Joey Fleishman
Technologist

National Insecurity Council
1400 Pennsylvania Ave
Washington, DC 10014

(201) 123-9876

*Centered, Right
Indent of 10p*   *Centered, Left Indent of 10p,
Baseline shift of 24 points*

Figure 4-16
Centering a block of text

Figure 4-17
Hanging indents

➥ Some people like to hang wall-
paper.   ¶

➥ Some people like to hang out-
laws.   ¶

➥ Me, I can't be bothered with
either of those, but I sure do
love to hang indents.

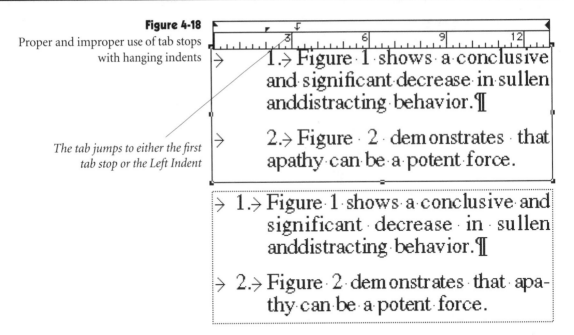

Figure 4-18

Proper and improper use of tab stops with hanging indents

The tab jumps to either the first tab stop or the Left Indent

Figure 4-19

Hanging footnotes

Grazing Goose Records

"It's a Cadillac, dear."

Securities	$223
Properties	152[A]
Cash	(148)[B]
Shoebox fund	33

[A]This month's rent is paid
[B]We owe that guy for the pizzas

STYLE SHEETS

Automatically Generated Bullets

The standard handing-indent approach to bullets works great, but sometimes it's a pain to add bullets in text. Here's how you can get XPress to add bullets to paragraphs for you automatically, just by applying a style (see Figure 4-20).

1. In the Edit Style Sheet dialgo box, click Formats. Give the paragraph a hanging indent; for example, set Left Indent to "1p6" and First Line to "-1p6".

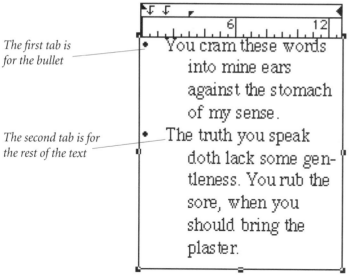

The first tab is for the bullet

The second tab is for the rest of the text

Figure 4-20
Automatically generated bullets

2. Set a left-aligned tab stop between the left margin and the Left Indent value. In this example, let's say at one pica. Choose the bullet character (a standard round bullet is made by pressing Option-8) as Fill Character.

3. For each paragraph you want bulleted, precede the text with two tab characters. The bullet will "type itself" as the fill character in the first tab.

Note that this tip only works when there's room for only one bullet in the first tab. If you see more than one bullet, make the tab smaller (move the stop to the left) until only one bullet appears. Also, note that this tip only works with pretty basic bullets; there's no way to automatically set a different font or size for that bullet character.

GRIDS

Making Use of the Baseline Grid

People who work with leading grids should be thrilled with the Baseline Grid feature in QuarkXPress. Once you set your grid up in the Typographic Preferences dialog box (Command-Option-Y), you can lock text to the underlying grid in the Paragraph Formats dialog box.

TABS

Pure Hanging Tab

The problem with the "More Hanging Tabs" tip is: what if you have a piece of text like "94c2.4" and you want it to align on the decimal point, not on the "c"? Quark added a more specialized version of the decimal tab in version 3.2, which is the Align On tab. Align On lets you specify the *only* character which is used for alignment, which can be a period, a "c", or any other character.

GRIDS

GRIDS
Constant First Baselines

When you're working with a leading grid, you might be frustrated by where Quark-XPress places the first line in a text box. That's because XPress generally moves the baseline of the first line up or down to accommodate the size of the text, rather than sticking to your baseline grid (see Figure 4-21). But if you explicitly set the First Baseline value for the text box in the Text Box Specifications dialog box (Command-M), the first baseline always appears at the same place, and your leading grid isn't messed up. Note that the First Baseline value has to be bigger than the type itself in order for the line to be moved down.

So don't go adding multiple carriage returns or trying to do weird things with leading, Space Before, or Baseline Shift. Just use the First Baseline setting.

Note that First Baseline Offset aligns all the columns of a text box

Figure 4-21
First Baseline maintains an even leading grid

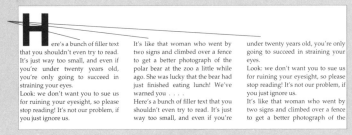

Yuko Hayakawa Kills Godzilla

TOKYO (AP) – Hayakawa-san, in a sudden burst of power, finally achieved victory over the terrible beast today in a battle that few will ever forget. Fortunately

Yuko Hayakawa Kills Godzilla

TOKYO (AP) – Hayakawa-san, in a sudden burst of power, finally achieved victory over the terrible beast today in a battle that few will ever forget. Fortunately

First Baseline Offset is the best way to adjust the placement of the first line in a text box.

Here's a bunch of filler text that you shouldn't even try to read. It's just way too small, and even if you're under twenty years old, you're only going to succeed in straining your eyes.

Look: we don't want you to sue us for ruining your eyesight, so please stop reading! It's not our problem, if you just ignore us.

It's like that woman who went by two signs and climbed over a fence to get a better photograph of the polar bear at the zoo a little while ago. She was lucky that the bear had just finished eating lunch! We've warned you . . .

Here's a bunch of filler text that you shouldn't even try to read. It's just way too small, and even if you're under twenty years old, you're only going to succeed in straining your eyes.

Look: we don't want you to sue us for ruining your eyesight, so please stop reading! It's not our problem, if you just ignore us.

It's like that woman who went by two signs and climbed over a fence to get a better photograph of the polar bear at the zoo a little while ago. She was lucky that the bear had just finished eating lunch! We've warned you . . . .

Here's a bunch of filler text that you shouldn't even try to read. It's just way too small, and even if you're under twenty years old, you're only going to succeed in straining your

Here's a bunch of filler text that you shouldn't even try to read. It's just way too small, and even if you're under twenty years old, you're only going to succeed in straining your eyes.

Look: we don't want you to sue us for ruining your eyesight, so please stop reading! It's not our problem, if you just ignore us.

It's like that woman who went by two signs and climbed over a fence to get a better photograph of the polar bear at the zoo a little while ago. She was lucky that the bear had just finished eating lunch! We've warned you . . . .

Here's a bunch of filler text that you shouldn't even try to read. It's just way too small, and even if you're

under twenty years old, you're only going to succeed in straining your eyes.

Look: we don't want you to sue us for ruining your eyesight, so please stop reading! It's not our problem, if you just ignore us.

It's like that woman who went by two signs and climbed over a fence to get a better photograph of the

If you want to lock objects, rather than type, to that grid, you have to have the grid showing (select Show Baseline Grid from the View menu or press Option-F7). When the grid is visible and Snap to Guides is turned on, objects snap to the baseline grid and to guides. We don't like the standard color of the baseline grid rules, so we typically change them to something else (click on the Grid color swatch in the Application Preferences dialog box, then set the color you like; we like hue: 45,000, saturation: 10,000, brightness: 65,000).

One other trick: Don't forget about XPress's ability to do math for you. If you use a grid of 14 vertical lines to an inch (agates), you can type "1"/14" in the Increment field of the Baseline Grid area in the Typographic Preferences dialog box. Then, if you want to place a picture box 30 of these units down, you can type 30 times the grid amount or "30*1"/14" in the vertical origin of the Measurements palette.

TABS

Scrolling the Tab Ruler

As the old Zen master said, "Frustration dissipates like the morning fog when light is shed on the problem." (Actually, we don't know any Zen masters, so we just made that up.) One frustration we've seen people get caught in is the issue of formatting past the boundaries of the text box.

For example, when you open the Paragraph Formats dialog box, QuarkXPress adds a ruler along the top of the text box so that you can manually add or edit the tab stops and indents. However, if the box is too wide, you can't see the left or right side of the ruler because it runs right off the document window.

However—and here's the shedding-of-the-light part—it turns out that if you click in that ruler and drag to the left or right, the page scrolls with you. Pretty soon you get to where you want to go and you can stop dragging. Note that when you do this, you sometimes add a tab stop, and you have to get rid of it by dragging it off the ruler.

SPACE BEFORE/AFTER

Use Space Before Not After

Look: you can do whatever you want to with XPress—you can use it as a bathtub toy for all we care (it floats—for a while—if you leave the shrinkwrap on). But that won't stop us from making suggestions, kibitzing, and telling you how we use the program. That's our contractual obligation, as authors. For instance, we almost never use Space After in the Paragraph Formats dialog box. Instead, we use Space Before.

For instance, in this book we use Space Before for the headings. We could apply Space After to the last paragraph of each tip (which would do the same thing), but what if one of the tips changes or we

LEADING
Leading Shortcuts

Back in the good ol' days, whenever we wanted to change the leading of a paragraph (or a bunch of selected paragraphs) from Auto to some absolute number, we'd bring up the Leading dialog box (Command-Shift-E), type a number, and press Enter or Return. Now we've learned better: we just type Command-Shift-semicolon or straight quote. These keystrokes decrease and increase leading by one point. Add the Option key, and you change the leading by $1/10$ of a point.

LEADING
From Automatic to Absolute

If you press Command-Shift-straight quote when the selected paragraph is set to Auto leading, XPress switches the leading to the absolute value that corresponds to the automatic value. For instance, if you've got 10-point type and Auto leading is set to 20 percent, if you select a paragraph that has automatic leading and press Command-Shift-straight quote, XPress changes the leading to 12 points (120 percent of 10 points). This is the fastest way to switch from automatic to absolute leading.

cut the last paragraph in a last-ditch scramble to make it fit on a page? No, Space Before is simply more reliable and logical.

(We do use Space After for one thing, however: lists and bulleted items. In this book, for example, each of the items in a list has space after it, and only the first item of the list has space before it.)

DESIGN
Leading Tips

Here are a few tips and tricks for adjusting your leading. Remember, though, that ultimately it is how easily the text reads and how comfortable the color is that counts.

▶ Increase the leading as you increase the line length. Solid leading may read fine with a line containing five words, but may be awful for a line containing 20 words.

▶ Generally use some extra leading for sans serif or bold type. It needs the extra room.

▶ Note the x-height of your typeface. Fonts with a small x-height and/or long descenders can often be set tighter than those with a large x-height. (In case you're curious, this is because the words already have more "air" in them, between the x-height and the top of the ascenders and/or between the baseline and the bottom of the descenders, than do words with a larger x-height and/or shorter descenders.)

▶ Set display or headline type tightly. Very big type can and should be set tightly, using either "+0" relative leading or even absolute leading smaller than the point size you're using.

▶ When you're using really tight leading, be careful not to let the ascenders of one line touch the descenders of the line above it.

A corollary tip to all of these: Break the rules if doing so makes the design look better!

Zero Leading

If you set a paragraph's leading to zero, QuarkXPress decides you really mean that you want Auto leading (see above). But what if you really want no leading at all from baseline to baseline? If you set leading to .0001 points, the program rounds down to exactly zero. The next highest value is .001 points. The truth of the matter is that these are equivalent for all intents and purposes, but we wanted to be clear anyway.

Why would anyone want to use zero leading? Well, it wouldn't be common (see Figure 4-22), but it's sometimes quite useful for special typesetting effects. A paragraph with zero leading has effectively zero height, so it overlaps the previous paragraph (there's zero space between the baselines of this paragraph and the previous line). It's especially good for those postmodern designs where you don't really need to read any of the words.

Of course, the disadvantage of zero leading is that it's very difficult to place the cursor in the line. To do it, use the arrow keys: place the cursor in the previous paragraph and press the Down Arrow key several times. As soon as you find the line in which the screen cursor doesn't move, you're on the zero-leading line.

Two Paragraphs on a Line

This tip has countless variations and uses. Essentially, it involves putting two short paragraphs (of length less than one full line) on a single line. The primary reason you'd do this is so you can have more than one style sheet for what looks like a single line of text (see Figure 4-23).

The key is to set the leading of the second paragraph to .001 point (see the previous tip), and then adjust the indents or the horizontal alignment of the two paragraphs (so the text doesn't overlap).

One of the paragraphs might be reversed out of a paragraph rule and the other not, for instance. Or you might have two different character formats. Of course, you could do this with three or more lines, too—if you can keep them all straight! Style sheets, of course, are crucial to using these techniques without going mad.

Figure 4-22
One use of zero leading

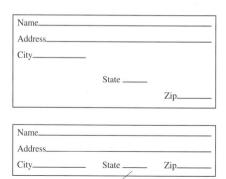

Leading set to zero

These settings make an underscore that doesn't underline the text

Figure 4-23
Two paragraphs on a line

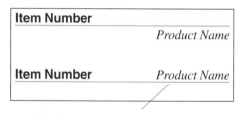

Zero leading on this paragraph pulls it up to the previous line

Don't Forget Your Relatives

Most people who use XPress overlook a subtle and useful leading mode: relative leading. Relative leading lets you specify leading as a number of points larger than the current point size (or the largest point in the paragraph). You can set relative leading by typing a plus sign followed by the desired value.

For instance, body copy is often leaded two points above its size. So if you're using 10-point Times, you can type "+2" in the Leading dialog box (Command-Shift-E) or in the Paragraph Formats dialog box (Command-Shift-F).

The most useful part about relative leading is when you change your type size. With absolute leading, the leading doesn't change until you change it; with relative leading, the leading always follows along.

Jump to Next Column or Box

As we said in "Multiple Tabs," later in the chapter, you should almost never type more than one of a character in a row. That includes carriage returns. If you find yourself typing six returns in a row to force some text to jump over to the next column or into the next text box of a chain, slap yourself and say "there's got to be a better way." There is: the Enter key is an invisible character that jumps to the next column or box (whichever comes first). Shift-Enter jumps to the next box, bypassing any columns in its way. You can see either of these by selecting Show Invisibles under the View menu. Delete all those returns, and type the appropriate single character.

Indent Here Versus New Text Box

In versions of XPress before 3.3, the program ignored the indent here formatting when the text flowed from one linked text box to another, or from one column to the next. If you were relying on the paragraph staying indented to where the indent here character (Command-\) was, and the paragraph happened to break over two text boxes, you were in for a disappointment. Fortunately, QuarkXPress 3.3 finally fixed the problem, and the paragraph stays indented.

Check for Rivers

Often the first problem that arises when people set their text to justified alignment is that their documents start looking like a flood just hit; all these rivers of white space are flowing around little islands of words. Because our eyes are so good at seeing patterns of lines, too much space between words is disturbing to the eye (we see the space rather than the words).

We told you about several ways to check the color of a text block in "The Color of Type," earlier in this chapter, including turning the page over and holding it up to the light, flipping the page upside down, or looking at the page from a distance. It's also a great way to check for rivers in your text. This way your eye isn't tricked into actually looking at the words—just the spaces.

XTENSIONS

Line Check

Don't forget to use the Line Check feature (part of the free Thing-a-ma-bob and FeaturesPlus XTensions) to find overset text boxes and other problems that might slip by your eye. Nobody's perfect; that's what computers are for.

MEASUREMENTS

H&J Percentages Versus Tracking Units

Brad Walrod, author of *QuarkXPress Unleashed* (a good book, especially if you want to learn more about XPress Tags and how to use some of the utilities mentioned in Chapter 5, *Copy Flow*), taught us a good tip about the letterspacing percentage value in the H&Js dialog box. These values use the same increment as kerning (one percent equals one kerning unit). This enables you to perform a quick and easy test when you're trying to figure out what letterspacing you want in a document. If you're thinking about increasing the letterspacing value, use kerning to apply that same value to a paragraph of text, so you can see what it looks like.

As Brad says, "I guarantee that if you do this test you will never again use a maximum [letterspacing] value of 15 percent."

H&JS

Making Letters Tight

If you determine that the typeface you are using is looser than you'd like (we think that many faces are), you have two choices for tightening it up.

LEADING

Minus Leading

As mentioned in an earlier tip, you can set a paragraph's leading using relative numbers such as "+2" or "+5" or "+0". But don't forget that you can also use negative numbers. You rarely need to, but sometimes—with headline type—you want to set lines close together.

XPress stops you from going too far, though. Using negative leading values, XPress never lets you set the type so tight that the ascenders of one line touch the baseline of the other (though the ascenders and descenders bounce into each other). If you need to do this, you should use an absolute leading value instead of a relative one.

SPECIAL CHARACTERS

Toggling Smart Quotes

Smart Quotes is really cool if you type a lot in QuarkXPress. However, if you ever want to enter a single or double "neutral" straight quote character, it's a hassle to turn off Smart Quotes first. Instead, hold down the Control key when typing the quote (single or double). When Smart Quotes is on, you get a straight quote; when it's off, you get a curly quote.

Adjusting Word-spacing with H&Js

There are two other ways to adjust word-spacing, in a slightly more global manner. First, you can create a new H&J setting and apply it to the paragraphs that you want changed (or alter the "Standard" H&J to change all the paragraphs in a document). If you increase the optimum wordspacing value in the Edit H&Js dialog box, the wordspacing increases.

Or, if you want to get clever with XPress Tags, you can export the text you want to alter, then perform a quick search and replace to change all the spacebands to "<k-5> " (that's the XPress Tag code for "kern the next two letters -5 units," followed by a single space). When you import the text back into XPress, every space is kerned -5 units.

▶ Lower the optimum values (Opt. column) for wordspacing (Space row) and letterspacing (Char row) in the Edit Hyphenation and Justification dialog box.

▶ Use negative tracking.

The first is better for changing the "color" of the font throughout much or all of the document. The second is better for adjusting smaller amounts of text.

How Big Are Those Percentages?

Have you ever wondered what those justification percentage values in the Edit Hyphenation and Justification dialog box mean? What, exactly, is the difference between "5%" and "10%" letterspacing?

While we always thought that the percentage of character spacing was based on an em space, it's actually based on an en space—half an em. That means that each percent is $1/100$ of an en, or $1/200$ of an em. Kerning and tracking are also defined based on $1/200$s of an em. Therefore, each character percentage is one unit of kerning or tracking.

Tighter and Looser H&Js

David almost always works with a minimum of three H&J settings in his document: "Standard", "Tighter", and "Looser". First, he edits the "Standard" H&J setting, turning on Auto Hyphenation, and tightening up (lowering the values) on the letterspacing and wordspacing parameters. The "Tighter" and "Looser" settings are for specialty cases. If a paragraph looks better with slightly tighter than normal H&Js, then he applies "Tighter". If the "Standard" settings are too limiting for a paragraph, and having looser spacing wouldn't hurt it, then he applies "Looser".

Phil typically works with even more H&J settings than that, depending on the layout. For instance, for setting text in narrow columns, he creates a setting with tight justification and liberal hyphenation rules, so he won't get oddly spaced type and rivulets of white. For display type, he turns off Auto Hyphenation, and sets tight word- and letterspacing.

One of the most important things to remember when fooling around with these types of settings is the color of the page (see "The Color of Type," earlier in this chapter). If setting a tighter H&J makes one text block look noticeably darker than the rest of the page, you may need to alter the paragraph with manual tracking rather than let the H&J settings do it for you.

H&JS

Reasonable H&J Values

Olav Martin Kvern, book designer extraordinaire and generally cool guy down the hall from David's office, says that he usually starts working on spacing settings for normal book line lengths (19 to 22 picas) at around 95/100/110 for word spacing and -1/0/5 for letterspacing (the three values correspond with minimum, optimum, and maximum values). As he puts it, "I'm generally more concerned about letterspacing that's too tight over letterspacing that's too loose—and the other way around about word spacing." Phil has similar biases, but tends toward setting like 85/100/125 for word spacing, and -2/0/2 for letterspacing.

However, Ole and Phil both stress that space settings are entirely subjective and are completely dependent on the font, size, and line length, among other things.

H&JS

Single-Word Justify

You have to understand that some features in QuarkXPress are added simply because some large newspaper or magazine chain (one that owns a *lot* of copies of the program) requested it. For instance, the Single Word Justify checkbox (in the Edit Hyphenation and Justification dialog box) accommodates people in some Scandinavian countries, but almost nowhere else.

If you turn Single Word Justify off, single words in a narrow column of justified text might not stretch across the entire column even with elaborate H&J settings. This might sound like it'd be a good thing, but it actually makes it difficult for the reader to

H&JS

Different Hyphenations

If you're as conservative in typography as we are, you probably hate to use more than one hyphen in a row. However, when we've got a *really* bad rag, we'll sometimes break down and allow two or three. To speed up this process, we create duplicate H&J settings, each with a different value for Hyphens in a Row.

To do this, you can duplicate your "Standard" H&J setting (click Duplicate in the Edit Hyphenation and Justification dialog box), and name the new H&J something else, like "Standard with 2H's". Then, when you encounter a layout situation requiring two hyphens in a row, you can—reluctantly—select the paragraph, press Command-Shift-F to bring up the Paragraph Formats dialog box, and select "Standard with 2H's" from the H&J popup menu.

see where the end of the paragraph really is. We recommend that you always leave Single Word Justify on (in fact, you can just forget it's even there).

Phil, presenting the dissenting opinion here, says that you shouldn't find yourself in a situation where two words don't fit in a single column; it's just poor design. However, if you *do* find yourself in this dilemma, he'd say leave the word flush left and immediately march down the hall to the art director and get the layout changed.

H&JS

Multicolumn Insert Space

Earlier in this chapter, in "Insert Space," we gave you advice on faking the old insert-space typesetting control with flush left and right text. But what if you want to add an equal amount of space between each word across a line of text? You can do this by using forced justification and adjusting the H&J settings.

1. Go to the H&J dialog box (Command-Option-H) and create a new H&J setting called something mnemonic like "InsertSpace".

2. Make sure the letterspacing (Char) fields in the Justification Method area of the dialog box are all set to zero. That means that QuarkXPress won't add extra space between any characters in the paragraph, only between words. You might need to increase the values in the wordspacing (Space) fields as well.

3. Save this new H&J setting.

4. Use the Paragraph Formats dialog box (Command-Shift-F) to apply the "InsertSpace" H&J setting to the paragraph and set the paragraph to Forced alignment.

The paragraph should now be spread across the text box, with an equal amount of space between each word. If you want a normal word space between some words, add a flex space (which, despite its name, is actually a fixed width) by pressing Option-Shift-Space (see Figure 4-24).

One   **Two**   **Three**   **Four**

One Two   **Three**   **Four**

Here, no letterspacing is allowed, and a non-breaking space sits between the first two words.

H&J's letterspacing set to default value allows letterspacing.

Figure 4-24
Inserting equal space between words

H&JS

Finding and Changing H&Js

There's just no way to find and replace H&J settings throughout a document. Or is there? Let's say someone was working on your document and applied an H&J setting called "Really Tight" to paragraphs when you weren't looking. You want to clear them out, but keep the "Really Tight" setting for future use. Here's how. (You can also use the technique described in "Replacing Style Sheets" in Chapter 5, *Copy Flow*.)

1. Create a new temporary document and bring the overly tight H&J into it. The easiest way to do this is probably to apply the "Really Tight" H&J to a dummy paragraph in a dummy text box, then drag that text box over to the new dummy document (or you can use Cut and Paste). When the text box comes across to the new document, it brings the "Really Tight" H&J setting with it.

2. Delete the tight H&J from your original document. When you do this, QuarkXPress asks you which H&J setting you want to apply to paragraphs that contain the deleted H&J. In this example, when you delete "Really Tight" from the H&J list, you can replace it with "Standard", or something else. This effectively does a complete search and replace throughout the document: everywhere the "Really Tight" setting was applied, it gets changed to something else.

3. The "Really Tight" H&J setting was saved in the temporary document, so you can retrieve it by dragging that dummy text box back across (or by using Cut and Paste). Then you can close that dummy document.

A couple of caveats to this tip. First, note that this changes all the paragraphs in a document that use the offending H&J setting.

H&JS

Breaking H&J Rules

The most important thing about how any program's H&J routine works is: What specifications will it violate if it has to?

In QuarkXPress's case (PageMaker is no different, by the way), it will honor *all* settings—except that, if it absolutely has to violate one setting because it's unable to justify the line otherwise, it will violate the *wordspacing maximum* setting. This makes perfect sense, since a too loose line is much more readable than a too tight line; and if only the wordspacing is too loose (i.e., the letterspacing isn't), you'll still be able to tell where the words start and stop.

There's still no way to change some and not others automatically. Also remember that this only works in versions 3.2 or later; before then, H&J settings, when deleted, were always reset to "Standard".

H&JS

How XPress Does H&J

Just in case you've ever wondered, here's the order in which QuarkXPress's H&J routine does its stuff.

1. It tries composing the line using the optimum (Opt. column) word- and letterspacing values. With justified text, of course, it's almost never successful.

2. Next, it tries hyphenation (if hyphenation is turned on).

3. If hyphenation doesn't do the trick, XPress tries adjusting the wordspacing between the allowed maximum and minimum values. It tries both expanding and squeezing, and, if it finds values that work in both directions, uses the one that requires the least adjustment. Things almost always progress at least this far before justification is achieved.

4. If it's still not quite right, XPress tries adjusting the letterspacing between the allowed maximum and minimum (Max. and Min. columns) values. Again, it uses the one that requires the least adjustment.

5. Only if nothing has worked to this point does it violate anything (see the tip to the left).

DESIGN

Orphan and Widow Controls

It's all very well and good to let QuarkXPress avoid widows, orphans, and runts for you (runts are what some people call one or two words which sit on the last line of a paragraph by themselves) using Keep with Next ¶ and Keep Lines Together in the Paragraph Formats dialog box. But for most documents you still need to painstakingly peruse each page, making adjustments as you go. You have many other tools to help you avoid widows and orphans. Here are some of our favorites.

▶ Adjust tracking by a *very* small amount over a range of text, but try to do at least a whole paragraph or a few complete lines so the color of the type doesn't vary within the paragraph. Typically, nobody can tell if you've applied -.5 or -1 tracking to a paragraph or a page, but it might be enough to pull back a widow or runt.

▶ Adjust horizontal scaling by a small amount, such as 99.5 percent or 100.5 percent.

▶ Make sure Auto Hyphenation and Auto Kern Above are on. Kerning can make a load of difference over a large area of text. Auto Hyphenation has to be changed in all of your H&Js, while Auto Kern Above affects the entire document.

▶ Use an H&J with a smaller optimum wordspacing value. If it's at 100 percent, try 98 percent.

▶ Set up different hyphenation and justification settings that you can apply to problem paragraphs. You might apply a tighter or a looser setting for a paragraph, for instance, or allow more hyphens in a row.

If none of these works for you, don't forget you can always just rewrite a sentence or two (if it's yours to rewrite). A quick rewrite of a sentence can fix up just about any word over- or underrun problems.

KERNING
Quick Kerning for Families

Applying kerning pairs to a number of typefaces using Quark's Kerning Table Editor can be very time-consuming and tiresome. (The editor shows up only if you have Quark's Kern/Track Editor XTension in the XPress folder (or in the XTension folder starting with version 3.3.) You can speed up this process by using the Export command to save to disk a set of kerning pairs you've created for one typeface, and then using the Import feature to apply the same kerning table to other typefaces. Once you've imported the kerning tables, you can always go back and edit them to account for specific vagaries of that typeface.

The more similar the faces, the better this will work. At any rate, you always have to make adjustments (but at least you're not starting from scratch).

HYPHENATION
Watch Those Hyphens

There's nothing like giving your document a good once-over before you print it out. One of the things you want to look for is a badly hyphenated word. Remember that QuarkXPress uses an algorithm to hyphenate words rather than a lookup dictionary like some other programs. Because of this, it can hyphenate more words than other programs, but it doesn't always do it right.

For example, XPress hyphenates the word "Transeurope" as "Transeu-rope" rather than "Trans-europe." If you find these problem words, you can either change them manually (by adding discretionary hyphens—see the next tip), or make a global change using Hyphenation Exceptions.

Kern-Pair Limitation

Just in case you're kern-pair happy, you should note that XPress's built-in Kern/Track Editor cannot create more than 8,000 pairs per typeface and style. We don't know anyone who's ever approached this number, though (not even Phil has approached it!). Of course, there are about 40,000 possible kerning pairs in a font, so there's always a chance you'll be frustrated.

Also, the Kern/Track Editor cannot access more than about 100 installed fonts at a time. So, if you've got a whole mess o' fonts open at one time, you might find yourself in trouble (we try to avoid this problem by using font-management utilities such as MasterJuggler or Suitcase). Both these limitations are limitations of the system-level Macintosh List Manager, by the way, not of XPress. There is no limitation (at least none we know of) for the number of *fonts* the XPress Preferences file can store kerning pairs for.

Adding Hyphenation

When you need to add your own hyphenation to some text, don't go in and add regular hyphens. Why? What would happen if the text had to reflow for some reason (like you added a word)? Suddenly you would have hyphens scattered throughout your text (see Figure 4-25).

Instead, use discretionary hyphens (also known as "dishies"; they're entered with Command-hyphen). These will break into real hyphens if they need to, but will disappear when they're not needed (even Find/Change ignores a dishy).

Why Won't This Word Break?

It's really quite frustrating: you've got your document all laid out and it's looking beautiful, except that you're having trouble with a few words. They just won't hyphenate properly. Here are a couple things to check for.

▶ A discretionary hyphen placed just before the word makes it a nonbreaking word. The problem is that there's no easy way to search for these characters. One method is to export the text as XPress Tags, search for spaceband plus "<\h>" (the tag for discretionary hyphen), and replace the found text with nothing.

If, as in the example above, there's a specific word you want to check, try placing the cursor just before the word and using the arrow keys to move forward and backward. If there's a place that you hit the key but the cursor doesn't move, there might be an invisible character (such as a discretionary hyphen) there.

▶ We also often forget about the Hyphens in a Row value in the Edit Hyphenation and Justification dialog box. XPress counts dashes as hyphens when checking this amount. If Hyphens in a Row is set to "2" and you already have two in a row, XPress won't hyphenate the next line. David keeps

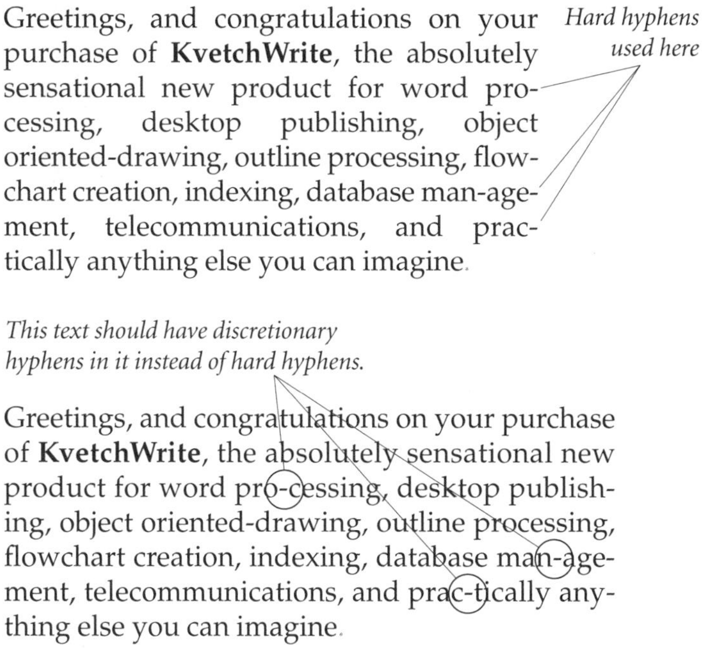

Greetings, and congratulations on your purchase of **KvetchWrite**, the absolutely sensational new product for word processing, desktop publishing, object oriented-drawing, outline processing, flowchart creation, indexing, database man-age-ment, telecommunications, and practically anything else you can imagine.

Hard hyphens used here

Figure 4-25
Reflowed hyphens

This text should have discretionary hyphens in it instead of hard hyphens.

Greetings, and congratulations on your purchase of **KvetchWrite**, the absolutely sensational new product for word pro-cessing, desktop publish-ing, object oriented-drawing, outline processing, flowchart creation, indexing, database man-age-ment, telecommunications, and prac-tically anything else you can imagine.

another H&J setting around that allows three hyphens in a row, and applies that (with discretion) where necessary (see "Different Hyphenations," earlier in the chapter).

LIGATURES

Using Automatic Ligatures

We remember the bad old days, when we had to "hard wire" the ligatures in QuarkXPress: find "f i" and then change to the "fi" character; then do the same thing with "fl". There were all sorts of problems with this; XPress's spelling checker would think words with ligatures were spelled wrong, the words wouldn't hyphenate correctly, and it was hard to search for these words with Find/Change. Fortunately, since version 3.2, you can dispense with this primitive method and use Automatic Ligatures.

The Ligatures feature found in the Typographic Preferences dialog box (press Command-Shift-Y) solves all these problems. When you turn it on, every "fi" and "fl" combination in the document is converted for you, but hyphenation, spelling checks, and Find/Change work as usual. Best of all, you can still click between the two characters for editing (see Figure 4-26).

Officially, the finalists were affluent flounder

With ligatures

Officially, the finalists were affluent flounder

Without ligatures

Figure 4-26
Automatic Ligatures

Some people prefer not to use the fi and fl ligature as part of a longer ffi or ffl pair (like in "office" or "waffle"). If you feel this way, or a client does, check the "Not ffi or ffl" box (we think it looks just fine, so we leave it unchecked).

The Ligatures feature is the kind of thing you should turn on in Typographic Preferences when no documents are open, then just leave it on (if no document is open when you set this, it gets applied to every new document you create from then on).

LIGATURES

Finding and Replacing Ligatures

If you're still in the Dark Ages, or have a particular reason for performing manual Find/Change searches instead of using automatic ligatures, make sure you're careful about replacing them correctly. Especially make sure you turn off Ignore Case from the Find/Change dialog box. If you don't, capitalized "Fi" or "Fl" combinations get changed, too! If you're using the Ligatures feature, you don't have to worry about this.

LIGATURES

Breaking Automatic Ligatures

In the last tip couple of tips we discussed how great automatic ligatures are. Nonetheless, there are times when you *don't* want to have ligatures. For instance, in justified text, when you're allowing spacing between each character, if there's no space between the ligature pair, it looks really odd. Similarly, in some headlines, a ligature might look wrong. You can defeat XPress's Ligatures feature for particular text by adjusting the Break Above field in the Typographic Preferences dialog box.

When Break Above is set to one (the default), any ligature with more than one unit of tracking ($\frac{1}{200}$ of an em) applied to it breaks into the two separate characters. Note that this can surprise you if you're not careful: if Break Above is set at too small a value, too many of your ligatures in justified text will break, defeating the purpose of the tool. A value of one or two is too small for us;

we usually raise this to four or five, which breaks the ligatures so they don't stick out, but keeps them intact in most instances. However, the value you choose really depends on your typeface and design.

In headline type, where you don't want to change tracking values, you can disable automatic ligatures by adding a very small kerning value between the two characters. For instance, you can add .01 units between an "f" and an "i" and the ligature immediately break into two characters.

UTILITIES

Key Caps and PopChar

Anyone who can remember every character in a font, including all special symbols and characters, is no one to borrow money from. We can never remember most of the characters we need, so we use Key Caps and PopChar. Key Caps comes with your system—it's automatically installed under the Apple menu—and shows you a keyboard map for every character in any font you choose from its menu (see Figure 4-27).

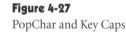

Figure 4-27
PopChar and Key Caps

To use Key Caps, select it from the Apple menu, then select the font you want to see from the Key Caps menu. When you hold down the Shift key, you see the map of all the uppercase characters. When you hold down the Option key, you see the Option characters, and so on.

One-Stroke Font Change

QuarkXPress has so many keystrokes and shortcuts that we can never remember them all. Here are two that David always forgets about. Pressing Command-Shift-Q sets the next character you type in the Symbol font, while pressing Command-Shift-Z sets it in Zapf Dingbats (providing you have these fonts installed, of course). After you type the character, XPress automatically reverts to the typeface you were in. If you have one or more characters selected when you press these keystrokes, XPress changes them to the desired font.

PopChar is a little freeware utility written by Günther Blaschek (one of our favorite names), that does the same thing but better (see Figure 4-27). When it's loaded in your system, you only have to click in a corner of your screen and you can immediately see the whole character set (and how to type the characters) for whatever typeface you're working in. This is superior to Key Caps, since you don't have to manually select the typeface. It also shows you little technical details, like the ASCII number of the character. We use PopChar all the time (and it's on the disc bundled with this book).

Get It Right for Overseas

We in the United States grew up with the ethnocentric viewpoint that the way we write and typeset is the way everybody does it. Not so. For example, double quotation marks are used in America where single quotation marks are used in Britain. In some European countries, our quotation marks are replaced with guillemets («, », ‹, and ›—Option-\ and Shift-Option-\, and Shift-Option-3 and Shift-Option-4; note that XPress's Smart Quotes feature lets you set these to appear automatically when you press the quote keys). The Spanish language sets a question or an exclamation point at both the beginning (upside down, keyed with Option-Shift-/ or Option-1) and at the end of sentences. Figure 4-28 shows examples of each of these styles.

If you do a lot of foreign-language work, and especially work that has multiple languages in the same document, you should check out Quark Passport—the multilingual version of XPress. This program lets you set a language as a paragraph attribute and will then check spelling and hyphenate that language properly. It

Figure 4-28
Foreign punctuation

¡Mi perro se llama Spot!

¿Dónde está la casa de Pépe?

Spanish inverted exclamation and question marks

Il dit «La fromage, ça va bien?»

European guillemots

"He said, 'totally, dude' and walked off into the sunset."

'He said, "totally, dude" and walked off into the sunset.'

American (left) and British (right) quotation marks

comes with about 12 languages built in. (You may run into some difficulties exchanging files in those languages with Passport if you don't have all of the versions synchronized.)

Other languages, such as Hebrew, Farsi, Russian, and Greek, must be typed using a non-Roman font specific to that language and may require specialized software. QuarkXPress is presently available in 14 languages, including Japanese and German. (In case you're curious, Passport does not include Japanese.)

SPECIAL CHARACTERS

Setting Inches and Feet

You've probably heard it from everyone now: don't use straight quotes! However, some people *do* use them . . . for the feet and inches (or minutes and seconds) symbols. If you're going to do this, please go so far as to italicize the straight quotes so they're slightly obliqued. But better yet, use the ′ and the ″ characters from the Symbol font (press Command-Shift-Q to switch to Symbol for just the next character). If you don't like the looks of those characters, you could use either the characters in the Universal News and Commercial Pi font or the marks from an Expert Set. Of course, there's no keystroke to jump to these fonts automatically, so if you have a lot of them to type, you may want to do a search and replace using either the Find/Change feature or XPress Tags. (See Table 4-1 for the keystrokes.)

Font	Inch mark press	looks like	Foot mark press	looks like
Symbol	Option-4	′	Option-comma	″
Universal News	8	′	9	″
Expert Set	′	′	″	″

KEYSTROKES

Nonbreaking Spaces on Foreign Keyboards

Apple pulled a fast one on us: in System 7.1, they appropriated the keystroke Command-Option-spacebar for switching keyboard layouts (located in the Keyboard control panel). There's no way that we can figure out for turning this off. Fortunately, Quark has

KEYSTROKES

Getting Your Quotes Straight

When Smart Quotes is turned on in the Application Preferences dialog box (this feature was new in version 3.2), every time you type a single or double quote it comes out curly. QuarkXPress is replacing the straight quote with the Option-[or -] and the Shift-Option-[or -] keys behind the scenes.

However, if you really need a straight quote someplace, you can get it by pressing Control-' or Control-" (that's Control, *not* Command). This keystroke does just the opposite when Smart Quotes is turned off; then you get curly quotes. Unfortunately, this feature doesn't work with some foreign-language keyboard layouts (we've even had complaints about the UK keyboard not working).

If you're using XPress version 3.1 and want the same sort of functionality, try using Smart Keys II (it's on the disc bundled with this book).

Table 4-1
Inch and foot mark keystrokes

added a back door: you can use the Control key instead of the Command key when typing various nonbreaking spaces (flex space, punctuation space, and en space).

Ballot Boxes and Custom Dingbats

Some people think that the best way to create blank "ballot" boxes is either to type a Zapf Dingbats lowercase "n" and set it to outline style, or to buy a separate font package such as Bullets and Boxes from Caseys's Page Mill. The problem with the first method is that imagesetting the outline often results in a hairline that is too thin to reproduce well. The problem with the second method is that it costs something to buy it (not that much, though, and the package itself is great). Nonetheless, QuarkXPress gives us a better option.

1. Create a picture box of any size.

2. Give the picture box a border (Command-B); we like to use half a point.

3. Select the box with the Item tool, and cut it to the Clipboard (Command-X).

4. Use the Content tool to select the point in the text where you want the box to go. Paste the box in (Command-V).

5. Resize the box to suit your needs.

Also, by importing a graphic into the picture box (either before you cut and paste it or after it's anchored), you can even create your own custom dingbats (see Figure 4-29).

Using Letters and Graphics

Dingbat characters in a font may be suitable for ornamentation in text or on your page. For instance, you could put a swash character or dingbat at the beginning or end of a story. You can even make a dingbat sit as a drop cap at the beginning of a paragraph (see Figure 4-30).

And re<u>mem</u>ber!  The *"cornier"* your Presentation, the less likely it is to be *Taken Seriously!*

Custom dingbat created by placing an EPS (Encapsulated PostScript) file within an anchored picture box. Picture box has been resized, and its baseline shifted, until the block of text looked appropriately corny.

☐   *Ballot box made with an outlined Zapf Dingbat ("n")*

☐   *Ballot box made with an anchored (square) picture box having a 0.5-pt frame.*

Figure 4-29
Custom dingbats and ballot boxes

DINGBATS

Boxed Type

Here's some fun you can have with the ever-useful Zapf Dingbats: extreme uses of kerning. By careful use of kerning and baseline shifts, you can have regular type overprint a Zapf Dingbat box character, creating boxed type without the headaches of creating each box as an inline graphic.

1. Type the letter "n" and set it to Zapf Dingbats, a few point sizes bigger than your body type. Apply a slight negative baseline shift to this box.

2. Next, type the character you want, and make it white.

3. Put the insertion point between the box and the character, and kern them until the character is centered in the box. It's best to work at a 400-percent view for this sort of adjustment, of course.

You can be quite creative with this technique, overlapping multiple boxes for an outlined and stroked effect, or using one of Zapf Dingbats' ballot boxes instead of a simple solid box (see Figure 4-31). And once you create a boxed-text alphabet, you can save it and paste the characters in whenever you need them.

Figure 4-30
Dingbat character as initial cap

This is a dingbat and the letter "W"

Whereas, the Society of Good-for-nothings is ultimately a useless institution; whereas, the members present have attempted to make something of themselves and failed; whereas the group at large is found to be fundamentally good for nothing; we, the committee hereby make a motion that nothing change and that we all go watch "Three's Company" on our special rerun cable channel.

Get fancy with Dingbats!

There are so many things to try.

Crazy!

Figure 4-31
Boxed sets

Each of these lines were created using tab with Zapf Dingbat fill characters.

Figure 4-32
Dingbat tab leaders

Creative Tab Leaders

You don't have to be content with the size and font of a tab's leaders (otherwise called *fill characters*). If you want the characters to be smaller, select the tab character itself and change the point size. If you want the characters to be in another font, change the font of that tab character. People don't often think of the tab character as a character, but that's just what it is. If you turn on Show Invisibles (select it from the View menu or press Command-I), you can see the character as a gray arrow.

Changing the font and size isn't all you can do; you can even change the amount of space between the leader characters. Select the tab and adjust its tracking or kerning value. Typically, when you change the kerning value for a single character it only changes the space between it and the next character. In this case, however, it changes the space between each iteration of the leader character (see Figure 4-32).

Multiple Tabs

If you are setting up a table and want to place tabs between each column, follow the same rule as spaces: don't type multiple tabs in a row to make your columns align. Set one tab stop for each column. Then just press Tab once to jump from column to column. In fact, it's probably safe to say that you should never type two of the same character in a row unless you're typing "balloon" or "bookkeeper" or something like that.

Selecting and Changing Tab Stops

While it's easy to drag a tab stop, it appears harder to change its alignment or fill character. When you click on the tab stop and change the alignment or fill character, nothing seems to change. The trick is to click Apply or OK. Only then is the tab stop changed. Don't fret; this subtlety has confused more than one power user, including Phil (that's "Mr. Type," to you!). If you have continuous Apply on (Option-click the Apply button) you'll never notice this problem, because the tabs are updated the second you click in or tab to any other field.

TABS

Clear All Tabs

Have a lot of tabs you want to clear in a hurry? You could drive yourself nuts dragging each tab stop out of QuarkXPress's tab ruler, or you could simply Option-click in the ruler bar in the Paragraph Tab dialog box (Command-Shift-T) to remove all set tabs for the selected paragraphs at a single stroke.

TABS

Evenly Spaced Tab Stops, Part I

You want equal spaces between each of your tab stops across a text box? Unless your math skills are ultrafast and ultrafine, you probably don't want to spend the time trying to figure out where to place each tab stop. Like we always say, "Let XPress do it for you."

1. Duplicate the text box and delete all the text out of the copy.

2. Go to the Text Box Specifications dialog box (Command-M or Command-double click on the text box) and set the number of *columns* to the number of tab stops you want. Then change the gutter width to three points (the smallest you can make it).

3. Select the first text box (remember you can select through the top box by Command-Option-Shift-clicking) and open the Pargraph Tabs dialog box (Command-Shift-T with the Content tool selected).

4. Add the tab stops where the column markings are (see Figure 4-33).

TABS

Formatting Tabs Quickly

One reader, Barry Simon, pointed out to us that you can format tabs for a number of paragraphs more easily by just working on a single paragraph. If you set the proper tab settings for the first paragraph, you can quickly apply those settings to the rest of the paragraphs if you select all the lines (including the first one), open the Paragraph Tabs dialog box (Command-Shift-T), and click OK (or press Return). The tab settings for the first paragraph are applied to the rest of the paragraphs (also, see "Copying Paragraph Formatting and Styles," in Chapter 5, *Copy Flow*).

You can also use the copy formatting keystroke: with your cursor in the paragraph(s) you want to change, Command-Option-click on the paragraph with the formatting you want to copy. It copies tabs, leading, indents, and style sheets.

TABS

Clean Tab-Stop Numbers

Adjusting tab stops in the Paragraph Tabs dialog box can be a hassle if you want nice, even numbers. The solution: set up your measurements to work in picas or points, then set tabs only at 100-, 200-, and 400-percent views.

Figure 4-33
Adding tabs equally

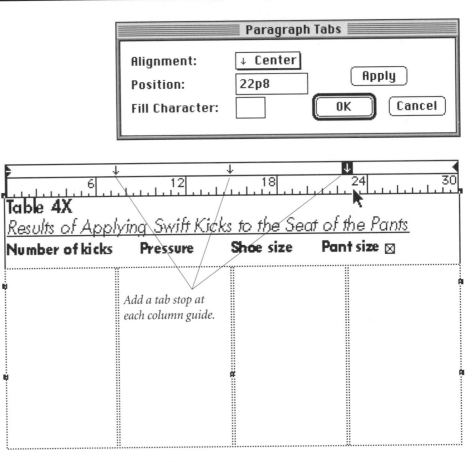

TABS

Evenly Spaced Tab Stops, Part II

Don't forget that you can use arithmetic in dialog box fields. This includes the Paragraph Tabs dialog box.

If you want evenly spaced tabs, place each tab by adding an increment to the previous tab position. For instance, let's say you want a tab stop at .5 inch and every inch from there.

1. Type ".5" into the Position field of the Paragraph Tabs dialog box (or ".5"" if your measurements aren't inches).

2. Press Command-A or click the Apply button. This applies the tab stop to the paragraph without leaving the Paragraph Tabs dialog box.

3. Position the cursor after the ".5" (you can just press the Right Arrow key) and type "+1".

4. Press Command-A or click Apply again.

5. Continue until you have all the tab stops you need. Then press OK.

Note that if the equation gets too long in the Position field, you can click on the last tab stop you added (the little arrow icon in the tab ruler). This simplifies the equation to save space.

This tip might not sound like a big deal. But what if your initial position was .637 inch, and you wanted to add a tab stop every .598 inches from there? This tip saves you from having to perform all that backbreaking arithmetic yourself. Let the computer do it!

SPECIAL EFFECTS

Shadow Tip

If you make a custom shadow style as described in the previous tip, it's a good idea to loosen the tracking of your type first so that each letter just touches the shadow of the previous letter. Normal letterspacing frequently overlaps the background "shadow" characters so they are difficult to read (see Figure 4-34).

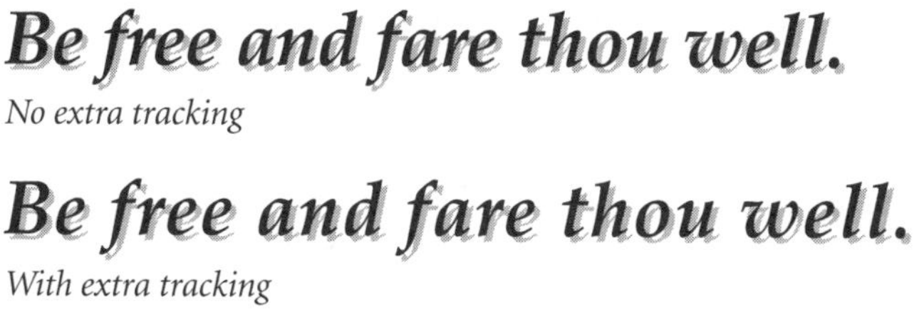

Be free and fare thou well.

No extra tracking

Be free and fare thou well.

With extra tracking

SPECIAL EFFECTS

Alternate Shadows

It's easy to apply the Shadow type style to text. But what if you want a shadow of a different color or shade? Or a shadow of a different size and location? Then you have to get clever, or at least careful.

Select the box containing the text you want to have shadowed. Make it transparent by setting both its background color *and* its runaround (Command-T) to None. Now duplicate the box, and offset the duplicate. Select the text, and change its color. Select the original text box and bring it to the front. There you have it; instant (well, almost instant) custom drop shadows.

Figure 4-34
Space out shadows

DESIGN

Narrowing Em Dashes

Perhaps typeface designers get overzealous every now and again with their characters. Certainly, the em dash might fall into this category, not in flourish but in width. Simply put, they're often just too wide. We'll sometimes make them narrower by setting them to a horizontal scaling of 75 or 80 percent of their original width. If you have a *lot* of them, you might consider doing this using XPress Tags (search for the em dash and replace with "<h80>—<h100>").

Weightier Small Caps

Only a few typefaces available on the Macintosh come with small capital letters. QuarkXPress makes up for this by transforming full-size capital letters into small caps based on the specifications you set in the Small Caps section of the Typographic Preferences dialog box. However, the standard settings, with vertical and horizontal scaling at 75 percent, often create small caps whose weight is noticeably lighter than surrounding, full-size type. Try keeping the 75 percent vertical scaling, but increasing the horizontal scaling to 80 percent, for a better, weightier look (see Figure 4-35).

Since QuarkXPress lets you save typographical preferences with each document, you can tailor the Small Caps settings to look best for each job you work on. Of course, nothing beats a custom-designed small cap like those in Expert Set and Small Caps fonts.

Figure 4-35
Small cap weights

"Oh! It's a DOS machine. . . how quaint."

75-percent vertical
and horizontal

"Better than CP/M, ducky."

75-percent vertical and
80-percent horizontal

"Well, I hope there's enough RAM in it."

Custom-made Expert Set

Type in the Margin

Usually in QuarkXPress, the edges of text boxes are inviolable. There's no margin release, no handy command for moving one line an eentsy bit over the edge. Or is there? This tip shows a clever way of fooling QuarkXPress into hanging text at the beginning of a line beyond the left margin of a column or text box (see Figure 4-36). The example we use is for a drop cap, but you could use it for hanging punctuation or any other character.

1. Instead of a single-character drop cap, specify a two-character drop cap for your paragraph, spanning as many lines vertically as you like.

V alen: if, by your art, you haves
Put the wild waters in this roar, allay them.
The sky it seems would pour down stinking pitch,
But that the sea, mounting to th'welkin's cheek,
Dashes the fire out. O, I have suffered
With those that I saw suffer! A brave vessel,
Who had, no doubt, some noble creature in her,
Dashed all to pieces.

———————————— Edge of the text box

Figure 4-36
The amazing hanging drop cap

2. Add a space to the left of the first character in the paragraph. If your paragraph is justified, this should be a nonbreaking space, such as Option-Shift-spacebar.

3. Select the first character (we usually press Command-Up Arrow and then Shift-Right Arrow, which jumps to the beginning of the paragraph, then selects the first character) and apply negative tracking like crazy. You'll find you can tighten the tracking on that first character so much that the drop cap character actually moves to the *left* of the space. Keep on tracking till the left edge of the character starts to disappear beyond the left edge of the text box. Adjust the tracking as necessary.

Although the first letter appears sliced off on the left side, it actually prints properly.

You could even use variants of this trick to move an inline graphic off into a margin. Of course, once it's there you won't be able to see or select it (except with the cursor keys) unless you first remove the kerning (the Command-Up Arrow, Shift-Right Arrow is a quick way to get where you need to go, even when the character is hidden).

Two-Paragraph Drop Caps, Part I

It's easy to extend a drop cap below its paragraph into the following one. Just start the second paragraph with a line break (Shift-Return), not a plain return. The second paragraph will really be part of the first, but with some fiddling, you can simulate the effect of a true paragraph break (see Figure 4-37).

Figure 4-37
Two-paragraph drop cap

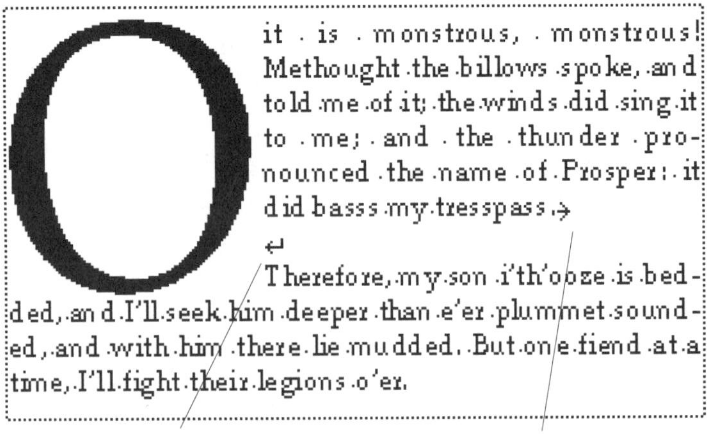

Soft returns break the line but
keep the paragraph intact.

The Option-Tab forces the
line not to justify.

If your paragraphs are justified, add an Option-Tab at the end of the first "paragraph," which will force that line flush left. If you need a paragraph indent for the second "paragraph," you'll need to fake it with spaces of some kind, perhaps dedicating your flex space to this purpose. If for any reason any of this doesn't work for you, we suggest going back to the old way of creating drop caps: create the letter in a separate text box and lay it over the box containing the rest of the text.

DROP CAPS

Adjusting Space After Caps

We often find that the space between the initial cap and the text that's flowing around it is too small. People have tried all sorts of weird workarounds for moving the two apart, but we prefer the simple method: add kerning between the drop cap and the character after it. The more kerning you add, the farther away the runaround text is set (see Figure 4-38).

DROP CAPS

A Caveat About Drop Caps

You're probably aware that the size of the automatic drop caps generated by QuarkXPress is measured not in points, but as a percentage of its "normal" size, based on the number of lines allotted to the cap in the Paragraph Formats dialog box. Well, what if you

DROP CAPS
Two-Paragraph Drop Caps, Part II

Another way to create a multiparagraph drop cap is to revert to the method we used in the good ol' days: just slap that drop cap in a separate text box and flop it down where you want it (the text runs around it when runaround is set to other than None; press Command-T). One step better: Cut the text box out with the Item tool and paste it in as the first character of the text block as an anchored box (with the Content tool). Of course, you can't do any fancy runaround this way.

want to apply a baseline shift to the cap? If you specify a two-point baseline shift for an initial cap, you'll be in for a surprise. Just as the drop cap is scaled up from its original point size to fill the number of lines specified for it, so too are baseline shifts. If you have 12/14 type and a drop cap set for three lines, a two-point baseline shift actually becomes something like eight points. Why not six points? It's a puzzlement.

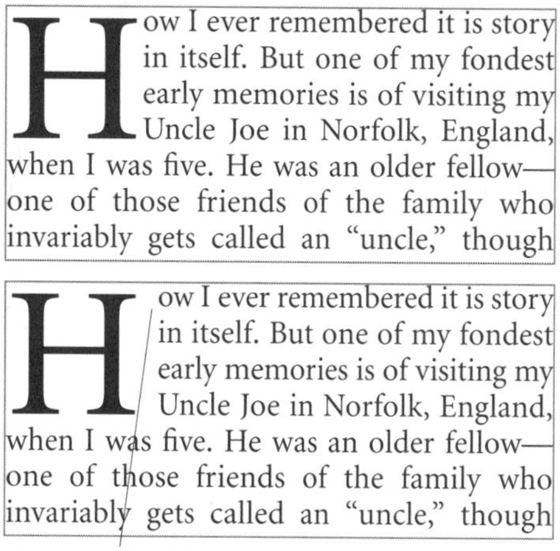

Wraparound Drop Caps

When using letters such as "L", "W", or "A" as drop caps you may want to wrap the text block around the shape of the letter (see Figure 4-39). While there is no way of doing this automatically, there are three workaround techniques you can use (see next two tips).

The first method is the two-text-box trick.

1. Copy the drop cap letter(s) of the paragraph into a new, smaller text box.

2. Size the initial letter to approximately fit the number of lines you want.

3. Set both the background color and runaround of your text box to None.

4. Place your drop cap text box over your paragraph text box. The body copy won't reflow if you remembered to set the runaround to None.

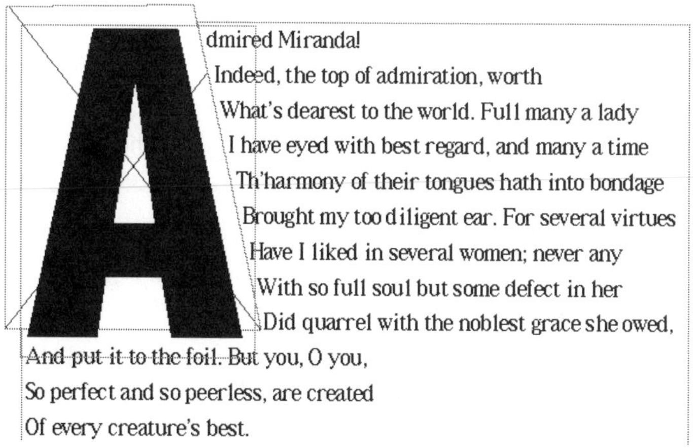

How I ever remembered it is story in itself. But one of my fondest early memories is of visiting my Uncle Joe in Norfolk, England, when I was five. He was an older fellow—one of those friends of the family who invariably gets called an "uncle," though

How I ever remembered it is story in itself. But one of my fondest early memories is of visiting my Uncle Joe in Norfolk, England, when I was five. He was an older fellow—one of those friends of the family who invariably gets called an "uncle," though

Kerning added here pushes all the lines to the right.

Figure 4-38
Adding kerning after a drop cap

Figure 4-39
Wraparound drop caps

Admired Miranda!
Indeed, the top of admiration, worth
What's dearest to the world. Full many a lady
I have eyed with best regard, and many a time
Th'harmony of their tongues hath into bondage
Brought my too diligent ear. For several virtues
Have I liked in several women; never any
With so full soul but some defect in her
Did quarrel with the noblest grace she owed,
And put it to the foil. But you, O you,
So perfect and so peerless, are created
Of every creature's best.

5. Draw a line or a polygon around the drop cap, creating a border where you want the text to wrap.

6. If you drew a line, change its shade to zero percent, make it white, or turn on Suppress Printout in the Line Specifications dialog box. We usually like turn on Suppress Printout because it's easier to find and select later.

7. Make sure the wraparound object is in front of the paragraph but behind the initial cap.

Note that QuarkXPress lets you make a text box containing a single character (such as for our example) as small vertically as you like, without forcing the text to overflow the box. We wish we could also have the option of turning this feature on for multiple-character text boxes (are you listening, Tim Gill?).

DROP CAPS

Graphic Drop Caps

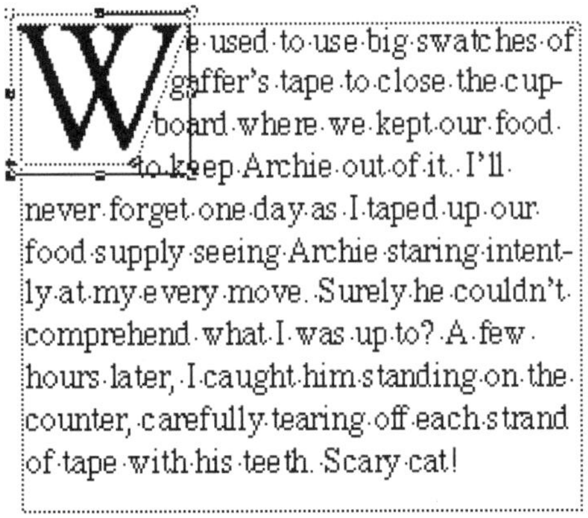

Another method for wraparound drop caps is to bring the initial cap in as a graphic (see Figure 4-40). This lets you use QuarkXPress's automatic or manual runaround features to control the text runaround. You can, of course, create the letter as a graphic in just about any Macintosh graphics program. But, if you're in a hurry, you don't even have to leave QuarkXPress.

1. Make a brand new QuarkXPress document with small page dimensions, as close as possible to the size of the initial cap you'll be creating.

2. Create a new text box on that page and type the initial caps in the new document.

3. Select Save Page as EPS from the File menu (see "Saving a Page as EPS," in Chapter 6, *Pictures*). Save the EPS file to an appropriate name and location.

4. Return to your original document. Create a picture box, and import the EPS graphic that you just created into a picture box.

5. Give the letter an automatic or manual runaround, and position it over the appropriate paragraph.

Note that EPS pages that have EPS pages embedded in them can sometimes cause printing problems.

Figure 4-40
Manual wraparound of EPS drop cap

DROP CAPS

Wrapping Drop Caps with Soft Returns

The previous two techniques work fine, but with one drawback. There's no way to properly anchor these initial caps to their paragraphs. These techniques require that you create the runarounds with irregular polygons, lines, or automatic or manual runarounds. None of these can be made part of an inline picture or text box, and if your text reflows, you'll have to manually move the caps so they'll stay with their paragraphs.

However, by making clever use of QuarkXPress's automatic drop caps, soft returns, and spaces, you can make "anchored" wrapped initial caps. Here's how:

1. Using the Paragraph Formats dialog box, apply an automatic drop cap to the paragraph.

2. Place the insertion point to the right of the cap, and adjust the kerning (Command-Option-Shift-[) so that the line closest to the cap is the correct distance from it. For instance, if you use a three-line drop cap with the letter "A", you kern so that the first line almost touches the "A".

3. Move the cursor to the end of the first line (you can do this quickly by pressing Command-Option-Right Arrow) and insert a new-line character (also known as a soft return) by pressing Shift-Return.

4. Adjust the space between the initial cap and the second line by adding flex spaces, a tab (and set a tab stop), or— our favorite—a single space with tracking (select the space character and add tracking).

5. Repeat steps three and four for each line of text that sits next to the drop cap.

If the cap is the letter V or W, or some other character that's the opposite shape of an A, you'll need to do the single-space tracking method in step 4 (you can also use kerning, or a combination of kerning and tracking; see Figure 4-41).

Figure 4-41
The soft return and space technique

As literally dozens screamed with the blood lust and *ennui* to which the Romans of those times were so often given, without fear an unrepenting Androgynous strode onto the filthy floor of the Desultorium, there to meet his fate before the sinister person of GLUTEUS MAXIMUS, vice-tonsil of Rome, one of the not-nicest guys ever to pack iron in the Big SPQR. *"Aha!* So at last

*Each of these lines is broken by a soft
return and indented with fixed spaces*

Adding Extra Space Between Paragraphs

Recently, David witnessed one of his esteemed officemates using multiple carriage returns to control the space between paragraphs and almost went apoplectic. Let's see if we can pound this idea into your head as strongly as we did with "Don't use multiple spaces between words or punctuation."

Don't ever use an extra carriage return to add space between paragraphs. Not only will you offend the people at Quark who spent long hours implementing the Space Before and Space After features, but you will—nine out of 10 times—mess yourself up with extra blank paragraphs hanging out at tops of columns or in other places where you don't want them. If you want a full line of space between paragraphs, apply it through Space Before or Space After in the Paragraph Formats dialog box. Even better, build it into a style.

Closing Up a Box to the Type's Baseline

How many times have you run into this one? You've set a headline or some callout type all in caps. You want a nice border around the type, close to the characters. You try to move the bottom edge of the headline's text box up till it's close to the type's baseline and . . . you can't do it! As soon as you move the bottom edge anywhere close to the baseline, and—*poof!* That line of text gets bumped out of the box altogether.

The problem is that even though you're working in all caps, QuarkXPress looks at the descender length built into a typeface to determine whether a block of type will fit in a box. As you moved the bottom edge of the text box up, the box cut off the descender length, so QuarkXPress naturally assumed there was no more room in the box for that line of type. You can see approximately where this descender depth is by highlighting the line of type.

Other than using a typeface that doesn't have any descenders, such as Hobo or Peignot (just joking), your choices are pretty limited. Usually, we just place the headline in a separate text box and position it where we want it (if the box's background color and runaround are set to None, then the headline won't interfere with the body copy's text box). Another solution would be to kern and track the type to your satisfaction, move the headline to a blank page, then save the page as an EPS file (see "Saving a Page as EPS," in Chapter 6, *Pictures*). You can then import the EPS into a picture box, and resize and crop the box as close to the type as you wish.

White on White Type

Sometimes we find it difficult to find white type when it's on top of a white area, especially when the text is only a small portion of a larger text box. One way to work around this is to place a colored character right next to the type. For example, you might place a right angle bracket (Shift-comma) colored black on the same line as the white text. When the white text is over the white page, the black character stands out clearly. When the text is over a black background, the white text is clear and the black character disappears (see Figure 4-42).

Figure 4-42
White on white type

The white text is invisible when it's not over the background.

The colored marker blends into the background.

Fractions, Part I

Setting fractions can be a real pain in the buttocks, especially if you have a lot of them (see Figure 4-43). If you have just a few fractions to create or the fractions are multidigit (like $^{16}/_{128}$), the Make Fractions feature in the Thing-a-ma-bob XTension works pretty well. Also, the "Fake Fractions the Tags Way" tip in Chapter 5, *Copy Flow*, explains one method of changing a bunch of fractions using the Find/Change feature and XPress Tags.

Here's some information relevant to either method: the numbers in the fractions usually look best at about 60- or 65-percent vertical size, and 65- or 70-percent horizontal size. Remember that each factor in fraction creation, such as kerning and baseline offset, needs to be decided based on the typeface you're using.

Figure 4-43
Fractions

$$\frac{1}{2} \qquad \frac{7}{8}$$

$$^{15}/_{16} \qquad 3/4$$

Fractions, Part II

The Make Fractions feature that comes in the FeaturesPlus and Thing-a-ma-bob XTensions is pretty good. But sometimes you want to process a lot of text all at once, changing fractions throughout the document. You can use QuarkXPress's Find/Change feature to make single-digit fractions quickly.

1. Set the superscript and subscript values in the Typographic Preferences dialog box (Command-Option-Y) to a vertical and horizontal scaling of approximately 67 percent. Set the Superscript offset to 33 percent and the Subscript offset to zero percent. You can adjust these depending on the typeface you're using.

2. Bring up the Find/Change dialog box (press Command-F). Turn Ignore Attributes off. Check the Plain type style on the Find What side and check Superscript on the Change To side. Also uncheck the Text box in the Change To side so what you find is replaced with the same text.

3. Enter "\?/" for a wildcard (you can also press Command-/) followed by a slash. Press Option-Return to Find First. Click Change All.

4. Check the Superscript box under Find What and Plain under Change To. Enter "/" in the Find What Text field, and do the Change All procedure in step three.

5. Check Plain in Find What and Subscript in Change To. Search for "/\?" (a slash followed by a wildcard), and change all instances.

6. Check Subscript in Find What and Plain in Change To, and search for "/". Change all instances.

This sounds much more confusing than it really is (read it over a few times until you get it).

Note that this procedure could easily screw up phrases like "and/or". We usually make sure that all the fractions are set up with fraction bars (Option-Shift-1) rather than normal slashes. If you don't start up with these fraction bars, you should include a Find/Change in the above procedure to change the normal slash to a fraction bar. Then go through your document selectively changing only the slashes in fractions into fraction bars.

FRACTIONS

Stacked Fractions

QuarkXPress also lets you create stacked fractions, such as $2\frac{1}{2}$ and $\frac{5}{6}$. Here's a quick formula for making them.

1. Type the numerator and denominator, separated by an underline (Shift-hyphen).

2. Change the point size of these three characters to 50 percent of original size. For example, 12-point type gets changed to six-point type.

3. Select the numerator and the underline, and apply a baseline shift equal to the point size (50 percent of the original).

4. Leave the numerator and underline highlighted and apply -90 units of tracking.

5. At your discretion, apply extra kerning between the characters to achieve a more precise look. You may want to zoom to a 400-percent view, or print a test sheet.

You may need to adjust the numbers we provide for different typefaces and number combinations.

ANCHORED BOX

Changing Underscore Position

There are very few ways to change the position or size of the underscore style (the line that runs under text). Most people don't care about this because it's often considered a typographic abomination. Nonetheless, some people need to use it (or at least *think* they need to), so here's a tip for how to adjust the position, size, color, and so on. Note that this is a useful tip for large display type; it's not so useful for body copy.

1. Place the text to be underlined in a separate text box and paste that box back as an anchored box. Make sure that the baselines of the anchored text match the baselines of the text around it (see "Aligning Anchored Text Boxes" in Chapter 6, *Pictures*).

FRACTIONS

Son of Fractions

One easy way to make fractions is to apply the superior style to the numerator (the top number) and *both* the superior and the subscript style to the denominator (the bottom number). Sounds weird, doesn't it? Try it once, and you'll see how well this works. You'll need to tweak the settings in your Typographic Preferences dialog box, the exact amounts depending on the font you want and the effect you're trying to achieve. Also, we recommend using the virgule character (Option-Shift-1) between the numbers. Just leave that character unstyled; it's fine the way it is.

Note that you can type this formatting in as XPress Tags like this: "<v>2<v> /<-v>3<-v>" (this produces $\frac{2}{3}$).

2. Give the text inside the anchored text box a Rule Below. Set the Rule Below to whatever size, offset, style, and color you want (see Figure 4-44).

Figure 4-44
Rule Belows for underscore characters

His mother was a witch, and one so strong
That could control the moon, make flows and ebbs,
And deal in her command without her power.

The Rule Below is applied to the paragraph in the anchored text box

His mother was a witch, and one so strong
That could control the moon, make flows and ebbs,
And deal in her command without her power.

Another, significantly easier technique is to use the Custom Underline feature of the free Stars & Stripes XTension from Quark found on the disc in the back of the book (see Figure 4-45).

Figure 4-45
Using Stars & Stripes for underscores

RULE ABOVE/BELOW
Double Underscores

We tend to shy away from using underscores for emphasis, preferring a more subtle type style instead, such as italic or bold lettering. However, this is ultimately an aesthetic question. If, for the sake of argument, you're the kind of person who likes using underlined type, you're probably going to <u>love</u> this tip.

Here's how you can put *two* underscores under some text (see Figure 4-46). Note that this really only works for one-line paragraphs, like headlines (though if you get tricky, you can get more useful results).

Underline Attributes

Color: ▮ Cyan
Shade: ▶ 70%
Width: 0.5 pt
Offset: -2 pt

[OK]   [Cancel]

Custom Underline is found under the Style submenu in the Style menu

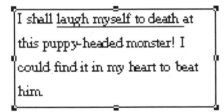

1. Place an extra return after the paragraph you want to double underscore.

2. Give this new, empty paragraph a Rule Above (Command-Shift-N). You can set it to a thick double or triple line, or whatever else your heart fancies. Set the offset to some small amount, perhaps three points, and make sure Length is set to Indents.

3. Bring up the Paragraph Formats dialog box (Command-Shift-F) and turn on continuous Apply (Option-click Apply). Now drag the left and right indent triangles in the

text-box ruler in until only the word you want is under-lined (you may have to drag the dialog box out of the way of the text box to do this). If you want the entire line underscored instead of just a selection of words, skip this step.

4. Change the leading on the ruled, empty paragraph to zero leading (type .001 for leading; see "Zero Leading," earlier in this chapter).

Thunder Lizards Unite!

Make it *Conspicuous...*

Figure 4-46
Double underscores

Making Combs

Drawing lots of rules in QuarkXPress is facilitated by the Step and Repeat function (Command-Option-D), but if you have too many rules on a page, the screen redraw can take forever! If you need to make a form with lots of text-entry combs on it, this slow-down can be a problem. Instead, try this method for making combs (see Figure 4-47).

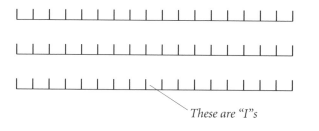

These are "I"s

Figure 4-47
Combs

1. In a text box, type a row of the capital letter "I" in a sans serif typeface (we usually use 11-point Helvetica), each separated by a space.

2. Apply a Rule Below to that paragraph; make it .5 point thick, with an offset of -.2 point.

3. Go to H&Js under the Edit menu and create a new H&J setting with Auto Hyphenation turned off and a flush zone almost as wide as your text box.

4. In the Paragraph Formats dialog box (Command-Shift-F), apply this H&J setting to the capital-"I" row.

5. Adjust the left and right indents for the Rule Below so that it doesn't stick out to the left and right of the first and last "I". In this example, try .75 point on each side.

Making Great Ellipses

After years of testing, our laboratories have found that you can get a really good-looking ellipsis by typing "[f].[f].[f].[f]". Each of those "[f]" symbols is a single, nonbreaking flex space—Command-Option-Shift-spacebar. (Use the Control key instead of the Command key if you're having troubles.)

We typically set the flex space to about 40 percent of an en in the Typographic Preferences dialog box (Command-Option-Y). You can allow a break after the ellipsis (at the end of a line) if you use a standard flex space (Option-Shift-Space), instead. Of course, you can add an additional period and flex space at the end, if you want a four-dot ellipsis at the end of a sentence.

You can also be slick and do this with XPress Tags by searching for all of your ellipses (you may have to look for the ellipsis character, Option-semicolon) and replacing them with the right coding. Search first for four period ellipses (or a period plus an Option-semicolon) and replace what you find with "<\!q>.<\!q>.<\!q>.<\!q>."; the exclamation point makes the flex spaces nonbreaking. Next, search for three periods (or Option-semicolon) and replace with the same string minus the last flex space and period.

This comb is much faster for QuarkXPress to redraw than a bunch of rules. It also is much easier to adjust; if you want it wider, just change the paragraph's width or adjust the width of the text box. Depending on the size of the comb, you'll need to adjust each of these measurements. We'll often also apply 90-percent horizontal compression to the I's, so they aren't as thick.

Line and Paragraph Numbers

Are you a legal clerk? Do you format contracts all the time? If so, you probably need a line number before each line of text or before each paragraph. Here are a couple of our favorite tips to achieve this.

Line numbering. There are two good ways to number each line in a document.

▶ If you don't care about the formatting of your text, try exporting it as a Microsoft Word document. Open it in Word, and then save it again as Text Only With Line Breaks. This places a return at the end of each line, but it also kills any formatting (italic, bold, font info, sizing, and so on). Then use Word's Renumber command to add a number and a tab to each paragraph (each line is a new paragraph now because of the line breaks).

▶ Probably a better way to do this is to create a narrow, tall text box on your master page (the master page that the text-to-be-numbered is based on). Put all your numbers in this box, with the same leading as the text on your pages.

Don't type the numbers in yourself! You can use Word or Excel to generate a whole mess of consecutive numbers for you. Then save that file as text and import it into your tall, narrow text box (you can link the boxes together to speed this up).

Paragraph numbering. Numbering each paragraph is easier. Export the text into Microsoft Word, use the Renumber feature, and then reimport it into QuarkXPress.

Quick and Easy Tables

Tables. Your idea of fun, right? No one likes to make tables, but many of us have to. Here's a method we use sometimes. Note that this is only for basic tables, in which each cell has the same number of lines, and each column is the same width (see Figure 4-48).

1. Type all the table values in a word processor (or into a text box in XPress) one column at a time, from top to bottom, and left to right. You don't need any tabs; just type a return after each table entry (if a cell has two or more lines in it, type Shift-Return to break the lines).

2. Make a text box in XPress and give it the number of columns you want in the table (in the Text Box Specifications dialog box or in the Measurements palette).

3. Flow the table data into this text box, and adjust the height of the text box until each column has the proper number of rows in it. (Or, you could press Enter after the bottom item of each row; that forces the text to jump to the next column.)

4. Select all the text and assign a table style sheet. Make sure the style sheet has a Space Before value. That way you'll add space between each row in the table.

5. If you want lines to delineate the table cells, you have to draw them yourself (or use the script on the disc bundled with this book).

Admittedly, there are some potential problems with making a table this way.

▶ It's difficult to make changes (such as adding or deleting rows) in QuarkXPress.

▶ It's a hassle if some cells have more lines than others. Nonetheless, you can make a one-line cell act like a two-line cell by adding a Shift-Return after the first line.

▶ Different column widths are also difficult. You can do it, though: instead of a multicolumn text box, flow the text into several linked text boxes.

Figure 4-48
Quick and easy tables

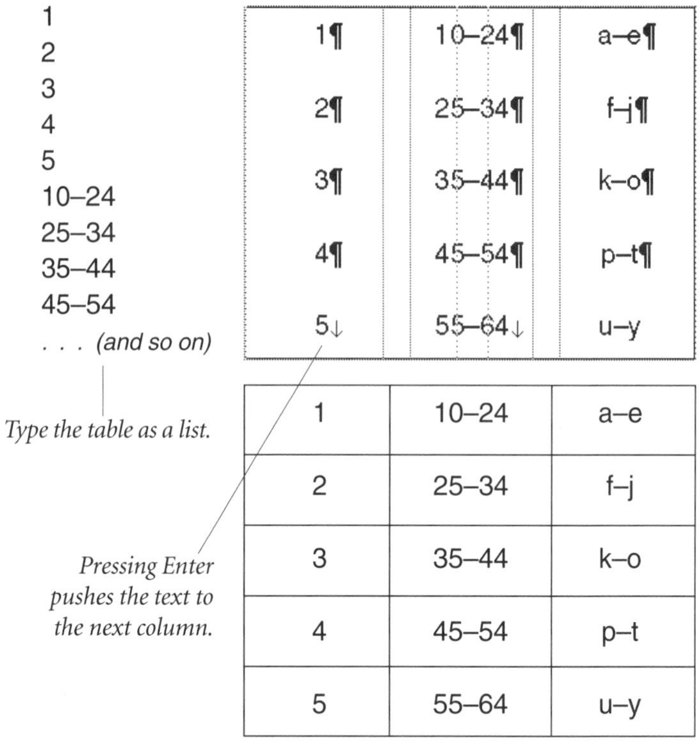

```
1
2
3
4
5
10–24
25–34
35–44
45–54
. . . (and so on)
```

Type the table as a list.

Pressing Enter
pushes the text to
the next column.

1¶	10–24¶	a–e¶
2¶	25–34¶	f–j¶
3¶	35–44¶	k–o¶
4¶	45–54¶	p–t¶
5↓	55–64↓	u–y

1	10–24	a–e
2	25–34	f–j
3	35–44	k–o
4	45–54	p–t
5	55–64	u–y

However, there are also advantages.

▶ It's relatively quick to prepare and import.

▶ No cutting and pasting is necessary.

▶ It only uses one text box, which leads to faster performance, smaller file sizes, and easier alignment.

TABLES

Funky Tables Made Easy

You can create tables by making a number of text boxes, but it's often a hassle manipulating them one by one, especially if they each have some kind of background that appears in all the boxes. Instead of making separate boxes, try putting the shared image or blend in one large picture box behind the table, and break it up with lines (see Figure 4-49).

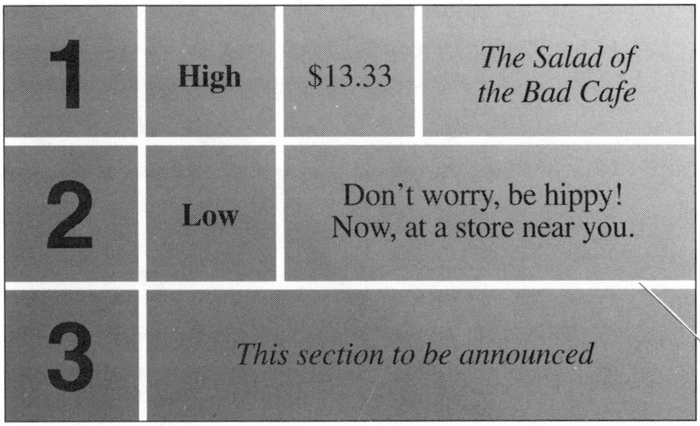

1	High	$13.33	*The Salad of the Bad Cafe*
2	Low		Don't worry, be hippy! Now, at a store near you.
3			*This section to be announced*

Figure 4-49
Shared image behind a number of boxes

The table's grid is made with white lines overlapping a blend rather than with separate boxes

DESIGN

Hanging Punctuation, Part I

QuarkXPress does not make it easy to create hanging punctuation. This tip is perhaps the easiest way we've seen—but automatic, it ain't. In fact, it's downright painful. But it *does* work if you've got time to spare.

Hanging punctuation, by the way, is where the punctuation extends out into the gutters (past the margins). The reason for doing this in the first place is that most punctuation is smaller than a full-sized character, so a perfectly aligned punctuation mark at the left or right margin looks odd; "hanging" the punctuation out into the gutters creates—believe it or not—a cleaner look.

This method works on either side of a text box, though the one we describe here is for the left side (see Figure 4-50).

1. Draw a picture box on the left side of the text box. The picture box should be the same height as the text box, and can be any width (we usually make it about a quarter-inch wide). The runaround for this box should be set to Item, and all of the runaround fields should be set to zero.

2. Place the right edge of the picture box exactly where you want the left margin of the text to sit.

3. Extend the text box to the left so that the picture box overlaps the text box slightly (because the runaround is set to Item, the text should run around the picture box).

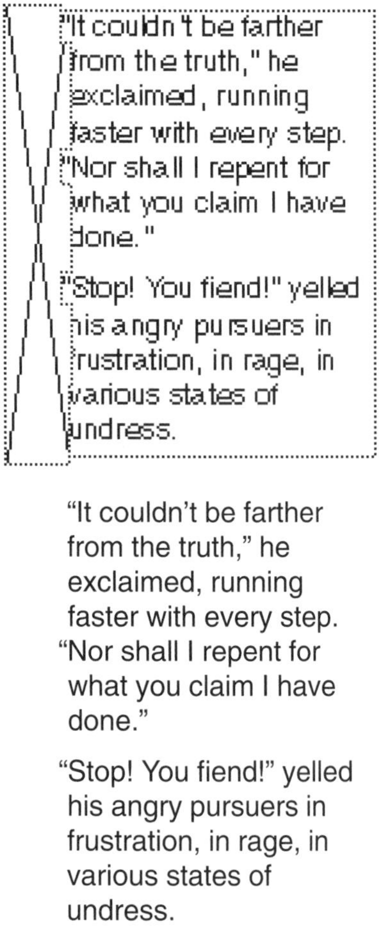

"It couldn't be farther
from the truth," he
exclaimed, running
faster with every step.
"Nor shall I repent for
what you claim I have
done."

"Stop! You fiend!" yelled
his angry pursuers in
frustration, in rage, in
various states of
undress.

Figure 4-50
Hanging punctuation with a picture box

4. Place a vertical ruler guide where you want the punctuation to hang. For instance, if you want the punctuation to hang three points, place a guide three points from the right edge of the picture box.

5. Convert the picture box to a polygon (select the last item in the Box Shape submenu under the Item menu) and turn on Reshape Polygon.

6. For every line which should have hung punctuation, insert four new polygon handles in the picture box and then drag the middle two of those handles so that you've got a small rectangular intrusion into the "margin." Use the vertical guide you placed in step three to keep your indents consistent (the new polygon points snap to that guide).

As you go along making these hanging indents, there's a good chance that the line breaks will change. If you don't want this to happen, you need to insert soft returns (Shift-Return).

For obvious reasons, you want to be sure that your text won't change after you perform this painful task. In other words, perform this trick as late in the job cycle as you can.

DESIGN

Hanging Punctuation, Part II

Of course, there are other methods of creating hanging punctuation. Here's a way we think is harder, but you might prefer it (hey, everyone's different).

1. Make the text box wide enough to accommodate the text column along with the hung characters. (We can't tell you how much to add; you'll just have to measure.)

2. Select all the text and indent it on the right and left to return it to the proper column width (if you made the text box six points wider, then add three points each to the left and right indents). You're going to want to include this in a style sheet if you do it more than once.

3. Insert return characters before and after the lines that contain the characters you will be hanging. You typically have to change the horizontal justification to Forced to keep these paragraphs justified.

4. Cancel out the indent where you want something to hang. For example, if you want a line to hang slightly off the right margin, reduce that line or paragraph's right indent.

Of course, if any text flow changes after you do this, you're in hot water and will have to backpedal (and search and replace) furiously. Therefore, be as sure as possible that nothing's going to change after you go to all this work.

DESIGN

Hanging Punctuation, Part III

If you just want to hang the occasional character into the left margin (for example, an initial cap or quotation mark), you can do it by kerning.

1. If the character is on a line in the middle of a paragraph, place returns before and after the line so that the line is its own paragraph. (If you're working with justified text, you'll have to force justify that line or paragraph.)

2. Type a fixed space (like Option-spacebar) as the first character on the line (before the character to be hung).

3. Place your insertion point between the fixed space and the character to be hung (that is, to the *right* of the fixed space), and apply a negative kern value (in the Measurements palette, or type Command-Shift-[). You have to apply a large kern value, like -200. The more you kern, the more the "first" character is pulled into the margin.

The main drawback to this method—besides the fact that it's labor-intensive—is that you can't see the character once it gets outside your text box. It'll print fine, though. However, it might just take you a printout or two to ensure you've used a proper amount of kerning.

DESIGN

Hanging Punctuation, Part IV

If you find yourself wanting to hang punctuation off the right side of text that is flush right (right aligned), this can help: place a right-aligned tab stop just slightly in from the right margin of your text column. Each line without punctuation should be preceded with a tab; each line with punctuation at the end should not. There are other variations on this same technique that we leave to your own imagination.

PRE-3.3

Flowing Side-by-Side Paragraphs

David likes to keep a bottle of champagne around for those special occasions when he finds a really cool tip that lets him do something he thought was previously impossible to do with QuarkXPress. The problem is that he's usually so busy playing with the new trick that he never gets around to opening the champagne! Such was the problem when someone told him how to create side-by-side paragraphs that would reflow with body text.

The problem which plagued QuarkXPress users for years is how to get a paragraph such as a multiline subhead to sit out in the left margin next to a paragraph *and* to follow that paragraph whenever it reflows. The obvious method was to use an anchored text box with a hanging indent. However, Quark refused—until version 3.3—to fix a very strange "feature" that made this method seem impossible (see "Anchored Boxes as Initial Caps," in Chapter 6, *Pictures*).

The breakthrough idea was to use the indent here character rather than a hanging indent (see Figure 4-51). (Sure, it's a simple idea; but then we're pretty easily excited.)

1. Create a separate text box that contains the subhead. Make its width smaller than the margin you're fitting it into and set Text Inset to zero.

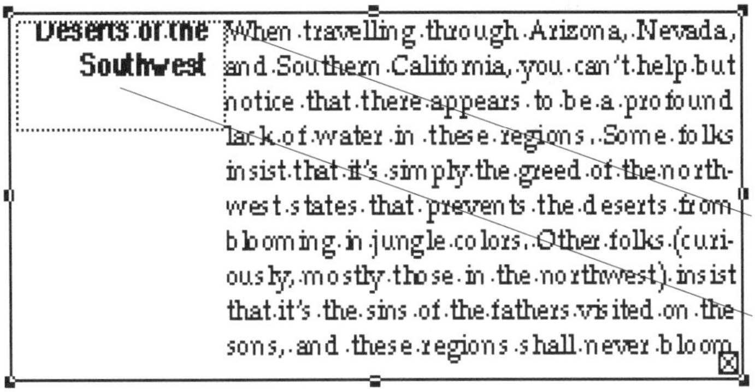

Deserts of the Southwest When travelling through Arizona, Nevada, and Southern California, you can't help but notice that there appears to be a profound lack of water in these regions. Some folks insist that it's simply the greed of the northwest states that prevents the deserts from blooming in jungle colors. Other folks (curiously, mostly those in the northwest) insist that it's the sins of the fathers visited on the sons, and these regions shall never bloom.

Figure 4-51
Side-by-side paragraphs

Indent to Here character placed here.

Anchored text box; note the slight baseline shift.

2. Cut or copy that text box with the Item tool and paste it using the Content tool as the first character in the paragraph. It's now an anchored box.

3. Select the anchored box by clicking on it (rather than selecting it as text), and change it to Align with Text Ascent (in the Measurements palette or the Anchored Text Box Specifications dialog box).

4. Make sure that the Left Indent and First Line values for the paragraph are zero in the Paragraph Formats dialog box.

5. Place the cursor between the anchored box and the first word of the paragraph, press Tab, and then press Command-\ (the indent-here character). Set a tab stop for that paragraph, placed where you want the left margin to begin (this value should be the same as the left indent of other paragraphs on the page).

6. The baselines of the subhead and the paragraph probably aren't the same—we can't figure out why this is. But that's the way it is, so you need to compensate for it. Select all the text within the anchored box and apply a baseline shift using whatever value it takes to align the baselines. The top of the text may look like cut off, but it prints fine.

That's all there is to it! We sometimes select the anchored text box and lock it so that its width doesn't get changed accidentally. And we often save one of these text boxes in a library so that we can quickly copy it out and paste it where we need it.

Note that all this hoopla isn't necessary if you're using version 3.3. In that case, you can make the anchored box a normal hanging indent (give the whole paragraph a large indent with an equally large negative first line indent).

ANCHORED BOXES

More Flowing Anchored Boxes in the Margin

Here's another technique, which is, by all reckoning, more flexible and perhaps easier than the last. It's more flexible because it lets you place subheads or graphics in either the left or right margin of your text (see Figure 4-52).

1. Set large left and/or right indents for all the text in your story. This margin is where the graphic or subhead is going to sit, so it needs to be big enough to accommodate it. If you only want to hang items off the right side, you only need to add a right indent, and so on.

2. Copy the picture or text box with the Item tool, and paste it in to its own empty line in the text using the Content tool. Now it's an anchored box on that line. Set the anchored box to align on the ascenders in the Anchored Box Specifications dialog box or in the Measurements palette.

3. Remove the left and right indents from that anchored-box paragraph.

4. If you want the box in the right margin, set it to flush right (right-aligned).

5. Set the leading for that one paragraph to .001 (effectively, zero leading).

You may need to adjust the anchored box's baseline shift to place it properly. Note that if you use Auto leading in your text, this tip may not work (but why would you use Auto leading, anyway?).

FONTS

Renaming a Font (Difficult)

Warning: This is a serious power-user trick. Do not attempt it at home.

This procedure was put together by Kip Shaw, with help from Jim Lewis (author of the programs theTypeBook and the-FONDler), Greg Swann (author of many utilities, including FONDetective), Greg Dunn, and Phil. It is very complex and sensitive. If you're going to try it, do it *only* on copies of fonts; one false keystroke and you've most likely ruined what you're working on. This procedure requires ResEdit version 2.1 or later.

Figure 4-52
Hanging graphics or text in the margin

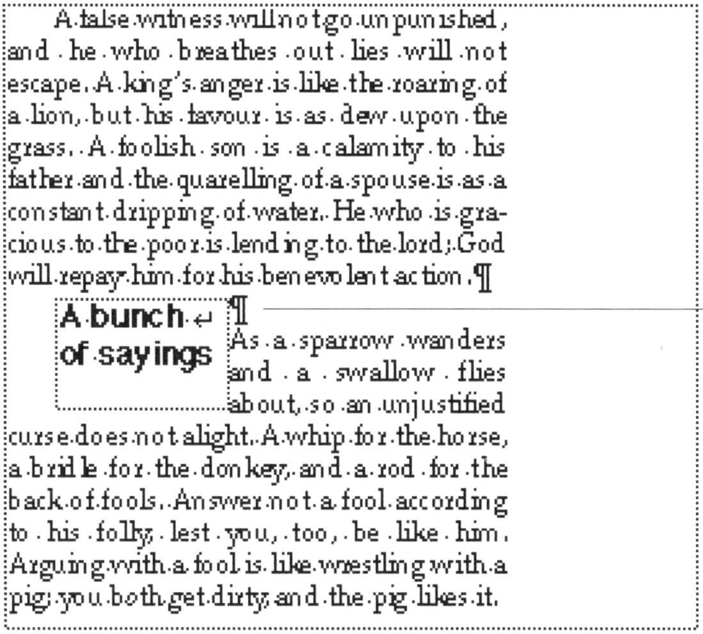

A false witness will not go unpunished, and he who breathes out lies will not escape. A king's anger is like the roaring of a lion, but his favour is as dew upon the grass. A foolish son is a calamity to his father and the quarelling of a spouse is as a constant dripping of water. He who is gracious to the poor is lending to the lord; God will repay him for his benevolent action. ¶

A bunch ↵ of sayings ¶ As a sparrow wanders and a swallow flies about, so an unjustified curse does not alight. A whip for the horse, a bridle for the donkey, and a rod for the back of fools. Answer not a fool according to his folly, lest you, too, be like him. Arguing with a fool is like wrestling with a pig; you both get dirty, and the pig likes it.

The anchored box is pasted in on its own line.

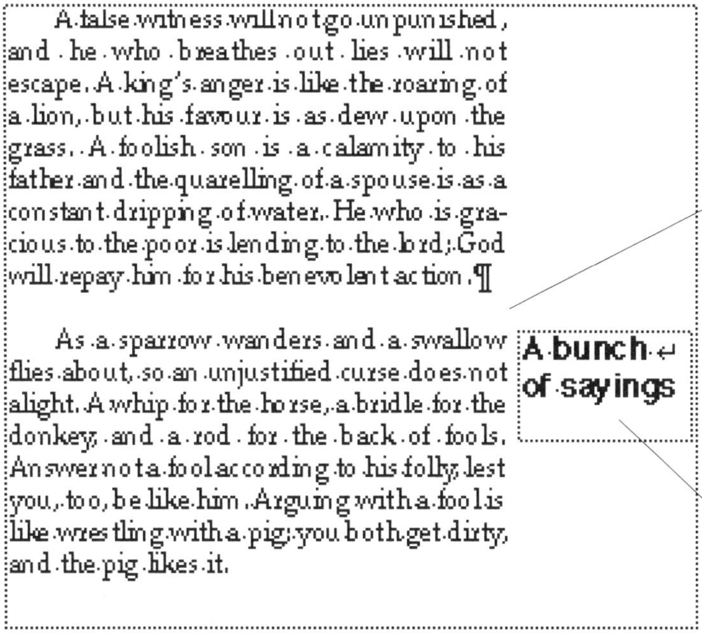

A false witness will not go unpunished, and he who breathes out lies will not escape. A king's anger is like the roaring of a lion, but his favour is as dew upon the grass. A foolish son is a calamity to his father and the quarelling of a spouse is as a constant dripping of water. He who is gracious to the poor is lending to the lord; God will repay him for his benevolent action. ¶

As a sparrow wanders and a swallow flies about, so an unjustified curse does not alight. A whip for the horse, a bridle for the donkey, and a rod for the back of fools. Answer not a fool according to his folly, lest you, too, be like him. Arguing with a fool is like wrestling with a pig; you both get dirty, and the pig likes it.

A bunch ↵ of sayings

The paragaph with the anchored box has Space Above applied to it.

The anchored box has zero leading, right alignment, and no indents.

The requirement for a renamed font can stem from any of several needs: for example, you might want to have two (or more) different tracks available for a font; or you might want to have automatic kern pairs set up differently for different sizes of a font; or you might have fonts from different vendors, but with the same name, that you want to be able to use at the same time.

Here's how you do it:

1. Make a copy of the font suitcase and the printer fonts for the font family whose name you want to change.

2. Change their filenames. Suitcase filenames, remember, can be any old thing, but outline font filenames have very strict and important rules; keep the same number of letters as in the original filenames, and simply change one letter (example: change "HelveBolObl" to "HelvaBolObl").

3. In ResEdit, open one of your new printer font files, then open its lowest-numbered "POST" resource (501).

4. Find the listing for the original filename in "POST 501", and make the same change you made to the filename itself in step two.

5. Make sure this filename isn't listed anywhere else in the "POST" resources. It shouldn't be; but if you do find it, change it as in step four.

6. Save your changes and close the file.

7. Repeat steps three through six for all other printer fonts in the family whose name you're changing.

8. In ResEdit, open your new screen-font suitcase file. Then open its "FOND" window, which lists all the "FOND" resources—one for each screen font in the suitcase.

9. Select the "FOND" for a screen font you want to change, and press Command-I. In this Get Info window are listed both the ID number and the name of the "FOND" (the name of the "FOND" is what appears in your font menus). Change the name by making the same change you made in the printer font's name, retaining all spaces (if any), capitalization, and number of characters. Close the Get Info window.

10. Holding down the Option key, open the newly named "FOND" resource. Find the old name's text string, and replace all instances with the new name.

11. Save your changes and close the "FOND".

12. Repeat steps eight through 11 for all other "FOND" resources in the suitcase.

13. Now we must renumber the screen fonts, especially if you plan to have both versions (original and new) open at the same time. There are several ways:

▶ If you aren't using MasterJuggler or Suitcase, drag one suitcase icon on top of the other. This copies all of the bitmap fonts into one suitcase. Then drag that suitcase onto your System Folder.

▶ If you are using Suitcase or MasterJuggler, let the utility resolve the conflict by itself: open both font suitcases.

That's it. If you've followed these directions carefully, you have two differently named, functional copies of the same font.

FONTS
Renaming a Font (Easy)

There's another solution for renaming a font, and this one is simple but costs some real money. Buy a copy of Altsys Fontographer, a font-editing utility that can open any existing font and lets you save it under another name. Their excellent manuals explain the ins and outs of font-naming conventions (and font numbering conventions) and don't involve *any* resource hacking. Fontographer is under $200, but that's a high price to pay unless you want to get into making special characters or fonts. See Robin Williams's book, *How To Boss Your Fonts Around*, for advice on this subject.

FORMATTING
Text on a Curve

To be honest, there's no good, cheap, easy way to put text on a curve in XPress. But that doesn't stop us from trying.

1. Draw a circle (hold down the Shift key while dragging out an oval picture box to constrain to a circle).

2. Make a small text box at the top of the circle that has only one letter in it. Center that letter and format it the way you want the whole word or phrase to look.

3. With the Rotation tool, click in the center point of the circle and drag the mouse until the character is in the right position.

4. Step and Repeat with zero offsets, change the letter, and rotate it again. Continue this until all the letters of the word or phrase are completed (see Figure 4-53).

Figure 4-53
Text on a curve

Now, this is not a *good* way, nor is it an *easy* way. In fact, it may just drive you crazy (especially if you need to change the curve in any way). However, it *is* a cheap way.

Better ways? Our favorite way to place text on a curve within XPress is to use the SXetchPad XTension from Datastream (there's a demo of it on the disc in the back of the book). Or do it the way you do it now: create the text in Illustrator and FreeHand and import it as an EPS.

copy
FLOW

If you use more than just a little text in your documents, you probably should be using a word processor to type and edit it before bringing it into QuarkXPress. If you have more than two pages of text, you should probably be using style sheets to format and reformat that text. And if you have more than just a few pages of text, there's a good chance you'd be more efficient if you knew how to use XPress Tags. Each of these has to do with moving copy in, through, and around QuarkXPress. And, while in many tips in this book you can speed up your work a little here and there, this is an area where you can save hours of time with a few simple tricks.

Text Reflow Between Versions

Each version of QuarkXPress flows text slightly differently, because Quark keeps changing features. Don't worry about how the text will change when you open an older-version document in a newer version of XPress. Each file is tagged with a version number, and XPress is smart enough to check that tag before starting to reflow the text. If you open a 3.1 file in 3.2 or 3.3, the program uses the 3.1 algorithms and feature set.

However, if you want to update the file to take advantage of the latest and greatest features and algorithms, hold down the Option key as you click Open in the Open dialog box. The old text flow is ignored, and XPress flows it the way it thinks it should. Often, there's no difference. But sometimes there's lots. It all depends on your document, how it's laid out, and what features you took advantage of (from justification to smart ligatures). The best thing to do is to peruse your file carefully after Option-opening it.

STYLE SHEETS

Creating Styles by Example

Instead of using the Edit Style Sheet dialog box to define the format of a style, you can create a style based on an existing paragraph in your document (see Figure 5-1). This way you can format a paragraph just the way you want it, and then create a style that has all those attributes.

To create a style based on an existing paragraph's formatting, position the insertion point anywhere in the paragraph, then create a new style. When you get to the Edit Style Sheet dialog box, you'll see all of the formatting that's applied to the current paragraph listed at the bottom of the box. All you have to do is name the new style, click OK, and save your changes. Note that this doesn't automatically apply the style sheet to that paragraph; you have to then apply that style to the text using the Style Sheets palette or the Style menu.

Figure 5-1

Creating a style by example

Lady Lovelace's Idea¶

Place the insertion point in a paragraph.

When you click the New button from the Style Sheets dialog box, you'll see an Edit Style Sheet dialog box listing all the attributes of the selected paragraph.

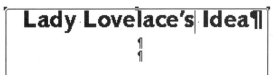

Redefining Tabs in Styles

Although you can define tabs inside of a style, it's a pain in the left buttock going back and forth between editing a style and looking at the effects on your page. An easier solution takes advantage of creating style sheets by example (see the previous tip) and the ability to merge styles together. This tip assumes you've already created a style sheet, and you need to edit the tab stops.

1. Apply the style sheet to a paragraph.

2. Change the tab stops of that paragraph to where you'd like them to be.

3. Create a new style sheet based on this new paragraph (see the previous tip). Name this style sheet slightly differently than the original style sheet (we usually just append the word "new").

4. In the Style Sheets dialog box, select the old style sheet and click Delete; when you're prompted with a dialog box asking for a replacement style, select the new style sheet and click OK.

5. Finally, select the new style, click Edit, and rename it without the "new" attached.

Note that this only works with a style that isn't defined based on another style.

QuicKeys Styles

Style sheets are powerful, but we don't always find them accessible enough. So we've created macros using QuicKeys (our favorite macro-making program) to automate two actions that don't have keyboard shortcuts in QuarkXPress.

▶ Command-Control-N for selecting "No Style" from the Style Sheets submenu

▶ Control-Option-S to open the Style Sheets dialog box (and then press Enter to edit the currently selected style sheet)

Chapter 10, *Macros and Scripts*, lists several other macros that can make your life easier.

Create New Styles Fast

Command-clicking on a style listed in XPress's Style Sheets palette (see Figure 5-2) brings you to the Style Sheets dialog box, you can quickly create a new style by clicking the New or Duplicate buttons instead of the Edit button. This is faster than selecting Style Sheets from the Edit menu, but perhaps not quite as fast as creating a QuicKey macro to do it for you (see "QuicKeys Styles," below).

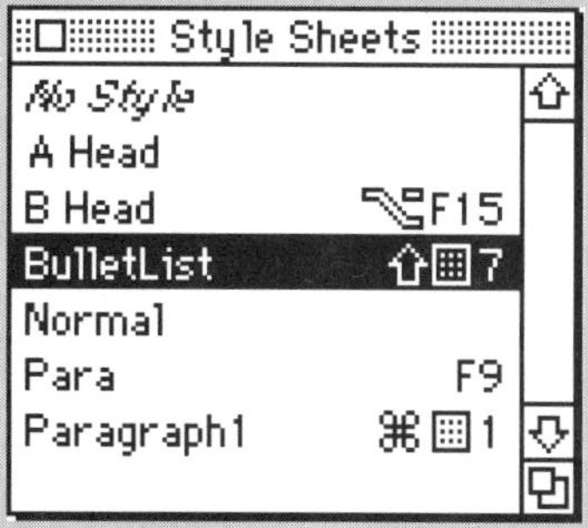

Figure 5-2
The Style Sheets palette

STYLE SHEETS
Quick Text Styling

While we think making style sheets is a great thing, sometimes it's just not worth the trouble. If you want to type a new paragraph with the same character and paragraph formatting as another paragraph, you can copy and paste the entire paragraph, and then delete the text. That way, the new text that you type is already in the appropriate style.

STYLE SHEETS
Giving Style Sheets a Color

Sometimes when we have lots and lots of style sheets in a document, and they're all somewhat similar, we like to change the type color of each one. One might be blue, another might be red, and so on. This allows us to see on screen, at a glance, which style sheets have been applied where.

Of course, if you do this, don't forget to change them all to the proper color before you go to final output.

STYLE SHEETS
Legal Style Keystrokes

Only certain keys are "legal" or allowable for applying styles: the function keys (F1 through F15) and the numbers on the numeric keypad. In combination with the modifier keys—Control, Command, Shift, and Option—that provides for a lot of keyboard shortcuts. However, because QuarkXPress, starting with version 3.2, uses many of the function keys for its own shortcuts (both with and without Option and Shift), we suggest that you use function keys as style sheet hot keys only in conjunction with the Control key.

There's no way to print a listing of what keystrokes go with what styles (see "Printing Your Style Sheet," later in this chapter) so we just print a screen shot of the Style Sheets palette and tape it to our wall. If you have a really long style sheet, you may have to take a couple of screen shots.

FORMATTING
Seeing Local Formatting

If there are any local paragraph-formatting or character attributes in the selected text or paragraph containing the insertion point—formatting that overrides that of the current style—a plus sign appears to the right of the style's name in the Style Sheets palette. This is a handy way of knowing if you're looking at a paragraph formatted according to its style, or at formatting that's been applied locally (see Figure 5-3).

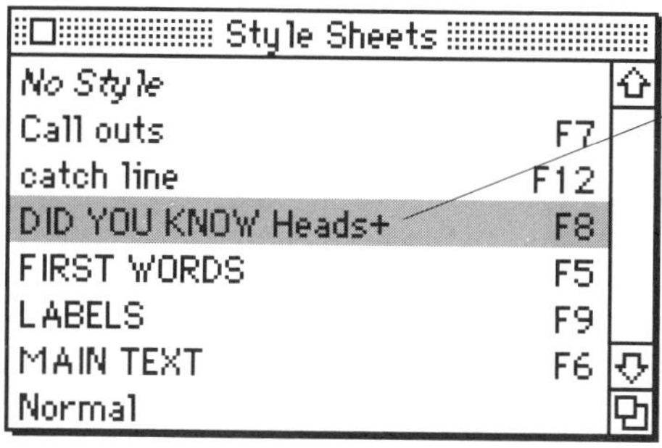

The plus sign following the style name shows that local formatting is present in the current selection.

Figure 5-3
Local formatting flag

STYLE SHEETS
Overriding Local Formatting

Any paragraph that has "No Style" applied to it loses all local formatting (such as font changes, bold and italic, and so on) when it's tagged with another style. This, more often than not, is a pain in the butt, and causes much confusion. However, there are some powerful uses for this feature, such as stripping out all local formatting that some dumbbell put in for no good reason. XPress can apply "No Style" and then another style in one stroke when you Option-click on the style name in the Style Sheets palette. This removes all paragraph formatting that doesn't conform to the style.

STYLE SHEETS
Removing Some Formatting

In the previous tip, we learned that "No Style" is great for eliminating all local formatting in a paragraph. However, what if you want to get rid of only *some* local formatting?

Instead of using "No Style" to get rid of all local formatting wherever it occurs, you can get clever with the way the document's paragraph styles are defined. The trick is that QuarkXPress is built in such a way that it forgets about any local formatting that equals the formatting in a paragraph style. So, first change the style sheet so that it contains the formatting you want to remove, then remove that unwanted formatting from the style sheet.

This is much easier to understand with an example. Let's say you have a whole bunch of text that has a "BodyText" style sheet applied to it, but some bozo selected the whole thing and changed

STYLE SHEETS
Is it Local Formatting?

The little plus sign that appears in the Style Sheets palette is great because it tells you when local formatting has been applied over a style sheet. But sometimes you can't tell whether it's character formatting or paragraph formatting that's been applied. However, if the plus sign only appears when the text cursor is in some places in the paragraph, then it's definitely local character formatting. If it shows up anywhere in the paragraph, then it may be that paragraph formatting was applied. On the other hand, it could be that character formatting was applied to the whole paragraph.

Another way to check is to place the text cursor in the paragraph, then Option-click on the style name in the Style Sheets palette. If the paragraph changes, then you know it had local formatting over it. If it didn't change, there's no local formatting. Then you can press Command-Z to Undo the reapplication of the style (important if you've inadvertently wiped out *some* local formatting that you wanted to keep).

the typeface to 18-point Futura (this kind of error happens a lot when you copy and paste text from one document to another and the style sheets are slightly different in each file).

If you apply "No Style" to everything, then apply the "Normal" style again, you would wipe out any bold and italic attributes in the text, and you'd have to go back and reapply them by hand. However, using this technique saves the day (see Figure 5-4).

1. Edit the "BodyText" style so that the style definition includes all the formatting that you *want to get rid of.* In this example, it entails making "BodyText" 18-point Futura.

2. Save the change to the style sheet.

3. Edit the "BodyText" style again. This time define it to the way you like. In this example, you'd define it back to the original typeface and size.

4. Save the change to the style sheet.

At this point, all the text is formatted properly: you've gotten all the text to be the original typeface and size, but you've retained the bold and italic local formatting. You don't have to select the text; just adjust the style sheets.

Figure 5-4

Removing some formatting

She is like a <u>tree planted by streams</u> of water, that yields its *fruit* in its **season;** whose *leaf* does not wither, and everything she does shall *prosper.* The ungodly <u>are not so, but</u> are like **chaff** which the wind blows away.

1. Someone has gone in and changed some text to a different font and added underline style.

<u>She is like a tree planted by streams of water, that yields its *fruit* in its **season;** whose *leaf* does not wither, and everything she does shall *prosper.* The ungodly are not so, but are like **chaff** which the wind blows away.</u>

2. Change the paragraph style to match the local formatting

She is like a tree planted by streams of water, that yields its *fruit* in its **season;** whose *leaf* does not wither, and everything she does shall *prosper.* The ungodly are not so, but are like **chaff** which the wind blows away.

3. Change the style back; the unwanted formatting is lost, but the wanted local formatting remains.

Overriding Style Sheets on Import

We wish that there were more control over how XPress handles importing style sheets. But take heart: There are always workarounds. For example, here's a little number that lets you import style sheets which override the ones within your document.

1. Import the new style sheets from another document by clicking the Append button in the Style Sheets dialog box. When it asks you whether you want to rename the incoming styles or use the existing styles, click Rename. XPress adds an asterisk after the name of each renamed style. For instance, if the style were named "Callout", the program would add a new style called "Callout*".

2. Delete the original style (in this case, "Callout"), and tell QuarkXPress to replace all instances of that style with the new asterisked style ("Callout*").

3. Select "Callout*", click Edit, and remove the asterisk from the Name field.

4. Click Save.

Now the old style is the same as the newly imported style. In effect, the old style sheet name has been overwritten by the new one. This technique works great as long as you don't have to go through it for 125 different styles. We still wish there were an Override Existing option when importing styles.

Based On Differences

Note that styles that are based on other styles are primarily defining differences between the base style and the new style. Let's say you have a style called "Head1" and it's 18-point Futura with the bold style applied, and a style called "Head2" that's based on "Head1", except that it's 12-point Futura and is not bold. The difference between the two is the point size and the style.

Fast Word Imports

Here's a hidden and wonderful feature. When you're importing a Microsoft Word file into QuarkXPress and it has any same-named styles, Option-clicking Rename New Styles or Use Existing Styles applies renaming or override to all incoming styles. We wish this would work when appending styles from other XPress documents!

The newest version of the Word filter that shipped with the Power Mac release makes this explicit. They added a checkbox labeled Apply to All Duplicates that does the same thing as the Option-click.

Copying Paragraph Formatting and Styles

If you want to copy all the local paragraph formatting and the style from one paragraph to another, first click in the paragraph whose format you want to change. Then Option-Shift-click the paragraph whose format you want to copy. Not only is the paragraph's style copied, but any local paragraph formatting (margins, tabs, leading, and so on) is also applied to the destination paragraph. No local character formatting in the destination paragraph is changed.

If you only want to copy tab stops from one paragraph to another, see "Formatting Tabs Quickly" in Chapter 4, *Type and Typography*.

If you change the font of "Head1" to Franklin Gothic, then the font of "Head2" changes, too, because they're linked by their differences. There's one exception: if you change the parent style to have attributes that are *the same* as the child style, the difference link is broken. If you change "Head1" to "not bold," for example, then there's no difference in style between the two and the link is broken. Then, if you go back and change "Head1" to bold again, "Head2" follows suit and becomes bold. This is much the same as what happens when local formatting within a paragraph matches the formatting of the style.

Why to Avoid "Normal"

The one style that QuarkXPress is guaranteed *never* to be able to append from another document is the "Normal" style. You can't delete QuarkXPress's "Normal" style, so you can't ever automatically replace it with a different "Normal". So if you're not careful, you can end up importing text that becomes incorrectly formatted once QuarkXPress's "Normal" style is applied to it.

One way (we think it's the best way) to avoid potential problems is simply not to use "Normal" at all. Instead, religiously create and use an alternative default style, such as "BodyText".

Not only do we not like tagging paragraphs with the "Normal" style, we think you shouldn't even base other styles on it. It's dangerous. Just don't do it.

Replacing Style Sheets

We find it rather odd that you can search and replace style sheets in Microsoft Word but not in QuarkXPress. Or can you? Here's a quick search-and-replace procedure to change all instances of one style to another. Let's say you want to replace every instance of "Heading3" with "RunInHead".

1. Open the Style Sheets dialog box (from the Edit menu or press Shift-F11) and duplicate "Heading3" (select the style and click the Duplicate button).

2. When the Edit Style Sheet dialog box appears, leave the name set to "Copy of Heading3" and click OK.

3. Select the style you want to replace (in this case "Heading3") and click the Delete button. Don't worry; because you created a duplicate of this style, you'll be able to get it back after deleting it.

4. QuarkXPress asks you what style you want to give to the paragraphs tagged "Heading3"; specify the replacement style in the popup menu (in this case "RunInHead"). This is the key to this tip.

5. Click Save.

6. Go back to the Style Sheets dialog box and edit the duplicate style sheet: remove the "Copy of" from the front of the name, and click OK.

You have now replaced all instances of "Heading3" with "RunInHead", and retained "Heading3" so you can use it again. You can also find and change styles using the technique described in "Finding and Changing H&Js" in Chapter 4, *Type and Typography*. Note that this tip also works for replacing colors and H&J settings.

Page Breaks

PageMaker has a kind of cool feature that we like; you can specify a paragraph attribute that forces the paragraph to start on a new column or page. That is, any paragraph tagged with this attribute will always start at the top of a page or column. As it turns out, you can do a similar thing in QuarkXPress. Many readers pointed out that you can simply make the Space Before value in the Paragraph Formats dialog box as large as the height of the text column. For example, if your text box is 45 picas tall, make the Space Before value 45 picas. You can set this as a paragraph style or as local formatting for particular paragraphs. (We, of course, recommend having a special style.)

FIND/CHANGE

Faking Character Styles

Although QuarkXPress doesn't have named character styles, it is possible to use QuarkXPress's Find/Change feature to achieve some of the functions of character styles.

1. In Microsoft Word or XPress, assign a seldom-used type style, such as Underline, Outline, or Shadow, to the text to which you want to apply your special local formatting. You can apply these with a keystroke.

2. If you prepared the text in your word processor, bring the text into QuarkXPress.

3. Select the Find/Change command from the Edit menu (or press Command-F). Make sure Ignore Attributes is unchecked. Check the appropriate boxes to replace the style you originally applied with the new formatting you want.

4. Click the Change All button.

For example, you could search for all instances of text that is in Outline style and reformat them with 12-point New Baskerville

Bold. Then, later, if you needed to, you could search for all instances of 12-point New Baskerville bold and reformat them with a different style.

Unfortunately, you can't use this method to apply the more sophisticated of QuarkXPress's typographic controls, such as tracking or horizontal scaling, because they're not accessible from the Find/Change dialog box.

RUN-IN HEADS
Combining Paragraphs for Run-In Heads

Another way to fake character styles—this time to create run-in heads—is by combining paragraphs. If you have two consecutive paragraphs with different text formats, and you combine them by deleting the carriage return that separates them, each of the two, now-joined sections within the new paragraph will retain the formatting of the paragraph it originally belonged to (see Figure 5-5).

For example, you could create a head using a paragraph style calling for 14-point Futura Bold, and follow it with a body paragraph using 12-point ITC Garamond. By deleting the return after the Futura Bold paragraph, you'll end up with the Futura Bold text as a run-in head for the body text set in ITC Garamond.

Note that if you put some special character (or series of characters) at the end of paragraphs that you want to be run-in, you can use the Find/Change dialog box (Command-F) to get rid of their carriage returns. For example, if you ended each run-in head with three asterisks, you could search for "***\p" and replace it with a space.

Figure 5-5
Automating run-in heads

When a body meets a body.

If you plan on coming through the rye—or just visiting—you might think about the package deal in which we provide you—no extra charge—with a genuine imitation camel's hair jacket

Heading as it's typed in the text—styled on a separate line.

When a body meets a body. If you plan on coming through the rye—or just visiting—you might think about the package deal in which we provide you—no extra charge—with a gen-

Heading after being run-in.

RUN-IN HEADS
Anchored Run-in Heads

If you need to change the formatting of the run-in heads in the last tip, you're in for trouble. While you can use the Find/Change ability in "Faking Character Styles," above, it's kind of a hassle. Instead, you might want to take the extra time to make robust run-in heads out of anchored text boxes (see Figure 5-6).

As we point out in "Aligning Anchored Text Boxes" in Chapter 6, *Pictures*, make sure that the leading of the text in the different boxes are equal, and that the anchored box has a text outset of zero (you have to set this in the Runaround Specifications dialog box before you paste the box into the text flow) and a text inset of zero (set in the Text Box Specifications dialog box). And, again, note that if the

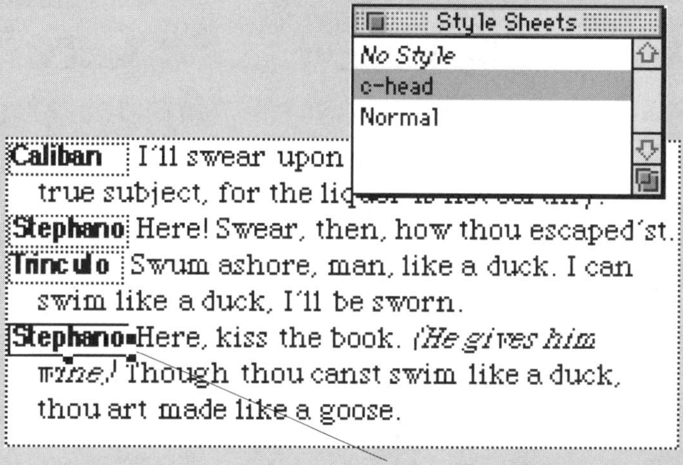

Figure 5-6
Run-in heads using anchored boxes

The text in the anchored boxes are set to a different style sheet.

typeface of the run-in head is different than the text around it, you'll probably have to adjust baseline shift. Of course, all of this can quickly be set up in a special run-in style or a box you keep in a library.

There's a drawback to this paragraph combination trick, however. You must be aware that you're basically fooling Quark-XPress. As with fooling Mother Nature, this isn't a nice thing to do, and XPress, like Nature, has a nasty habit of getting even at the worst possible time.

When you combine two paragraphs, QuarkXPress applies both the style and all the paragraph-level settings for the first paragraph to the new, combined paragraph. So in our example, QuarkXPress thinks that the 14-point Futura Bold is the default font for the entire new paragraph, even though part of it is 12-point ITC Garamond. For some reason, QuarkXPress doesn't consider the Garamond formatting to be local formatting, so if you apply a new style to this paragraph, *both* the Futura and Garamond are changed to the typeface and size called for in the new style. So don't use this technique unless you're certain that you won't have to ever change the style that's applied to the combined paragraph.

Breaking Up Galleys

Sometimes it's faster and more convenient to enter the text for a multiple-story publication in one big "galley" file in a word processor, rather than to create one file for each story. One large file takes up less space on your hard drive than many small ones (and also requires less time and effort to keep track of).

But how do you import that multiple-story galley into your page layout without creating a labyrinth of linked text boxes? The best way is to turn that one huge linked file into many nonlinked stories. Just bring the galley text into a new XPress document, with Automatic Page Insertion turned on. Then cut and paste one story at a time from the text into your final document.

Printing Your Style Sheet

We can't find any way to print a listing of every style on our style sheet along with descriptions without using an XTension such as QuarkPrint. However, if you export the styles as described in the last tip, you can print the styles from Word. When you've opened your Word document with each of the styles, go to the Define Styles item under the Format menu (Command-T), and select Print from the File menu (Command-P). A lot of the formatting in QuarkXPress styles doesn't get passed through to Word, of course, so the listing isn't complete. But it's better than nothing.

Be Careful When Pasting Text

One of the reasons it's so important to save text using XPress Tags before importing it again is the way QuarkXPress handles text that's pasted between documents—especially documents that use styles with the same names but different definitions.

If you copy some text from one document and paste it into another, you'd think the text would automatically conform itself to the different style definitions in the new document. Instead, QuarkXPress retains all the differences between the old and the new styles as local formatting. However, if you save the text from the first document in the XPress Tags format and then use Get Text to import that file into the second document, the old style formatting is stripped away, the text is styled properly, and hard local formatting is retained.

Exporting Styles to Word

We often use QuarkXPress's Save Text feature to export all our styles to Microsoft Word format. This saves us from having to recreate every style name in Word. We can design a whole book or magazine, export the styles for writers and editors to use when creating copy, and be assured that the style names will match when we import the files into XPress.

To export styles, create a one-line paragraph for each style (you can just type a carriage return). Apply the style and export that text in Word format. When you open the file in Word, all the styles are there.

You can change the formatting of the styles in Word to your heart's content because XPress's style formatting overrides Word's when you import the file. This means you can set up Word's formatting so the text is easy to read and edit on screen and in output.

Of course, you can also perform the opposite task: if you already have a file in Word and you want those style sheets to come into QuarkXPress, import some styled text from that file. Once it's in XPress, you can delete the text and the style sheets remain. And again, you can edit their formatting to your heart's content.

Don't Forget to Include Style Sheets

When you don't have Include Style Sheets turned on in the Get Text dialog box (Command-E), QuarkXPress styles text imported from Microsoft Word (and any other text editor that uses and saves paragraph styles) with "No Style". If you have any intention of applying other paragraph styles to these paragraphs, you're in for a surprise: all your local formatting—even italics—disappears as soon as you apply a paragraph style (see "Totally Overriding Local Formatting," above). Instead, if you import text with Include Style Sheets turned on, the word-processor styles come with the text. Even if you don't have any other style besides "Normal" applied to the text in the word processor, you'll want to take heed of this.

However, it doesn't matter how you import *nonstyled* text (saved as Text Only) from a text editor or a word processor. No matter what you do, QuarkXPress styles it as whatever style your cursor is set to (usually "Normal").

From PageMaker to QuarkXPress

Getting information from one application to another is sometimes tricky. Getting it from PageMaker into QuarkXPress can be a real problem! The PageMaker Import Filter that Quark released a few years ago can sometimes help. Most people don't read the online file that comes with it, though, so they miss two facts: first, it only works with PageMaker 4 files; second, you must do a Save As from PageMaker before you try to import the file into QuarkXPress.

If you just need to import text from PageMaker, we suggest that you export the text from PageMaker in Microsoft Word format and then import it into QuarkXPress using Get Text. This preserves more type formatting and paragraph styles than cutting and pasting text.

Don't Worry About Word Styles

Remember that QuarkXPress overrides Microsoft Word's formatting for style sheets if you have identically named styles in your QuarkXPress document. That is, if your Microsoft Word document's "Normal" style is 16-point Geneva and your QuarkXPress document's "Normal" style is 12-point Palatino, the text that is tagged as "Normal" is imported as Palatino (like you'd want). The implication of this is that you never really have to worry about what the styles look like in Word. For example, in the word-processing files for this book, our text was all in Helvetica and Palatino, but when we imported the text files into QuarkXPress—where we'd carefully predefined all of our styles with the same names—they came out in the fonts you're reading (Adobe Minion and ITC Kabel).

TeX into XPress

TeX (pronounced "tek") is a code-based typesetting system, invented by the legendary Donald Knuth, that does great mathematical equations. Several versions exist; most are for UNIX-based workstations, but there are a few for Macintosh and Windows. If you're doing a math textbook, or any other piece that requires a lot of equations, you may want to import TeX equations into a QuarkXPress document.

It's not easily done.

In fact, the only way we know of is to get a program called Lightning Textures from BlueSky Research. Lightning Textures eats TeX files and spits out Adobe Illustrator files that can be imported as graphics into QuarkXPress or edited in either Illustrator or FreeHand.

Warning: Textures is supposedly really difficult to learn (of course, so is TeX). So don't make the mistake of thinking this is going to be an easy process. Unless you're going to do a *lot* of this, we suggest finding a consultant to do it for you.

At this writing, Aldus just released the XPress-to-PageMaker document converter. This might put the pressure on Quark's R&D department to update the PageMaker Import filter.

When Nisus files Are Word Files

Quark gets many calls from frustrated Nisus users because Quark doesn't sport a Nisus filter. The answer is typically: Save in Word format. Nisus lets you save its files in Microsoft Word format. XPress then sees them as Word files, and you can import them perfectly. However, there's one problem with this: style sheets don't export correctly from Nisus to Word, so they can't get imported into XPress. This is a mess (to say the least) if you're doing any job over two pages.

Adam Engst (friend and author of *The Internet Starter Kit* and the editor of *TidBITS*) to the rescue. Here's a little step-by-step that he uses to get his Nisus files ready for XPress.

1. In Nisus, you can name your character styles anything you want, but link them to named rulers. The combination of character styles and named rulers are more or less the equivalent of Microsoft Word's paragraph styles. Note that if you use character styles for characters—as opposed to paragraphs—you lose the style information on the way to Word (though the actual character formatting is retained).

2. Write a macro in Nisus that searches for "(paragraph start)(any char)(1+)(return)" in the first named character style. Make sure that Any Font, Any Size, +Any Styles, Any Color, and +Any User Styles are turned on (otherwise the program only finds paragraphs that contain no extra formatting).

3. Replace the found text with "<FT>(found)" (or something like it) using the same style. Also make sure all the +Any's are checked.

   Essentially, this macro says, "Find every paragraph with such-and-such style and replace it with the same paragraph but with the '<FT>' tag in front of it."

In case you like looking at complex codes, the Find/ Replace statement looks like this: "Find/Replace "^.+\r" "<FT>&" "tgGaW-O-o" ".

4. Note that you need a Find/Replace statement like this in the macro for each paragraph style that you use in the document. If you only change one or two of these, it's a hassle; but once you've got one working, it's easy to duplicate for every other style. After you run the macro, every paragraph in the document is preceded by a text tag, such as "<H1>", "<H2>".

5. Save the files from Nisus in Word format.

6. In Word, replace all the instances of each tag with the proper paragraph style. For instance, replace all instances of "<H1>" in the "Normal" style with the "Heading 1" style. Adam wrote a bunch of QuicKeys macros to do this for him, which speeds up this process considerably.

7. Finally, in Word, erase all the text tags, such as "<H1>". The best way to do this is to search for the text tag and replace it with nothing (just leave the Replace field blank).

Clearly, this is not a trivial task, though once you've figured out how to do it for one document, it's much faster for subsequent ones. However, it does work, and it's better than anything else we've come up with. (If you know of a better way, let us know!).

IMPORTING

Text from Ventura Publisher

XPress Tags uses almost the same coding format as that power-house of DOS-based desktop publishing, Ventura Publisher. That's right! If you have a tagged, coded ASCII file from Ventura Publisher, you can import that file into QuarkXPress using the XPress Tags filter. You won't get the proper formatting, and you certainly won't get page layout, but you can save yourself a bundle of time in applying style sheets.

The trick is to alter the tags slightly before importing the file. Here's what you do.

1. Open the Ventura text document in a word processor, or import it as straight ASCII text into an XPress text box.

Conflicting Tag Filters

The Style Tags filter quietly disappeared in version 3.2, but some people still have it floating around in their XPress folders. If you're one of these people, do not under any circumstances have both the Style Tags and XPress Tags filters in the same folder with QuarkXPress (or in the XTensions folder). You can have one or the other, but if both are there, you have a good chance of crashing when you import text with Include Style Sheets turned on.

You can probably just throw away the Style Tags filter. That's what Phil recommends, unless you have some old text files around in the Style Tags format that you may need to work with in the future. If that's the case, you may want to convert them now, and then get rid of the filter.

2. Search for all instances of " = " (there's a space on either side of that equal sign) and replace it with ": " (that's a colon followed by a space).

3. Save that document as ASCII text (Text Only) again.

4. Import it into a QuarkXPress text box with Include Style Sheets checked.

When you import the file, all of the style sheet names are automatically brought into the QuarkXPress document. However, if you've already created style sheets with the same names as the Ventura document, then QuarkXPress uses the style definitions that you've created in QuarkXPress.

You can also perform a reverse procedure to bring tagged text from QuarkXPress into Ventura.

Database Publishing

Creating a telephone directory? Cataloging thousands of products? Formatting information taken from a database or spreadsheet? These all fall into the category of database publishing. Whether you're formatting 50 pieces of information or 50,000, a database-publishing tool can be of great help.

One method of manipulating lots of data is to program your database to export text in XPress Tags format. If your database can handle that and you know how to do it (or know someone who does), this can be very powerful. (For example, even relatively common database programs such as FileMaker Pro can be programmed to export in XPress Tags format without much hassle.)

A second method is to use the mail merge functionality in a program like Microsoft Word and then import the merged document into XPress. This works surprisingly well in some cases. We know of people who do whole catalogs using this method.

However, since we usually like to keep things simple, even when we're doing complex jobs, we love the Xdata XTension (see "Power Formatting with Xdata" in Chapter 11, *XTensions*). That's not only because it is a Quark XTension and works well with QuarkXPress, but because it has made our lives so much easier.

David once produced a 17,000-name directory using Xdata and QuarkXPress. Just when he thought he was stuck with applying paragraph styles to 17,000 names, he heard about Xdata. Each person's name, address, telephone number, and e-mail address was formatted precisely the way that he designed it, and, additionally, he could take advantage of almost every typographic feature in QuarkXPress.

Auto Linking

And then there was the guy who imported a text file and spent 15 hours filling each text box in his document with the appropriate amount of text without bothering to link the text boxes together. His 20-page document consisted of pages that were totally independent of each other, and although the text read from page to page, as soon as he added a word on the first page, he had to move the last word from that page to the beginning of the second page, the last on the second to the first on the third, and so on. Oy...

Linking is a blessing from god, and should be revered as such. It was sent to make our lives easier, and it can—if we take advantage of it.

One of the great features of text linking is automatic page insertion. This feature makes it possible for QuarkXPress to add as many pages as necessary to accommodate the amount of text you're trying to import into your document. We usually turn Auto Page Insertion off (in the General Preferences dialog box, or press Command-Y), not because it's bad, but because it can confuse us (we're already confused enough). When 30 extra pages get added in the middle or end of our file and we're left trying to figure out why they're there and not where we want them to be, we know we forgot to turn this feature off.

When Auto Page Insertion is off, the easiest way for us to handle a lot of text is as follows.

1. Pour in the text file. With Auto Page Insertion off, you get an overset mark in the lower-right corner of the text box.

2. Check the text to make sure something strange hasn't happened in the importing.

3. With that text box selected, select Insert (on the Page menu) and add new pages to the document where you want them. Make sure you have Link to Current Text Chain checked.

4. Only the number of pages that you specify in the Insert Pages dialog box are added. If there is still more text to come, you'll see another text overset mark in the last text box of the chain. If you added too many pages, you'll have to delete some.

On the other hand, when we're just trying to pull in a lot of text all at once (see "Breaking Up Galleys," earlier in this chapter), automatic page insertion is a natural for the job.

XPRESS TAGS

Learning XPress Tags

We've got a bunch of cool XPress Tags tips in this book, and there are truly hundreds (if not thousands) of other things you can do with this tagged language. People often ask us what the best way to learn the codes is. Our answer: Create some text styled different ways in XPress, then export the text in tagged format (Save Text from the File menu, or Command-Option-E). When you open that exported text in a word processor (or, if you'd rather, reimport it into XPress; however, make sure Include Style Sheets is unchecked, or the program interprets the codes rather than displaying them) you can read the codes with no trouble (see Figure 5-7).

To decipher the codes, look up each of them in the table in Appendix A, *XPress Tags*.

Note that XPress defines its tags much more often than is actually necessary, so there's a lot of redundancy in its coding. That's not bad; you just need to take it with a grain of salt. But otherwise, you'll get a very good overview of tagging.

Figure 5-7
XPress Tags coding

How the text looks on the page

Whether the weather is *cold*, whether the weather is *hot*, we'll be together, whatever the **weather**, whether we like it or not.

How the text looks in XPress Tags

@parastyle:Whether the <k-10>w<k0>eather is <BI>cold<BI>, whether the <k-10>w<k0>eather is <BI>hot<BI>, <k-10>w<k0>e'll be together, whatever the <Bz9f"Helvetica">weather<Bz10f$>, whether we like it or not.

QUICKEYS

QuicKey Tags

Once again, it's QuicKeys to the rescue! If you're into XPress Tags, you know that it can get very monotonous typing the same tag over and over again throughout a document. Instead, you can set up a QuicKey that types the coded information for you. For example, if you want to make some words italic, you can create a sequence that jumps to the beginning of the word, types "<I>", then jumps to the end of the word and types "<I>" again.

If you work with people who type copy in word processors that don't handle style sheets (most word processors don't, surprisingly enough), you can have them type style sheet XPress tags for each paragraph. While this would be tedious normally, using QuicKeys it's no problem at all. They could just press F1 (for example) and "@Heading1:" would type out. Then, on the next line, they'd hit F2, and "@BodyText:" would type out. That's all QuarkXPress needs to apply the style sheets properly when you import the document.

Even more complex sequences can be created, depending on how far you want to go and how many QuicKey extensions you want to use.

Tags to Replace Tabs with Leaders

As we said back in "Spaced-Out Leaders," in Chapter 4, *Type and Typography*, we sometimes like to format period-leader tabs with extra tracking at a smaller type size. Usually we just create one of these modified tabs, copy it, and paste it wherever we want. However, in a situation where there are many of these tabs to change, XPress Tags can really come in handy.

The method is simple.

1. Export the text you want to edit using Save Text with XPress Tags selected from the Format popup menu.

2. In a word processor (or even in QuarkXPress) search for all instances of the tab character in the XPress Tags text and replace it with "<t60z7>^t<tz>" in Microsoft Word, or with "<t60z7>\t<tz>" in XPress (the character in the middle turns into a tab character).

3. Save the text as Text Only from Word or ASCII Text from XPress and reimport it into QuarkXPress. Make sure that Include Style Sheets is checked in the Get Text dialog box.

Based On and Next Styles in XPress Tags

Here's one that David even forgot to put in his definitive XPress reference book, *The QuarkXPress Book*: XPress has the ability to base a style sheet on another and to specify the next style when you make style-sheet definitions in an XPress Tags file. The code for this is:

@stylesheetname=[s"based-on name", "next-style name"]stylesheet_definition

Yes, this is in Appendix A, *XPress Tags*, but since so few people know about it, we thought we'd bring it to your attention more blatantly here.

Quotes and Conversions

When you want to edit XPress Tags text in QuarkXPress as if it's plain text, be sure that both Convert Quotes and Include Styles Sheets are unchecked in the Get Text dialog box. If Include Style Sheets is on, the tags get interpreted. If Convert Quotes is checked, you'll get a mess because of all the codes that contain straight quotes around font names, style sheet names, and so forth. The tags filter can't recognize curly quotes correctly, so your tagged text becomes unusable.

Later, when you import the Tags as final text, you need to check both boxes in the Get Text dialog box, and the tags get interpreted and only the quotes not inside codes get fixed.

All the tab characters are now set to seven points with 60 units of tracking. You can alter other formatting using the same techniques (see Appendix A, *XPress Tags*, for a list of the XPress Tags codes). Note that if you don't know exactly what codes to type, you can simply format one line the way you like it in XPress, export that line in XPress Tags format, and use the resulting codes for your Change To or Replace With string.

Overprinting Accents with Tags

Working in non-English languages can be a complicated proposition, especially when you're working with an American or English computer system. Microsoft Word has a few nice features for creating accented characters that may not be available in most typefaces. For example, you can type a š character in Microsoft Word by using the overprinting function (type Command-Option-\, "O", Command-Option-\, "AC(s,ˇ)"—which looks like "\O\AC(s,ˇ)" on screen when you have Show ¶ turned on).

However, when you import the Word file into XPress, the overstrike characters turn back into the backslash code (kind of like the carriage turning back into a pumpkin, but different). Here's a way you can use XPress Tags and the Find/Change feature in a word processor to magically turn these back into accented characters.

1. Import the text from Microsoft Word into QuarkXPress with Include Style Sheets checked.

2. Export this text in XPress Tags mode.

3. Open this text file in a text editor (such as Word), and replace all instances of "\O\AC(s,ˇ)" with "<k-80>s<k0>ˇ". The amount of kerning between the two characters (in this case, -80 units), depends entirely on the width of the letter you're trying to overstrike. For example, an "o" usually takes a good bit more kerning than an i (or a dotless "i", Option-Shift-B).

4. Import the new text file back into XPress, using Include Style Sheets (so that the XPress Tags import correctly).

Of course, you'll need to go through the Find/Change procedure for each type of overstrike pair. Ultimately, if you do a lot of this sort of work, you may want to look into getting a foreign-language typeface from a company such as Linguist's Software (see Appendix B, *Resources*). If you're typesetting just Western European Latin alphabets, the Expert Set fonts that Adobe and other foundries put out have some of the necessary characters.

Return of Overprinting Accents

In the previous tip, we talked about converting a Microsoft Word overstrike format into an XPress tag format. Perhaps more frequently, however, is the case where your text is already in XPress and you need to overstrike a bunch of characters.

1. Create the overstrike character to look just like you want it somewhere in your document, using baseline shift, kerning, sizing, or whatever.

2. Export the sample "character" and the text story that contains all the characters you want to overstrike as XPress Tags.

3. Open the XPress Tags files in a word processor. The sample you did looks something like "<k-90>s<k11b0.2>ˇ<k0b0>".

4. Perform a Find/Change between the overstrike pair and the XPress Tag version.

You often need to *positively* kern *after* the accent character, because it's narrower and therefore the following character will be too tight without kerning. Try it; you'll see what we mean.

Here's a trick we use to get the spacing *after* a haček right: pick a letter like capital "I" (one that's nice and vertical) and enclose samples of the letter you're putting your macron over (an "o", for example) between each "I", so that you've got "IoIoIoI". Then position your haček over the middle "o" (using kerning, baseline shifting and so on). Keep your eye on one of the other "IoI" groups and try to match that spacing.

Remember, these kerning and baseline-shift figures will only necessarily be good for the one font at the one size (and for those specific characters, since different letters have different widths); to do other combinations, or at other sizes, repeat the whole trick.

Fake Fractions the Tags Way

Although the Make Fractions feature in the Freebies and Thing-a-ma-bob XTension is great, a similar XPress Tags search-and-replace procedure can save hours when you have to create a large number of well-set fractions. For example, you can search for all instances of "1/2" and replace them with "<z7k-10b-3>1<z12k-8b0>/<z8k0>2<z$>". This set of codes sets the size to seven points, the kerning to 10 units, and the baseline shift to three points, then types "1". It then changes the type size to 12 points, the kerning to -8 units and the baseline shift to zero before typing a fraction bar (Option-Shift-1). Finally, it sets the size to eight points, sets no kerning, and types "2" before resetting the type size back to its original value.

This may seem like a lot to you, but once you get the hang of it, it's extremely easy and can save you enormous amounts of time.

Also, see "Son of Fractions" in Chapter 4, *Type and Typography*, for another XPress Tags fraction tip.

FRACTIONS

Expert Fractions with XPress Tags

The tip "Fake Fractions the Tags Way," above, is useful for making "made" fractions: fractions that are created by resizing type and moving it around. What if you want "drawn" fractions—numerators and denominators pre-designed just for this use? Expert Set fonts with these sort of characters are available for many type families (Minion, Utopia, Bembo, and several others). Using XPress Tags, you can automate their substitution, too.

The first case works for the fractions shown in Table 5-1. Export your text as XPress Tags and open the file in a word processor. Let's say you want to convert all the "1/4"s. Then, in the word processor, search for "1/4" and replace it with "<f"Minion-Exp-Regular">G<f"Minion-Regular">".

The Expert Sets also contain the numerals zero through nine in the numerator and denominator positions so you can create any other fraction, too. Press Shift-Option-0 through Shift-Option-9 to get the raised numerators, and Option-0 through Option-9 to get the baseline denominators. The correct fraction bar is the slash in the Expert Sets. You can automate this process somewhat with XPress Tags, but you have to do a special case for each fraction. For instance, to make the fraction $^{13}/_{16}$, you would search for "13/16" and replace with "<f"MinionExp-Regular">" followed by Option-Shift-1, Option-Shift-3, slash, Option-1, Option-6, and finally "<f"Minion-Regular">". One step too complicated? Maybe—but not if you've got oodles of text with fractions.

Table 5-1

Ready-made fractions in Expert Sets and their keystrokes

Fraction	Expert keystroke
¼	G
½	H
¾	I
⅛	J
⅜	K
⅝	L
⅞	M
⅓	N
⅔	O

XPRESS TAGS

Using XPress Tags in a Word Processor

We use Microsoft Word as a word processor all the time, but that doesn't mean it gives us everything we want. For instance, there are times we want to apply some XPress formatting to text while in a word processor. Here's a way to extend the formatting power of the word processor by using XPress Tags.

1. Prepare the file, including the tags, in the word processor. Save the file in the native format (Word or whatever); don't save as text only. The XPress Tags codes you've typed won't be interpreted yet.

2. Use Get Text to import the story into a QuarkXPress document, making sure that Include Style Sheets is checked.

3. Save the text (from the File menu or press Command-Option-E) as XPress Tags.

4. Edit the text file back in your word processor, replacing these combinations.

   replace   <\<>   with   <

   replace   <\>>   with   >

   replace   <\@>   with   @

5. Save the file in Text Only format and reimport it into your QuarkXPress document while Include Style Sheets is turned on. All your codes should be interpreted this time.

Voila! Word with Tags. Not elegant, but it's cheap.

Confusion About the '$'

The "$" code in XPress Tags is really cool because it acts as a reset for formatting. For instance, you can type "<h80>T<h$>o". The first code sets horizontal scaling to 80 percent, and the second code resets it to whatever horizontal scaling is spec'ed to in the style sheet (or the document default, if no style sheet is applied to the current paragraph). This is generally more versatile than hard coding the kerning back to zero or some other value (think about it: What if the definition changes in your style sheet?). However, the "$" code resets *some* attributes to the definitions of the current style sheet, but not all. The only formatting codes that can be reset with the "$" code are the following.

► Font

► Size

► Color

► Shade

Shorter Tags

Are you tired of typing long tags, such as "@Bodytext=<*J*p(7.2,0,7.2,11,0,3.6,g)*t(148,2,"")*d(1,2)z9>"? Then stop! Instead, substitute a unique brief placeholder for each long tag in your coded document. For instance, type "*bb" instead of the code above. Then, later, search for the placeholder and replace it with the real thing. You can use a word processor to make this change or a utility such as Torquemada or Add/Strip, where you never have to type anything more than once.

Of course, make sure you use unique sequences of characters for your placeholders (that is, sequences that don't appear anywhere else in your text).

Those Silly Ol' Case-Sensitive Tags

Don't forget that all XPress Tags are case sensitive. Typing "<H>" rather than "<h>" can mean the difference among small caps, horizontal scaling, and failure. Style, color, and H&J names are the same way. If you forget, it's easy enough to search and replace in Word or a case-sensitive text editor.

Confusion About the '<\p>' Tag

Sometimes we take on the responsibility for simply clearing up the confusion that Quark or other people have created. One such confusion (in the realm of XPress Tags) is what the "<\p>" code gets you. Quark, Inc., has finally confirmed that the "<\p>" tag imports as the punctuation space, not as the flex space, which is "<\q>". We suppose this is just another example of "minding your peas and queues."

Commas in XPress Tags

If you're just now updating from version 3.0 and are used to typing commas in your XPress Tags (or if you're using old XPress Tags files from an archive), note that you can no longer type commas in codes. For instance, you used to be able to separate items in a code like "<I,c"Red", f"Palatino">" but this has changed since 3.1. The same list, now that you can no longer use commas, would read "<Ic"Red "f"Palatino">".

▶ Horizontal Scale

▶ Kerning

▶ Tracking

▶ Baseline Shift

The "$" code does not reset any attributes that are not on this list to the paragraph style sheet settings.

Care with Tags, Part I

Using XPress Tags can be lifesaving—but coding them wrong can result in serious troubles. Unfortunately, until the XPress Tags filter that shipped with XPress version 3.3, the program didn't check for illegal or improper coding on import of tagged files; it either choked (that's a common term for stopping, crashing, freezing, or spitting up) or messed stuff up really badly in your documents.

For example, the following mistake is a real killer. If you use a character that begins a tag definition (like "@" or "<") and then neglect to close the definition properly (that is, by typing a colon, a definition, or a right angle bracket, depending on what you're coding), you're bound to regret it. Not only does QuarkXPress try to read *everything* past that point as a code, but it might also (in the case of an unterminated "@") create a very corrupt style sheet. Corrupt style sheets are bad news: you often cannot get rid of them, and have to trash your document entirely.

The tip? First, be *very* careful not to do this in the first place. Second, use the newest XPress Tags filter (the one that shipped with version 3.3 is version 1.7; you can find out what version an XTension or filter is by clicking on it on the desktop and pressing Command-I or selecting Get Info from the File menu). This version has some built-in error checking that usually stops you from screwing up your files too much.

On the other hand, if you still have the text file that had the unterminated tag call, you can, of course, fix the problem and import the text file into another QuarkXPress document. And, if you haven't saved your QuarkXPress file yet (since you corrupted it), you can revert it back to its noncorrupted state.

Care with Tags, Part II

Via the indefatigable Mike Arst's experimentation, here are some more ways you can screw up your tags, and some things that (surprisingly) *don't* mess you up.

► One "<" followed by a space simply disappears in version 3.2 and earlier.

► Two or three in a row of "<" followed by a space become a single "<" in version 3.2 and earlier.

► In version 3.2 and earlier, one or more "<" followed by an alphanumeric character (i.e., not a space) messes you up, as described in the previous tip.

► At the beginning of a paragraph, of course, a "@" is a style sheet call, with the attendant requirement that it be properly terminated. Elsewhere, "@" or "@@" simply becomes itself.

As we said in the previous tip, the newest XPress Tags filter has better error checking, so some of these problems have gone away.

XPRESS TAGS

Care with Tags, Part III

This tip deals with spaces in style sheet names. Are they legal, or aren't they? Answer: Mostly. It depends on which version of XPress you have.

In 3.0, spaces in style sheet names are stripped when you export the story from XPress (i.e., if you had a name like "@Body Text", it becomes "@BodyText" on export). Spaces are legal in imported tagged text. This can obviously lead to confusion if you are exporting and importing text, since now you've got two versions of the same style sheet.

In 3.1, 3.2, and 3.3, spaces are legal in both directions.

XPRESS TAGS

Xtags

Xtags, an XTension from Em Software is a superset of Quark's own XPress Tags format. It has several additional capabilities.

MAC/PC

PC Text Files with Control-L

By the way, if you're bringing XPress Tags files from some PC system, you'll be happy to note that the Control-L character—which is the form-feed character on the PC—is correctly interpreted by XPress as the new-box character.

UNDERSCORES

Messy XPress Tags

If you use the Stars & Stripes XTension to alter your underscores (a really neat feature, if you must use underscores), and you export some text with those altered underscores in XPress Tags format, and you look at that exported file in a word processor, you're in for a tiny surprise. It appears as though XPress has several undocumented XPress Tag features that XTensions such as Stars & Stripes can use. However, they're clearly pretty bizarre and we wouldn't mess with them.

▶ Character-based "styles" on import

▶ Embedded text boxes

▶ Embedded picture boxes

▶ XPress Tags error checking

TEXT MANAGEMENT

Converting Columns with Torquemada

Once upon a time, Greg Swann (author of Shane the Plane and other masterpieces) wrote a little utility called Torquemada the Inquisitor. With such a descriptive name (not!), some people *still* don't know what this incredible program does. To call Torquemada (or Torq, as many people call it) a search-and-replace utility is like saying QuarkXPress is a fun little program that lets you put text and graphics on the same page. Torq is a powerhouse of a search and replace engine, and has become an essential tool for text massage—especially when you're working with XPress Tags.

Torq lets you perform up to 640 searches (and make respective replacements) on a document, and it does it very fast (see Figure 5-8). If you have a list of 100 words that need to be spelled a certain way, it'd be a hassle and a half to perform all those searches manually. Instead, you can load the words into Torq and just let it flog away at the files (you can even batch run multiple text files by drag and dropping a folder-full on Torq's desktop icon).

But there are some more obscure ways of using Torquemada, too. For instance, let's say you receive a text file from an author who was trying to be a little too helpful and has typed a list of names like this:

Arnold	Frank
Becky	George
Catherine	Hiromi
Doug	Igor
Eggboard	Jacqueline

Of course, in order to format this in XPress, you probably need it in one long column of text (you can handle the columns yourself, thank you very much). If this list were much longer, it'd be a nightmare to pull apart with cut and paste. Here's where Torq can show its stripes.

Figure 5-8

Torquemada the Inquisitor

Note: Torquemada the Inquisitor can appear very intimidating to the uninitiated because of all its obscure codes. Don't worry; it's really pretty easy once you pull it apart.

1. Copy the offending lines and save them as a text file.

2. Using Torq, search for "^t^*^p" in the text file and replace it with "^p". To decode that: this searches for a tab followed by anything that ends in a return and replaces all of that with just a return. In other words, it systematically throws away every item in the right column.

3. Next, run a new search on the original file (not the one you ended up with in step one; Torq always prudently retains your original file, giving you a new file as the result of your Torquing. Search for "^p^*^t" and replace it with "^p". That searches for every instance of a return followed

Commenting Torq Sets

One of the problems with Torquemada's search-and-replace sets is that they're often really hard to read and decipher on screen. One way to clear up the mess is by commenting the sets. That is, you can insert "human-readable" comments to help you remember what each code (or set of codes) means.

To add a comment to a Torq set, type it in the Replace string column (the right column in the search/replace set). As long as the Search string column (the left one) is left blank, Torq ignores the right one entirely; but the comment remains there for you to read on screen. Phil heartily recommends you add extensive, thorough comments to your Torq sets; he can testify from sad experience that it's very easy to forget just what you were trying to do, especially in your more complex search/replace strings.

by anything that ends in a tab and replaces it with simply a return. In other words, it throws away everything in the left column and preserves the right column.

4. Merge the resulting files together, and you're in business.

This might seem like a couple of steps too many, but in fact, it's very fast indeed. If the original author's list used multiple spaces instead of tabs between the columns (horror of horrors), you can use another Swann utility called XP8 to clean that up quickly.

(To be fair in this particular case, you can do this in Microsoft Word by opening the file, Option-dragging a selection around the right column, and using copy and paste.)

Note that all these utilities are on the disc that's bundled with this book (the version of Torquemada that's on the disc is shareware; however, you can buy a fuller-featured commercial version directly from Greg's company; see Appendix B, *Resources*).

Styling Every Other Row

Back in "Alternating Tint Stripes" in Chapter 4, *Type and Typography*, we said you can create cool tables by placing stripes behind every other row using Rule Below. Of course, the best way to format a mess o' text is to use style sheets. However, applying a particular style sheet to every other paragraph is a real hassle. Torq to the rescue.

1. Export the text from XPress as XPress Tags (using Save Text from the File menu).

2. Search for "^*^p^~^p" and replace it with "@firststyle:^*^p@secondstyle:^~^p". To decipher: first this searches for any amount of any text (^*) followed by a return (^p), more text (^~) and another return. Then it replaces all that with the same text and returns, but with the XPress Tags coding for "apply this style sheet." Of course, you would replace "firststyle" and "secondstyle" with whatever style sheet names you're using.

3. Reimport the resulting Torqued file back into XPress. (Make sure Include Style Sheets is turned on in the Get Text dialog box so that the tags are interpreted back into their proper formatting.)

A Complex XPress Tags Example

We'll throw in one more XPress Tags example, just to show what a little extra work by a bit-head programmer can do. Let's say you've just received some text files from someone who just LOVES to type LOTS of words in ALL CAPITAL LETTERS. If you're like us, you'd rather these words be in small caps.

You've got three choices: First, retype each of these words in lowercase and then apply a small caps style to them. Like you've got nothing better to do, right? The second choice is to use a macro such as the one outlined in "Changing to Small Caps" in Chapter 10, *Macros and Scripts*.

The third choice is to use XPress Tags. This technique should not be tried by children without parental guidance; it's truly industrial strength, designed for processing a lot of text at once.

The trick is to use a program such as Nisus or "sed." Nisus is a very cool text editor on the Macintosh. Sed is a textstream editor developed for UNIX and then ported to the DOS environment.

Sed's strength is that it supports regular expressions—methods of describing text patterns that would otherwise have to be described literally (and therefore at considerable length). The trouble with it is that, on account of its complexity, it takes a long time to learn the syntax. For example, the following hideous-looking sed instruction will find all occurrences of capitalized words (two or more characters) in a file, change them to lowercase, and insert XPress Tags codes for small caps (<H>) to either side of them: "s/\(\<[A-Z][A-Z]+\>\)/<H>\L&<H>/g".

In English: "Find every whole word consisting of two or more capital letters in the range of A to Z. Convert it to lowercase and insert the character string '<H>' on either side of the word."

If a line in the source file reads: "This is DEFINITELY a BIG pain in the NECK," then the final output will look like this: "This is <H>definitely<H> a <H>big<H> pain in the <H>neck<H>."

See? Nothing to it.

WORKGROUPS

Workgroup Publishing with QPS

Workgroup publishing is another one of those phrases that has been bandied about for some time now. It's really pretty simple: If you're working with a bunch of other people to publish stuff, you're doing workgroup publishing. The biggest problem with workgroup publishing is moving files, pictures, and text from one person to another in an organized way. It seems like something's always getting lost or the wrong version of a file's getting used, and hardly anyone knows where things are (or even should be).

Quark has come to the rescue with a product called Quark Publishing System (or QPS for short). This is a whole networked system that's designed to solve many of these workgroup issues. If you're in such a situation, we urge you to call Quark and ask them about QPS and how it can help you. It's not inexpensive—it's estimated at a minimum of $1,100 per user for the basic setup—but it's cheaper than the high-end, proprietary systems like Atex. Plus, it's centered around QuarkXPress, a program you already know.

pictures 6

For several chapters now, we've been discussing words, words, words (what's good enough for Shakespeare is good enough for us). But words ain't all there is to XPress, of course. Pictures make up the other half of the story—some say the better half.

In this chapter we're going to explore how QuarkXPress works with both bitmapped images and object-oriented graphics. Then we'll take a diversion and discuss how graphics and text interact with each other, through runarounds, paragraph rules, and anchored boxes.

LITTLE GEM
Watch 'Em Change

Back in Chapter 1, *QuarkXPress Basics*, we told you about how to watch the changes you're making to pictures as you perform them (see "Viewing Changes as You Make Them"). In case you don't remember, the key is to hold down the mouse button for about half a second until you see the cursor flash once. Then, when you scale or crop the image by dragging, you can actually see the image get scaled or cropped (otherwise, QuarkXPress shows you a gray-outline box).

Table 6-1
Color levels versus file size

Bit depth	Gray levels	File size
32	256	935K
16	256	368K
8	256	252K
8	16	252K

IMPORTING

Huge Files When Importing Graphics

It was kind and generous of Quark to offer us the ability to import images at higher bit depths (in the Application Preferences dialog box), but we urge you—plead with you: if you don't *need* to, then don't go above eight-bit color. The problem is that your document's size on disk balloons when you raise the color bit value (changing the Gray TIFFs value from 16 levels of gray to 256 levels of gray is fine, though). Table 6-1 shows how file size increases depending on your settings. The document size is based on a single document with five grayscale images and five color images.

IMPORTING

Changing Color TIFF Setting

Changing the Color TIFFs or Gray TIFFs display settings in the Application Preferences dialog box doesn't do anything to pictures that have already been imported into a document. It only affects images when they're imported. Therefore, to see a change in an already imported image, you have to reimport it. Remember, you can do this quickly by holding down the Command key when you press the Open button in the Open dialog box (all the images in the document get reimported automatically).

Why would you care about the bit depth of the preview setting? Remember that if you print to a non-PostScript printer, XPress uses this preview setting rather than the high-res data on disk. Therefore, increasing the bit depth on the preview image improves your output for those devices. We just use PostScript printers, so we don't worry about this.

IMPORTING

Upgrading Screen Quality

QuarkXPress normally imports a screen representation of a high-resolution TIFF (or the largely obsolete RIFF) file at 72 dpi. This low-resolution screen image provides for a relatively quick screen refresh rate (when, for example, you move around the page). However, if the image on the screen takes slightly too long to redraw, you may want to sacrifice speed for screen quality.

You can cut the screen resolution in half by holding down the Shift key while clicking the Open button in the Get Picture dialog box. This won't have any effect on your printed output, but it takes less time to redraw (those of you who have a Power Mac can stop chuckling). In version 3.1 and earlier, XPress imported images at 36 dpi and the Shift key imported them at 72 dpi.

IMPORTING

Changing TIFF Depth

If you are heavily into image editing and control, you will undoubtedly want to change the bit depth of a TIFF or RIFF image at some point. Here are two tricks for changing depth while you import the image.

▶ Holding down the Option key when clicking Open in the Get Picture dialog box changes a TIFF line-art (one-bit) image into an eight-bit grayscale image.

▶ Holding down the Command key when clicking Open in the Get Picture dialog box changes a TIFF grayscale image to line art (one-bit), or a TIFF color image to grayscale.

Neither of these techniques actually changes the source file. XPress just does the conversion for its own benefit (and yours) whenever you open or print the document.

Do's and Don't's

Here are a few suggestions pulled from the dusty vaults of experience on working with pictures.

▶ Don't delete your picture file after importing it, assuming that it's placed for all time. QuarkXPress only *links* to EPS and TIFF images saved on disk.

▶ Do be sure you know where your picture files are.

▶ Do keep your picture files together to avoid confusion if you need to move your document some place (like a service bureau). You may want to visually segregate the document from its pictures, but keep them in the same folder.

Grayed-Out Style Menu

Don't forget that the Style menu only applies to bitmapped images. If you have the Content tool active and a picture selected, and the Style menu is grayed out, you have probably imported an EPS file, or a PICT file that contains more than just a single bitmapped image. If you're sure you have the right file format, it may be that you either have the Item tool selected (instead of the Content tool), or that you don't have the picture box selected. If none of this works, we suggest plugging the machine in.

Low Resolution TIFF

Have you wondered why your version of XPress might import pictures with a low-resolution, 36-dpi screen preview, while your colleagues import at 72 dpi? You may have turned on Low Resolution TIFF back in version 3.1. Unfortunately, this feature no longer appears in the Application Preferences dialog box. If you turned it on in version 3.1 then upgraded to 3.2 or 3.3, you're stuck with the choice, and the only way to import a higher resolution image is by holding down the Shift key when you click Open in the Get Picture dialog box.

Or, if you find yourself doing this all the time, try throwing away your XPress Preferences file and restarting XPress. Of course, when XPress builds you a new one, you'll have lost many of your other preferences, including hyphenation exceptions, custom frames, and so on (if you've made them); but your import resolution should be reset to the new way of doing things. With a fresh, new preferences file, all your documents will import images at the higher resolution (unless you hold the Shift key down).

Making Multiple Changes to Pictures

If you know you are going to make multiple changes to your graphic image—changing the skew, rotation, scale, and offset, for example—and you use the Measurements palette, you'll have to wait for XPress to redraw the picture each time you change an entry. Instead, you can speed up your formatting by making those changes in the Picture Box Specifications dialog box (Command-M, or double-click on the object while holding down the Command key) so that QuarkXPress will process all changes at once rather than one at a time.

Turning Text into Pictures

You can bring text into QuarkXPress as a PICT image by using a feature of Microsoft Word. First, select the text you want in Word and press Command-Option-D. This converts the text to a PICT image and places it in the Clipboard. Then move into Quark-XPress, select a picture box with the Content tool, and press Command-V. What you paste may look odd and bitmapped on the screen, but it will print out much smoother than it looks. You can also manipulate the picture, by rotating or scaling it. This tip suggests a handy way to get a table from Word into QuarkXPress, though you won't be able to edit the table, simply position it as a graphic. One word of warning: The PICT file format is notoriously unreliable. Fonts and character widths may change at any time, line weights can go berserk, and some PICT graphics just won't print.

Another method is to paste the copied PICT image into Aldus FreeHand, which has the very cool ability to convert PICTs into text and graphics. You can even paste a whole table into FreeHand (however, it'll probably need some cleanup work before you make an EPS out of it).

Ultimately, the best way to create a picture of text is to use Free-Hand or Illustrator to create an EPS image. You can copy an EPS picture from either of these programs by holding down the Option key while selecting Cut or Copy from the Edit menu. Note that any text that you copy from the illustration program may or may not have the outline font information saved with it; if the font isn't available in the printer, the text may come out in Courier. Check out the next tip to eradicate this potential bugaboo.

Another Reason to Avoid PICTs

We hate PICT images, and almost never use them for files we have to import into QuarkXPress. One reason is that they're infamous for poor printing. But here's another good reason: XPress doesn't link to PICT images on disk when you import them. Rather, it embeds the entire image in the QuarkXPress file itself. That doesn't seem like such a bad thing (it might even be helpful sometimes), but the reality is that this can get out of hand quickly.

When you import a two-megabyte PICT image, your document file size increases by two megabytes. That's a lot of unnecessary data being saved. Sure, you don't have to take the image files with you when you go to the service bureau, but do you really want to risk bloating your documents like that? We won't tell you that it's not safe, but we would never do it.

TEXT
Convert Text to Curves

When a service bureau or a colleague tries to print your document, they might get a surprise: if they don't have the proper fonts installed on their machine, the text might come out all in Courier (an uglier sight is hard to imagine). One answer is to send the fonts along with your document. However, this is both a hassle and may be illegal (there's no ruling on this) if the service bureau doesn't already have a license for those fonts.

If the offending text is not extensive, you might try converting it to outlines in an illustration program, saving it as an EPS, and importing it into a picture box in XPress. Converting to outlines (both FreeHand and Illustrator can do this as long as you're using either TrueType fonts or have Adobe Type Manager installed) removes the need for the original font because the text is described as a graphic: curves, lines, and so on.

This might work well for headline text, but it would be a mess for body copy for two reasons. First, text converted to curves often prints much more slowly. A full page of text might take 30 seconds to print; when you convert it to curves, it could easily take several minutes or more. Second, text that is converted to curves won't look as good in small point sizes when printed on desktop laser printers. This is because the font cannot be hinted (hinting makes small text—like under 18 points—look better on lower-resolution printers). Large point sizes don't typically need hinting, so this isn't an issue.

POSTSCRIPT
Saving a Page as EPS

There can be times when you need to bring part or all of a Quark-XPress page into another document, or even into another program altogether, such as PageMaker, Illustrator, or FreeHand. The Save Page as EPS command under the File menu lets you save

PICTURES
Preformatting Picture Boxes

You can select an empty picture box and apply formatting to the picture that you're *going* to import into it. Select an empty picture box and change the picture attributes, such as rotation, skew, offset, and scaling, in the Measurements palette (or the Picture Specifications dialog box; Command-M or Command-double-click on the box). Then, when you import a picture into that box, XPress automatically applies those settings to it.

Why should you care? Well, if you need to apply the same attributes to a number of different images, you can create one picture box, apply the desired settings, then duplicate the picture box as many times as you have pictures (or store it away in a library for future use). Now, each time you import one of those pictures, it has the formatting you wanted already applied to it.

PostScript Copy and Pasting

QuarkXPress can't understand the native Illustrator or FreeHand formats, so when you copy an object out of those programs and paste it into QuarkXPress, you either get an error or a simple PICT image. Neither one will do.

XPress does, however, understand the PICT/EPS format. You can create a PICT/EPS version of an object within Illustrator or FreeHand and put it on the Clipboard by holding down the Option key while selecting Cut or Copy from the menu (you have to do it from the menu, not using the Command-C or Command-X keyboard shortcut). This is usually reliable, but we have heard of some problems with it—especially images getting distorted when you Option-copy them out of Illustrator 5.0. You can also run into problems with font downloading using this method. Once again, saving as EPS and importing using Get Picture is more reliable (also, images pasted in—even like this—cannot be color separated).

a document page as an EPS file, which you can import into any Mac program that supports EPS.

However, sometimes (especially with earlier versions of XPress) EPS files saved in landscape mode don't print well (or at all). We haven't had any trouble with versions 3.2 or 3.3, but if you *do* have trouble, you might keep this in mind and export it again with Orientation set to Portrait. Also, it's generally unsafe to embed one EPS image inside another.

For instance, a friend of ours recently called us with a "weird" printing problem. She had saved an image out from Photoshop as EPS, imported it into XPress, then saved that page from XPress as EPS and imported it into another document. When she tried to print: El massivo PostScript crashola. When she saved the original image as a TIFF and repeated the process, the page printed fine. It was the nested EPS that caught her. It should work fine, but often it doesn't.

Getting XPress EPS Files into Photoshop

Wouldn't it be great if you could save a QuarkXPress page as an EPS file, and then open and edit it bit by bit in Photoshop? Too bad the EPS format that QuarkXPress creates is incompatible with Adobe Photoshop.

As it turns out, there really is a way. The trick is to rasterize the PostScript file so that applications such as Photoshop can read and edit them.

In order to rasterize (turn into a bitmap) the EPS file, you need a PostScript interpreter. Freedom of Press, a software-based PostScript-interpreter clone, can create a bitmap TIFF file which Photoshop can open. Scitex's SmartVIP software can also rasterize the EPS file into an editable bitmapped image. However, the least expensive method is to use Transverter Pro (see Appendix B, *Resources*), which can convert almost any PostScript file into a bitmap or Illustrator-editable file.

If you don't have any of these in-house, you can probably find service bureau in your area that has them; often they charge a flat fee for this sort of process.

However, perhaps the most elegant way to bring XPress EPS files into Photoshop is through the Epilogue plug-in from Total Integration. It's actually a real, licensed-from-Adobe PostScript Level 2 interpreter built into a plug-in, so you can open and rasterize *any* PostScript file you want (see Figure 6-1).

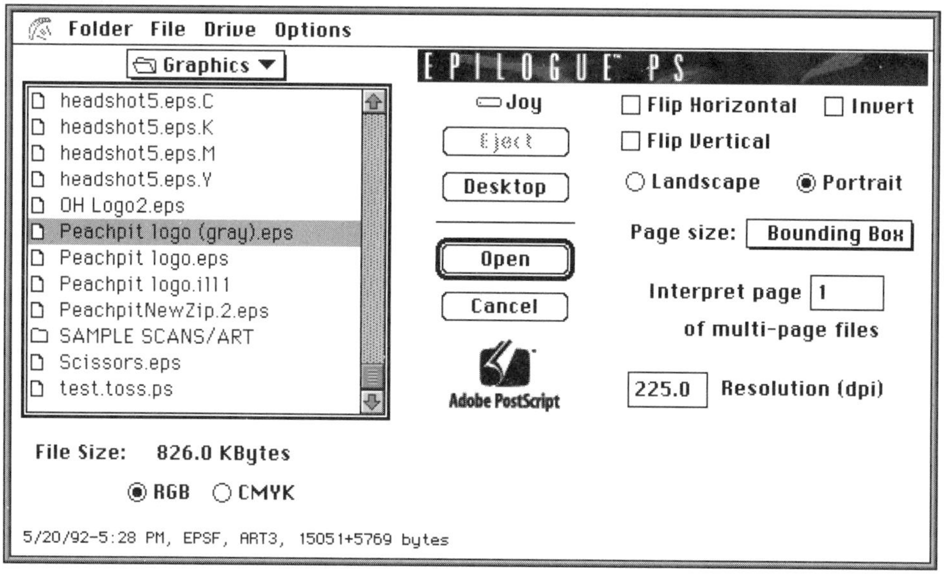

Figure 6-1
Epilogue plug-in filter for Photoshop

EPS Preview PICT in Photoshop

This isn't really an XPress Tip, but it's an interesting tip nonetheless, so we threw it in: You can open a preview of any Macintosh EPS in Adobe Photoshop by selecting Open As and select PICT Resource as the format. The image is displayed in all its 72-dpi glory. If you try to open the EPS itself, Photoshop tries to turn it into a bitmapped image (it succeeds if it's an Illustrator file).

Invisible EPS Images with ResEdit

There can be times when you want to print a picture, but not see it on screen. For example, you might want to place a particular

Using EPS to Redimension a Job

Suppose you have a very complicated page layout in QuarkXPress, and your client suddenly decides on a slight change in page size that requires repositioning and resizing every element on the page. You could spend hours fixing the document, or do what an enterprising designer did in similar circumstances: save the page as EPS, import the EPS into a document with the new page size, and scale the EPS to fit. Slight changes to a page's proportions can sometimes be an acceptable tradeoff against simply getting a job done on time.

image on your master pages that needs to print out on every page, but displaying it on every page would be distracting and time-consuming. Rather than greeking the display of all pictures, which replaces every non-selected picture on screen with a gray box, you can create a screen-invisible EPS document (one which doesn't show on the screen but prints out properly) by using ResEdit.

1. Copy the EPS file (when working with ResEdit, always use a copy of the file you're editing).

2. Use a paint program such as DeskPaint or MacPaint to select a white rectangular area of any paint document and copy it into the Clipboard.

3. Open the copy of the EPS file within ResEdit.

4. Open the file's "PICT" resource by double-clicking its icon.

5. Select Clear from the Edit menu.

6. Create a new PICT resource by pressing Command-K, and then paste the white square into it.

7. Go to the Get Resource Info dialog box by pressing Command-I; change the "PICT" resource number to 256.

8. Save the changes to the file.

Now when you import this EPS file into your QuarkXPress document, you won't see anything, but it will print out.

Inaccurate Screen Previews

Most EPS files have screen previews that let you see what the PostScript is going to look like, more or less, when the image is printed. The problem is the "more or less" part. Typically, people rely pretty heavily on these previews. That's a mistake. First of all, the previews are usually only 72 dpi, while the final piece is printed at a higher resolution (the preview is jaggy, the final is not). Secondly, applications often cannot create perfect previews because of QuickDraw technology.

For instance, EPS files from FreeHand are often off by as much as a point. If a point doesn't matter to you, then don't worry about it. But if a point is important, you may have to print a lot of proof pages to make sure your layout is correct. Even the bounding box of the image may be off as much as a point or two, so you can't trust that either.

Precision Placement

One way to achieve better precision in placing EPS graphics from FreeHand or Illustrator is to build crop marks around the image before exporting it as an EPS. Once you import the EPS into XPress, you can adjust the placement of the picture so that the crop marks lie just outside the picture box frame.

CLIPBOARD
Retaining Picture Box Specs

Here's a little knowledge that you should store in the back of your brain; it'll come in useful some day. When you cut or copy a picture out of a picture box, the specifications that the picture box had been set to (skew, scaling, offset, and so on), are "saved" with the copied image. When you paste the picture into another picture box, these specifications are transferred, too (even the link information—where the high-resolution image is on disk—is retained).

IMPORTING
Retaining Picture Modifications

At some point, you'll undoubtedly find yourself in a situation where you want to import a picture into an already-used picture box. But if you do, you'll lose the original specifications (scaling, offset, rotation, and so on) for the picture box you're importing to.

One method of retaining those settings is to take the low-tech road—find a pencil and jot down all the specs for the previous picture (nice of XPress to show them to you in the Measurements palette); then, after you bring the new picture in, retype the original specs in (remember, if you have multiple changes to the picture box, it's usually quicker to make them in the Picture Box Specifications dialog box all at once).

EPS FILES
It May Contain Binary Data

Do you ever see the "Page could contain EPS pictures which include binary data. OK to continue?" dialog box? It's sort of weird, huh? It's very rare that it would matter that your EPS pictures contain binary data; in fact, we *always* use binary data and never have problems. The best way to deal with this dialog box is to ignore it. The second best way is to quit QuarkXPress and then start up again. Chances are, the messages will go away. Don't know why.

PROOFING
Printing Rough

There are times that you want to see your page on paper without bothering with all those pictures. The easiest way to do this is to select the Rough setting in the Print dialog box when you print. However, the one nuisance with this technique is that all the pictures are replaced with "X"s.

If you want output of your page showing the locations where the pictures are, but you don't want the pictures *or* an "X," you can give each picture box a frame (if it doesn't have one already; a half-point is thick enough), and then suppress the picture (either check Suppress Picture Printout in the Picture Box Specifications dialog box—Command-M—or click the checkmark in the Picture Usage dialog box's last column). Note that Suppress Picture Printout suppresses the picture but not the frame; Suppress Printout stops both from printing.

PICTURES

Replacing Images with Different File Types

What do you do when an image shows up as Missing in the Picture Usage dialog box? You click Update and go looking for the image, right? Let's say your original image was a TIFF, but after you imported it into QuarkXPress, you opened it in Photoshop and saved it as an EPS with a different filename. As it turns out, when you go looking for the missing file, XPress doesn't display any files with a different file type. In this case, it only lets you see—and therefore replace—the original image with TIFF files. (XPress is trying to be helpful, believe it or not.)

This catches us especially when we're replacing a low-res TIFF image with a high-res DCS file.

Luckily, we finally found the trick: make sure the new file has exactly the same name as the old file, and then place the new file either where XPress is expecting to find the old file or in the same folder as the document you're working on (these are the two places the program always looks for files). At that point, the Picture Usage dialog box lists the file as Wrong Type rather than Missing. Click Update, and you're in business.

You could also go to the Finder and move, rename, or delete the original picture file. Then QuarkXPress will let you relink the picture box to a new picture, as described in the next tip.

However, perhaps the best way to retain the picture attributes is to use the free PictAttributes XTension (which is on the disc bound into this book).

LINKING

Relinking with a New Picture

When you update an image in the Picture Usage dialog box, you don't have to relink with the same picture! You can relink with any other picture, and that new image inherits the picture specifications (scaling, skewing, and so on) from the old image's picture box. Unfortunately, the Update button is only available when QuarkXPress can't find a picture.

So, to fool QuarkXPress (you're smarter than a mere piece of software, aren't you?), move, delete, or rename the file you want to replace (we constantly use PrairieSoft's DiskTop for this, but switching to the Finder works just as well). QuarkXPress notices the change when you select Picture Usage, and lets you use the Update button.

However, there's one catch: XPress won't let you update to an image with a different file type. If the original image is a TIFF, then the update image needs to be a TIFF, too.

PICTURES

Wrong Type

Every now and again someone calls, complaining that their Picture Usage dialog box is listing the status of a picture as Wrong Type (usually it just says OK, Modified, or Missing). This cryptic message usually means one of two things.

▶ The file has been compressed with a utility such as TimesTwo or DiskDoubler.

▶ The file has been saved in a different format since it was originally imported into XPress. For instance, if you import a TIFF image into XPress, and then go back to Photoshop and save it as an EPS image with the same file name, you'll get this message.

The remedy is simple: click Update in the Picture Usage dialog box just as though the status read Modified.

Finding Picture Paths

The Picture Usage and Subscriber Options dialog boxes are especially helpful in an indirect way. If you're trying to find where a picture came from—that is, where it is on disk—you can select the picture on the page and open either of these dialog boxes. In the Picture Usage dialog box, the picture is highlighted in the list, so if you have a whole mess o' pictures in your document, you don't have to go scrolling through the list to find the one you want (this also works if you have multiple picture boxes selected). The disk path name is displayed on the left side of the dialog box. Unfortunately, long path names get shortened. However, you can see the whole path in the Subscriber Options dialog box (from the Edit menu or double-click on the picture with the Content tool). Click on the file name in the popup menu, and the path is displayed just as it is in a standard file dialog box (see Figure 6-2).

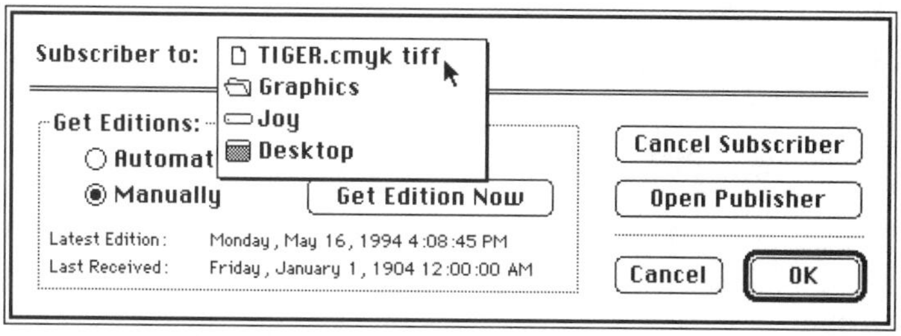

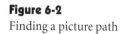

Figure 6-2
Finding a picture path

Screen Capturing

A screen shot is simply a picture of your screen (or part of what's showing on the screen). Taking screen shots is sometimes helpful in XPress, especially as a workaround for printing out something that you couldn't otherwise print (the list of master pages, the Document Layout palette, and so on). The capability of taking a

Transferring Pictures

Often, we'll need to get screen shots or pictures that were created on a PC into a Mac QuarkXPress document or vice versa. Fortunately, the latest version of XPress can read most of the file formats of the opposite platform. For instance, you can open a PC TIFF or BMP file on the Mac with no problem. On the other hand, sometimes a particular file or format won't open easily. Adobe Photoshop saves the day. It opens all sorts of files—including PCX files—from a PC and can save them as Mac TIFF files. Conversion programs such as HiJaak can also help, but remember that—as Steve Werner put it— "when doing conversions, the shortest path is usually the best." If you have a lot of images that you need to do this to, it's probably worth buying a copy of De-Babelizer (incredibly powerful translation software). There's a trimmed-down version (the Lite LE edition) on the disc in the back of the book.

screen shot is built directly into your Macintosh's system software, but there are also a number of commercial and shareware utilities that give you more control than the System does.

To use the System to take a picture of the entire screen, press Command-Shift-3 at any time. After you hear the sound of a shutter clicking, the cursor freezes for a short while (the time it takes depends on how large a screen you have, how fast your computer is, and how many colors are showing—color can take considerably longer than black and white, especially on older machines). When the machine unfreezes and you get your cursor back, the contents of your screen have been recorded in a file named "Picture 1" (or "Picture 2", if there already was a "Picture 1", and so on), and saved at the top level of your startup disk.

Once you've taken the screen capture, you can edit it in Photoshop or any other image-editing program (we like Zedcor's DeskPaint for this sort of thing).

Commercial and shareware screen-capture utilities usually have additional features like onscreen editing, the ability to add captions, and other useful features. There are loads of these programs available, including the commercial Exposure Pro (what we used to create most of the figures in this book) and Capture, and the shareware programs Flash-It and Screenshot. On the Windows platform, we often use Tiffany (another commercial program).

Finding a Bunch of Missing Files

If you move image files or rename the folders they reside in (or even rename the disk they're on), you can wind up with XPress thinking all of your pictures are missing. There are two easy ways to relink images to a number of pictures XPress thinks are missing.

The first method is the coarser solution, and works if all of your image files are in one folder (or, of course, if you can *move* them into one folder). Move your QuarkXPress document inside that folder and open it. QuarkXPress looks for missing pictures first inside the folder where the document is located; it automatically relinks them. Save the document, and then move it wherever you like; the images stay linked.

The second method is just slightly more subtle, and works if you have clumps of missing files in one or more folders. When you find one missing file inside a folder, QuarkXPress "sees" the other missing files and prompts you whether or not you want to relink them all in one fell swoop (see Figure 6-3). You can then repeat this for other folders with missing images in them.

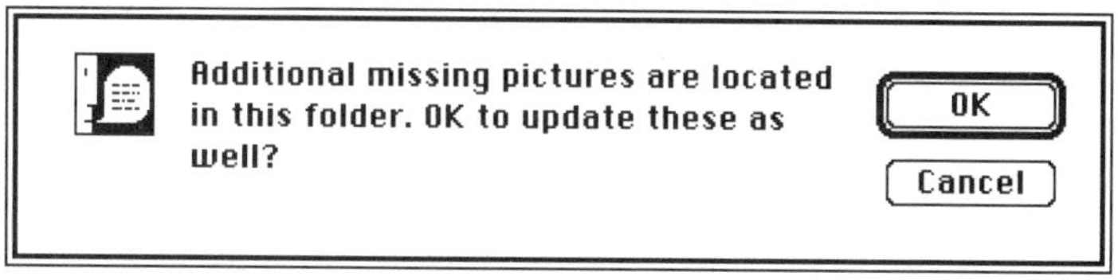

Additional missing pictures are located in this folder. OK to update these as well?

OK

Cancel

Figure 6-3
Updating
missing files

POSITIONING

Precision Picture Movement

When you have the Content tool selected and have selected a picture box, you can "nudge" the picture within the box in tiny increments by clicking the arrows in the Measurements palette. Each click moves the image one point in that direction. Holding down the Option key while clicking moves the picture in .1-point increments.

However, we typically find it even more useful to use the arrow keys on the keyboard. Again, each time you press a key it moves it one point; each time you press the key with Option held down, the selection moves .1 point. There are XTensions, such as NudgeIt, that let you customize how far each click or press moves the selection; see Appendix B, *Resources*, for specifics.

Note that if you have the Item tool selected when you do this, you're actually moving the picture box itself.

SCALING

Quick Scaling and Positioning

The quickest way to get a picture properly sized and positioned is to follow these steps.

1. Crop the picture.

CROPPING

Use Cropping Sparingly

Remember that XPress doesn't forget the parts that you've cropped out of a picture. That's why you can always go back and change your cropping or picture specifications. The flip side to this adaptability is that QuarkXPress often must process the entire image when printing your page, which can take a lot of time and printer memory. If you import a scanned photograph of the graduating class of 1995 and crop it down to only one face in the crowd, you could be spending a lot of time waiting for the page to print.

The key is this: because XPress can't alter an EPS image, it must always send the entire image to the printer. However, XPress *can* alter TIFF files. That means it's smart enough to only send the portion of the image that it needs. In version 3.1 and 3.2, the program forgot to crop the TIFF image's information if the image was rotated; however, that's been fixed in version 3.3.

Nonetheless, it's still better to use cropping judiciously. If you only want a small portion of the picture, use an editing program such as DeskPaint or Photoshop to cut out the other parts before you import the image.

2. Position it with one corner in the correct location on your page.

3. Command-Option-Shift-drag on the opposite corner to scale the picture box while keeping its proportions.

SCALING

The Right Way to Resize Bitmaps

You may have noticed that changing the size of simple black-and-white bitmaps often yields unpleasant results—ugly, plaid patterns appear (see Figure 6-4). This is especially a problem with dithered black-and-white scans—those that are halftoned during the scanning process—and black-and-white Paint clip art that has patterns in it (such as Mac screen shots). You can avoid these patterns by carefully resizing your bitmap images to have an integral relationship between the resolution of your printer and the final image resolution (bearing in mind the size to which you scale the image). You can use the following equation to determine the proper scaling.

(Picture resolution ÷ Output resolution) × Any whole number × 100 = Acceptable scaling percentage

Figure 6-4
Nonintegral scaling ratios can cause patterning

Note that this is true *only* for one-bit black-and-white images. For common bitmap and printer resolutions, you can use the values in Table 6-2.

When printer resolution is	Scale 72-dpi bilevel images to
635 or	34.02%
1270 or	56.69
2540	79.37
	96.38
	102.05
	119.06

When printer resolution is	Scale 72-dpi bilevel images to
300 or	12.00%
600	24.00
	48.00
	72.00
	96.00
	120.00

When printer resolution is	Scale 300-dpi bilevel images to
635 or	23.62%
1270 or	47.24
2540	70.87
	94.49
	118.11
	141.73

Table 6-2
Integral scaling for bilevel bitmapped images

LITTLE GEM

Faking Perspective

To make a picture look like it's lying horizontally, change the picture rotation to -15 degrees, the picture skew to 45 degrees, and the vertical scaling (Scale Down) to 70 percent (see Figure 6-5). Of course, this is just one of many permutations between scale, skew and rotation. Adjust your pictures as necessary.

Figure 6-5
Pseudo-perspective

Figure 6-5
Pseudo-perspective

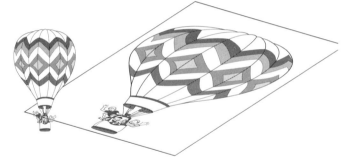

SILHOUETTES
Making Grayscale Pictures "Transparent"

The simple answer to "How do I make my grayscale TIFFs transparent?" is, "You can't." Grayscale TIFFs are not and cannot be transparent. The reason for this is that every pixel has been assigned a gray level. (In one-bit TIFFs, whites are usually transparent. If you save a one-bit EPS from Photoshop, you have the option to make the whites transparent in the Save As dialog box.)

Figure 6-6

Making a fake transparent grayscale TIFF

happiness runs in a circular motion; life is like a little boat upon the sea; everything is a part of everything anyway; you can have everything if you let yourself be; happiness runs in a circular motion; li̇ boat upon the sea; every of everything anywa thing if you let yoursȧ s in a circular m a little boat upon the se part of everything ve everything if yo l happiness runs in a circula on; life is like a little bo t upon the sea; everything is a part of everything anyway; you can have everything is you let yourself be ❦

This image is inside a polygonal picture box

However, you can fake a transparent look in some situations by importing the picture into a polygon which just wraps around the edges of the graphic. One way we've found to do this is to import a graphic into a rectangular picture box, trace the edges using the Polygon Picture Box tool, then cut the graphic out of the first box and into the new picture box (see Figure 6-6).

Of course, the problem with polygonal boxes is that they can only have straight-line segments. If you need to clip the image out with curved lines, we suggest using clipping paths in Photoshop. Make a path, save it, and set it as a clipping path (this is all done in the Paths palette). When you save as EPS, the clipping path is saved with the image.

You can also use a mask in Illustrator or a Paste Inside in Free-Hand to do a similar sort of clipping (but we think Photoshop's approach is the most elegant).

SILHOUETTES
More Transparent TIFFs

You create a grayscale image in Photoshop, save it as a TIFF, import it into QuarkXPress, set the background color of the picture box to "None", and put it on top of a colored box. When you print it, it looks awful (see Figure 6-7). What went wrong? Quark-XPress is not very good at figuring out what should or shouldn't be transparent in TIFF images, but when you set the picture box background color to "None", it tries its hardest anyway.

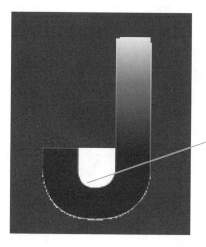

Edges get jaggy when Quark-XPress tries to make the edge around a TIFF transparent. Also note the white space at the bottom of the J, where the program got confused.

Figure 6-7
Grayscale TIFFs with background color of "None"

QuarkXPress makes something "transparent" in a similar way to the polygon tip above, though it uses lines and curves behind the scenes to "cut out," or clip, the image. However, because it has only the 72-dpi screen image to work with, the program cuts a very rough outline around the picture. This has tripped up more than one unsuspecting soul. The solution? Same as we talked about in the last tip: either save the image as an EPS (with or without a clipping path), or set the background color to something other than "None".

SILHOUETTES

Making the Background of EPS Files Transparent

Bitmapped EPS images that have a white background can fool you into thinking they're transparent in QuarkXPress, when they're really not.

If you place a grayscale bitmap EPS image (like one from Photoshop) over a gray or colored background, XPress does one of two things: if the background color is applied to the picture box, it blends the color right into the image; if the background color is in a box behind the picture box, the picture appears to cut neatly out of the background. Both of these are illusions.

What really happens in both cases is that the entire EPS image, including its rectangular bounding box, knocks out of the background (this has nothing to do with trapping; it does this even in black-and-white documents; see Figure 6-8).

Figure 6-8
EPS images appear
different on screen

*What it looks
like on screen*

*What it looks
like on paper*

Background of White

*Background is
colored gray*

*Gray picture box behind
the image*

If you want the image to knock out the background, this is a problem because it doesn't look right on screen. If you don't want it to knock out the background, then it's a problem because it looks right on the screen but doesn't print correctly. Either way, you just need to be aware of it.

There are a couple ways to get around this.

▶ Draw a clipping path around the image, like we talk about in "Making Grayscale Pictures 'Transparent,'" above. This has the effect of making the image both appear and print the same way: just the image knocks out the background.

▶ Convert the grayscale image to a bitmap (one-bit) image in Photoshop by selecting Bitmap from the Mode menu. You can create a standard-looking halftone by selecting

Halftone from the Bitmap dialog box, or pick a different sort of bitmap to work with. The key here is the output resolution. If you're *only* printing on a desktop laser printer, you probably don't need a resolution any higher than 300 or 600 (depending on your printer). However, if you're taking this image to film, you should probably increase the output resolution to between 1,000 and 2,000, making a rather large file in the process.

For example, a 500K grayscale image only becomes a 140K bitmap image at 300 dpi (so you actually save space on disk, but the image is only good for a desktop laser printer). The same image balloons to 2.18 Mb when converted to a bitmap at 1,200 dpi (suitable for imagesetting).

You can save the file as either a TIFF or an EPS, though if you save it as EPS, you need to check Transparent Whites in the Save as EPS dialog box. Note that this image overprints its background, and lets color through the "white" areas of the picture.

BACKGROUND COLOR

Matching the Background to the Image

Often, when you use a TIFF image in a nonrectangular box (and sometimes even when you use rectangular boxes), the background of the image doesn't blend in with the background of the box (see Figure 6-9). Trying to place a background color doesn't help, because the background color affects the image itself (this is either a bug in the program or simply a counterproductive feature—either way, it's annoying). But we've got a solution! Try the following steps.

1. Make a duplicate of the picture box using the Step and Repeat command. The horizontal and vertical offset fields should both be set to zero.

2. Delete the image from this duplicate box and give it a background color that matches the edges of the TIFF image (you may have to adjust the tint: usually between 90 and 100 percent does the trick).

Figure 6-9
When a TIFF image doesn't fill its box

Background color set to white

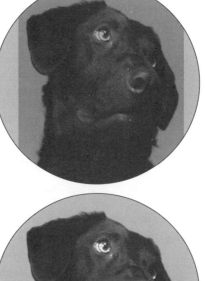

Background color set to 20-percent black (same value as the background color of the image)

Background color set to "None" with a 20-percent gray box behind it

3. Send the duplicate box behind the original picture and change the original picture box's background color to "None" (transparent).

This also works to blend inverted images into the background of a box.

CONTRAST

Adjusting the Break Point on a High-Contrast Image

When you select a bitmapped image (like a TIFF) and apply the High Contrast feature to it (under the Style menu), every sample point that is 30 percent or lower gets set to white; the rest are set to black. This 30-percent cutoff value does hardly anyone any good because the resulting image is almost always too dark. Using the Hand tool in the Other Contrast dialog box, you can adjust this point horizontally to anywhere on the scale. Try moving the vertical line over to around 60 percent. This cuts out most of the lower gray values and gives you a clean and recognizable image for many grayscale or color pictures (see Figure 6-10).

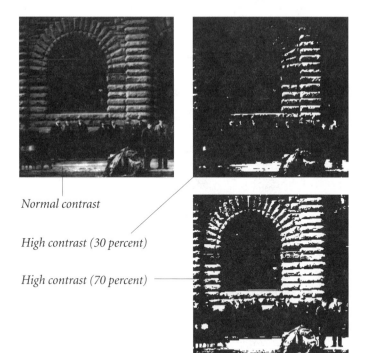

Normal contrast

High contrast (30 percent)

High contrast (70 percent)

COLORIZING

Making Bitmaps Negative

Here's a way to invert an image besides selecting the Invert item from the Style menu: color it white. This is often not only easier, but also more desirable. For example, if you want a white image on a blue background, you can select the picture box with the Content tool, change the shade of the picture to zero percent (or change the color to "White"), then change the background color to some shade of "Blue" (such as 100 percent).

Figure 6-10
Adjusting the high-contrast break point for a grayscale image

This technique is also of great help when working with line art which was scanned as a grayscale image. By adjusting the cutoff point, you can alter the line thicknesses in the artwork (see Figure 6-11). Remember that holding down the Shift key while using the Hand tool constrains the movements to horizontal or vertical.

Figure 6-11
Line art scanned as grayscale image

High contrast (30 percent)   *High contrast (60 percent)*

Of course, to get a really good-looking image, you'd have to start with an 800-dpi grayscale image (because you want to end up with a minimum of 800 dpi for line art). This would be a really enormous file! So, once again, the caveat to the tip is: this grayscale-to-bilevel bitmap conversion is better done in Photoshop or other image-editing program.

CONTRAST

Shading Grayscale and Color Pictures

In versions of XPress earlier than 3.3, the Shade item is grayed out (unusable) for grayscale and color TIFFs and PICTs. If you need to tint—or ghost, or screen back, or whatever you want to call it—a grayscale or color image but are using an earlier version, you can adjust shading through the Picture Contrast Specifications dialog box. Use the Hand tool to move the contrast curve vertically (see Figure 6-12). Moving the whole curve up makes the image darker, and down makes it lighter (lower gray levels).

Note, however, that when you move the curve up or down, you're likely to cut out possible gray levels. If you make the image darker, for instance, dark areas go black; make it lighter, and light areas go white. In either case, you lose detail. Because of this, you may want to adjust the curve using the Pencil or Spike tool instead (or use an image-manipulation program).

If you are using version 3.3 or later, you can set the tint of a grayscale image using Shade in the Style menu, but you still have to use the technique described above for color images.

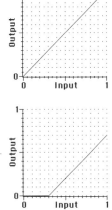

Figure 6-12
Shading a grayscale or color TIFF

COLORIZING

Changing One Part of an Image

Have you ever wanted to colorize or desaturate (ghost back) one part of an image, leaving the rest of the image alone? The obvious answer is to do it in Photoshop. But you can do many of these sorts of manipulations with great precision directly in Quark-XPress. The following steps assume you already have a picture box with a TIFF image in it.

1. Clone the picture box (Step and Repeat with offsets at zero).

2. Adjust the size of the new, top picture box. As long as you only adjust the corner or side handles and don't move the picture itself, the cloned images remain aligned perfectly.

   You can also change the picture box shape using the Box Shape submenu under the Item menu. For instance, if you want to colorize a polygonal shape within the image, you can make the top picture box into a polygon, then reshape it by turning on Reshape Polygon in the Item menu.

3. Finally, make whatever change you want to the top image. You can colorize or tint grayscale and black-and-white TIFF images easily. To ghost back a color TIFF, you have to use the Picture Contrast Specifications dialog box (see "Shading Grayscale and Color Pictures," above).

Correcting Errors in the Curve

You can make changes at any time to the contrast filter which XPress applies to color and grayscale pictures in the Picture Contrast Specifications dialog box. This means that if you use the Pencil tool and you can't keep your hand steady (we sure can't), you can smooth out the curve by going back over the rough parts after you've finished the basic line. It also means that if you don't like the change you made, you can press Command-Z to revert to the last state. It also means that if you hit OK and then decide that the image looks like crud, you can either press Command-Z to revert, or just select Normal Contrast from the Style menu to get back to the picture's original state (at time of importing).

Note that this tip won't work with EPS images, because you can't make any adjustments to that sort of picture (you can still clone it, and so on, but it won't do you any good).

CONTRAST
Don't Use Other Contrast

There are a half-dozen problems that make the contrast controls in XPress less than useful, the most essential of which is sharpening—or more precisely, lack of sharpening. Scanned images always need to be sharpened (preferably using Photoshop's Unsharp Mask filter) before they're printed and *after* tonal correction. Since XPress doesn't have a sharpening filter, that's impossible.

So if you need to perform tonal correction on a scanned image (you almost always do), don't use the controls in QuarkXPress. Do it in an image-manipulation program, which probably has better tonal-correction tools, and where you can also sharpen the image. Then save the file and place it in QuarkXPress, fully corrected, sharpened, and ready to print.

HALFTONES
Gray Levels in Halftones

Each spot in a screened halftone image is made up of tiny dots, and different gray levels are achieved when electronically screening the halftone by turning various dots on and off (at a 10-percent tint, 10 percent of the dots within a spot's cell are turned on). Okay, now remember that the lower the screen frequency, the bigger the spot, and the more dots are used per spot; the higher the frequency, the fewer dots are used. Thus, the higher the screen frequency, the fewer possibilities for levels of gray there are.

To find out how many levels of gray you can achieve, divide the resolution by the screen frequency, square it, add one, and drop any fraction. For example, you can get 92 levels of gray when you print a 133-line screen at 1,270 dpi ($(^{1270}/_{133})^2+1$), but only 6 levels of gray when you print a 133-line screen at 300 dpi ($(^{300}/_{133})^2+1$). The output is clearly posterized. To get 92 levels of gray on a 300-dpi laser printer, you would need to print at 30 lines per inch! It's an unfortunate fact, but this is one of the inherent tradeoffs in digital halftoning.

Printers such as the Apple LaserWriter Pro 630 among others, can use a special process that modifies the size of dots, giving an effective resolution of approximately 600 dpi for the purpose of imaging halftones. However, because of its special halftoning algorithms, you can't use this formula on these printers (or printers like them).

David covers this topic in much more depth in the book he wrote with Steve Roth called *Real World Scanning and Halftones* (for instance, that book includes a whole chapter on why you get banding in blends).

BLENDS

Avoiding Banding

Making blends in QuarkXPress is very cool, but if you've made many (or you've made blends from any other program) you probably know the disappointment of seeing those beautiful smooth blends print out in harsh bands across the page. Why does it sometimes do that?

Most banding occurs because of the physical limitations of the printer. PostScript printers only allow a maximum of 256 different levels of gray (that means each step is only .39 percent). This refers to the entire range from zero- to 100-percent screen values. Therefore, if your blend is from 20 percent to 30 percent (or any other 10-percent change), the printer can only supply you with 25 different steps (10 percent ÷ .39 percent). If you spread those steps over four or five inches, there's a reasonable chance you'll see banding.

Note that we said there's a "maximum" of 256 levels of gray. Very often, you're handed even fewer than that (see "Gray Levels in Halftones" above), which can cause even more banding problems.

You will see very visible banding with this small a change over a large distance.

We recommend that you turn off Calibrated Output in the Print dialog box when printing blends because the calibration sometimes accentuates banding (actually, we typically just turn it off for everything).

OTHER CONTRAST

Why Can't I Apply Other Contrast Settings?

We've heard from a slew of people who insist that—no matter what kind of color image they select—the Other Contrast feature (in the Style menu) never changes from its grayed-out state. The answer is typically simple: the images were imported while the Color TIFFs popup menu in the Applications Preferences was set to either 16 or 32 bit. At those values, XPress won't let you change the contrast settings. (The technical explanation is that the program stores contrast settings in the higher channels of the image's preview, so if you tell XPress to fill those channels with preview data, there's no room for other contrast settings.)

ROTATION
Rotate Images First

Whenever you modify an imported picture in QuarkXPress, you're increasing the amount of work the program has to do when it prints. Ask QuarkXPress to jump through too many hoops, and you may find your jobs take forever to print, or don't print at all. Rotating bitmapped pictures, in particular, can slow printing to a crawl. If you need to rotate a picture, it's far better to rotate the picture in a program like Photoshop, and then import it into QuarkXPress. This way, you only have to wait for the picture to be rotated once; otherwise, you have to wait for QuarkXPress (or actually, the printer's PostScript interpreter) to rotate it every time you print.

BLENDS
Color Blends in Black-and-White Bitmaps

Carlos Sosa, that hip heartland designer, turned us on to a very odd and potentially useful technique of putting blends inside of images. (This tip only works with one-bit images such as those in Bitmap mode in Photoshop.)

1. Import a one-bit (black-and-white) image into a picture box and set its color to "White".

2. Set the image to Invert (Command-Shift-hyphen).

3. Give the picture box a blended background.

The background blend actually pokes through the image itself, making it appear as though the image were blended (see Figure E in the color pages after this chapter). Note that you can fake this effect for a grayscale image by first converting the image into a bitmap in Photoshop (change Mode to Bitmap, and select the Halftone Screen technique). Also, if you want the blend to be "on top of" a colored background, replace that color for "White" in the first step above.

PHOTOSHOP
Considering Photoshop's Settings

When you save an image from Photoshop (or another image manipulation or paint program), take a moment to consider each choice that that program gives you.

TIFF versus EPS. One question we're asked all the time is, "Which should I use: EPS or TIFF?" Our answer is typically, "Use the one that suits you best. There is nothing inherently better or worse about either format." Some people say that one or the other prints better or more reliably. That's dingo dung, as far as we're concerned.

Note, however, that you can do different things with each. For instance, an EPS can contain halftone screening and transfer function information; TIFF can't. EPS can also contain object-oriented information, such as type or lines, which TIFF can't. TIFF, on the other hand, is typically more versatile from within QuarkXPress. You can colorize it, crop it without a printing performance hit (see "Use Cropping Sparingly," earlier in this chapter), change its contrast, and set halftone screens for it using Other Screen; you can't do any of that for EPS images.

ASCII versus binary. When you save an image as an EPS, you can save it in either binary or ASCII formats. You should use ASCII if you are printing the image over a serial network cable (such as those sometimes used between PCs and printers), if your service bureau doesn't use a Mac to talk to their imagesetter (perhaps they're using a PC or a UNIX-based computer), or if you have a lot of extra disk space that you don't mind filling up and loads of cash that you want to give to your service bureau.

EPS versus DCS. Another question we're often asked is, "Which is better: DCS or EPS?" The answer is that DCS is just a type of EPS, and they're both reliable. DCS (desktop color-separation format) was created by Quark, but that's no good reason to use it. Probably the only good reason to use DCS is if you want to work with a low-resolution composite image in QuarkXPress and put the high-resolution images on a print server (or let your service bureau hang on to them). When you print to a color printer, XPress uses the master file with the low-res image. When you print separations, XPress replaces the master file with the high-resolution images.

Another good reason to use DCS was developed by In Software: It's called PlateMaker, and it's a plug-in module for Photoshop. It lets you create DCS files that contain spot colors or varnish plates based on additional channels in your Photoshop file. It's very impressive, and if you need this sort of thing, this is just the thing you need.

Including screens or transfer functions. Perhaps more important to think about is the Include Halftone Screens and Include Transfer Functions checkboxes in Photoshop's EPS Options dialog box. If you check Include Halftone Screens, Photoshop includes specifications for the halftone screen, angle, and spot shape in the file, so that nothing you do in QuarkXPress can change them. If you leave it unchecked , QuarkXPress prints with its default angles and spot functions, plus the screen frequency that you specify in the Page Setup dialog box. If you use a printer with Accurate Screens or Balanced Screens, this decision is crucial because you want to set the proper screen angle and frequencies for each color.

The situation with transfer functions is similar. Transfer functions are primarily used for dot gain compensation. Note that QuarkXPress's internal dot-gain compensation does not affect EPS files at all; if you want dot-gain compensation, you need to set the values in Photoshop.

We make these decisions based on the situation we find ourselves in. If we're printing to a calibrated imagesetter and then to glossy paper, we probably won't worry about transfer functions. In other situations, we may require that DCS EPS files include Photoshop's elliptical spot function (much better than XPress's ellipse), and so we include it.

COLOR SEPARATION
Separating Color TIFFs

While QuarkXPress 3.1 won't separate color TIFFs that use the common RGB format, versions 3.2 and later will, using EfiColor. However, you should think carefully before you use this method. There are typically two methods for separating RGB images into CMYK: separate them before you import them into QuarkXPress and separate them after you've imported them. Note that most scanned images begin life in an RGB format.

Preseparating files. The way that most people have separated images in the past is to use a program like Photoshop, Color-Access, Cachet, ColorStudio, or Aldus PrePrint. These programs let you import an RGB file and convert it to CMYK. Then you can save the image as EPS, DCS, or TIFF.

Postseparating files. Other people like to separate their images using a separate utility *after* the image is imported into Quark-XPress. For instance, you can import a number of scans into XPress, save the file a page at a time as EPS, then run those EPS files through Aldus PrePrint to make the separations. Sound like a hassle? It is! Why do people do it? Beats us.

The newest way to separate files is to use a color-management system like EfiColor. EfiColor has the benefit of actually shipping with XPress, so it's "free." However, there's a basic problem with letting it do your separations for you. Converting from RGB to

CMYK can take a long time, especially for larger scanned images. Doing it once in Photoshop is painful enough. Doing it with Efi-Color means you have to convert the file every time you print separations. For many people, that's impossible, at best.

What do we do? We use Photoshop or ColorAccess to preseparate all our files, then save them as CMYK TIFFs. It's easy, it's convenient, it's flexible. Note that your needs may be different than ours, though, so don't just follow us slavishly.

SCALING

Scaling Pictures and Resolution

When you scale a bitmapped image up or down in QuarkXPress, the number of sample points (pixels, or dots) in the image never changes. XPress is just placing the same number of sample points in more or less space. So if you scale an image, the resolution of the image *does* change.

For instance: if you have an image with 150 sample points per side, and at 100 percent it's one by one inch, you have a resolution of 150 samples per inch (spi). If you scale the image down to 50 percent (half an inch per side), the same number of sample points is packed into half the space, so the resolution of the image doubles: you now have 300 spi. Similarly, if you double the size of the image in QuarkXPress, the resolution is cut in half, because each sample point has to cover twice the area it did (see Figure 6-13).

Why should you care about all this? Image resolution has a major effect on three things: file size (on disk), printing speed, and quality. If the resolution is too low, it looks awful (but prints quickly and takes up little room on disk). If the resolution is too high, it takes up way too much space on disk and prints slowly (there's almost a three megabyte difference between saving a four-by-five-inch color image at 200 dpi instead of 300 dpi).

PHOTOSHOP

Preparing Images for Print

If you think you can just scan in some picture, throw it on your page, and print it . . . you're right. However, if you think you can do this and make it look *good*, you're wrong. We can't cover everything you need to know here, but here are a few tips.

Figure 6-13
Resolution versus scaling

Figure 6-13
Resolution versus scaling

100 percent = 72 dpi

200 percent = 36 dpi

50 percent = 144 dpi

*50 percent =
144 dpi*

100 percent = 72 dpi   *300 percent = 12 dpi*

Levels and sharpening. We feel pretty confident in saying that *every* image you scan (or have scanned for you) will need tonal adjustment and sharpening. If a service bureau is doing the scanning, they'll sometimes do this for you. If not (or if you're using Photo CD or your own scanner), you'll have to do it yourself. The key to tonal adjustment is the Levels control in Photoshop. The key to sharpening is Unsharp Masking in Photoshop (see Figure 6-14).

Halftone screens and resolution. The second item which you should pay attention to is the resolution of the image. The resolution of the final image (after scaling) should never be more than two times the screen frequency you're printing at. That means if you're printing at 133 lpi, you never need more than a 266-dpi image. If you up your screen frequency to 150 lpi, you may need a 300-dpi image. However, we typically recommend that people use a multiple of 1.5 rather than two. That means that a 150-lpi image wouldn't need more than 225 dpi, and a 60-lpi image only needs 90 dpi to print well (see the previous tip for why you should use lower-resolution images when possible).

Figure 6-14
Preparing an image for print

Original scan

BACKGROUND COLOR
Runaround Links

We don't know why, but when you set the runaround of a picture box to None, XPress automatically sets the background color of the box to "None", too. Perhaps some Quark engineer was just trying to be helpful. However, this "feature" can get you in trouble if you're not careful with it. Of course, you can always go back and change the background to an opaque color manually.

TEXT WRAP
Vertical Alignment and Text Wrap

The Centered, Bottom, and Justified Vertical Alignment popup menu items (in the Text Box Specifications dialog box; Command-M) do not work when some runaround object intrudes into the text box. Instead, XPress always uses Top alignment. This can be very frustrating. However, as soon as we understood *why* it can't work, we felt better about not being able to do it.

After tonal correction and sharpening in Photoshop

The reason, if you think about it, is simple: the program could lock itself into an endlessly repeating (recursive) routine. For example, let's consider a vertically justified text box.

The intrusion (runaround object) forces a change to a line break which makes the text block a line longer, which reduces the effective leading (fitting a larger number of lines into the same space), which makes the original line *not* break any more, which changes the leading back to what it was at first, since we're no longer a line longer than we were, which takes us right back to the beginning again.

And, even if we don't end up in a hopeless situation like the above, it would still take the program a lot longer to sift through all the combinations and permutations which the intrusion causes; in other words, performance would take a big hit.

Picture Wrap with No Picture

After you have built a text runaround polygon around a graphic image, you can delete the picture and the polygon remains (see Figure 6-15). Remember to delete the picture while the Content tool is selected, or else you'll delete the picture box (and the picture and polygon with it) instead of just the contents of the box.

Figure 6-15
A runaround with no picture

Of course, polygonal text boxes have the same problem (polygonal text boxes are just rectangular text boxes with an intrusion).

Note that, as far as XPress is concerned, all this is true regardless of whether the intruding box actually touches any text. The mere fact that there's something intruding at all into the text box is enough to cause this behavior.

Polygons from Empty Boxes

If a picture box is empty when you apply Manual Image text runaround, the text-runaround polygon is created in the shape of the picture box itself. We find this handy for creating quick, custom text runaround paths that don't necessarily have anything to do with a graphic. It's useful, for example, to force a block of text to justify at an angle or wrap around a large drop cap (see Figure 6-16). However, in version 3.3, XPress lets you make polygonal text boxes. This is typically a more elegant solution for odd text runarounds (see "Use Polygonal Text Boxes," below).

Speed Up Polygon Editing

Every time you change a corner or a line segment of a text runaround polygon, QuarkXPress redraws the polygon and recomposes the text to go around it. This can quickly become tedious. You can make the program hold off on reflowing the text until you've finished editing by holding down the spacebar (you can even add or delete points using the Command key while the spacebar is held down). When you're finished, let go of the spacebar, and QuarkXPress reflows the text. Note this only works for text runaround polygons, not other kinds of polygons.

Use Polygonal Text Boxes

Instead of using complicated inverted text wraps to get polygonal text blocks, we like to use the polygonal text-box feature introduced in QuarkXPress 3.3. Make a regular text box, then select the last item in the Box Shape submenu (under the Item menu). This

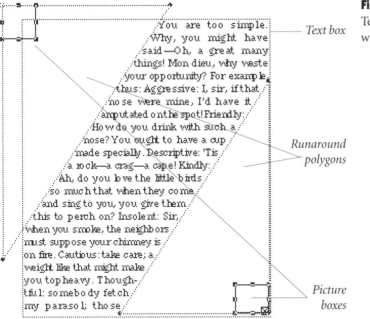

Figure 6-16
Text runaround polygons
with no pictures attached

Text box

Runaround
polygons

Picture
boxes

turns the text box into a polygon, although it's still in the shape of
a rectangle. To alter its shape, you have to turn on Reshape Polygon (select it from the Item menu).

Some XTensions, such as PiXTrix, let you convert polygonal
picture boxes into text boxes, retaining their shape automatically.
This could be very helpful if you wanted to make a complicated
polygonal text box (see Figure 6-17).

Figure 6-17
Polygonal text boxes

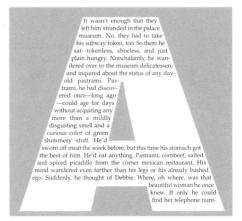

TEXT WRAP
Smooth Auto Image or Manual Image Runarounds

If you've imported a picture with an irregularly shaped outline
into QuarkXPress, but want smooth, curved text runarounds surrounding the picture, you can manually edit the runaround in
QuarkXPress. But you can't define curves when editing a manual
runaround, so you'll end up adding more and more points to the
runaround, creating a choppy line that only roughly approxi-
mates a curve (see Figure 6-18).

Here's another approach.

1. Bring the picture into Illustrator or FreeHand.

Figure 6-18
Smooth runarounds

Automatic runaround

Here, the EPS has a white line around it giving it a smoother runaround

2. Draw a path around the picture that matches the runaround you want to create in QuarkXPress. Give the path no fill, and a white stroke.

3. Bring the picture back into QuarkXPress, and set the runaround to Auto Image, with no outset.

Even though the path you made is white, and won't show against the background, QuarkXPress sees it and smoothly runs text around it.

There's a corollary to this tip: just because you can't see an object in an EPS file doesn't mean that it won't affect your output or your text flow!

Shaped Text Blocks

You don't have to have a picture in a picture box to create an interesting text runaround. Text can run around almost any page element. For example, you can draw diagonal lines on either side of some text and control how the text flows (see Figure 6-19). This is a great way to create diagonal text blocks. When you're ready to print, either set the lines to Suppress Printout in the Line Specifications dialog box (Command-M), or color the lines "None" (we

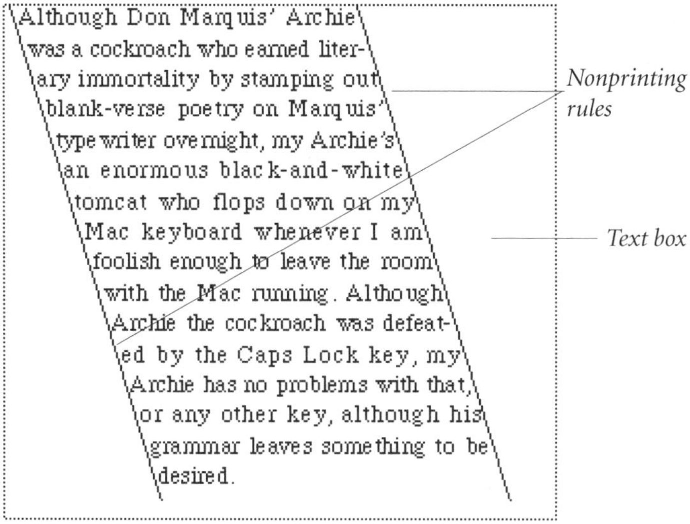
Although Don Marquis' Archie
was a cockroach who earned liter-
ary immortality by stamping out
blank-verse poetry on Marquis'
typewriter overnight, my Archie's
an enormous black-and-white
tomcat who flops down on my
Mac keyboard whenever I am
foolish enough to leave the room
with the Mac running. Although
Archie the cockroach was defeat-
ed by the Caps Lock key, my
Archie has no problems with that,
or any other key, although his
grammar leaves something to be
desired.
Nonprinting rules
Text box

Figure 6-19
Shaped text blocks

usually check Suppress Printout and set the lines to some interesting but subtle color; the color lets us easily see the lines when we want to select them). The next tip shows you even more ways to handle interesting picture-free text runaround.

TEXT BOXES

Skewing Text and Text Boxes

If you want to skew a whole column of text, you can enter a value in the Box Skew field of the Text Box Specifications dialog box. That's simple enough. But what if you want the text box to skew but not the text itself (see Figure 6-20).

1. Select the text box and turn it into a polygon (this is new in version 3.3) by selecting the last item in the Box Shape submenu (under the Item menu).
2. Turn on Reshape Polygon (also in the Item menu)
3. Grab the top or bottom segment of the text box (the line between the corner points) and drag it to the left or right.
4. Turn Reshape Polygon off.

Of course, you can also do this to picture boxes, but you typically don't need to. Let's say you skew the picture box by 15 degrees. To straighten the picture out, you can make the picture skew -15 degrees.

Figure 6-20
Skewed boxes

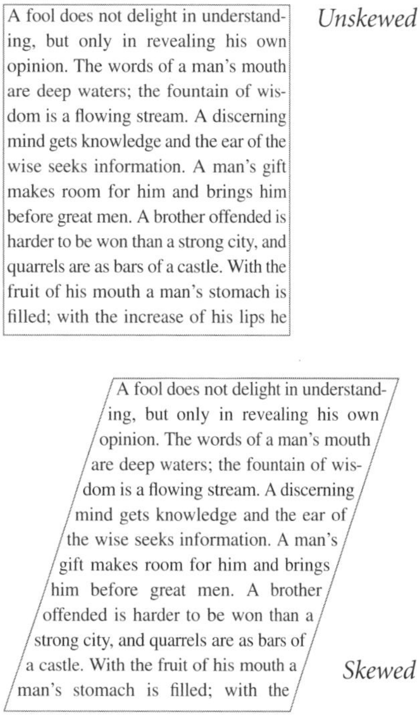
A fool does not delight in understanding, but only in revealing his own opinion. The words of a man's mouth are deep waters; the fountain of wisdom is a flowing stream. A discerning mind gets knowledge and the ear of the wise seeks information. A man's gift makes room for him and brings him before great men. A brother offended is harder to be won than a strong city, and quarrels are as bars of a castle. With the fruit of his mouth a man's stomach is filled; with the increase of his lips he
Unskewed
A fool does not delight in understanding, but only in revealing his own opinion. The words of a man's mouth are deep waters; the fountain of wisdom is a flowing stream. A discerning mind gets knowledge and the ear of the wise seeks information. A man's gift makes room for him and brings him before great men. A brother offended is harder to be won than a strong city, and quarrels are as bars of a castle. With the fruit of his mouth a man's stomach is filled; with the
Skewed

TEXT WRAP

Disappearing Runaround Text

Remember that text runaround is based entirely on box layering. A picture box must be on top of a text box in order for Auto or Manual Image text runaround to have any effect. One problem many seasoned veterans of QuarkXPress have is that they forget they can assign a runaround to a picture box while the box still has an opaque background. If you assign a text runaround and find that you can't see the text behind the picture box, make sure the box has a background color of "None".

TEXT WRAP

Two-Column Runaround

More than one text box can wrap around a single graphic, of course, leading to some very interesting effects. Figure 6-21 shows how a single curved line in an EPS image can make two columns of text run in an interesting pattern. Note that the graphic is set to suppress printout, so it doesn't print.

TEXT WRAP

Inverted Runaround Tips

There may be no other procedure in QuarkXPress more confusing than creating an inverted text runaround. To clarify the method, you need to know one thing: XPress always puts text where it has the most space to put it. Lets say you draw a diagonal line across a bunch of text (see Figure 6-22). At the top of the text block, the text runs around the left side of the line because there's more space there. Lower, the balance shifts and the text jumps to the right side of the line.

Inverted runarounds work the same way, but are a couple more steps more complex. First of all, to create an inverted runaround (a runaround in which the text runs inside a runaround polygon rather than around it), you have to have Manual Image runaround selected and the Invert Runaround checkbox turned on in the Runaround dialog box.

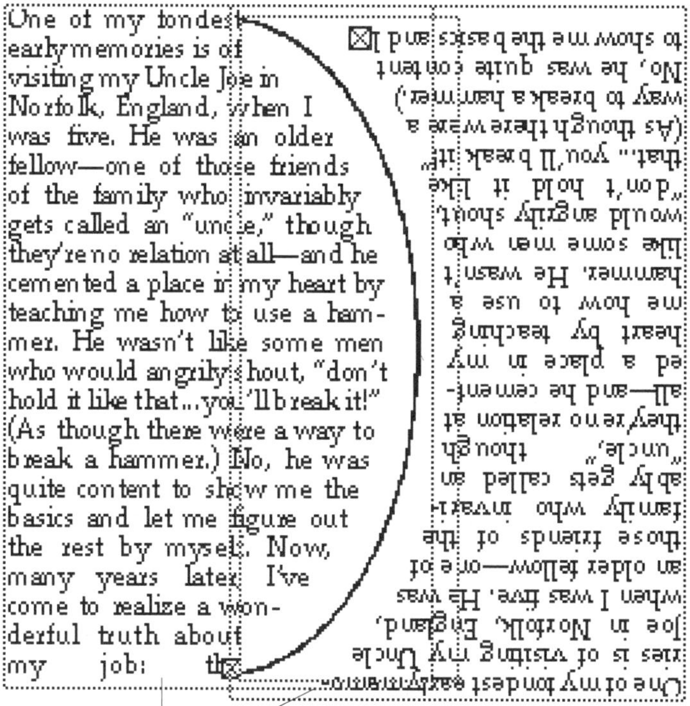

One of my fondest early memories is of visiting my Uncle Joe in Norfolk, England, when I was five. He was an older fellow—one of those friends of the family who invariably gets called an "uncle," though they're no relation at all—and he cemented a place in my heart by teaching me how to use a hammer. He wasn't like some men who would angrily shout, "don't hold it like that... you'll break it!" (As though there were a way to break a hammer.) No, he was quite content to show me the basics and let me figure out the rest by myself. Now, many years later, I've come to realize a wonderful truth about my job: the

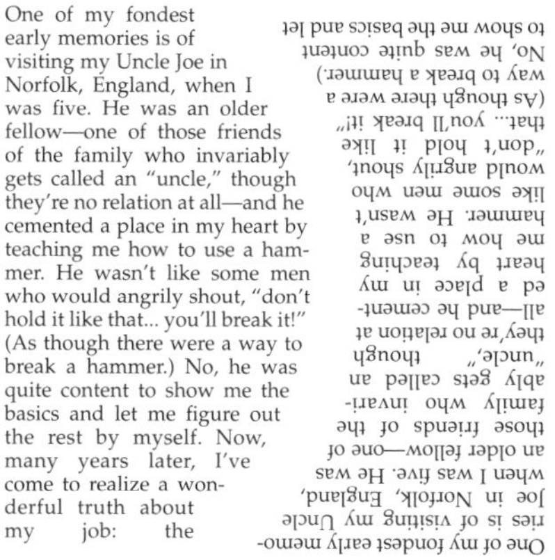

Figure 6-21

Two boxes running around one graphic

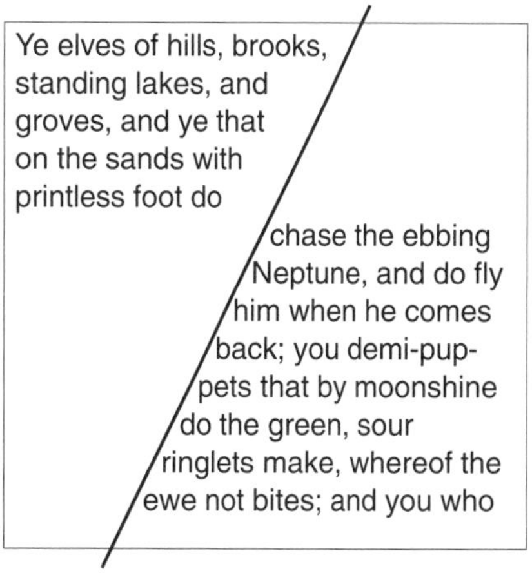

Both of these text boxes wrap around the circle graphic

One of my fondest early memories is of visiting my Uncle Joe in Norfolk, England, when I was five. He was an older fellow—one of those friends of the family who invariably gets called an "uncle," though they're no relation at all—and he cemented a place in my heart by teaching me how to use a hammer. He wasn't like some men who would angrily shout, "don't hold it like that... you'll break it!" (As though there were a way to break a hammer.) No, he was quite content to show me the basics and let me figure out the rest by myself. Now, many years later, I've come to realize a wonderful truth about my job: the

Next, you have to make the picture box that contains the runaround polygon bigger than the text box itself. That typically means making sure that the picture box is a rectangle (change it to one—if it's not one already—by choosing the rectangle in the Box Shape submenu under the Item menu), and adjusting the corner handles of either it or the underlying text box (see Figure 6-23). This is important because you want to give the text no room to flow around the item itself (then the text will flow where there's the most room: inside the runaround polygon).

Ye elves of hills, brooks, standing lakes, and groves, and ye that on the sands with printless foot do chase the ebbing Neptune, and do fly him when he comes back; you demi-puppets that by moonshine do the green, sour ringlets make, whereof the ewe not bites; and you who

Figure 6-22

Text flows where it has the most space

Figure 6-23

Avoid broken inverted runarounds

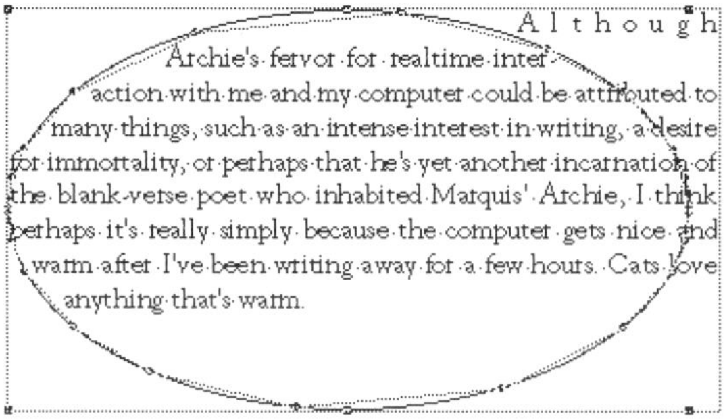

Although Archie's fervor for realtime interaction with me and my computer could be attributed to many things, such as an intense interest in writing, a desire for immortality, or perhaps that he's yet another incarnation of the blank-verse poet who inhabited Marquis' Archie, I think perhaps it's really simply because the computer gets nice and warm after I've been writing away for a few hours. Cats love anything that's warm.

An elliptical picture box with manual picture runaround

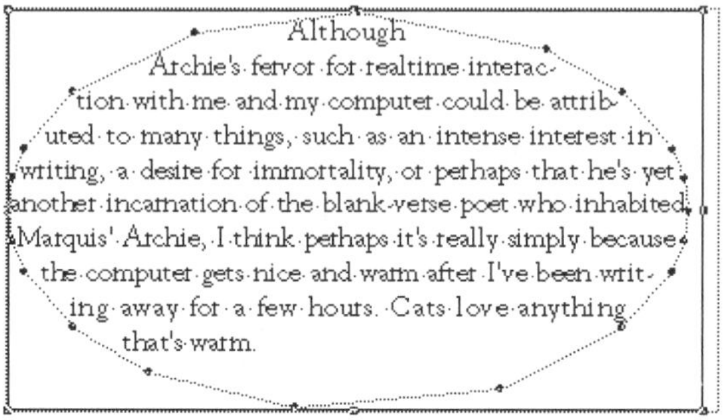

Although Archie's fervor for realtime interaction with me and my computer could be attributed to many things, such as an intense interest in writing, a desire for immortality, or perhaps that he's yet another incarnation of the blank-verse poet who inhabited Marquis' Archie, I think perhaps it's really simply because the computer gets nice and warm after I've been writing away for a few hours. Cats love anything that's warm.

When the picture box is turned into a rectangle, the text reflows, and the manual runaround stays the same.

However, now that XPress has polygonal text boxes, inverted runarounds are less important because you can just make the text box the shape you want.

TEXT WRAP

More Inverted Runarounds

If you use version 3.3, you can use polygonal text boxes to make really interesting text box shapes. If you haven't upgraded yet, though, you're still stuck with weird workarounds. Here's a good one for you. If you want to shape a text block, try creating a polygonal text box around it (see Figure 6-24). Then you don't have to worry about manual text runarounds or other difficulties.

TEXT WRAP

Wrapping Around Two Sides of an Object

We find that, occasionally, we'd like to have text wrap around both sides of an object. Is that so much to ask? Unfortunately, Quark-XPress wraps only on one side or the other of a graphic, but not around both sides. We have a few ways to get around this, but—to tell you the truth—none of them is really that great. The best way (in our humble opinion) is just to tell your designer to design it differently! Barring that, you could try a method that uses a bunch of one-line-high text boxes (see Figure 6-25).

1. Your text box should be only one column wide, with a graphic somewhere in the middle of it.

2. Adjust the text box so that it ends just above the graphic.

3. Add a new text box below the graphic, reaching down to the bottom of the column, and link the two boxes together.

4. Make two text boxes directly under the first box. Each box should be half as wide as the first, and as tall as your text's leading value. For instance, if your text is 12 points high with 14 points of leading, make a 14-point tall text box. This box should go just below the top text box (overlapping the graphic slightly).

5. Duplicate these boxes several times using Step and Repeat so that there are two columns of text boxes reaching from the original, top box, to the new bottom one.

6. Link all of the text boxes together using the Linking tool (remember that you can hold down the Option key when you select the tool to keep it selected beyond one use). The links should run from the top box on the left to the top box on the right, then to the second box on the left, the second box on the right, and so on.

7. Adjust the width of the line-high text boxes one at a time so the graphic can be seen in the middle of them.

You can make life easier by selecting Show Baseline Grid from the View menu when you draw the line-high text boxes. This grid of horizontal "snap-to" guides makes it easy to create and adjust the series of text boxes.

If this tip sounds overly complex, it's only because it's a kludge. However, after trying it once or twice, we find that we can do a half-page column in about five minutes.

Note that if you move your graphic, you're sunk! You'll probably have to recreate the entire grid from scratch.

Figure 6-24

Inverted polygons for text runaround

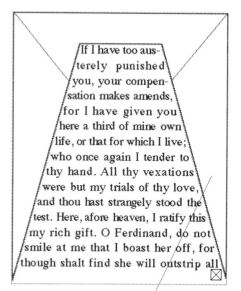

This polygon sits around the text box

Figure 6-25

Wrapping text around a graphic

If I have too austerely punished you, your compensation makes amends, for I have given you here a third of mine own life, or that for which I live; who once again I tender to thy hand. All thy vexations were but my trials of thy love, and thou hast strangely stood the test. Here, afore heaven, I ratify this my rich gift. O Ferdinand, do not smile at me that I boast her off, for though shalt find she will outstrip all praise, and make it halt behind her. Then, as my gift, and thine own acqui- sition worthily purchased, take my daughter; but if thou dost break her virgin- knot before all sanctimonious ceremonies may with full and holy rite be ministered, no sweet aspersion shall the heavens let fall to make this contract grow; but barren hate,

The text is actually linked through a whole mess o' text boxes to give the illusion of wrapping around the graphic

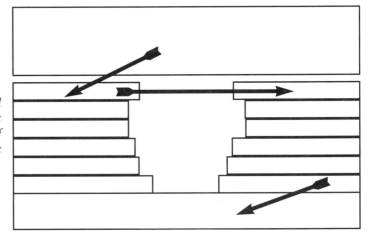

REPLACING IMAGES

Replacing Pictures While Locking Text in Place

Here's a typical procedure, especially at magazines: Scan a photo on an in-house, low-resolution scanner, and then send the photo out to a color house to get scanned on a high-end system (the high-end scan may take a day or two; the low-res version can be used immediately).

The low-res image gets rotated, skewed, scaled, positioned on the page, and—most importantly—text is flowed precisely around it. The high-res image is adjusted at the color house or on a fast machine elsewhere, so that it can be imported at 100 percent with no rotation (see "Rotate Images First" earlier in this chapter).

The problem? When the high-res image comes back from the color house and is imported in place of the low-res version, it's always slightly different (sometimes more than just slightly), and the text reflow gets totally screwed up. How can you maintain the text runaround and still replace the picture? Here's how.

1. If the runaround for the picture is not set to Manual Image, then set it to that (Command-T).

2. Using Step and Repeat with offsets of zero, duplicate the picture box once on top of itself.

3. Delete the picture from one of your two picture boxes using the Content tool. Note that the picture disappears, but the text-runaround polygon remains.

4. If the empty picture box has any background color or frame, remove them. You want this picture box to end up in front of the text, so that the runaround works, but you want it to be totally invisible. Since this box is transparent, it really doesn't matter which picture box is in front of the other.

5. Replace the image in the other picture box with the new image and adjust the settings the way you'd like them (offset, scaling, and so on). This box should have no runaround, but you'll probably want to ensure it has a background color (unless it's an EPS image, in which case it doesn't matter).

After this procedure, you'll have two picture boxes where you only had one before. One has a runaround based on the low-res image, but is invisible; the other has a high-res image but no runaround, so the text won't reflow.

Backgrounds of Anchored Boxes

Note that the background color for an anchored box is not necessarily the same as that of the text box in which it is located. For example, if your text box has a 10-percent gray background and you anchor a zero-percent black picture box into it, the anchored picture box won't match its surroundings (you'll get a white box on a gray background). If you can think of a better word than "tacky" to describe this, let us know. Instead, be sure to specify "None" for the background in all anchored boxes.

ANCHORED BOXES

Anchored Figures on Their Own Line

You might use anchored boxes within a line of text for symbols, complex dingbats, or company logos, but more frequently you'll use them as single "characters" within their own paragraph.

We know we said we hated automatic leading and that you should never use it, but here's an exception. Setting the paragraph that contains the anchored box to Auto leading ensures that there is enough space above the image so that it doesn't overlap any text. The anchored box's alignment should be set to Baseline, too (see Figure 6-26).

Adjusting Runarounds for Anchored Boxes

It took us almost forever to figure out that QuarkXPress ignores any runaround specification you give an anchored box except for one: the Top field when its runaround is set to Item. If you want to set a runaround for an anchored box, you have to set it before you paste it into the text block (you can't change it once it's pasted in). Whatever you have set for the Top runaround value is set for all four sides of the runaround box.

Aligning Anchored Text Boxes

If you're trying to align the baselines of text within an anchored text box with the baselines of text that surrounds it, you need to make sure of three things.

► The leading in the anchored text box and the surrounding text box must be equal.

► The anchored text box must be set to a text outset of zero in the Runaround Specifications dialog box. Note that this is *not* the same as selecting None. Because you cannot specify runaround for a box once it's anchored, you should set this before you cut and paste it.

► The anchored text box must have a text inset of zero. You enter this value into the Text Inset field in the Anchored Text Box Specifications dialog box.

► If the type size or font of the anchored text is different than its surrounding text, then you'll probably have to adjust the baseline shift of either the anchored box or the text within the anchored box.

The night was uncommonly dark, and a pestilential blast blew from the plain of Catoul, that would have deterred any other traveller however urgent the call: but Carathis _____ s with dread. Nerkes conc_____ cafour had a particular pr_____ morning this accomplished _____ directed their route, halted _____ from whence so noxious _____ troyed many animal but A_____ se malignant fogs with deli_____

The night was uncommonly dark, and a pestilential blast blew from the plain of Catoul, that would have deterred any other traveller however urgent the call: but Carathis enjoyed

Absolute leading

The night was uncommonly dark, and a pestilential blast blew from the plain of Catoul, that would have deterred any other traveller however urgent the call: but Carathis enjoyed most whatever filled others with dread. Nerkes concurred in opinion with her; and cafour had a particular predilection for a pestilence. In the morning this accomplished caravan, with the woodfellers, who directed their route, halted on the edge of an extensive marsh, from whence so noxious a vapour arose, as would have destroyed many animal but Alboufaki, who naturally inhaled these malignant fogs with delight.

The night was uncommonly dark, and a pestilential blast blew from the plain of Catoul, that would have deterred any

Automatic leading

Figure 6-26
Set anchored boxes to Auto leading to prevent the graphic from overlapping the text

ANCHORED BOXES

Anchored Boxes as Initial Caps

In the past, we've implied that you could use anchored boxes as initial caps simply by pasting them in as the first character of a paragraph and setting their alignment to Ascent. However, you may run into a problem if you're using a pre-3.3 version of QuarkXPress. In those versions, if your paragraph has any sort of left indent, some text lines that wrap around the anchored box are indented from the anchored box itself (see Figure 6-27).

Figure 6-27
Anchored boxes can cause
problems in pre-3.3 versions

Now my charms are all o'rethrown
And what strength I have's mine own,
Which is most faint. Now 'tis true
I must be here confined by you,
Or sent to Naples. Let me not,
Since I have my dukedom got
And pardoned the deceiver, dwell
In this bare island by your spell;
But release me from my bands
With the help of your good hands.
Gentle breath of yours my sails
Must fill, or else my project fails,
Which was to please. Now I want
Spirits to enforce, art to enchant;
And my ending is despair,
Unless I be relieved by prayer,
Which pierces so, that it assaults
Mercy itself, and frees all vaults.
As you from crimes would pardoned be,
Let your indulgence set me free.

*The anchored box
causes strange
reflow problems*

*This text is set up
with a hanging
indent.*

There are a few workarounds for this problem (including using a combination of setting the offsets to zero, adding a tab stop, and using the Indent Here character), but no other method is so easy and elegant as this one: upgrade to the newest version of the software.

ANCHORED BOXES

Dragging Anchored Boxes

While David hates using drag-and-drop text editing (it always gets in his way), there is one use for it that he likes: dragging anchored boxes to where he wants them. It's so much easier than trying to select them, then copying, pasting, and so on. The problem is that typically it doesn't seem as though you can drag-and-drop anchored boxes. Not true; you just need a little ingenuity.

When Drag and Drop is turned on in the Application Preferences dialog box (Command-Option-Shift-Y), you can select a range of text and drag it to where you want it. If an anchored box is part of that text, it goes, too. However, because there's no way to drag only the anchored box—with no other text going along for the ride—you have to select at least one other character (even a spaceband or carriage return) and then drag *that* character.

Nesting Anchored Boxes

Have you ever tried to make a text box that contains an anchored box into an anchored box itself? Can't do it, can you? Well, here's one way you can nest anchored boxes inside each other.

1. Anchor a text box in some text.

2. Select the text that the anchored box is in, and copy it.

3. Paste it inside another anchored text box.

You shouldn't overdo this tip: one level of embedding is probably okay, but we don't really recommend any further levels. At best, you'll get slow screen redraw. At worst, you'll corrupt your whole document and render it unusable. Make you nervous? It should. Don't use this tip unless you need to.

Anchored Picture-Box Rules

Nope, there's no way to cajole, coerce, or configure QuarkXPress to paste or place an anchored vertical line in a text block. Or is there? We work around this problem with the following technique.

1. Create a picture box as thin (or thick) as you want your rule to be.

2. Give the picture box the background color you want the rule to be (for example, 80-percent magenta).

3. Copy and paste this empty picture box into the text block. You'll probably want to paste it either at the beginning of a paragraph or on a line on its own.

4. Set the anchored box to Ascent alignment, and the text in the text box to absolute leading, so it wraps around the picture box/rule.

Making an Anchored Box into a Regular Box

It can be truly frustrating: you paste an anchored box into a text flow and then can't get it "out" again as a separate text or picture box. As it happens, there are actually two ways to turn an anchored box into a standalone box. The first way is to select it with either the Content or the Item tool (click on the box rather than dragging over it like a character) and select Duplicate from the Item menu (Command-D). This makes a copy of the box, but in a standard (nonanchored) form.

The second method is to select the anchored box with the Item tool (click on it), copy it, and then select Paste while still using the Item tool. Both of these methods duplicate the anchored box; if you don't want it in the text any more, just delete it.

> Every·man·being·gone·out·of·sight,·the·gate·of a·large·inclosure,·on·the·right,·turned·on·its harmonious·hinges;·and·a·young·female,·of·a slender·form,··came·forth.··Her·light·brown hair·floated·in·the·hazy·breeze·of·the·twilight. A·troop·of·young·maidens,·like·the·Pleiades,' attended·here·on·tip-toe.··They·hastened·to the·pavilions·that·contained·the·sultantas and·the·young·lady,·gracefully·bending,·said to·them:·'Charming·princesses,·every·thing·is

Figure 6-28

Anchored vertical rule

Figure 6-28 shows a sample vertical rule made using this method. Note that in this example, the rule appears as if it is set off from the left text margin. Actually, the text is set off from the rule using a nine-point left indent together with a negative nine-point first-line indent. The picture box/rule is the first character in the paragraph.

VERTICAL RULES

EPS Rules

If you need a vertical rule below one point, you're out of luck with the previous tip, because one point is the minimum thickness of a picture box. It's obviously time to resort to drastic measures: build the rule in another program and then import it into a picture box before anchoring it in a text box. If you need to lengthen or shorten the rule, just change the vertical scaling of the picture.

VERTICAL RULES

Vertical Rules with Rule Above

Here's an easy way to use the Rules command to create vertical rules that move along with a paragraph, as shown in Figure 6-29. The secret of this trick is to fool QuarkXPress into making a vertical rule out of a horizontal paragraph rule that's much, much thicker than it is long. Here's what you do.

1. Give the paragraph a left indent wide enough for the length of rule that you want, plus some extra for white space.

2. Add a second paragraph below the first, with no left indent.

3. Use Paragraph Rules (Command-Shift-N) to set a rule above the second paragraph. Set the rule's offset equal to the distance between the baseline of the first line of the second paragraph and the last line of the first. If you set your offset using percentages, this trick won't work.

4. Set the width of the rule equal to the depth of the paragraph above. So if the paragraph above contains five lines with 10-point leading, set the rule's width to 50 points.

Cyan

Magenta

Yellow

Black

Figure A
Process colors
broken out

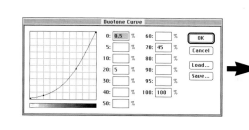

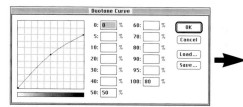

Figure B
Duotones from
Photoshop

Figure C
Color tricks the eye

This color looks different over different-colored backgrounds

Figure D
Faking duotones

Background color of 100-percent cyan

Background color of 40-percent cyan

50-percent cyan in a box behind the TIFF

Two TIFFs (the top one overprints)

Three cloned TIFFs (the top one overprints)

Figure E
Blend inside a one-bit image

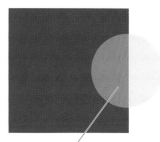

40-percent cyan

25-percent yellow

A 20-percent magenta
circle–set to overprint–
sits on top of this square

When the page is separated,
the 20-percent magenta
knocks out of the darker
magenta background

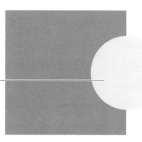

80-percent magenta

10-percent black

This shadow is
set to overprint

100-percent black

Rich black (includes
cyan and magenta)

Figure 1
Tricky silhouettes

*The original cut-out cow.
Saved as a CMYK TIFF from Photoshop*

*CMYK TIFF from Photoshop, background
color of "None", colored box behind*

Note the slight
jaggy edges ———

*The original cut-out cow.
Background color of None*

*CMYK EPS from Photoshop, saved with a
clipping path; process-color background color*

*Background colored the same in Photoshop as
the process-color background in XPress. Note
that the screen image (shown here) makes it
look like two different colors.*

*When the image on the left is printed, however,
you can see that the colors are exactly the same.*

Figure J
Setting your own
outline stroke width

The beast I saw resembled a leopard, and his feet were like those of a bear, and his mouth like that of a lion. One of his heads seemed fatally wounded. His mortal wound was healed, however, and the whole earth followed the beast in wonder.

Figure K
Expanding reversed
text using trapping

White text knocking out of a black background

The beast I saw resembled a leopard, and his feet were like those of a bear, and his mouth like that of a lion. One of his heads seemed fatally wounded. His mortal wound was healed, however, and the whole earth followed the beast in wonder.

The text is set to 1 percent Black, with a .25-point spread

Figure L
Halftone screen
frequencies

60 lpi   *120 lpi*   *150 lpi*

Traditional AM (amplitude-modulated) halftone

*Stochastic FM (frequency-modulated) halftone made using Isis Imaging's
ICEfields software. Note the lack of patterning, the increased detail, and
the heightened saturation of colors.*

*Cyan plate from
traditional screening
enlarged to 300 percent*

*Cyan plate from ICEfields's
stochastic screening
enlarged to 300 percent*

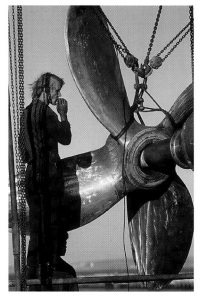

Figure N
Scaling images

Scaled down in Photoshop and imported at 100 percent (1.1 Mb)

Imported at full size (21 Mb) and reduced to 30 percent in QuarkXPress

Figure O
Blending tip

Blend from 100-percent magenta to 100-percent black

(Note: these two blends look the same on screen)

Blend from 100-percent magenta to 100-percent black and *magenta*

Figure P
JPEG compression

(Note: using Storm's PicturePress compression on a SuperMac Thunder II card)

Original image File size: 580K

10:1 compression File size: 56K

20:1 compression File size: 32K

32:1 compression File size: 20K

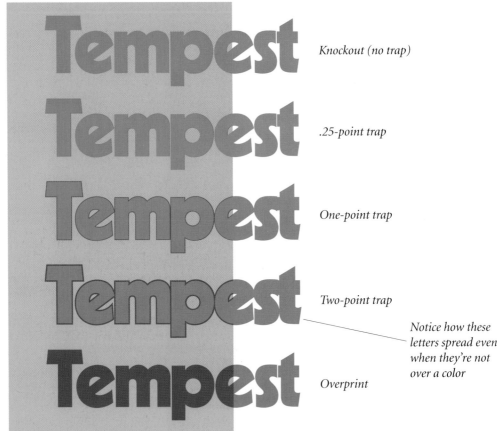

Knockout (no trap)

.25-point trap

One-point trap

Two-point trap

Notice how these letters spread even when they're not over a color

Overprint

XPress can't trap to this blend because it has trap conflicts.

XPress can't trap graduated blends to anything.

Objects can spread over scanned images.

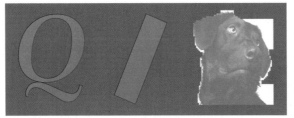

Type traps okay   Lines trap okay   Images don't trap

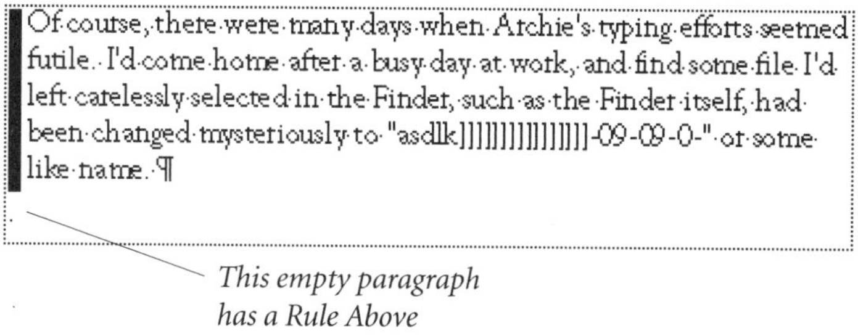

Of course, there were many days when Archie's typing efforts seemed futile. I'd come home after a busy day at work, and find some file I'd left carelessly selected in the Finder, such as the Finder itself, had been changed mysteriously to "asdlk]]]]]]]]]]]]]]]-09-09-0-" or some like name. ¶

This empty paragraph has a Rule Above

Figure 6-29
Anchored vertical rule

Now you can experiment with the three following methods for setting the "width" of the vertical rule.

▶ Set the length of the rule equal to the paragraph's indents, then specify a large right offset.

▶ Even better, set the length to Indents, then go to the Paragraph Format dialog box, and drag the right indent triangle in the ruler over to the left, till you've got a very skinny paragraph. Option-clicking the Apply button lets you see the effect of your dragging on the width of the vertical rule. As the right indent gets wider, the rule gets narrower.

▶ Set the length to Text, and type a period, hyphen, or some other narrow character in the second paragraph. The rule will instantly become as wide as the character. You can then make the character white, or zero-percent black, so it won't print. This also works with the tab character.

VERTICAL RULES

Using Text for Rules

Here's one more way to make a vertical rule that flows along with your text.

1. Place a fixed space (Option-spacebar) and the capital letter "I" from a sans serif typeface, such as Helvetica, at the beginning of a paragraph.

2. Set the size, horizontal scale, baseline shift, color, and any other attribute you want to the letter "I". Make it as tall as you want the rule to be.

Use Subscriber Options for Any Picture

What David likes most about the Subscriber Options dialog box is that it works with *all* kinds of imported pictures, not just with edition files. That's right, you can access Subscriber Options for any picture you've imported into your document using the Get Picture command as well as the Subscribe To command. Therefore, Auto Update can work for any picture, rather than just for editions (David never uses editions). Subscriber Options makes working with all of your pictures easier and faster.

3. Place the cursor between the space and the "I" and kern until the "I" is pulled into the margin (if there's no margin to pull into, it'll go right out of the text box; you can't see it on screen but it *does* print).

You can also create this sort of drop cap by making a two-character drop cap (the space and the letter "I"), and then kerning as noted above.

Subscribing to Non-Native Formats

Since the Open Publisher command works equally well on artwork you've imported or subscribed to, what's the advantage of subscribing? Not much, if your graphics program can directly edit the file you've brought into your QuarkXPress document. Let's say that you have an EPS file from Adobe Illustrator that you import onto your QuarkXPress page. If you select Open Publisher from the Subscriber Options dialog box, the system launches Adobe Illustrator and opens the file so that you can change it. When you're done, you simply save it again, and QuarkXPress can update the picture. This works because Adobe Illustrator can properly open its own EPS files.

But some programs (such as Aldus FreeHand before version 4.0) can't properly read their own EPS format. They can export the EPS file with no problem, but can't open that EPS from within the program. Instead, you have to keep the original file separately, find it, open it, make changes, and then export a new EPS that can be updated in QuarkXPress.

However, like many things, there's a simple solution. If you *publish* your picture from FreeHand or TypeStyler as an EPS rather than *exporting* it as EPS, the Open Publisher command usually works just like it does with an Illustrator or Photoshop EPS.

So while subscribing to editions from Adobe Illustrator or Adobe Photoshop is an often-needless complication, publishing and subscribing from programs such as Aldus FreeHand (pre-4.0) or Brøderbund's TypeStyler can be quite effective.

PUBLISH & SUBSCRIBE

Changing Subscriptions

QuarkXPress can subscribe to edition files that have been published from other programs. However, most programs only publish PICT image editions, which we consider pretty worthless. The newest versions of FreeHand and Illustrator (at the time of this writing) can publish EPS/PICT editions, which are much more usable. Note that double-clicking on the image with the Content tool brings up the Subscriber Options dialog box. Double-clicking with the Option key held down launches the application that published the edition (you need a *lot* of RAM or the RAM Doubler extension for this to work, though).

LINKING

Phantom Graphic Changes

If two or more people are sharing QuarkXPress files and graphics on a server, they may have strange problems with QuarkXPress thinking a graphic has been modified since the last time it was imported, even if no modifications actually were made. The problem usually occurs because either the file is busy when QuarkXPress is checking its status, or the various computers' clocks are out of sync.

Waiting for the graphic to become available again or resetting clocks in time with one another (give or take a few minutes) usually fixes this oddity. One other thing about clocks on the Macintosh: it appears that if various Macs are set to different time zones (using the Map control panel), QuarkXPress may also have difficulty figuring out which graphics have been modified. Note that Retrospect Remote and utilities such as Timelord can automatically synchronize all the clocks on a network.

PICTURES

Finding the Last Modification Date

Every now and again, especially if you're working in a workgroup over a network, it's helpful to know when a picture in Quark-XPress was last modified. That is, I may know that my art

PUBLISH & SUBSCRIBE

Out of One, Many

We can think of one good reason to use Publish and Subscribe with applications such as Illustrator. The reason lies in the ability to create many editions from a single file. Suppose you have a large, complicated Illustrator picture, and you want to get different parts of it into different places within your QuarkXPress document. You could just import the entire picture to each location, and crop it as desired. But that's wasteful: your printer still has to image the whole picture, no matter what's cropped out. Typically, in this situation, we'd suggest cutting and pasting each element from the main picture into smaller picture files, but that can be a hassle.

An easier solution is to simply select each discrete area of the picture you want to bring into your document, and publish it as an edition. Whenever you change the master, all the published editions get updated, and then are automatically updated in your XPress document as well.

department did some image retouching on a picture of the Pope yesterday but I don't know if I have the latest version in my document. You can find the last-modified date for an image in an unlikely place: the Subscriber Options dialog box (choose Subscriber Options from the Edit menu or double-click on the picture with the Content tool; see Figure 6-30). Look at the Latest Edition line, even though it isn't an edition.

Figure 6-30
The Subscriber
Options dialog box

*The date and time that this
image was last modified on disk*

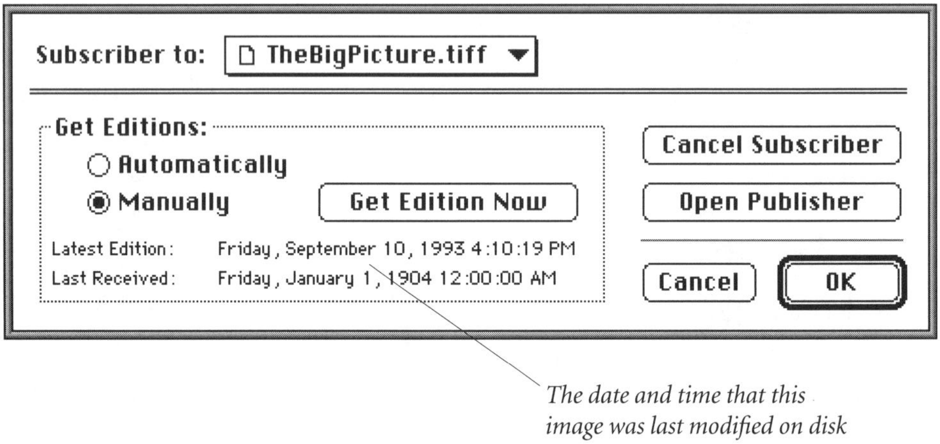

Note that you can also use an XTension such as TIFFormation or WhatzIt? or select the image in the Finder and choose Get Info from the File menu.

IMPORTING
There's CT and Then There's CT

QuarkXPress can import both Scitex CT (continuous tone) and LW (line work) files. However, it can only separate CT files. Note that when we say CT files, we're actually referring to CT HandShake files. We know of at least one guy who got burned because he asked a color house for CT files and got Scitex's proprietary format instead of the open-format CT HandShake files.

EPS FILES
Bleeds in EPS Images

If your page has items that bleeds off the sides, don't expect the bleed to appear in EPS files created using the Save Page as EPS command. When you save a page as EPS, QuarkXPress cuts the edges of the EPS off right at the edge of the page (the objects still jut out, but PostScript's clip command doesn't let the printer image them). Unfortunately, there are times when you want to export an EPS and take the bleed with you. For instance, you need those bleeds if you're printing an EPS with OPI comments from Aldus PrePrint or Aldus TrapWise.

You've got two choices in this case. First, there's a great little shareware utility called EPS Bleeder that lets you move the clipping boundary farther out. Second, Quark has promised us that they'll release an XTension very soon (perhaps even before you read this) that will let you specify a bleed distance. This might take the form of an additional field in the Save as EPS dialog box.

You can get these utilities from various online services or on the disc in the back of the book.

DROP SHADOWS

Transparent Drop Shadows

Have you ever tried to get a drop shadow in a TIFF or EPS to sit on top of a colored background in QuarkXPress? It looks horrible, doesn't it? That's because no matter what you do, you cannot make an image (or part of an image) transparent in QuarkXPress. However, you *can* make them transparent in other programs, such as Adobe Photoshop. That, along with a basic grain of information that most people seem to forget, makes it possible to create images that appear to blend in with colored backgrounds on your pages. That grain of information is: identical CMYK values print identically.

1. Make an image in Photoshop and place it on top of a solid color background. Make sure you know what the CMYK values of the background are (write them down). Note that you have to be in CMYK mode already when you do this.

2. Within Photoshop, you can adjust transparency. If part of the object is transparent (let's say a drop shadow), then you'll see it lying *on top of* the colored background.

3. Save the image as either EPS or TIFF.

4. Import it into a QuarkXPress picture box, and place that picture box on top of a larger box.

5. Make a color in QuarkXPress that has the same CMYK values as the background color you made in Photoshop, and apply this color to the background of the larger background box.

The two colors—the one made in Photoshop and the one made in QuarkXPress—will almost undoubtedly look different on the screen. However, if the CMYK values are the same, they *will* print the same (unless EfiColor changes them for some reason. And because there's no break of color between the smaller picture box (the one with the picture in it) and the larger one, the transition is seamless (see Figure I in the color pages).

EPS FILES

Better Onscreen EPS Files

As you know, EPS images typically have some sort of preview image so you can see them on the screen. On the Mac, the preview is an embedded PICT image. On the PC, it's a TIFF. Either way, it's almost always a bitmapped image. And if we know anything about bitmapped images, it's that they stretch and scale poorly.

Therefore, whenever you're making EPS images—whether it's from Free-Hand, Illustrator, or XPress itself—you should strive toward making them at approximately the size you're going to use them. Then again, if you can deal with a lousy screen preview, don't bother. It's still all PostScript, so it'll print fine.

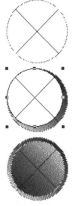

The process   *The result*

Figure 6-31
Three-dimensional buttons

A New Dimension

Okay, maybe we're just easily amused, but we think this trick for creating three-dimensional buttons in QuarkXPress is pretty keen.

1. Draw a rectangle or oval (we think it looks best with a square or circle).

2. Give it a straight Linear blend. We like to set it at 45 degrees, but it's up to you.

3. Duplicate the object, and make it smaller. The amount you make it smaller is up to you. Remember that if you want to reduce it to 80 percent, you can simply type "*.8" after the measurement in the W and H fields.

4. Reverse the angle of the blend. The easiest way to do this is to reverse the order of the blend colors. If you were blending from "Black" to "White", set the blend of the second object from "White" to "Black" instead. Or—if you feel like getting messy—you could just add 180 to the first object's blend angle. So if the first object had a 45-degree blend, the second object should have a 225-degree blend (45 + 180 = 225). You don't have to do the math if you don't want to; just type "45 + 180" in the angle box of the Color palette.

5. Space/Align the two objects so that their centers are equal (set Vertical and Horizontal alignment to zero offset from the objects' centers in the Space/Align dialog box).

You can really see the effect best when the page guides are turned off (see Figure 6-31). It's even nicer when you add a .25-point white frame around the inside object (sort of a highlight to the button's ridge).

3-D Boxes

While you *can* create rectangular 3-D boxes using the last tip, it's not the only way to create them. Here's one more method.

1. Make a rectangular picture box (the closer to a square it is, the better) with a background shaded to 40-percent of some color.

2. Clone it (Step and Repeat with zero offsets), and change the shade of the new top box to 80 percent.

3. While the top box is still selected, change it into a polygon (by selecting the last item in the Box Shape submenu under the Item menu). Turn Reshape Polygon on so you can modify this rectangle.

4. Delete the upper left corner point of this rectangular polygon (Command-click on the corner point).

5. Now draw a new rectangular picture box, shaded at 60-percent of that same color. Make sure that the corners of the box align with the diagonal line of the triangular picture box (see Figure 6-32).

Once again, this may be a process more easily performed in an illustration program. But for a quick-and-dirty, this technique can come in handy.

Making a Cube

It seems like everyone has their own favorite way to make 3-D objects. Here's one for making cubes.

1. Draw a box (hold down the Shift key to constrain a rectangle to a box).

2. Give it a blend from 100 percent to 10 percent of some color, at 135 degrees.

3. Clone it (Step and Repeat with zero offsets), and change the new box's blend to start at 70 percent and end at 10 percent at 260 degrees.

4. Move the new box up so that the bottom of the new box is at the same places as the top of the first box. You can do this using guides, Space/Align, or even subtracting the height of the box from the vertical origin.

5. Clone the first box again and change this new box's blend to a 45-degree angle.

6. Move this new box to the left so that the right side of the new box is at the same place as the left side of the first box. Again, there are a number of ways to do this.

Figure 6-32
3-D boxes

7. Change both the second and third boxes to polygons by choosing the last item in the Box Shape submenu; turn on Reshape Polygon from the Item menu.

8. Grab the top box by its top side (not the corner points), and drag it down and to the left. Grab the left box by its left side and drag it up and to the right. The upper right corners of the two boxes should be at exactly the same point.

When you select Hide Guides from the View menu, you should see a pretty good cube. You can also make pyramids and cylinders within XPress using polygons and ovals (see if you can figure out how; see Figure 6-33).

Figure 6-33
3-D objects made with pictures boxes

color 7

If we could see the whole spectrum of electromagnetic radiation, we'd be bombarded with a light show of color from almost every object around us. We'd see X-rays, radio and television signals, and even electricity emanating from objects like telephones. Fortunately (for our sanity), we can only see a tiny fragment of the whole spectrum of light. Those wavelengths we can see are labeled the visible spectrum, and they appear to us as a rainbow of color.

While many people have avoided using color in their XPress documents, most of us print documents with at least one or two spot colors, and quite a few people use XPress to create full-color work daily. In this chapter we'll discuss techniques you can use to make your life easier when working in color.

COLOR LIST
Changing the Default Colors

You can alter the default color list—the list which all new documents open with—by adding, deleting, and modifying colors while no document is open. These changes stick around forever, or at least until you either change them again or delete the XPress Preferences file. Changing the color list while a document is open only changes that document's list, and does not affect any other documents.

Jump to Edit Colors

The Colors palette is more like the Style Sheets palette than meets the eye. In both palettes, Command-clicking on an item in the palette quickly brings you to a dialog box. In this case, Command-clicking on any color brings up the Colors dialog box, in which you can edit, duplicate, append, delete, or create new colors. This is also a fast way to the Edit Trap dialog box.

Spot-Color Pinch Hitters

You don't *have* to create your own spot colors in your documents. If your job contains only black and one to three spot colors, you can use a process color (cyan, magenta, or yellow) to pinch-hit for each spot color.

When you take your film to the printers, give them written instructions such as "Print all film labeled 'Cyan' as Pantone 234 and all film labeled 'Magenta' as Pantone 567." If you do this, though—to avoid confusion down the line—clearly label each piece of film with a piece of white tape with the correct color written on it (such as "PMS 567") If you're extra cautious, use a black permanent marker to black out the original color name on the film.

This trick makes it easy for periodicals who use a new set of spot colors each month. You don't have to painfully respec your imported graphics that use the spot colors; spec them once as the same process color as you're using in XPress, and it gets mapped automatically.

Put Black Type on a Fifth Plate

While process color is printed in four colors, that doesn't mean you have to only have four pieces of film for each page. Especially if you're running the type of operation where last-minute type changes are frequent, you might find it helpful to make your black type a spot color, instead of normal black. You can spec this fifth color to look black, and set it to overprint. When you print separations, all the type ends up on a fifth plate all by itself. Then, when you take the film to the printer, tell them to burn that extra piece of film on the black plate.

While you increase your film costs at first (five plates instead of four), you'll find that last-minute changes are much *less* expensive (you only have to reprint that one plate instead of four). It's up to you to determine which method will be the more cost-effective for you and your operation.

Drag-and-Drop Color Application

Sometimes we think the folks at Quark like to toss in features just because they're cool—for example, drag-and-drop color application. Try it: Hold your mouse down on one of the tiny color squares on the Colors palette, and drag it over your page. Notice that as you drag, the image of that color square stays attached to your pointer.

As you move the pointer over objects, their color changes to the color you're dragging. Move the pointer past an object, and its color reverts to whatever it was before. To apply a color to an object, let go of the mouse button. If you decide not to apply the color swatch, let go of the mouse button while the swatch isn't over anything.

It really doesn't add a tremendous amount of what we in the software-pontificating business like to call "functionality," but it's a heck of a lot of fun to play with.

Note that you can apply a color in this way to backgrounds and borders, but not to text, even if you have the text icon selected in the Colors palette. And since the palette is grayed out until you select an object, you can't drag anything until you've selected at least one object.

Libraries of Colors

Here's one more way to save your colors so that you can use them in new documents. Place an object (even just a picture box with a colored background) in a Library file. David has a Library file named "David's Colors" into which he places colors he knows he'll use in various documents, but which he doesn't want to place in the default color palette. When he wants a particular color, he'll open the library, pull that color's object out onto the document page, and then delete it. The object is gone, but the color stays in that document's color palette. Within the Library file, you can group your colors into types such as "Warm Colors," "Cool Colors," or "Newsletter Colors" using the Library's labeling feature.

Adding Default Colors

Back in the first edition of this book we told you that the best way to add colors from a document to the default color palette was to use Uncle Izzy's Notepad Method: open the color by clicking the Edit button, write down the CMYK or other values on your handy-dandy notepad, close the color, the Colors palette, and all your documents, and then add the color back into the Colors palette with no documents open. Boring procedure. But it works.

Fortunately, we realized the error of our ways. Here's a much better way: with no document open, click the Append button in the Edit Color dialog box, and select the document you want to copy a color from. If you don't want all the colors from that document, simply delete the unwanted ones after appending them. That's much easier, no?

Append Colors by Dragging

If you want just one or two colors from another file, and don't want to append the entire list, you can copy and paste, or drag across an object filled with that color from another document. The color and its specifications come across too, and are added to the list of available colors.

EDITING
Tinted Colors

You already know that you can apply a color (let's say red) to a grayscale TIFF image. And you know that you can shade the colorized image using Shade from the Style menu (this is new in version 3.3). Here's one other way to apply a tinted color: make a new color that's defined as a tint of the color you're using. For instance, you could create a new color that's set as 40 percent of red, and apply it at 100 percent to a TIFF image (or type, or a background, or whatever). What's the difference? No difference, really. Just another way to go about your business.

COLOR DISPLAY
Accurate Blends

If you've got an eight-bit color monitor (256 colors), QuarkXPress lets you speed up your screen redraw by sacrificing onscreen color blend quality. You do this by turning Accurate Blends on or off in the General Preferences dialog box (Command-Y).

When Accurate Blends is on (the default), all blends appear on the screen as smoothly as QuarkXPress can make them (some are better than others; it depends on what colors you use). When you turn it off, the program just spits out a quick-'n'-dirty representation of the blend. This feature doesn't affect printing at all—just the speed at which your screen redraws. Note that if you're using a 16-bit (thousands of colors) or 24-bit (millions of colors) monitor setting, this feature doesn't do anything.

COLOR DISPLAY
Make Your Pantones Display Right

If you're working with spot colors, you can change the color specifications (in the Edit Color dialog box) for any Pantone color to make it look better on screen or on a color printer. The color specifications have no effect when you print the color separations (spot overlays); they come out as black, as they should.

Be aware, though, that if you're relying on QuarkXPress to separate the Pantone swatch into process colors (if you have Process Separation turned on in the Edit Color dialog box for that color), there's a good chance that you'll screw it up (but we don't recommend separating Pantone colors like this anyway).

SPOT COLOR
Pantone Libraries

There's actually a good deal of controversy, amid official statements from Quark and claims from users, as to how accurate XPress's Pantone color libraries are and what they're good for.

Here's our two cents' worth:

▶ No color, from any program, anywhere, any time, at least in this universe, is going to perfectly match on screen what you'll see when it prints. Monitor calibration can help this, of course, and so can the proper lighting conditions (both for viewing your screen and your printed matter). But, due to the totally different natures of the color-reproduction technologies involved, you'll *never* get a perfect match.

▶ If you take a Pantone color and separate it, you won't, in the vast majority of cases, be able to get an exact or even near match of what the Pantone color looks like when printed as a spot color. Again, it's the nature of the beast. For confirming evidence, look at Pantone's Process Color Imaging Guide swatch book, which shows Pantone inks printed next to their process-color simulations. You'll see some good matches, some that are mediocre, and quite a few that are very poor.

All that having been said, XPress's ProSim library is designed to give you as good a reproduction as possible when printed as separations rather than as spot colors. Just be advised, again, that it won't be perfect.

EDITING COLOR
Switching Between Color Models

We include this tip with a caveat: it's fun and somewhat educational to play with color on the screen, but it often has very little relationship to what you get on final output.

Sometimes you get a color just the way you want it using the RGB mode in the Edit Color dialog box, except you want a slightly darker tone. At this point you can switch to the HSB model by selecting it from the popup menu, then simply lower the brightness level slightly. The same applies for any combination of models. For example, you can start with a Pantone color, then get the CMYK values for it by selecting CMYK from the popup menu, alter it, then translate to RGB for further changes. Every color model can be translated into the others.

FIND/CHANGE
Search and Replace Colors

Because QuarkXPress can merge colors—that is, you can replace one with another when you delete—you can search and replace all the colors in your document pretty quickly with a little workaround. However, instead of repeating the whole workaround here virtually word for word, just look back at the tips called "Replacing Style Sheets" in Chapter 5, *Copy Flow* and "Find and Change H&Js" in Chapter 4, *Type and Typography*. Everywhere it says "Style Sheet" or "H&J," mentally replace it with the word "Color." The tips work in just the same way.

LITTLE GEM
Color Tricks the Eye

Placing a colored object next to a differently colored object makes both colors look different from what each would if you just had one color alone (see Figure C in the color pages). In the same way, a color can look totally different if you place it on a black background rather than on a white one.

These facts should influence how you work in two ways. First, when you're selecting colors from a swatch book, isolate the colors from their neighbors. We like to do this by placing a piece of paper with a hole cut out of it in front of a color we're considering. Second, after you've created the colors you want to work with in your document, try them out with each other. You may find that you'll want to go back and edit them in order to create the effect you really want.

Editing 'Registration'

If you use the "Registration" color regularly, you might want to change its color so that you can tell it apart from normal "Black" on screen. You can use the Edit Color feature described earlier to change the onscreen color of "Registration" to anything you like. However, note that you can only use the color wheel to choose colors for "Registration". Also, because "Registration" is originally black, the Edit Color dialog box appears with the brightness scroll bar down to zero. Just raise the brightness to the level you want, and then change the color.

No matter what color you specify, objects with the color "Registration" always print on every plate. Changing the color changes nothing but the screen representation for that color. Use a color that is distinctly different from anything else in the document you're creating. That way you always know at a glance what's normal black stuff and what is colored "Registration".

A Rich Black

You can create a much richer black color by defining a separate black in your Colors palette which contains a bit of other process color in it. The standard rich black that many color strippers use is 100-percent black along with 40-percent cyan. You can get ambitious, though, and add 20 to 30 percent each of magenta and yellow, too. When a 100-percent black object overlaps multicolored objects, it can look inconsistent, due to density shifts in the ink. Adding color to your blacks solves the problem. (See Figure H in the color pages.)

This trick works not only for achieving richer black off a printing press, but also from a thermal color printer. However, if the thermal color printer is your final destination, you might boost the additional colors to between 50 and 100 percent each.

QuarkXPress has a nifty solution to a nasty problem with rich blacks. If you had an object knocking out this rich black, the slightest misalignment of the press could result in the process components of your rich black bleeding over the edge of the knockout, with predictably ugly results. QuarkXPress checks to see if an object is knocking out a rich black. If it is, it only spreads the object on the cyan, magenta and yellow plates of the rich black color, leaving the black plate alone.

You need this kind of help most when you're knocking out a white object (such as reversed text) from a rich black.

Trapping Rich-Black Boxes

As we noted in the last tip, rich black is often used to create a more even black, and XPress is somewhat intelligent in how it knocks type and other objects out of rich black. But if the press misregisters slightly, it's not just objects that knock out of the rich black that can look odd; it's the edge around the rich black, too.

Here's an easy way to trap the edge of a rich-black box.

1. Set Frames to Inside in the General Preferences dialog box (Command-Y).

2. Give the box a black frame equal to the trap you want (let's say one point).

3. In the Trap Information palette, set the Frame Inside to Knockout and the Frame Outside to Overprint.

Now, the inside half of the frame knocks out the nonblack colors of the background, and the outside half of the frame overprints whatever is behind the box (effectively trapping the box to its background).

Separating EPS and Duotone Spot Colors

To make sure QuarkXPress separates spot colors in EPS files you create, you must have a spot color defined within XPress with exactly the same name as the spot color in your EPS file. Whether or not the colors are actually defined identically is irrelevant. The same goes for the Pantone colors. If you use a Pantone color in your FreeHand or Illustrator file, make sure it's named the same as in your QuarkXPress file, and it'll print fine.

Many people create duotones or tritones in Photoshop, and then save them as EPS files before importing them into XPress

Getting Colors from Other Programs

It turns out that you don't have to create your colors within XPress. With version 3.3, you can just as easily import an entire color library from an illustration program such as Illustrator or FreeHand. Quark-XPress imports the colors and places them on the color list when you import an EPS file that uses them. The key is that the colors must be named colors in those programs. In Illustrator, you need to create the colors through the Custom Color item, or they don't come in as named colors (though the color specs come in just fine). Likewise, in FreeHand, only named spot colors (Custom or PMS) come across into XPress.

Only colors that are actually used in an EPS file are imported. If you just want to import the colors, but don't need the picture itself, you can make a few rectangles and apply the colors you want to those objects. Then save the page as an EPS file (with or without a preview). When you import the EPS into Quark-XPress, those colors are added to the color list. You can then delete the picture from the document, and the colors remain.

To Import or Not To Import

As we've said, XPress automatically appends any named colors you've used in an EPS graphic. However, unless you're really in control of the graphics you're importing, you may not want this palette update to happen. If not, hold down the Command key when you click OK in the Get Picture dialog box.

One note of caution: Since the name of the QuarkXPress color and the name of the color stored in the EPS file must match exactly, don't edit the name of an imported spot color. If you do, Quark-XPress won't be able to separate the renamed color onto the correct plate when you print separations.

(you have to save them as EPS files for duotones to work) If the duotone uses spot colors, such as Pantone colors, you have to make sure you've got the same-named color in your QuarkXPress document. People have had difficulty with this in the past because the two programs sometimes named their Pantone colors differently.

(A somewhat obscure example of this appeared when an acquaintance imported a duotone created with the American version of Photoshop into a Spanish version of QuarkXPress. XPress couldn't separate the black plate properly because XPress expected it to be called the Spanish word for black—"Negro".)

Fortunately, starting in version 3.3, XPress automatically imports the color names into your document when you import an EPS. Even though Photoshop's Pantone color names can be slightly different from QuarkXPress's (Photoshop's sometimes have an extra letter at the end of some the colors for uncoated or coated stock specification), XPress is smart enough to import them in the way it names them.

Also note that if your duotones are set to a spot color and a process color (like black), you have to adjust the halftone screen for the spot color (in the Edit Color dialog box) so that you don't end up with moiré patterns.

How to Make DCS Files

XPress can import and separate EPS files saved in the five-file Desktop Color Separation (DCS) format and the one-file DCS 2.0 format. The DCS format places a low-resolution (72-dpi) preview in a master file, and four higher-resolution process color images in their own files. DCS 2.0 typically merges those files together into one big file, plus it can include spot colors or varnish plates.

You can create DCS files from Photoshop in one of two ways: by saving as an EPS file (see Figure 7-1), or by using the Plate-Maker plug-in from In Software. PlateMaker has the added benefit of being able to save more than four process colors: it saves each alpha channel as a separate color. That means you can make well-registered six- or seven-color images, or add varnish plates to your job (see Figure 7-2). Remember that you have to already have converted to the CMYK mode to save in the DCS format.

You can also export a DCS file directly out of QuarkXPress (of an XPress document page) using Save Page as EPS. However, at

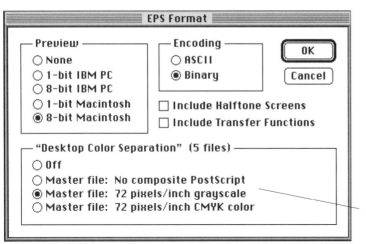

Figure 7-1
Photoshop's Save As EPS dialog box

Click one of these to create five DCS files

Figure 7-2
PlateMaker's export dialog box

least at the time of this writing, XPress 3.3 creates gigantic master files because it puts the entire image in both the master files and the process color files (so you get the same information twice), so it's a little less useful than if it created a low-resolution image in the master file.

PHOTOSHOP

Duotones

We really like the way Adobe Photoshop handles duotones (or tritones or quadtones). They're simple to make, they separate beautifully from QuarkXPress as EPS files (as long as you have the spot colors' names the same in both programs), and you can see what they look like in color. However, there's more than one way to spin a cat. Here's a way to make duotones right in XPress. The method relies on overprinting one TIFF image on another. We generally import a grayscale TIFF into a picture box, size it, and position it where we want it. Then we clone it (see "Cloning an Object," in Chapter 10, *Macros and Scripts*), change the color and

Quick and Dirty Duotones

Okay, we grant that a title like "Quick and Dirty Duotones" doesn't exactly make you want to rush out and try this one on anything too important. Nonetheless, we feel it's our duty to let you know about a method of creating duotones that might be perfect for you on a quick and dirty job. You can create a pseudo-duotone by placing a background tint in a box behind a grayscale TIFF (the TIFF can be colored, too). If the tint is in a separate box, you must remember to set the TIFF to overprint (see Figure D on the color pages).

the contrast curve for this second image, and make sure the background color of the overprinting image is set to "None". Last, we set the trap for the topmost picture box background to overprint in the Trap Information palette. (See Figure D in the color pages.)

Lithographers have all sorts of methods for creating duotones (they're the ones who traditionally made them). Some change the screen frequency of one plate. Others just change the contrast curve slightly. Ultimately, it's an aesthetic judgment that you'll just have to make yourself.

Overprinting Grayscale TIFFs

You may have noticed that XPress does some weird stuff to grayscale images when you import them into a colored box. When you import a grayscale TIFF, the program merges the picture with the background color. Let's say the picture box has a background color of "Red"; when you import a picture, all the whites of the image are turned to red, all the black areas are left as black, and everything in between is a mix of the two colors.

Unfortunately, when you print your separations, you find that the black areas actually knock out the colored areas. If your printer has perfect registration, this might not be a big problem. If you're a mere mortal, however, you'll find yourself with an ugly-looking image.

The problem is that you can't trap a picture to its own background because QuarkXPress no longer views the TIFF as separate from its background; rather, it sees it as part of the same object.

Here are a few possible alternatives.

▶ Place your grayscale image in a box with a background color of "None", and set the picture to overprint in the Trap Information palette. Then put a colored box behind the image. The grayscale image won't knock out of the colored box. This can be dangerous because of what XPress does to grayscale images with transparent backgrounds (it sometimes makes them very jaggy; see "More Transparent TIFFs" in Chapter 6, *Pictures*).

▶ Open the image in Photoshop and select Indexed Color or RGB from the Mode menu. Either way you're effectively making this an RGB color image (in Indexed Color mode, the image is the same size as the original grayscale; in RGB mode, it's three times as large). If you turn EfiColor on (it is on by default), the image gets separated into four process colors (not the result you want, we assure you). If you turn EfiColor off, the image appears on the black plate, which is how you'd want a grayscale image to appear (this happens with all RGB images, if EfiColor is turned off).

Now you can place it in a box with any background color and set the picture to Overprint in the Trap Information palette.

▶ Blend the two colors in Photoshop (perhaps in duotone mode) and save the file as either a duotone EPS or a CMYK TIFF (you'll need to save the file as a duotone EPS if you want to use a spot color such as "Red").

▶ See "Making the Background of EPS Files Transparent," in Chapter 6, *Pictures*.

TRAPPING

Default Trapping Information

There are many benefits to be gained from QuarkXPress's Trap Information palette. One particularly useful feature is the "reasons" QuarkXPress supplies for why it's applying a certain trap to an object, or part thereof.

Select the object, then click and hold down your mouse on the question-mark button in the Trap Information palette (see Figure 7-3). A balloon appears, explaining why a particular trap will be applied. These "reasons" are extremely terse, but can be a great help in understanding how QuarkXPress's traps work in general, and why particular objects and colors are being trapped in a certain way. Note that you'll only get the question mark button when Default trapping is specified.

TEXT

Trapping Text

You can use QuarkXPress's trapping (either color-pair trapping or the Trap Information palette) to apply spreads or chokes to

TRAPPING
Don't Forget to Click Trap

When you're defining traps for a color in the Trap Specifications dialog box, don't forget to click the Trap button after you enter a positive or negative trapping amount for a listed color. If you forget to do this before you click Save, the values you've entered will be lost. Forgetting this step has been the downfall of many a trapper.

TRAPPING
Don't Double Trap

If you are familiar with trapping using illustration programs such as FreeHand or Illustrator, you know that when you apply a trapping stroke to an object, your trap is really only one half of that thickness (the stroke falls equally inside and outside the path). But that's not true in QuarkXPress. If you're in the habit of entering two points when you want a one-point trap, break it when you use QuarkXPress. This program handles the conversion for you.

Figure 7-3
The Trap Information palette and
its popup information balloons

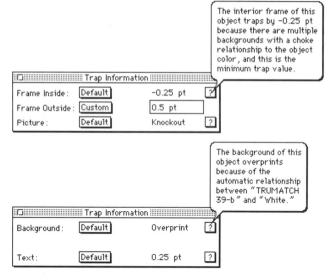

> The interior frame of this object traps by -0.25 pt because there are multiple backgrounds with a choke relationship to the object color, and this is the minimum trap value.

Trap Information			
Frame Inside:	Default	-0.25 pt	?
Frame Outside:	Custom	0.5 pt	
Picture:	Default	Knockout	?

> The background of this object overprints because of the automatic relationship between "TRUMATCH 39-b" and "White."

Trap Information			
Background:	Default	Overprint	?
Text:	Default	0.25 pt	?

colored text, but XPress can only think of the type as being completely surrounded by a single background color. Even if different parts of the text are over different colors, XPress traps all the text the same way.

Of course, trapping type is quite slow anyway. Printing a whole page of trapped type could take tens of minutes. Clearly, if you need to trap a lot of text, you'll have to take the performance hit. Otherwise, try to turn trapping off for nonessential text.

Note that whenever you have text that is set against an indeterminate background, it cannot be choked; you must knock the type out, spread it, or overprint it.

Trapping Small Type

You can run into trouble when you're trapping small type, especially serif type. Since the type is so fine—especially the serifs—even a small amount of trapping can clog it up. The counters can fill in, and the serifs can get clunky (see Figure 7-4). Bear this in mind when you're setting up your trapping preferences, and when you're specifying colors for type—and, for that matter, when you're specifying what fonts to use when they're going to get trapped.

Monsieur de Bergerac

Monsieur de Bergerac

Figure 7-4
Serif type can clog up and the serifs
can get clunky when trapped

Trapping and Stretching Photos

If your picture box has a border (also called a frame, even if it's just a rule), you can specify Frame Inside and Frame Outside trapping. The Frame Inside trap affects how the frame traps to the picture contents; a positive trap value here will spread the frame (thereby increasing its thickness) over the picture, whereas a negative value here will spread the picture (by up to one half the frame's thickness) without affecting the frame thickness. Of course, most frames are black and are therefore set to overprint. Therefore, half the frame overprints the background and half the frame overprints the image.

You probably know that if you place an image in a picture box and press Command-Option-Shift-F, the image is resized to fit into the box while retaining its aspect ratio. But what you may not know is that XPress takes the trapping value into consideration when stretching the image.

When you resize the image to fit the box, it only goes as far as the trap setting. If the frame is set to overprint, the image is stretched to halfway through the frame. If the frame is set to spread or knock out the image, then the picture only gets stretched to the border of the frame. Then if you make the frame width narrower, you may find a white edge around the image.

Trapping Small Stuff

Note that the engineers at Quark made some hidden allowances for particular trapping situations. One of these has to do with small type and objects. QuarkXPress tries to preserve the shape of small objects (defined as text at 24 points or less, and objects of 10 points or smaller in height or width) when trapping by not allowing spreads or chokes when the object's shape would be compromised.

The program compares the darkness of the object on each plate to the darkness of its background, and spreads only if that plate is less than or equal to half the darkness of its background; choking will occur only when the background plate component is less than or equal to half the darkness of the object. If this sounds confusing, just forget it; you hardly have to think about it; QuarkXPress does it automatically.

Trapping Frames

The Trap Information palette lets you set inside and outside trapping values for picture and text box frames, but only if you use one of the first seven frames in the Frames dialog box. These are object-oriented frames, not the bitmaps QuarkXPress uses for some of its fancier custom frames (the newer versions of XPress don't include these anymore). If you're using a bitmap frame, your only options are to either overprint or knock out the frame, regardless of what colors may be surrounding it.

Use Big Traps

An easy way to make sure your traps are working correctly is temporarily to set extremely large values for your color and object traps: anywhere from three to 10 points. Print your separations on transparencies or thin paper, align each plate, and you can quickly determine how well XPress is handling your trapping requests.

Another good way to check trapping is to use the enlargement feature in the Page Setup dialog box to magnify the trap area (see "Printer as Magnifying Glass" in Chapter 8, *Printing*). Don't forget to reset the traps to their normal values before your final imagesetting, though!

Note that if you apply a multiple-line frame, the spaces between the lines are *always* white if the runaround for the box is set to Item; they'll knock out of *every* plate. If the runaround is None, whatever is behind the box prints between the lines.

Trapping Imported Graphics

QuarkXPress only applies trapping to objects created within the program itself. It can't trap elements in imported graphics.

To ensure that elements of object-oriented EPS files trap correctly, you must manually create the trapping in Aldus FreeHand or Adobe Illustrator (or whatever your graphics program may be) by modifying the overprint and color settings for strokes applied to paths and objects. XPress honors any overprint settings in imported EPS files, so if you've specified a line to overprint in FreeHand or Illustrator, that line overprints whatever's behind it in XPress. Otherwise it knocks out.

You can apply a QuarkXPress color to imported Paint, black-and-white and grayscale TIFFs, and black-and-white and grayscale bitmapped PICTs. You can then specify that these colored elements overprint or knock out behind them, either by defining the traps for the color you apply, or by using the Trap Information palette to define a knockout or overprint for a given picture box. (See "Overprinting Grayscale TIFFs," above.)

Just (Don't) Trap

Trapping is as much art as science—in fact, if you look up "difficult" in the dictionary, it offers the synonym: "trapping." We often don't have time to mess around to make sure our traps are proper throughout a document, and sometimes even if we have time, it'd just be too much of a hassle.

QuarkXPress's trapping is pretty good, all in all, but it's lacking in some important areas, such as blends, choking type, and partially overlapped objects. Ultimately, QuarkXPress isn't designed to be a great trapper. If you want to spare yourself a lot of hassle, you can turn auto trapping off (see "Turning Off Auto Trapping," below), and use a program like Aldus TrapWise.

You may not want to buy TrapWise yourself (it costs several thousand dollars), but your service bureau probably already has it. Find out how much it costs for them to trap the page for you, and then compare that with how much it's worth to you not to worry about it anymore. (Especially because if they trap it and make a mistake, they pay for their mistake.)

PREFERENCES

White Is a Color, Too

In QuarkXPress 3.0, an object that is positioned partially over another object and partially on the white page is considered over an "indeterminate" color. This has screwed up more people than we can count. However, in later versions, the Ignore White feature in the Application Preferences dialog box (under the Edit menu) makes QuarkXPress ignore the white page, so the object traps based on the background object alone (see Figure 7-5).

OVERPRINTING

Overprinting Tints

If you want a tint to overprint, but the overprint limit is getting in your way, try creating a color that is the tint you want. For example, if you want a 40-percent cyan tint to overprint another color, create a process color built of just 40-percent cyan. When you apply 100 percent of this color, you get a 40-percent cyan that overprints.

DROP SHADOWS

Trapping Shadow Boxes

Drop shadows, while overused in today's designs, can look really cool. One way to create a drop shadow is to duplicate a box, place it behind the first box, and give it a background color. However, if the shadow box is over a tint or an image, the shadow can look really awful because you can't see through the shadow (see Figure G on the color pages).

TRAPPING

Turning Off Auto Trapping

Depending on your page design, trapping can occasionally cause problems or slowdowns at print time. You can turn it off entirely, however, by setting the Auto and Indeterminate trapping values to zero in the Trap Preferences dialog box. If you're having strange slowdowns at print time and are working with colored type on colored backgrounds, you might try this. Of course, you also won't get any trapping, which causes its own problems.

Figure 7-5
Ignore White

When Ignore White is turned on, the trap value for this circle is determined by its relationship to the box, rather than "Indeterminate".

To Overprint or Not To Overprint

Sometimes people get confused when a color they've specifically set up to overprint in the Trap Specifications dialog box doesn't overprint at all. Even when they check the Trap Information palette (always the first place to look for your trapping questions), they see that it's not overprinting.

Often, they've simply forgotten that XPress only overprints a color when it's above the overprint limit (in the Trapping Preferences dialog box). Usually the overprint limit is set to 95 percent, so any color tinted below 95 percent won't overprint automatically. You can change this limit's value, or select the object and tell it to overprint (override the Default setting) in the Trap Information palette.

If you're working in color, you can partially avoid this problem by overprinting the shadow box on whatever is behind it. Just select the box and set the background trap to Overprint in the Trap Information palette. Note that if the box has a frame, you can't overprint it (but why would you want a frame on a shadow box?). (Also, see "Creating a Drop Shadow over an Image" in Chapter 11, *XTensions*, for another interesting way to make shaded drop shadows.)

Centering a Frame on a Box's Edge

If you've chafed at being forced to draw frames inside or outside of a box, when you really want the frame centered, half inside and half outside of the box's perimeter, try this trick.

1. Create a frame on the inside of the box, with a width of one-half of what you'd eventually like the frame to be.

2. Go to the Trap Information palette, and set a custom spread for the frame outside the box, also equal to half your ultimate desired frame width.

3. Set a runaround for the box to be at least equal to the spread you specified, so you won't have text getting covered up by the frame.

So if you set a half-point frame inside a box, with a half-point spread outside, you'll end up with a one point frame centered along the edge of the box. QuarkXPress won't display the frame's spread, or consider it in determining the coordinates or measurements for the box, or in aligning it to page guides or other objects. Also note that because traps only print when you do color separations, you won't be able to see the full frame on screen or on nonseparated output.

Creating Masks

Okay, if the truth be told, we don't do everything via the desktop. Sometimes, even though we know we shouldn't, we actually send pictures off to be stripped in at the printer. However, to make up for it, we give the strippers perfect-sized masks that they can drop images into (see Figure 7-6).

The easiest way to make these masks is to create a spot color (call it whatever you like; we usually use MaskColor) and fill the picture box with it. The film that you get from the color separation is in register with the rest of your page, so the printer can quickly burn the plates properly.

If you have a frame around the picture, life is only slightly more complicated because you have to set up the trap. To do this we usually set Frame Inside in the Trap Information palette to Overprint. Then, when you print your separations, the frame traps perfectly with the mask.

Note that you should check with your printer before you go through the trouble of creating and imagesetting these additional masks; some printers—especially those outside of North America—can't use them because they require film positives rather than negatives.

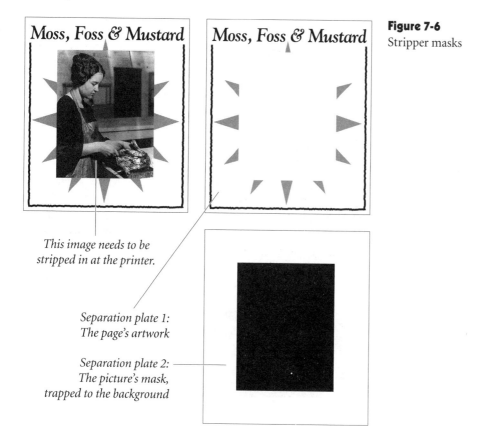

Figure 7-6
Stripper masks

This image needs to be stripped in at the printer.

Separation plate 1:
The page's artwork

Separation plate 2:
The picture's mask,
trapped to the background

Outlining Type

If you've ever set text in the Outline type style, you've probably figured out that it's useless because there's no way to specify how thick the outlines are. Here's a pretty kludgy workaround for getting better outlines (see Figure 7-7 and Figure J in the color pages).

Figure 7-7
Outlined type

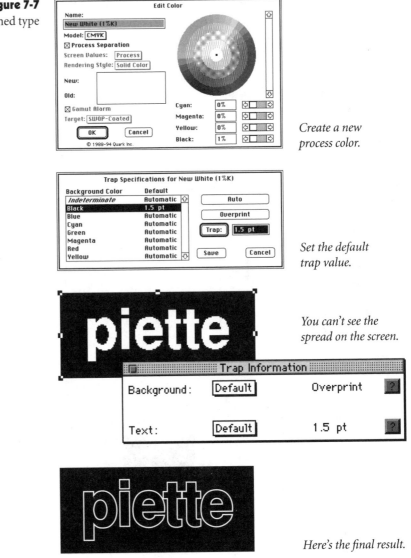

Create a new process color.

Set the default trap value.

You can't see the spread on the screen.

Here's the final result.

1. Create a new process color that's set to one-percent black.

2. In the Edit Trap dialog box, set the color to spread two points over black.

3. Apply this new color to your type.

4. Clone the text box (Step and Repeat with offsets set to zero) and change the new text to "Black" and the background color and runaround to None. In the Trap Information palette, make sure this text is knocking out or overprinting what's beneath it.

5. Turn Process Trap off in the Trap Preferences dialog box.

When you print, turn Separations on, even if you're only going to print the black plate. Because your new color is set to spread, the one-percent black (which is almost white) spreads over the background black.

If you change the background color, you have to change the foreground color, too. For instance, if you're printing on top of a colored tint box (say, 100-percent cyan and 40-percent magenta), your new color should reflect those colors (in this example, they should be one-percent cyan and one-percent magenta).

Of course, if your printer is so good that they can hold a one-percent dot, then you won't be getting a truly white outline. Oh well. In that case, do it the way you've always done it: use Illustrator or FreeHand, convert the text to paths, and spec your strokes explicitly.

Figure 7-8
Spreading reversed text

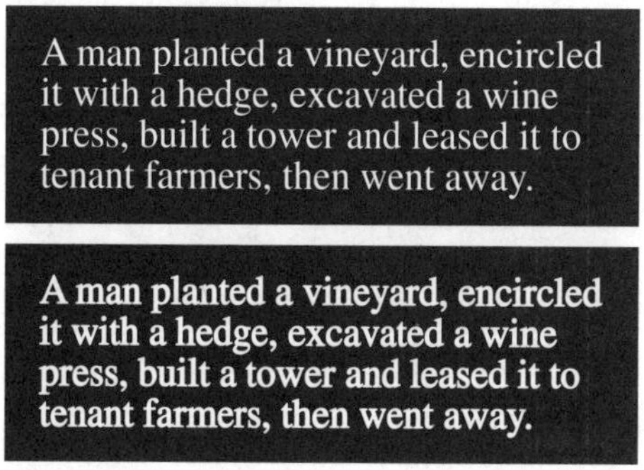

A man planted a vineyard, encircled it with a hedge, excavated a wine press, built a tower and leased it to tenant farmers, then went away.

A man planted a vineyard, encircled it with a hedge, excavated a wine press, built a tower and leased it to tenant farmers, then went away.

This text has a spreading trap value applied to it.

TEXT EFFECTS

Thicker Reversed Text

One of the problems with reversing text (like white text on a colored background) is that it often gets clogged up by the background ink spreading slightly. And even if it doesn't get literally choked, our eye perceives it as being choked.

One way around this is to spread the type's color slightly (see Figure 7-8 and Figure K in the color pages). Use the method in the last tip to create a white color with a spread value. In this case, however, you need to set the spread to a much smaller value—such as a quarter of a point.

QuickDraw Printers

If you're using a QuickDraw (rather than PostScript) printer, you can still specify an EfiColor profile. Once you've selected a QuickDraw printer in the Chooser, you can access an abbreviated Page Setup dialog box. Turn color printing on with the radio buttons, and select the EfiColor Profile you want from the EfiColor Profile popup menu. If the profile reference card for your printer profile has instructions for Special (or Printer) effects, make sure to apply them in this dialog box before proceeding with printing. Also, you'll get more accurate color if you use the inks and papers specified on the printer's profile reference card.

Don't Remove the XTension

With most XTensions, if you don't want to use what they have to offer, you can just delete them or, better yet, move them into another folder so that QuarkXPress can't "see" them. However, you shouldn't do this with the EfiColor XTension. That's because Quark actually uses part of the XTension to make preview images for pictures on your screen. So if you don't want EfiColor to function, don't move the XTension; just turn it off in the EfiColor Preferences dialog box. By the way, Quark-XPress still functions fine if you *do* move the XTension. It's just that it functions even better when the XTension is around.

Blending with Spot Colors

We were all *so* excited when XPress was first able to create blends in the background of text and picture boxes. Even better was the fact that the blends would print out properly, even if the colors were spot colors. However, as some people have noticed, they don't always appear in print exactly as we envision them in our minds.

For instance, if you make a blend from 100-percent magenta to 100-percent black, you would think you'd get a nice even blend between the two colors. But when you print separations and throw them on a printing press, you may find a big gray band right in the middle of the blend (see Figure O in the color pages).

Instead, try blending from 100 percent of magenta to a rich black (in this case 100-percent black plus 100-percent magenta). That way, the magenta simply appears to become darker and darker throughout the blend.

Blends in Illustrator

There are two ways to build a blend in Adobe Illustrator or Aldus FreeHand. First, you can use the graduated fill feature, specifying the angle and colors of a blend within a particular object. Or, you can blend two objects together (this is how all blends were done in Illustrator until version 5.0). In this second scenario, the program creates a blend as a series of grouped objects. This isn't a problem, but it *does* have some side effects, at least when using Illustrator.

Let's say you blend two objects; one is "Green" (a custom spot color) and the other is "White". Illustrator colors every intermediate step as a process color rather than a tint of the spot color "Green". While this technically makes some sense (if you think like an engineer), it's almost never what you'd expect nor want.

You can check this out yourself by making a blend like this in Illustrator and looking at one object in the blend (you'll have to ungroup the steps in the center and select just one of them). Then check the Paint settings and you'll see that it's a process mix of black, cyan, magenta, and yellow. When you try to separate this image from QuarkXPress, you get white on one end, the spot color on the other end, and a bunch of process colors in between.

Instead, to make a real spot-color blend, you need to have both ends of the blend be tints of the spot color. For instance, you could blend from 100-percent "Green" (or whatever spot color you're using) to one-percent or even .1-percent "Green". If you create a blend this way and look at the intermediate elements, you'll see that they are all tints of the PMS custom color.

EFICOLOR
Pre-EfiColor Documents

It's easy to take advantage of EfiColor's capabilities in a document created by previous versions of QuarkXPress. When you open an old document, the EfiColor XTension may be turned off. Go to the EfiColor Preferences dialog box and turn it on. Once EfiColor's on, and you've chosen appropriate profiles for the colors in your document, EfiColor converts the document's colors when you print. If you're not happy with the results, and would rather have the colors print as they did in previous versions of QuarkXPress, simply turn EfiColor off in the EfiColor Preferences dialog box.

EFICOLOR
Converting Pantone Colors

A funny thing happens if you convert a Pantone color to RGB and then try to print it using EfiColor: you get a different color. Now theoretically, this shouldn't happen. However, because of the way that EfiColor "sees" Pantone colors, you get a more accurate Pantone color by leaving it in Pantone mode (you *can* change the name if you want) rather than converting it to RGB or CMYK.

EFICOLOR
Turn Off Calibrated Output

If you're using the EfiColor XTension, we recommend that you turn off Calibrated Output in the Print dialog box. Some people use the calibrated output feature to adjust for dot gain, but the way that QuarkXPress handles it just isn't as powerful as other calibration software such as the Precision Imagesetter Linearization Software from Kodak. Whatever the case, if you leave Calibrated Output checked, then it may further adjust your color correction, messing up what the EfiColor XTension is trying to do.

EFICOLOR
Moving Profiles

EfiColor profiles are little pieces of software. And, like most pieces of software, they're copyrighted. Like fonts, you're not really supposed to copy them from one machine to another; you're supposed to buy a profile for each machine you use. However, EFI is being somewhat generous: they're encouraging people to freely pass around monitor and scanner profiles. But restraint is the name of the game when it comes to output-device profiles.

While this isn't supposed to be a commercial plug, EFI really makes its money through sales such as these, and we shouldn't begrudge them that. If you need a profile, call them (their number is in Appendix B, *Resources*) and order one. Plus, EfiColor Works includes a large set of output profiles, for a variety of color-proofing and printing methods.

printing 8

There's only so much fussing and fretting you can do over your XPress documents before you have to batten down the hatches and print those puppies out. After all, that's what desktop publishing is all about: getting the image on your screen onto paper or film. But it's rarely as easy as clicking OK in the Print dialog box. That's why we've compiled a mess o' tips here to make the process as easy and efficient as possible.

DRIVERS

Printer Driver Jamboree

The printer driver is a piece of system software that acts like a translator between your application and your printer; your application tells the driver what the page looks like, and the driver tells the printer. Because Apple and Adobe have revised their Laser-Writer drivers several times, if you're having printing problems, it's important to know your driver version to troubleshoot.

There are two fast ways to figure out what printer driver you're using on the Macintosh. First, you can go to the Environment dialog box in XPress (see "Your Environment" in Chapter 9, *Problems and Solutions*). Or, you can open either the Print or Page Setup dialog box. The number in the upper-right corner (near the OK button) is the version of the driver.

Or, if you'd prefer to waste some time, you can take the slow road to the printer driver's version number: select the driver in the Extensions folder (in the System Folder) and choose Get Info from the File menu (or press Command-I). Don't just look at the driver's name; the LaserWriter 8.1.1 and 8.1.2 drivers both are named LaserWriter 8. (You can rename them for clarity, though, and that new name shows up in the Chooser the next time you open it.)

Quick Tips for Speedy Printing

Here are some handy tips for optimizing printing speeds. Before you rip your network and workgroup procedures apart to follow these tips, though, you should consider whether the gains in print speeds, which may be modest in many cases, are worth completely overturning the ways most workgroups use networking and file servers. (Some of these tips are mutually exclusive. Our intention is not for you to use them all, but for you to look them over and perhaps pick up some good ideas.)

▶ Use a dedicated, fast Mac (even a Power Mac) for printing and nothing but printing. Remove any hardware and software from the Mac that's not necessary for printing. Bells and whistles like menu clocks can be entertaining, but steal processing cycles that could be better used in printing your document.

▶ Connect your dedicated Mac directly to your printer, and with no other machines on the network. Use removable cartridges to bring jobs to the dedicated printing Mac.

▶ Use Ethernet. It has 40 times the bandwidth—that is, it's *much* faster—than AppleTalk.

▶ If you're on a network, store EPS and TIFF files for a document on the machine you're working on, not on a file server. Storing images on a server slows down printing, as your copy of QuarkXPress must use the network to alternately read the graphics files and send information to the printer. When files are stored locally, QuarkXPress can read the files and send information to the printer over the network almost simultaneously.

▶ Scan grayscale and color images at no more than twice your final output screen frequency (you can almost always use a lower resolution—down to 1.5 times your frequency). If you're printing to a 300-dpi laser printer, and you know you won't print at a halftone frequency higher than 53 lpi, scanning at anything over 106 spi (samples per inch) is a waste, because the PostScript interpreter in your printer will have to spend time processing the excess data. If the file is saved as a TIFF, XPress automatically downsamples the image to two times the screen frequency anyway, but this takes extra time—and on an imagesetter, time is money.

▶ Similarly, scan your line art at a resolution no greater than your printer's maximum resolution. Any excess information wastes processing time. Of course, you need to scan at a higher resolution if you want to enlarge the image, because the resolution drops when you increase the size.

SPOOLING

Cheap Print Spooler

If you've got a machine that you're using as a server, or if someone on the network has a machine they're not using all of the time, you can turn it into a spooler with little fuss.

1. Choose a LaserWriter driver in the Chooser on the spooler machine. This should be the same driver as you're using (LaserWriter 8.1.2 is the best bet at the time of this writing).

2. Make sure Background Printing is turned on (click the On button in the Chooser with the proper driver selected on the left).

3. Open the System Folder on the spooler machine. Make an alias of the folder called "PrintMonitor Documents" (select the folder and choose Make Alias from the File menu).

4. Start file sharing on the spooler machine (from the Sharing Setup control panel), and then share the hard drive or the System Folder (select either one and then the Sharing item under the File menu).

5. Use AppleShare in the Chooser on your own machine to connect to the spooler machine.

SPEED

Speeding Up Image Output

Even on the fastest machines over the fastest networks, color images take a really long time to output. You can speed this process up by using systems that don't store the full, high-resolution image on your local hard drive, but store it instead on a server that you spool your files to.

There are a few different technologies that allow for this image-replacement stuff: OPI (Open Prepress Interface), DCS (Desktop Color Separations), and VIM (Varityper Image Management) are three of the most widely used. These systems work in one of two ways: they either look for a high-resolution image with the same file name at print time or they let you link to a high-res image manually.

6. Select the same LaserWriter driver on your machine in the Chooser, and make sure Background Printing is set to On.

7. Move the "PrintMonitor Documents" folder in your System Folder to a safe location (you may want to swap it back later). Drag the "PrintMonitor Documents alias" folder into your System Folder and rename it to "PrintMonitor Documents", exactly like the original.

When you print from your machine, your spooled documents will automatically be written to the spooler computer. It takes a little time, but not nearly as long as you'd think. Note that if you haven't mounted the server via AppleShare when you print, you'll get a dialog box that lets you do so the first time in a session that you try.

There's two caveats to this tip. First, you have to be sure the fonts you need are either resident on the laser printer or are loaded on the spooler computer. Second, this technique often goes berserk (strange spacing, odd symbols, etc.) when you print multiple collated or uncollated copies by typing a number into the Copies field of the Print dialog box.

SPOOLING

Background Printing

Turning on Background Printing in the Chooser (it's on by default when you install the drivers) means your document is printed in the so-called background while you do other work. But what's *really* going on? The pages get printed to disk first as a "spool document," and saved in a folder called "PrintMonitor Documents" in your System Folder (which means you better have enough room on your startup disk for it). Then, an application called PrintMonitor—which lives in your Extensions folder in your System Folder—takes over and prints the file for you in the background.

PrintMonitor has a RAM allocation just like any other application—except that it comes with a very small amount of RAM allocated as the default. PrintMonitor is almost clever enough to deal with this for you. If it discovers that it doesn't have enough memory to print a job, it will halt the spooled file and prompt you. The dialog box offers you the choice of canceling the job (bad), or "adjusting" the memory size upwards for PrintMonitor (a permanent change) and trying to print again.

It only makes these adjustments in small leaps, though, so if you're going to use background printing with XPress, we suggest you raise this value yourself.

1. Find your PrintMonitor application in the Extensions folder in the System Folder.

2. Select the application and choose Get Info from the File menu.

3. Raise that pitiful 80K to at least 150 or 200K; we've even raised it as high as 1,000K when it seemed to need it.

4. Close the Get Info window.

BITMAPPED IMAGES
Maintaining Resolution

When you print a document that includes TIFF images, Quark-XPress may downsample the image data behind the scenes. The program figures that you'll never need more resolution in your images than two times the halftone screen frequency or the resolution of the printer (as noted in the Page Setup dialog box), so it cuts off the data at that point.

If you have a 200-dpi image reduced to 50 percent on your page (which makes it a 400-dpi image because the same information is being crammed into half the space), and you're printing at an 80-lpi screen frequency, QuarkXPress chops off the image resolution at 160 dpi (two times the frequency). Typically, that's okay. In fact, it's great if you're proofing high-resolution images on a laser printer. However, every now and again, this feature can jump up and bite you.

For example, if you reduce an image considerably in a picture box, you can sometimes get mottling or jaggy artifacts from the downsampling (see Figure N in the color pages). Or, if you're purposely printing at a very low screen frequency because your color printer requires it (some do), your images may look really weird because QuarkXPress has downsampled them so much.

Fortunately, Quark has provided a workaround, even if it is a klunky one. Part of the Bobzilla XTension is a feature called Full Resolution TIFF. If you select a picture box and turn this on (by selecting it from the Item menu; it has a checkmark when turned

PAGE SETUP
Save the RC Trees

When you're printing onto a roll-fed imagesetter (more on these later), you can save film or paper by printing your letter-size pages landscape rather than portrait. That way you only use around 8.5 inches on the roll rather than 11. It may not seem like a great difference, but those two and a half inches really add up when you're printing a long document. For example, on a 100-page file you'll save an average of 250 inches of film or paper.

Printing the pages landscape also makes it easy to cut them apart and stack them (saving materials is also great for the environment). Check with your service bureau to see if they'll give you a discount for the materials, time, and energy you've saved them.

on), QuarkXPress won't downsample that image at print time. Unfortunately, you have to do this for each picture individually rather than set it for the whole document at once.

Here's another example: let's say you import a 300-dpi line-art (black-and-white) TIFF image and scale it down to a third of the size (the resolution goes up to 900 dpi). When you print to a 300- or 600-dpi laser printer, XPress throws out the extra data. We haven't seen any problems due to this, though. (Note that Full Resolution TIFF doesn't stop the downsample of line-art images.)

This effect (and the Full Resolution TIFF solution) only affects TIFF images. EPS pictures don't get downsampled because QuarkXPress can't touch the data that's encapsulated in them.

PRINT DIALOG BOX
Print Status

Back in versions 3.0 and 3.1 you had to hold down the Shift key while clicking OK in the Print dialog box to display the Print Status dialog box when you're printing. In version 3.2, they reversed the way it works; QuarkXPress not only tells you what page it's printing, but also what color plate, tile, and EPS or TIFF images it's working on (see Figure 8-1). However, if you ever tire of watching Print Status scroll by, you can turn it off by holding down the Shift key while clicking OK in the Print dialog box.

Figure 8-1
Print Status dialog box

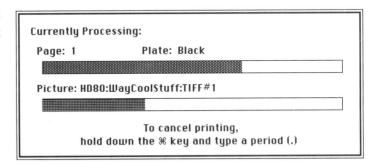

No program can know how long a page will take to print on a PostScript printer, so there's no way to show how much longer the print job will take (see "Estimating Printing Time Accurately" in Chapter 11, *XTensions*). Instead, the status bar in the Print Status dialog box only displays the percentage of pages that have been printed (for example, if you have two pages in your document, the status bar is 50-percent full after the first page, even if the second page takes 10 times longer than the first one to print). Nonetheless, we think there's some comfort in watching the Print Status dialog box while we're waiting for those long jobs to print—especially since we can watch the progress of the individual graphics.

If you're using LaserWriter 8, the Status Bar is kind of useless because it shows you the progress of the file spooling to your hard drive, not the progress of printing.

PAGE SETUP

Switching Printer Types

If you are creating a document on a machine with one type of printer attached to it and printing to a different printer for final output, make sure that you create your document with a printer driver compatible with the final output device. For example, if you are proofing on a Hewlett-Packard DeskJet and will later print to a Linotronic imagesetter, create your entire document with a Laser-Writer driver selected in the Chooser (you don't actually have to own the laser printer or have it on hand to use its driver). Then, when you want to print your document, switch to the DeskJet driver, and don't change your Page Setup dialog box settings.

Call it superstition, or what you like, but this approach has taken care of some major printing problems in the past for us. Note that when you're switching among printer drivers in the Chooser, you can press Tab to move between the various windows, and you can type a few letters of a driver or printer's name to select it (see Figure 8-2).

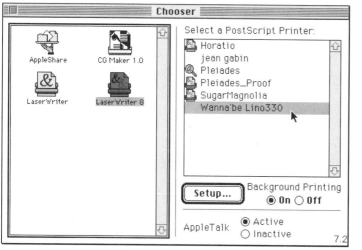

Figure 8-2
The Chooser

ImageWriter Tip

This is an obscure one, all right: To invoke bidirectional printing on the ImageWriter II, hold down Option-Command-Caps Lock when you click OK in the Print dialog box. However, if you actually use an ImageWriter, you've got more troubles than just this!

PAGE SETUP

Is it a PPD or a PDF?

QuarkXPress 3.3 can now recognize and use PPD (PostScript Printer Description) files. As one colleague commented, "That's nice of them to make a concession to reality." True enough, PPDs are the standard way to describe printers to software in the industry. PDFs (Printer Description Files), on the other hand, are how QuarkXPress has always gotten information about what sort of device it's printing to.

PPDs are nested three levels deep in the Printer Descriptions folder in the Extensions folder in the System Folder. You can "disable" a PPD (stop it from showing up in the LaserWriter 8 Set Up dialog box, in Quark's Page Setup, and in other places) by removing it from this folder and placing it outside the System Folder. You can install PPDs by dragging them into this folder. (PDFs, on the other hand, since they're only used by XPress, are always found in the XPress folder; starting in version 3.3, they're nested inside the PDF folder.)

Now that you can use both, though, they sometimes get mixed up (or at least we do) in the Page Setup dialog box. We learned that if you hold down the Shift key when you click on the Printer Types popup menu, XPress displays all the PPD files in italic. PDFs are in roman. Why they didn't make this the default, we'll never know.

PAGE SETUP

Check That Screen Frequency!

The Page Setup dialog box lets you specify the halftone screen frequency QuarkXPress uses for every tint in your document (except for those graphic images which you have set using the Other Screen features, and EPS graphics that have their screens specified internally). You should note that when you create a new document, the screen frequency may be automatically set to the last frequency value someone entered for a document on that copy of QuarkXPress. It's always a good idea to check the Page Setup dialog box, just to make sure you're getting a proper halftone screen.

A Great Screen for 300-dpi Printers

A couple of caveats to this tip, before we really get to it: this is helpful primarily if you're printing proofs which won't be reproduced, and if you don't need a wide spectrum of gray values in your output (in other words: don't use this for scanned images or graduated blends). That said, we think a great screen frequency to use for printing to a 300-dpi printer is 106 lpi. Go ahead and try it. We think you'll like the tone of the gray. Be aware, however, that tints and images printed with this technique may clog up in the reproduction process.

New PDF for Fiery RIP

If you have a Fiery RIP or another RIP designed for color printers such as the Canon Laser Copier, you should make sure you have the correct printer description file (PDF) for it. For instance, Quark released a PDF for the Fiery in July 1993 that fixed a load of problems people were having with blends and scanned images. We've included some of these PDF files on the disc in the back of the book. If the one you need isn't there, though, it can probably be downloaded from CompuServe, America Online, e•World, or AppleLink.

Choosing Print Colors as Gray

When you print 100-percent yellow to a black-and-white laser printer, you get 100-percent black. If you print 100-percent cyan, you also get 100-percent black. This isn't very helpful if you have both colors on the same page! Instead, try turning on Print Colors as Gray in the Print dialog box. This way, different colors are converted to different gray values. The gray values attempt to emulate the color-darkness values of the various colors, so 100-percent red prints darker than 100-percent yellow.

Color and the Printer Type

If you choose a black-and-white printer (like a LaserWriter or any other standard laser printer) in the Page Setup dialog box and then print to a color printer (like a QMS ColorScript), you still only get black-and-white output. This is because the PDF actually indicates to XPress, among other things, whether the printer supports color output. If it doesn't support color, XPress doesn't send color.

Note that this doesn't affect the ability to do separations, since printing separations is only black-and-white printing anyway (so it can be done on any printer).

Also, remember that to print in color, you need to click the Color/Grayscale button in the Print dialog box (in the LaserWriter 8 driver, you have to click Options in the Print dialog box to set this); otherwise your pages output in black and white.

BLENDS

Smooth Transitions

Blends can look awful on each piece of separation film, yet look perfect when the job is printed. In other words, if your calculations indicate that you have plenty of steps in your blend and that each step is small enough (under .03 inches), you really should be okay; what you're seeing on the negatives is just a function of the separation of the colors.

There are two caveats you need to be aware of.

▶ Print Colors as Grays only affects colors that are defined and applied within QuarkXPress, not colors belonging to imported graphics.

▶ This only works for black-and-white printers; using a PDF for a color printer overrides the setting, ensuring that color is sent.

PRINT DIALOG BOX

When Printing as Gray

Have you ever printed out a color piece in black and white (with Print Colors as Grays checked in the Print dialog box), handed it to a client, and tried desperately to explain, "this shade of gray is red, and that's sort of a PMS 286, and this one is . . . "? After 30 seconds, everyone in the room is confused. Instead, you might try adding a sample swatch of each color in the margin of each page for comparison (see Figure 8-3).

Figure 8-3
Printing color swatches on the page

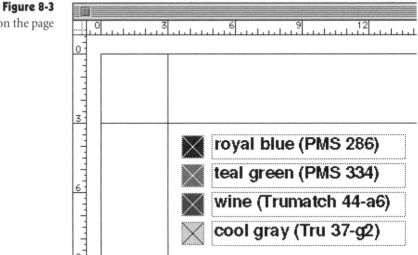

The other problem that happens is when the substitute gray levels for two or more colors are too similar (a light blue and a bright yellow may look exactly the same when you print them out in gray form). In this predicament, we'll sometimes save the document and go in and change the color specs for the offending colors—making them look totally wrong on the screen, but giving them enough contrast so that they'll print better in black and white on our laser printer. Then, after printing, we select Revert from the File menu and we're back at square one.

Avoid Unlimited Downloadable Fonts

Normally, QuarkXPress automatically downloads to the printer all the fonts it needs for a job as it needs them. If the printer runs out of memory, you get a PostScript error telling you that you can't print the job.

If you have the Unlimited Downloadable Fonts in a Document feature enabled in the LaserWriter 8 Page Setup Options dialog box, QuarkXPress downloads the font when it needs it, then flushes it out of printer memory when it needs to download the next font—so that there's only one font in printer memory at any one time. The next time the document needs the font, Quark-XPress downloads it again. The problem is, that might be 10 times on a single page, making your job print very slowly. So, while you gain the ability to print as many fonts as you want, you pay a hefty price in printing time.

And remember that the driver does the same thing when you're printing PostScript to disk; if you have Unlimited Downloadable Fonts checked, it inserts the fonts into the PostScript dump multiple times.

EPS Files and Unlimited Downloadable Fonts

EPS files that contain downloadable fonts (typefaces that require outline fonts to print correctly) print incorrectly when you import them into QuarkXPress and then print with Unlimited Downloadable Fonts turned on (in the Page Setup Options dialog box). The result? Courier is substituted for all the downloadable fonts but the last one.

The reason is that Unlimited Downloadable Fonts allows only one font to exist in the printer's memory at a time. Yet the EPS file

Printing XPress Blends

While most people still use QuarkXPress's blends feature successfully, we still hear from people who can't get them to print right. If you're in this bag, here are a couple of quick suggestions.

First, some printers just don't support XPress's blends properly, although the situation is improving as vendors update their software drivers or provide new PDFs or PPDs. If you're using a nonstandard printer (that is, any printer that doesn't show up in the Page Setup dialog box's popup list), call the manufacturer and see if there's a new PDF, PPD, or driver available.

Next, you can build your blends in Aldus FreeHand or Adobe Illustrator and import them into QuarkXPress.

Finally, the best way to do blends—in our humble opinion—is to create them in Photoshop (add a little noise for flavor) and import them as TIFF images.

From the Beginning or to the End

If you want to print from the first page to a specified page, you can leave the From field empty in the Print dialog box. Similarly, if you leave the To field empty, QuarkXPress assumes you want to print to the end of the document. Actually, this works in most Macintosh applications.

is printed as an entity; therefore, each font that is downloaded for the EPS flushes the previous font from the printer's memory. It can be frustrating, but then again there are few reasons to ever turn Unlimited Downloadable Fonts on. So, you're probably safe.

FONTS

Proper Printing of Embedded Fonts

Some applications are smarter than others when it comes to printing EPS files. For instance, if you save an EPS from a Quark-XPress page that contains downloadable fonts (fonts that aren't resident on your printer), those fonts might not print properly if you import the EPS into a program like FileMaker Pro (assuming you have the Claris XTND system's EPS translator). The problem is that these sorts of applications are not smart enough to look inside the EPS file to see what fonts are needed. So they don't download them automatically.

If you're running into this kind of problem, try this. Put a little block of text set to the necessary typeface somewhere else on the page that's getting printed (not in the EPS file). You can often even hide this off the page, or behind some other object, or you might even just type a single space character (which would be invisible). Sometimes that's enough to kick the program into downloading the typeface for you.

PAGE NUMBERS

Jump to Absolute Page Numbers

If you play around with sections and page numbers, you may find yourself in a quagmire when you try to print a page range. For example, let's say your document begins on page 56 and you want to print the 16th through the 20th pages. You could sit around and try to figure out what numbers to plug in to the Print dialog box's page range fields (71 and 75) or you could just type "+16" and "+20". The plus sign before the number means that the numbers are absolute; the first page in the document is "+1", the second page is "+2", and so on—no matter what their page numbers are.

This is also helpful when moving to a page using the Go To page command. You can quickly jump to the 20th page by entering "+20". (The plus sign in this tip has nothing to do with math; it's unfortunate and confusing that Quark used this symbol.)

Avoid Printing White Pages

When doing a lot of text editing in a document with automatic page insertion turned on, you can easily end up with many blank pages tacked on the end of your document. And if you're not careful, you'll end up printing all these white pages every time you run out a job—a nuisance with a laser printer, a major cost drain with an imagesetter.

QuarkXPress addresses this headache by adding a Blank Pages item in the Print dialog box. Uncheck this, and QuarkXPress won't print any blank pages—not even those that include objects that are colored white or set to Suppress Printout. It will, however, print pages that contain master page items, such as automatic page numbers, which might make the feature worthless in your particular situation.

Copying Your Document for Printing Sizes

If you're working with documents larger than the standard letter size, you can easily reduce them to fit on a letter-size page for proofing by entering the percentage you want in the Reduce or Enlarge field in the Page Setup dialog box (see Table 8-1). However, it's often very easy to forget that you've specified a size change, and waste paper by printing full size on too-small paper, or, worse, waste service bureau charges by sending a reduced-size document to an imagesetter.

To print this sized page	Onto this sized page	Reduce/Enlarge to
Legal	Letter	78%
Tabloid	Letter	64%
A4	Letter	94%
Letter	Tabloid	128%

Suppressing Picture Printout

When you need to suppress the printing of a whole mess o' pictures at a time, check out the Picture Usage dialog box. The last column in this dialog box lets you turn Suppress Printout on and off with a single click. When the column has a checkmark in it, the picture prints; no checkmark means suppressed printing.

Saving Print Settings

Every time you print a document, XPress remembers many of the settings you changed in the Print dialog box. If you turned Separations on, checked Spreads, or any one of a mess o' other items you can change, the program remembers those for the next time you print that document. But what if you want to tell QuarkXPress to remember a Print dialog box setup without actually printing anything?

Go to the print dialog box (Command-P), set it up the way you want, and press Print. Immediately press Command-period once or twice (or until it stops printing or spooling). Now save the document. The settings are saved with the document, and nothing has been printed. Simple, silly, but it works.

Table 8-1
Converting page sizes

Reduced-Size Rulers

If you print at a particular reduction or enlargement frequently, you can create a full-sized ruler in QuarkXPress and print that at the same (reduced or enlarged) percentage for easy measuring. For example, if you print at 75 percent a lot, create a full-size ruler on your QuarkXPress page in inches, picas, or whatever measurement you work in. Then print that page at a 75-percent reduction. Printing to film positive makes a handy transparent ruler for measuring those reduced proofs.

One solution is to save two copies of your document, each with a name reflecting the scaling percentages you've specified. This is a pretty extreme solution, and it takes up a lot of disk space. Ultimately, it comes back down to the bottom line that you just need to always, always check your Page Setup dialog box before printing.

If you use the $195 QuarkPrint XTension, this is the kind of thing you can easily set up print styles for (it's bundled with the CD-ROM version of Power Mac XPress).

PICTURE BOXES
Rough-Printing Transparent Boxes

By the way, version 3.1 made a subtle change in the way it printed in Rough mode. We've never heard anyone complain about it, but we thought we'd let you know nonetheless. When you choose Rough in the Print dialog box, picture boxes with "None" as their background color print blank, as opposed to printing with an "X" through them. Boxes with an opaque colored background, however, still print with an "X" through them.

(*Note:* At the time of this writing, there was a curious feature in XPress which looks like a bug: some picture boxes do not appear at all when you print in Rough mode. The key is that if the background color is White, less than 50 percent of a color, or color #1 of a blend is less than 50 percent of a color, an "x" won't appear. Yes, it's weird, but that's just the way it works.)

THUMBNAILS
Faster, Larger Thumbnails

We find the size that the Thumbnails option in the Print dialog box usually gives us pretty useless: they're just too small! And if we have pictures on the pages, the job takes too long to print. So we use this feature in conjunction with two others: Rough, and Reduce or Enlarge. Rough is nearby in the Print dialog box. Just make sure this is selected from the Output popup menu, and your thumbnails print with an "X" through the pictures, and with simplified frames. The Reduce or Enlarge feature is found in the Page Setup dialog box and is covered above. Use 200 percent, and your thumbnails are printed at 24 percent instead of a little over 12 percent. This is just about the right size for most letter-size pages. If you want your thumbnails much larger, check out the next tip.

Two Thumbnails per Page

If you want your thumbnails much larger, you can scale up to 375 percent and turn the page landscape in the Page Setup dialog box. With this value, you can get two letter- or legal-size pages on one page. You can get two tabloid-size pages on one letter-size landscape page with an enlargement of 300 percent. If your document is made of two-page spreads, then you can print letter- and legal-size pages up to 400 percent (the maximum allowed for enlargement), and tabloid-size pages up to 350 percent.

However, if you're using the LaserWriter 8 driver, there's an easier way to do this: just select 2 Up or 4 Up in the Page Setup dialog box and ignore QuarkXPress's Thumbnails feature altogether. That's our favorite method. (Remember to turn it back to 1 Up before sending it to be output later!)

Saddle-Stitch Imposition

While there are some great page imposition tools out there—including Aldus PressWise and the InPosition XTension—sometimes you want to do a quick little booklet for little cost. You can use the Spreads feature in conjunction with the Document Layout palette to "strip" together pages which will be double-sided and saddle-stitch bound. We think this is one of the coolest things you can do with the Document Layout feature anyway.

1. Create your document as usual, but with no facing pages.

2. When you're finished, use the Document Layout palette to move the last page to the left of the first page. Then move the second-to-last page (which has now become the last page) up to the right of the second page (which is now the third page). Then, move the next last page to the left of the next single page, and so on.

3. When you're done, every page should be paired with another page, and the last pages in the document should

Centering Your Page

Tired of your page printing in the upper-left corner of your sheet of paper? Wish it was centered instead? On some printers, you can get your page to do this (assuming, of course, that the page size is smaller than the paper size) if you select Automatic from the Tiling popup menu and enter zero in the Overlap field. This works with some printers, not with others.

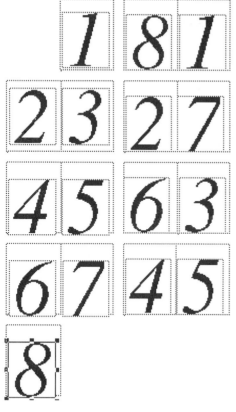

Figure 8-4
Saddle-stitched imposition

be the middle-most pages. For example, in an eight-page booklet, the final pages would end up being the spread containing pages four and five (see Figure 8-4).

4. Make sure the Spreads feature is selected in the Print dialog box when you print the document page.

Note that this method won't work if you are using automatic page numbering (because you're moving pages around; for example, the final page ends up being page one). You have to type in page numbers manually. If you want automatic page numbering, set each page to its own section (select Section under the Page menu and click Section Start). Then enter the page number before rearrangement into the Number field.

Ultimately, if you're going to be doing imposition like this very often, we do suggest using an XTension or utility (see Appendix B, *Resources*, for more information).

IMPOSITION

Printing Spreads

Here's a quickie if you need to print two half-sheets on one letter-sized page (like many booklets are arranged).

1. In the Page Setup dialog box, select landscape (wide) orientation and, in Options, Larger Print Area. If you need to shrink the page at all so it fits on half the sheet, select a reduction there, too.

2. In the Print dialog box, make sure the Spreads feature is turned on.

That's all there is to it.

IMPOSITION

Printing Double-Sided Documents

You can print double-sided pages with the following technique.

1. Print all of the odd-numbered pages using the Odd Pages option from the Print dialog box.

2. Place these pages back into the printer. Some laser printers require these to be face down, others face up. Test it first.

3. Select Back to Front from the Print dialog box.

4. Print all the even pages.

If everything is set up right, the second page should print on the back of the first, and so on. Check with your printer manufacturer before doing this, though. We've had no problems with Canon-engine printers, a few problems with the Ricoh (GCC) engine, and Varityper technicians roll their eyes in horror at the idea of running a page through twice.

You can also use this technique when photocopying documents in a two-side format. Print the odd-numbered pages first, then the even-numbered pages. Then you can photocopy the odd-numbered pages, turn them over, and feed them back through the photocopier while copying the even-numbered pages. Note that this can really mess you up if you don't have an even number of pages.

IMPOSITION
Printing Spreads Correctly

There's a potential problem in selecting Spreads in the Print dialog box, one that could cost you an arm and a leg.

Let's say you're laying out a magazine with a standard facing-page format, except in the middle of the document you have a fold-out, resulting in two three-page spreads. You send the file off to be imageset, specifying that Spreads should be checked. When you get the film or paper back you find everything worked just like you thought it would: two-page spreads spread across two pages, and the two three-page spreads spread all the way across three pages (never mind that this is definitely not how you'd want to print a magazine; it would be a stripping nightmare).

But when you get your bill, it's hundreds of dollars more than you expected. What happened? What went wrong? This is the dangerous part of printing contiguous spreads. When you specify Spreads, QuarkXPress tells the roll-fed imagesetter to advance the film the width of the widest spread in the page range specified. So in the example above, each two-page spread actually took three pages of film; hence it was much more expensive.

So don't waste paper or film when you print contiguous spreads from a multiple-page document; if for no other reason, it's expensive. If you have a multiple-page spread crossing pages

IMPOSITION
Should You Select Spreads?

If you're not familiar with the printing trade and how they like to receive printed artwork, you may be tempted to select the Spreads feature in the Print dialog box when you're printing facing-page documents. Don't. Unless you know what you're doing, printing spreads like this will probably cause your printer to hate you because he or she will have to cut them apart manually.

45 through 47, have your service bureau print the pages from one through 44 and 48 through the end as single pages or two-page spreads or whatever, and then print the three-page spread on a separate pass.

STRIPPING

Additional Job Information

Bleeds are typically objects that print mostly on the page, but bleed slightly off it. But you can also create items that are mostly off the page, and only slightly on it. This is ideal for adding additional job information on your documents. As long as at least a bit of a picture or text box overlaps the edge of the page, it will be printed along with what's on the page (see Figure 8-5). For this trick to work, the part that's touching the page has to be a non-printing color like white. For instance, if you hang a text box off the top of the page, the bottom of the box might touch the page, but the text at the top of the box sits off the page.

Figure 8-5
Hanging job information off the page

This item doesn't print because it's fully off the page.

ple can't pro-
ire their TVs,
interactive
) together.
s bundled as
l system, it's
onsumers.¶
le at Kodak
lt it to work
lards for CD-
ıly Memory).

Photo CD
Job
Page 11
Trim
right
to edge
on
this
page

This job slug and information prints because part of the text box is on the page. Note the automatic page number (Command-3).

STRIPPING

Better Registration Marks

The registration marks that QuarkXPress creates for you are okay, but not great, and certainly not optimal from a stripper's point of view. This is how you can make a better registration mark directly in QuarkXPress (you can also make one in FreeHand or Illustrator, and bring it in as an EPS; see Figure 8-6).

Figure 8-6
A more versatile registration mark

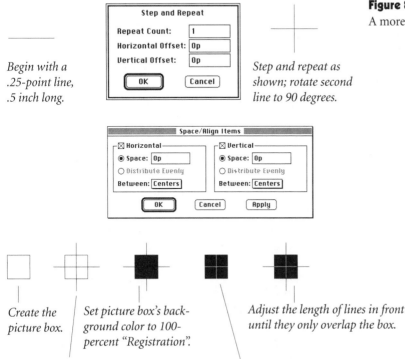

Begin with a .25-point line, .5 inch long.

Step and repeat as shown; rotate second line to 90 degrees.

Create the picture box.

Set picture box's background color to 100-percent "Registration".

Adjust the length of lines in front until they only overlap the box.

Use Space/Align as shown to position the center of the box directly over the lines' intersection.

Step and Repeat lines with zero offsets; bring duplicates to front; color them "White".

1. Draw a line about ½-inch long. Set width to .25 points with Midpoints selected in the Measurements palette. Color the lines "Registration".

2. Use the Step and Repeat feature from the Item menu to create one copy with no horizontal or vertical offset.

3. Make this second line perpendicular to the first by adding or subtracting 90 degrees from the line angle in the Measurements palette.

4. Draw a ¼-inch-square picture box (hold down the Shift key to maintain a square) and center it over the lines. You could center it by either using the Space/Align feature or by just aligning the box's handles directly over the lines.

Printer as Magnifying Glass

You can use Manual Tiling and Enlarge to blow up a particular area of the page for inspection (when 400-percent magnification on the screen still doesn't suit you). Change the enlargement factor in the Page Setup dialog box to 400 percent (or whatever enlargement you desire), then move the zero point of the rulers to the upper-left corner of the area which you want to inspect. Now print that page with Tiling set to Manual. *Voilà!* A super-size sectional.

This is great for inspecting anything small, including type and fine lines. You can also use this technique to inspect trapping values (see "Use Big Traps for Proofing" in Chapter 7, *Color*).

5. Set the box's background to 100-percent "Registration".

6. Select the two lines, and step-and-repeat both of them once with no offsets. Bring these lines to the front, if they're not already there.

7. Color the second set of lines "White", and shorten them so that they only overlap the box.

The great benefit of this registration mark is that when you print negatives, your printer can still align black crosshairs on a white background. After you create one of these, you can duplicate it as needed. Also, you can save it in a library or make an EPS out of it so that you can import it quickly onto other pages.

Going this route is clearly more work, as you sometimes need to build your page larger than necessary, then add your own crop marks and registration marks (and job info, if you want it), but it could be rewarding, depending on your situation.

Even better than going this route is using an XTension such as MarksXT, which gives you even more control.

Keyline Box for Page

As an aid to stripping—*only* if your commercial printer approves, of course—you can easily put a keyline box around each page by following these steps.

1. On your master pages, create a picture box the exact size of the page. (Fast way to do this: draw a little box and in the Measurements palette (you can make sure your zero point is reset by clicking once on the ruler origin), type zeros for the origins, and the page size for the height and width.)

2. To this box, apply a .1-point frame with color "Registration". (Of course, if it's only a one-color job, you can just color it "Black".)

3. On pages where there are bleeds, place (on the document page, not the master page) a small box with a background of "Registration" set to zero percent between the bleeding object and the keyline, to block out the keyline near the bleed area.

Note that most printers do *not* want their pages like this. Yours might, though. It's a nice option to offer them.

You Can't Trap Composite Prints

All the umpteen-zillion ways you can specify trapping in Quark-XPress only take effect if you're printing separations. XPress does *not* apply any trapping whatsoever for composite prints. So if you're printing to a full-color printer, such as color thermal-transfer printer like the QMS ColorScript, a Canon Color Laser Copier, or an IRIS, you won't see the results of any traps you've defined. Note that some printers—such as the 3M Rainbow—can actually receive process color separations; in these cases, they often *do* show you the traps.

Have Densitometer, Will Output

A densitometer is a piece of expensive equipment that you may not wish to spring for. The good news is that you shouldn't have to; it's the responsibility of the service bureau to check their output regularly (from once a day to once a month depending on how much output they do and how stable their chemical and imagesetter environments are) to make sure the density of their paper or film is correct, and that when you specify a 20-percent tint in your document, you get a 20-percent tint on your film (unless you're adjusting for dot gain).

If you are working with halftones or tints (and especially color separations) going to film, make sure your service bureau owns a *transmission* densitometer (as opposed to a *reflection* densitometer), knows how to use it, and does so frequently, especially when moving between film and paper.

The service bureau should use this information to linearize their imagesetter (make sure that the tints run evenly from one end of the scale to another) as well as keep the density at the right setting. Density is often controlled by the developing and fixing chemicals, while linearization is controlled through software in the PostScript RIP.

Check Your Compatibility

Fonts change, colors change, everything changes except change itself (if you've seen one cliché, you've seen them all). If you're working with a service bureau regularly, you'll want to make sure that their equipment and system setup is compatible with yours. The best way to go is to perform periodic tests; you can use a test sheet. On this sheet should be the fonts you regularly use, a gray percentage bar, some grayscale images, and perhaps some line art (just for kicks). The idea is to see whether anything changed much between your system and the service bureau's. If fonts come out different, the tints are off, or the density is too light or dark, you can either help them correct the problem or compensate for it yourself.

SERVICE BUREAUS

Some More Questions for Your Service Bureau

Here is a list of a few more questions which you may want to ask when shopping for a service bureau.

▶ What imagesetters do they have available, and what resolutions do they support?

▶ Do they have dedicated equipment just for film, and do they calibrate it using imagesetter linearization or other software? If they're using other software, do you need a component on your system when making files to output with them?

▶ Do they have an in-house color-proofing system? Is it a laminate system (like Match Print or Press Match) or digital composite (like the 3M Rainbow or Iris printers)?

▶ Do they have a replenishing processor, or do they use the same chemicals continually? If it's the latter, how often do they change their wash water?

▶ Do they have a customer agreement that lists what they're responsible for and what the customer is responsible for?

▶ Do they have a job ticket for output that lets you fill in all the details of your particular project?

▶ Do they inspect their film before it is sent out?

There are no right or wrong answers to any of these (well, the last one has a wrong answer; you can guess what it is). However, asking the questions not only tells you a lot about the service bureau, but also teaches you a lot about the process they're going through to output your film or RC paper.

The job ticket issue is extremely important, as it often constitutes the legal agreement between you and the service bureau. If the service doesn't provide one, then you may have difficulty resolving any problem situations.

You should make decisions about where to run each print job. For example, if a service bureau doesn't calibrate their equipment, you probably don't want to use them for halftoning or color separation work. If their top resolution is 1,270 dpi, you may need to go elsewhere for high-quality grayscale images. You can weigh these items against the cost of the film or paper output, the distance from your office, the friendliness of the staff, and so on.

Scitex RIP Tips

If you're printing to a Scitex RIP, we offer the following recommendations.

▶ Use the appropriate PDF, because it allows access to the Width field in Print Setup. XPress adjusts the height of a page depending on whether registration/crop marks are turned on or off, but—at least for Scitex RIPs—you have to adjust the width manually to reflect your "marks" choice.

▶ Turn off Calibrated Output in the Print dialog box.

▶ The halftone screen frequency setting in the Page Setup dialog box is very important. Although Scitex RIPs ignore PostScript halftoning information (Scitex's own values are substituted instead), if the screen frequency is left at the default setting of 60 lpi (or any other low value), your TIFF images get downsampled to twice the screen frequency setting, resulting in mottled images and jaggies. Scitex recommends setting lpi to 400, which pretty much ensures that XPress won't do any downsampling.

COLLECT FOR OUTPUT

Tagging Usage Reports

The best way to look at the Collect for Output report is within QuarkXPress itself, because XPress saves the report in XPress Tags format. If you want, you can create your own template to import these reports into, complete with style sheets. Every paragraph in the report is tagged with a style sheet name, so when you import it into a template that includes the proper style sheets, each paragraph gets formatted.

QuarkXPress ships with a file called Output Request Template that already includes all these style sheets, so if you're creating your own template, you can simply append them from there. However, if you've thrown that file away (we did), you can create your own using the information in Table 8-2.

COLLECT FOR OUTPUT

Listing Fonts and Pictures

You can find out what fonts and pictures you used in the Font Usage and Picture Usage dialog boxes. However, there's no way to print them without making screen captures. Or is there?

When you select Collect for Output from the File menu, XPress prompts you for a place to save a report file. If you click OK and then press Command-period as soon as you see the progress bar appear, the program saves the report file and then cancels the operation. You can open that report in a word processor and find the names of the fonts and the graphics (as well as a lot of other information).

You can also use the commercial QuarkPrint XTension to do this. This XTension is bundled on the CD-ROM Power Mac version of QuarkXPress.

Name	Description
color info	Each color defined in the document
color plate	What colors can be separated
doc fonts	Which printer fonts you used
doc fonts title	Title bar for fonts section
doc info	Overview of document
h and j	What H&J settings are defined
header	Heading for each section in the report
picture items	Lists each picture and it's specs
picture title	Title bar for pictures section
style sheet	Lists each style sheet that is defined
trapping	Trapping preferences settings
XT info	Which XTensions are loaded and/or required

If you only define one style sheet, it should be "header" so that you can more quickly scan the report.

FONTS

Telling Fonts Not to Download

When QuarkXPress prints a PostScript file to disk using Laser-Writer drivers before LaserWriter 8, it attempts to include any outline printer font information it can find. For example, if you used Courier in your file and have the Courier outline font in your System Folder, QuarkXPress includes that font's information in the file. However, if your service bureau already has the font, you don't need to include it in your PostScript file. It just makes the file bigger. Disk space might not be an issue to you, but if it is, you might want to *dis*include those fonts.

In the LaserWriter 8 driver, the default setting is not to include any fonts (see below). However, if you're using a pre-8.x version of the driver, you can still leave the fonts out. There are two ways to make sure QuarkXPress doesn't include any printer fonts you have floating about. The first option is to move the printer fonts someplace where QuarkXPress can't find them. This means putting them anywhere but in the System Folder (any system version), the Fonts folder (for System 7.1 and later), the QuarkXPress folder, or the folder where you keep your screen fonts (if you use MasterJuggler or Suitcase). This is another instance where Prairie-Soft's DiskTop seems impossible to live without. With it, you can quickly move these files anywhere you want, then return them after you create the dump.

LaserWriter 8 avoids this whole problem by offering you three options in a popup menu (see Figure 8-7).

▶ **None.** The default setting in this dialog box is None, and—just as the name implies—no fonts get included in the PostScript file when you choose this. If you and your service bureau are sure that they have all of the fonts downloaded to their imagesetter's hard drive (or if you provide the printer fonts so they can download them in advance of your job), then you may be safe selecting None. Your file will be substantially smaller with this option selected.

▶ **All.** The polar opposite of None is, of course, All. If you select this, then all the fonts get included in the PostScript dump. It makes for a big file, but we sometimes use this method because neither we nor the service bureau needs to worry about downloading fonts. They're all in the file.

Note that you should be sure Unlimited Downloadable Fonts is turned off in the Options dialog box (inside the Page Setup dialog box). When it's turned on, the fonts are usually saved in the PostScript dump more than once, creating a potentially enormous file.

PICTURES

Printing with Modified Graphics

If your picture status is listed as Modified in the Picture Usage dialog box and you go ahead and print anyway, you'll be printing using the modified graphic. If the status is Missing, on the other hand, you'll get the low-resolution screen version when you print. Either of these effects could be good or bad for you, depending on your situation. We just thought you should know.

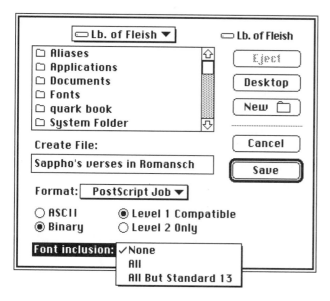

Figure 8-7
Saving a PostScript dump
using LaserWriter 8

▶ **All But Standard 13.** Almost every PostScript printer has a core of 13 basic fonts: Courier, Helvetica, and Times (each in four styles), plus Symbol. If you select All But Standard 13 from the popup menu, all the fonts in the document are included unless they're one of these 13 typefaces. When we send PostScript dumps to a service bureau, this is the method we prefer.

MAC/PC

Cross-Platform Dumps

A PostScript dump (also called a print-to-disk file) should always work perfectly whether going cross-platform or not, because it only contains PostScript instructions, and PostScript is device- and platform-independent. The computer that's downloading the PostScript file to the output device doesn't need to have the same program that you do, or the same fonts, or anything. They just need to be able to send the file to the imagesetter.

The one place this system breaks down, however, is that some programs on the PC insert a code in their PostScript files that causes havoc when you send the file to a printer on AppleTalk or Ethernet. It's the Control-D character: on the PC it stands for "end-of-file," but the PostScript interpreter tries to interpret it and send back an undefined command error.

You can delete the character yourself manually in any Mac word-processor. The Control-D character is normally found within one line of both the beginning and the end of the file; often the first and last characters in the file are Control-Ds. Sometimes it looks like a solid black diamond on the Mac; usually, though, it's invisible character. You have to select it using Shift plus the arrow keys. Delete the Control-Ds, and resave the file as text only or ASCII format.

If, of course, you look at a PostScript file and there's no Control-D to be found, you don't need to worry about it: it just means that your file was created by a program that knows better than to do that.

If you have to do a lot of this, you'd better get a utility to do it for you automatically. It's named "PM2LIN.ZIP" and it can be found on the disc in the back of the book, as well as in the DTP Forum on CompuServe.

Better Publications from Low-Resolution Originals

Here's an easy and inexpensive way to drastically improve the appearance of your documents from your 300-dpi printer. Just use the Page Setup dialog box to print them at 125 percent. Then have your lithographer reduce the image to 80 percent when he or she shoots your output. This gets you back to 100 percent, your correct document size, but with an effective resolution of 375 dpi. You can increase the final resolution to 600 dpi by printing at 200 percent and reducing to 50 percent, and so on. Anyway, it's amazing what even the seemingly minor resolution enhancement of 375 dpi will do for the look of your pages.

Another way to improve low-resolution output is to turn the darkness control on your 300-dpi printer to the lightest possible setting, then ask your lithographer to slightly overexpose the film when he or she shoots your originals to make negatives. This blurs the black area around type and other objects, greatly reducing those ol' 300-dpi jaggies.

Note that both of these methods can play havoc with tints! These really should only be used with documents that have no gray values or halftones (unless you're really careful with your screen frequency and dot gain settings).

Checking Pages with LaserCheck

LaserCheck is a utility that lets you print a document meant for an imagesetter on your desktop laser printer. That is, you can actually set up the Page Setup and Print dialog boxes just as though you were printing on an imagesetter, and your laser printer not only handles it correctly, it tells you—with the help of LaserCheck—more than you'd ever want to know about the Post-Script file it printed. We've found this handy for checking whether our tabloid-sized pages were going to come out lengthwise or widthwise on the L330, and for seeing whether a file would just plain print. Generally, if it prints with LaserCheck, there's a good chance it'll print on the imagesetter.

When Your File Is Too Big

It's easy to make PostScript dumps that are too big to fit onto a floppy. Add a TIFF or an EPS here and there, forget to turn off access to printer fonts (see "Telling Fonts Not to Download," above), or even just try to print a large file. Don't fret: there's always a workaround.

First of all, if you're going to work with the Macintosh, you must own a copy of Compact Pro. It's shareware, which means that you can get it almost anywhere (it's on the disc in the back of the book), but if you use it for more than a few days, you are honor-bound to send author Bill Goodman $25. Compact Pro has become the shareware standard on the Macintosh for compressing files. Some TIFF files can compress as much as 90 percent, but most files compress by around 30 to 60 percent.

There are many commercial compression packages, too, including TimesTwo, DiskDoubler, and StuffIt Deluxe. The central issue is often not which is better to use, but which program the person on the receiving side owns. If you're not sure what your service bureau has, save the compressed file as a "self-extracting archive" (".sea").

Let'er RIP!: a Good Software Spooler

While we're not really in the marketing business, we wanted to let you know about a cool little utility called Let'er RIP! This program is a combination software print spooler and print server. The software monitors a folder (any folder you want) for PostScript files that appear in it, then downloads them to a specific printer (note that Let'er RIP! doesn't necessarily use the printer selected in the Chooser, so you can set it up to use any printer you want). It's actually even cooler than this, but you should check it out yourself.

If you get an error with LaserCheck, you not only know that it probably wouldn't have output on the high-res device, but you get information on what PostScript problem caused the error. Your service bureau may be able to help you solve your problem if they know a little about PostScript.

For more advanced and detailed information, you might look into two PostScript error handlers: PinPoint XT from the Cheshire Group, and the Advanced PostScript Error Handler from Systems of Merritt (see Appendix B, *Resources*). David loves these, but he's a PostScript hacker and likes to muck about with "movetos" and "curvetos".

Color Bars on Your Separations

QuarkXPress automatically adds a strip of color bars to its process color separations at print time (when Registration Marks is turned on), but few people know what each color along the strip is. Along the bottom of the page are gray bars. In version 3.0, there were 16 bars set to six-percent increments. However, back in version 3.1, Quark got smart and changed it to 10 steps of 10-percent increments (which is what anyone other than a programmer who thinks in hexadecimal would want).

The color bar along the left side of each page of film is incomprehensible until you create a color proof of the page. Then you can see that the bars are broken down as follows.

- ▶ 100-percent black
- ▶ 100-percent yellow
- ▶ 100-percent yellow plus 100-percent magenta
- ▶ 100-percent magenta
- ▶ 100-percent magenta plus 100-percent cyan
- ▶ 100-percent cyan
- ▶ 100-percent yellow plus 100-percent cyan
- ▶ 100-percent cyan plus 100-percent magenta plus 100-percent yellow

▶ 50-percent cyan

▶ 50-percent magenta

▶ 50-percent yellow

▶ 50-percent black

If you have fewer than all four process color plates, you will have fewer than all 12 of these color squares. And note that you won't be seeing any of these on spot color plates.

CALIBRATION

Modified Calibration Curves in PDFs

Some of QuarkXPress's printer descriptions (the PDF files) have built-in calibration settings that alter gray levels when you print to those printers. The concept is to get better-looking images, but the truth of the matter is that this stuff is mostly a holdout of out-of-date technology. A few people still use the calibration settings to good use, but we mostly suggest people avoid them.

To avoid XPress's internal calibration, make sure Calibrated Output is turned off in the Print dialog box when you print (unfortunately, this checkbox isn't "sticky," so you have to turn it off for each new document).

Or, if you know that there's no calibration setting for the device you're printing to, you can simply ignore the checkbox altogether. To find out whether your PDF has a modified calibration curve, use the Printer Calibration XTension (it's on the disc). Then choose Printer Calibration from the Utilities menu.

You can select a printer and click Edit to see its calibration charts (see Figure 8-8). Click the No Gain button (this was "Reset" in version 3.1). If clicking the button produces no change in the graphs, then there's probably no calibration setting. If there *is* a change, then your PDF does indeed have a modified curve; if you save the No Gain version, it won't any longer.

COLOR SEPARATION
Separating Images from the Clipboard

XPress can separate grayscale or black and white images pasted from the Clipboard if they've been assigned a color. It can't separate a full-color image pasted from the Clipboard, though. The truth is that we generally don't recommend people pasting images into picture boxes; Get Picture is typically a better method.

Figure 8-8
Printer Calibration Curves

Figure 8-8
Printer Calibration Curves

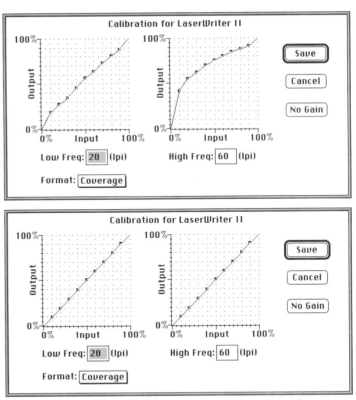

Figure 8-9
Flatness affects
smoothness of lines

Flatness: 0

Flatness: 5

Flatness: 80

Speeding Printing Through Flatness

You can often speed up print times dramatically and/or avoid PostScript "limitcheck" errors by raising the PostScript flatness value. If you've worked with flatness in FreeHand or Illustrator (before version 5), you know that the flatness value determines how hard the PostScript interpreter works to give you smooth curves. The higher the flatness value, the faster the graphic prints, but the more choppy your line gets. If you raise your flatness too high, the curve turns into a set of straight (read: ugly) lines (see Figure 8-9). However, you can almost always raise your flatness to between three and five and never see the difference.

FreeHand, Illustrator, and Photoshop all let you change flatness values. In FreeHand, you can change the flatness for any particular line (see Figure 8-10). In Photoshop, you can only specify flatness for the clipping path, if you have one selected (see

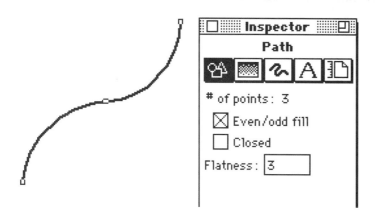

Figure 8-10
Setting flatness in FreeHand

Figure 8-11). Illustrator 5.x only lets you set flatness for an entire document, and indirectly at that (see Figure 8-12).

Setting a flatness value in XPress is significantly harder. In fact, there's no good way to do it other than printing PostScript to disk and then adding a line to the PostScript file using a text editor. To change the flatness value in a PostScript file, add a line just after the "%%EndComments" line in the header of the PostScript file (near the beginning of the file) that reads "5 setflat" (or insert whatever value you want to use; see Figure 8-13). Typically, the

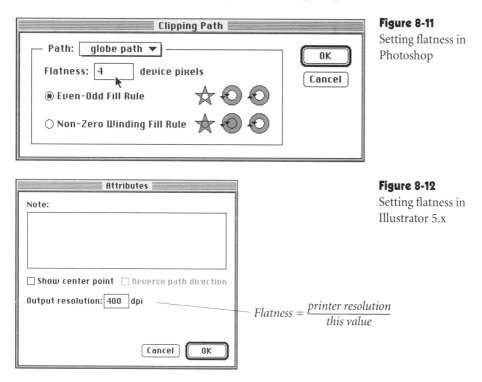

Figure 8-11
Setting flatness in Photoshop

Figure 8-12
Setting flatness in Illustrator 5.x

$$Flatness = \frac{printer\ resolution}{this\ value}$$

Figure 8-13

PostScript flatness statement

```
%!PS-Adobe-2.0 EPSF-1.2
%%Creator: QuarkXPress(R) 3.3
%%Title: 10-Worng.qx 1.0 (Page 135)
%%CreationDate: 12/10/90 10:47 AM
%%DocumentProcSets: QuarkXPress_3.3 0 0
%%DocumentSuppliedProcSets: QuarkXPress_3.3 0 0
%%DocumentFonts: Times-Roman
%%+ Survival
%%+ Lithos-Regular
%%+ Utopia-Regular
%%+ UtopiaExp-Regular
%%+ Lithos-Black
%%+ Utopia-Italic
%%BoundingBox: 0 0 504 648
%%EndComments
5 setflat
%%BeginProcSet:QuarkXPress_3.3 0 0
```

only time you need to set a flatness value for XPress files is if the file includes pictures inside oval picture boxes (flatness only affects curves).

The Coordinate System

If you know PostScript and you want to start playing around with PostScript dumps, you should be aware that in XPress' coordinate system, the 0,0 coordinate is in the upper-left corner of the printed page, and the entire page is inverted (1,-1 scale). The biggest problem you'll encounter is that it's difficult to pinpoint where the 0,0 coordinate is on the page, as it depends on whether you're using crop marks, bleeds, and so forth. However, if you're persistent in your searches, you'll work it out.

Regularizing Lines

If you're the brave sort who likes to experiment with the EPS files QuarkXPress makes when you save a page as EPS, or with the PostScript dumps it can make, you might consider adding these lines to your file, right after the "%%EndComments" comment at the beginning of the PostScript file.

If you have a number of thin lines next to each other, some may appear thicker than others on a low-resolution printer (such as a 300-dpi desktop laser printer). If you need them to look the same, insert the following code directly after the header (before the line "md begin").

```
/_R {.25 sub round .25 add} bind def
/_r {transform _R exch _R exch itransform} bind def
/moveto {_r moveto} bind def /lineto {_r lineto} bind def
```

COLOR SEPARATION

Changing the Color-Separation Angles

If you don't want to use the angles that QuarkXPress sets up for you (or that you get when Use PDF Screen Values is turned on), you have two choices: either go into the PostScript code and change them yourself (sounds painful, doesn't it?) or use an XTension to do it. Quark's QuarkPrint XTension lets you do this, as does the fcsAngles XTension (it's on the disc). Typically, unless you have a really good reason to do this, you shouldn't mess with it at all. Also, some imagesetters override these settings regardless of what you change them to.

POSTSCRIPT

Changing Halftones

QuarkXPress uses a standard round halftone spot when it tints type, rules, boxes, and other elements on the page (everything except halftoned bitmapped images, which you can control with the Other Screen feature under the Style menu). You can change the type of halftone spot that QuarkXPress uses by modifying the PostScript dump.

Search for "sp0 setscreen" (note that in earlier versions of the program, it was "xpspot0"). The first two numbers on that line are the screen frequency and the angle. The screen frequency should be the same as what you specified in the Page Setup dialog box. The angle should be 45 degrees. You can change both of these to whatever you want them to be.

If you change "sp0" to "sp1", your halftones are printed with a straight-line spot; "sp2" is an oval; "sp3" is a square spot; and

POSTSCRIPT

Finding the Fonts

Every once in a while we find ourselves with an EPS image on our hands without knowing what fonts are in it or required by it. Of course, we need to know the fonts to ensure that we have the printer fonts available for it to print properly. You can find out what fonts are in most EPS files in two ways. The first way is to open the file itself in a text editor. In Microsoft Word, you have to hold the Shift key down while selecting Open to be able to read the EPS file type (or just select All Files from the Open dialog box's popup menu). The fonts are probably listed at the beginning of the file after the structuring comments "%%DocumentFonts". If it says "atend", look at the end of the PostScript file.

If you've already printed a XPress file to disk that includes an EPS image, you can find this same information by searching through the PostScript for the word "EPS". The "%%DocumentFonts" comments are probably not too far away.

XPress can also do some of this looking for you. If you perform a Collect for Output (see "Catching all the Fonts and Pictures" earlier in this chapter), the report tells you what fonts are used in each of the EPS files.

"sp4" is a weird random spot. If you are working with a screen frequency of over 30 or 40, you probably won't be able to tell the difference between any of the spots, so this is mainly for special effects at low frequencies.

You can add your own spot functions by replacing the word "sp0" with a procedure. For example, you can create a triangular spot by replacing "sp0" with "{1 exch sub exch 1 exch sub sub 2 div}".

Note that if your PostScript file has multiple color separations in it, each plate has its own setscreen command. For more on spot functions (lots more), see David and his editor Steve's book *Real World Scanning and Halftones.*

problems
AND SOLUTIONS

No matter how careful you are in the creation and editing process, sooner or later *something* is bound to go worng. And at that time, it comes down to a question of character: are you ready to take the challenge, jump in, figure out what's wrong, and fix it? Or are you just going to call an expensive consultant? (If you answered the latter, you can skip this chapter . . . in fact, skip the whole book.)

We wrote this chapter to help you in the process of squashing whatever bug comes before you, even if it seems insurmountable. Note that sometimes even we can't figure out *why* something goes wrong. In these cases, our solution is often to work *around* the problem. Our motto: get it done and out the door.

PRINT ERRORS
Combating PostScript Errors

Is there a QuarkXPress user on the planet who hasn't seen the nasty "Sorry, a PostScript Error Occurred (-8133)" and wondered what the heck "-8133" means? Unfortunately, this message (and the number "-8133") simply means that some sort of PostScript error occurred. It doesn't tell you what the error was, and any of several errors could be the culprit. One is the infamous "stackunderflow" error. Another is the "undefined" command error. However, almost all PostScript errors are the result of printer-

Your Environment

If you ever run into problems with your copy of QuarkXPress, the first thing you should do is look at the QuarkXPress Environment dialog box. It contains tons of useful information about the version of QuarkXPress and its add-ons you're running. There are three ways to access this dialog box.

▶ Holding down the Option key while selecting the About QuarkXPress item on the Apple menu. However, if you've got a program that takes over Option-selecting in the Apple menu for its own use (Suitcase does this by default; you can change it), you have to get clever in order to reach the Environment dialog box.

The alternate method is to first hold down the Option key and click on any

menu other than the Apple menu. While holding the mouse button down, move over to the Apple menu, and select About QuarkXPress.

▶ If you have an extended keyboard, the process is even simpler: hold down the Option key and press the Help key.

▶ The third method is to press Command-Option-Control-E.

Note that in the Power Macintosh version of QuarkXPress, the list of XTensions in the Environment dialog box also shows you which XTensions are written with native PowerPC code: the ones with native code are in roman type; the others are italic.

memory problems (called "VMerror"), and almost all of them can be avoided with a few tricks.

Reset the printer. Our favorite technique for fixing memory problems is simply to turn the printer off, wait a few seconds, and turn it back on again. This flushes out any extraneous fonts or PostScript functions that are hogging memory.

Use minimum settings. Using the minimum settings means turning off all the printer options in the Page Setup dialog box, including those in the LaserWriter Options dialog box. You don't need them in most cases with QuarkXPress, and they take up printer memory that could be used better to image your pages.

Take care in your fonts. If you play around with a lot of different fonts trying to find one you like, you may inadvertently leave remnants of old fonts lying around in your documents. For example, a spaceband may be set to some font that you don't use anyplace else. Nonetheless, QuarkXPress must download that font along with every other font you use. This takes up memory that could be used for something else. Check the Font Usage dialog box to see which fonts are sitting around in your document. Then purge the ones you don't need.

Use Unlimited Downloadable Fonts. If you must have many fonts on a page, you might need to enable the Unlimited Downloadable Fonts feature in the LaserWriter Options dialog box under Page Setup. This feature makes the Mac download a font every time it needs to use it and then clears out the printer's memory. It can take much longer to print, but this type of memory management can be a lifesaver. (See Chapter 8, *Printing*, for more suggestions about using this feature.)

Print fewer pages at a time. We have successfully coaxed long documents out of an imagesetter by printing two to 10 pages at a time rather than trying to get all 500 pages out at once. Or, we've printed one plate of a process color job at a time. This is obviously a hassle, but it's better than not getting the job printed at all. Much of the work can be done early by creating multiple PostScript dumps, then queuing them up on a spooler at the service bureau.

Remove some graphics. One of the great promises of desktop publishing was that we could print an entire page out with every graphic and text block perfectly placed. Remember that promises are often broken. Case in point: large graphics (or even small graphics) sometimes choke the printer. These graphics often will print all by themselves, but when placed on a page they become the chicken bone that killed the giant.

See if you can isolate an individual element on a page that's causing the problem. If you can, try deleting the item and recreating it from scratch.

Remember that using every trick possible you might still get the page out, but is it really worth the time? Perhaps it's more efficient to just let your printer or stripper handle that graphic. Or, god forbid, just hot wax that puppy and paste it down yourself.

Save As. Logically, resaving your document under a different name doesn't make any sense, but it does work sometimes.

Reimport. If the problem turns out to be a graphic you've imported, you might try reimporting it. If the image is in a PICT format, you might have better luck using Get Picture rather than using Paste. Or, convert the PICT into a better format, like TIFF (for bitmaps) or EPS (for object-oriented graphics). Then reimport it. Remember that you can force XPress to reimport all the graphics in your document by holding down the Command key when you click Open.

Background printing. While background printing can be great, it's also been known to cause all sorts of problems at print time (some people never have a problem with it; others always do). If you're going to use it, make sure you give the PrintMonitor application (in the System Folder's Extensions folder) an additional memory allocation. If you still have problems, turn Background Printing off in the Chooser. (*Note:* This is also relevant for any other kind of print spooler you might be using.)

Memory. Nothing on a computer works well without enough memory. Make sure you've allocated more than enough memory to QuarkXPress. Also, you may need to add memory to your printer. We hardly have problems when we have six or eight megabytes of RAM in the printer, but any less than that and trouble is bound to visit us.

Fonts. Are you sure your fonts aren't corrupted? See "Are My Fonts Damaged?" later in this chapter.

Page Setup. In the Page Setup dialog box, make sure you've selected the same printer type as you've selected in the Chooser. Eric would like a dime for every time he's botched a print job by sending pages to a LaserWriter II NTX while having a QMS ColorScript 100 Model 30 selected in Page Setup. With the QuarkPrint XTension, it's become much simpler to specify printer settings such as these.

Last-ditch attempts. At the last minute, when we've tried just about everything else, here's a few last things we try (they shouldn't make much of a difference, logically, but sometimes they do).

▶ Quit from other applications (or even QuarkXPress) when printing.

▶ Delete everything you don't need from the page, and *everything* from the pasteboard.

▶ Delete all the overset text from text boxes (put the cursor at the end of the text box and press Command-Shift-Down Arrow to select to the end of the story; then hit Delete to kill it).

▶ Make sure you're running with the proper LaserWriter drivers from Apple or Adobe. We use the LaserWriter 8.1.2 driver at this writing. It's free, and if you have Internet access, you can get it at Apple's public-access Internet software site, *ftp.support.apple.com.* You can also download it from eWorld and AppleLink.

▶ After doing all of the above, simply try to print the document again. If it still won't print, reimport all your graphics, and try again.

▶ Once in a blue moon, you can get a document to print by saving it as a PostScript dump, and then downloading that file using a utility such as Font Downloader, LaserStatus, or SendPS.

▶ A clove of garlic over the AppleTalk port probably wouldn't hurt, either.

PRINT ERRORS

Those Nasty 'limitcheck' Errors

Another PostScript error that often lurks behind those ever-popular "-8133" errors is the "limitcheck" error. Limitcheck means that something in your QuarkXPress document was too complicated for your printer to correctly image.

Quite often you see this when one or more EPS files with long, complicated paths are included; these can simply require more of your printer than it's able to offer. If you get such messages and you have an EPS graphic on the first page that didn't print, here are some things you can try.

▶ In the drawing application you used to create the picture, open the picture again. Turn on automatic path splitting. FreeHand can be easily configured to automatically break an overly long, complicated path into several smaller paths that are easier for printers to image. Save the EPS again, and try printing it. If automatic splitting doesn't work, try splitting some paths by hand.

▶ In your drawing program, select long, complicated paths and increase their flatness. Usually, changing flatness from zero to two or three doesn't make a noticeable difference in the quality of your output, and can make a dramatic difference in a path's memory requirement (see "Speeding Printing Through Flatness," in Chapter 8, *Printing*).

PostScript Error on Level 2 Printers

Sometimes the strangest little things fix undefined PostScript errors. Here's one from one of our readers: If you get an undefined PostScript error when printing to a Level 2 PostScript printer, try selecting a non-Level 2 PDF (or PPD) in the Page Setup dialog box and then moving each object in XPress left or right one pixel on the page. (It may simply be the different PDF, or perhaps the combination of the two ... you might try standing on one leg, too!)

▶ If you have custom colors and/or patterns in an illustration, make sure to delete all the colors that aren't actually being used in the illustration. Use no more than three patterns in an illustration.

▶ If you have fancy blends, you may need to replace them with blends that use fewer steps.

▶ Simplify patterns in illustrations. Use the background as one of a pattern's colors, or as solid objects in a pattern rather than drawing the background as a separate object. Don't use the bitmapped PICT patterns in programs like FreeHand; they could choke a horse!

▶ Group objects within the pattern tile with common paint attributes. This may make the pattern print faster.

▶ Reduce the number of objects in a pattern tile.

▶ Use objects with simple paths as pattern objects.

▶ Remove details too small to appear in the final print.

You can also get "limitcheck" errors if you've cropped images inside nonrectangular picture boxes. Changing a circular or oval picture box to a polygon can save printing time, as it converts the box from curves to a bunch of short line segments. This requires much less processing to image correctly, with a subsequent reduced risk of "limitcheck" errors. In general, try to do any cropping *before* you import an image to QuarkXPress.

Another cause of "limitcheck" errors: saving a QuarkXPress page as EPS. Bringing that EPS into another QuarkXPress page. Saving *that* page as EPS, and bringing it into a third QuarkXPress page, and so on (you may also see save/restore errors in this situation). Though it's true that you can get some cool recursive and fun-house mirror effects this way, you probably won't be able to print them.

Bear in mind that even if your pages print properly from your laser printer, you may still run into problems from an imagesetter, as printing at higher resolutions requires significantly greater amounts of horsepower.

Handling Errors

As we noted in "PostScript Problems When Printing," above, QuarkXPress isn't great at telling you what sort of PostScript error may have killed your print job. Fortunately, there are a few tools out there that you can use to debug the problem.

LaserWriter 8. The first is part of the LaserWriter 8 driver (if you're not using this driver, you can't do this). When you're in XPress's Print dialog box, you can click the Options button (see Figure 9-1). Among other things, you can set the driver to give you some basic PostScript error handling. You get three choices.

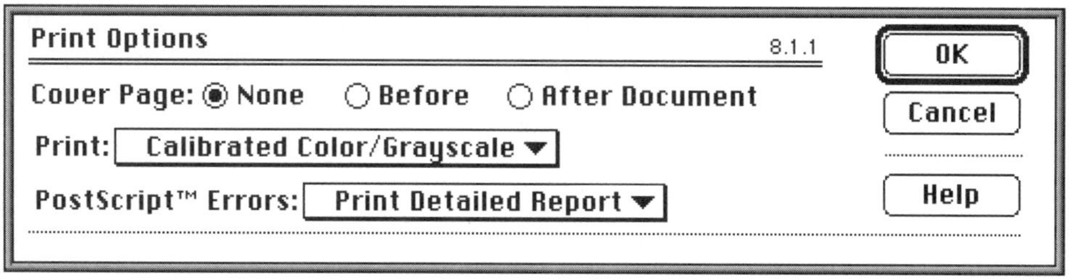

Figure 9-1
PostScript
error handling

▶ No Special Reporting (this is the default setting) gives you what you've always had: nothing. At best, you'll find out that a PostScript error occurred; at worst, you'll get an error number -8133 or the page just won't print at all.

▶ Summarize on Screen is the second level; when a Post-Script error happens, a dialog box appears telling you what the PostScript error was. This is helpful if you don't know much about PostScript and have to respond to someone's question, "Which error was it?"

▶ Print Detailed Report is the most thorough error handling, because it actually prints your page out (at least, as much of the page was imaged before the error came along), along with some detailed information about the state of the PostScript interpreter when it crashed.

XTensions and utilities. If you don't use LaserWriter 8 for some reason, your next tack should be to use some other XTension or utility. One such is an XTension called PinPoint XT from the Cheshire Group (see Appendix B, *Resources*). When a PostScript error is detected, PinPoint XT's special PostScript codes make the page print out with information such as what error it was, where on the page the interpreter was working when it encountered the area, and what sort of information was on the PostScript stack when the error happened. (This is similar in function to what LaserWriter 8 does.)

The shareware program "ehandler.ps" does a similar thing, though on a more basic level. The commercial program Advanced PostScript Error Handler does lots more, but you really need to know some serious PostScript before much of the information it gives you is of much help.

PostScript code. If you can't get any of these tools, here's some PostScript code that you can type into a PostScript dump to help you in your search. When a PostScript error is found, this code forces the printer to print out the page as processed so far, along with the PostScript error name and the offending command. Just put the following code at the beginning of the PostScript dump, just before the line that says "mddict begin" or after the line that says "%%EndComments".

```
true {
    errordict
    /handleerror
    {$error begin
    /chk{dup type /stringtype ne{=string cvs}if}def
        newerror
            { /newerror false store grestoreall initgraphics
            newpath 0 40 moveto 0 65 lineto 612 65
            lineto 612 40 lineto closepath
            gsave 1 setgray fill grestore newpath
            50 100 moveto /Helvetica findfont
            14 scalefont setfont
            (POSTSCRIPT ERROR:) show errorname
            chk show () show
            (OFFENDING COMMAND:) show
            /command load chk show
            (ioerror) errorname ne{showpage}if
        }if
    end
    }put
}if
```

We just keep this around as a text file so that we can quickly copy and paste it in when we need it (we've put it on the disc so you can just copy it from there). If you still don't get anything out of the printer when you download the PostScript to the printer, the error is probably a "VMerror" (run out of memory) or an "ioerror" (bad news…something's wrong in the input or output lines to or from the printer).

Troubleshooting Checklist

What's the first thing you should do when you can't get a page to print? If you answered "give up" or "call the local XPress guru," you need to think again. This whole chapter is dedicated to the memory of thousands of people who first tried every trick in the book and *then* called tech support. However, for each one of those people, there are hundreds more who actually succeeded with these tricks. (And tens of thousands who called tech support without trying anything.)

The very first trick you might try is to pinpoint what page element is causing the offending error by printing only certain parts of the page. For example, select Rough from the Output popup menu in the Print dialog box to avoid printing any pictures or complex frames. If the page prints, chances are one of the graphic images is at fault. You can also use Suppress Printout to specify that a single image should not print.

If the page still doesn't print after printing a rough copy, try taking out a text box at a time, or changing the fonts you used. If you are printing color separations, try printing a single color plate at a time.

One user we know had "limitcheck" and "undefined" Post-Script errors on two different files that contained a lot of Adobe Photoshop grayscale TIFF images. After he performed the following, his files printed without a hitch.

1. He first determined which photos were hanging the print cycle by checking the Print Status dialog box.

2. Next, he checked all the picture boxes and made sure each had a background of zero-percent black.

3. Even though he had a good idea about which image was causing the trouble, he went through the extra work of resaving each photo from Photoshop, naming it the same as before. That way, he could be sure he was getting "fresh" images. (If you have DeBabelizer, you can do this really quickly as a batch process.)

Circle-R in XPress EPS Files

It seems that EPS files created in some earlier versions of QuarkXPress won't print the ® (registered) character in some fonts. Instead, the character is left blank or you get the ® character from a different font.

If you have one of these EPS files, you can fix it with a little PostScript editing.

1. Open the EPS file in any text editor, and find "/register".

2. Change it to "/registered".

Once you've saved the file from your text editor, you need to change its type back to EPSF. You can use an utility such as ResEdit, DiskTop, Schizo, or Shane The Plane to do this (the last two are on the disc bundled with this book).

Note that the EPS files from more recent versions of XPress don't have this problem. Don't worry about it unless you actually see a problem.

Screen Freezes While Printing

If you've raised QuarkXPress's application memory allocation and your screen is still freezing when you try to print certain documents, try reducing the document window size and scrolling so that no part of the page is showing on screen as you print. Also try setting your monitor to display fewer colors, or even black and white (we use the shareware utility Pixel-Flipper to do this, but you can use the Monitors control panel). No, we don't know why this happens. We just know that sometimes this fixes it.

4. Each image was listed as Modified in the Picture Usage dialog box, so he updated them.

5. Finally, before printing, he made sure all the printer options were unchecked in the Page Setup dialog box.

Chances are, it was simply resaving the offending TIFFs from Photoshop that fixed the problems, but we thought we'd pass the whole process along to you since it worked for him.

Graphics Look Awful

One of the most common problems with print jobs from Quark-XPress has never had anything to do with QuarkXPress itself. The problem is with the person sending their files. Remember that QuarkXPress does not actually suck in any EPS or TIFF files that you have imported. It only brings in a low-resolution representation for the screen image, and maintains a link with the original file. If that file changes or is missing when QuarkXPress tries to print it, the graphic will look different from what you expected.

Here are two notes to write on your forehead.

▶ If you're going to send your QuarkXPress document, then send a folder, not a file. The folder should include the document and all EPS and TIFF images you used. You might even consider sending along your screen fonts. The Collect for Output feature can pull all this stuff together (except the fonts) for you.

▶ If you can, send PostScript dumps instead of the document itself. The PostScript dump *does* contain the information from the TIFF and EPS files, as well as all the information QuarkXPress needs from the XPress Preferences file and screen fonts, and so on.

PICTs from Hell

Occasionally, we've run into a problem with QuarkXPress freezing whenever it tries to display certain color PICT images. It'll load a document, but when it starts to image a particular PICT on screen, it simply locks up. Needless to say, this can be very frustrating. The next course of action might be to delete the PICT, but how can you delete an object if QuarkXPress freezes up every time you try to display it?

The best solution is not to use PICT files. Unfortunately, this sometimes even happens with EPS files that have a PICT preview built into them.

The next best solution is to use PixelFlipper extension or the Monitors control panel device to switch your Mac's display to black-and-white mode. Displaying the PICT files this way sometimes fixes things. After you have the document fully open, you can either delete the problem-causing PICT or EPS, or drag the problematic page in Thumbnails view into a new document with exactly the same dimensions (when you drag the page from one document to another, it rebuilds some of the underlying information from scratch).

Also, see "The Ol' Expanded Palette Trick," later in this chapter, for one more way to possibly solve this problem.

EPS FILES

Fonts Come Out Wrong

QuarkXPress must be able to find an outline font for every typeface you've used in the document. That means the fonts you selected and those that are stuck somewhere in an EPS document. Available means that they should be in your System Folder (any system version), your Fonts folder (System 7.1 and later), resident in your printer, or—if you're using MasterJuggler or Suitcase—in the same folder as the bitmap font.

Also, watch out for EPS files nested inside of EPS files nested inside of EPS files. Depending on which application created each EPS file, QuarkXPress may or may not be able to dig deep enough to find every outline font needed. One of the best ways to ensure that the fonts print out correctly is to download them to the printer in advance using a utility such as Font Downloader, Laser-Status, or the LaserWriter Utility to do this.

EPS FILES

When Pages Print in Courier

Sometimes, if you have EPS files in your document which use more than one downloadable font, and you have Unlimited

PICTURES

PICTs Appear Cut Off

For some strange reason, sometimes PICT images brought into QuarkXPress will appear with a large slice of their right and bottom edges sliced off. If you run into this, one potential solution is to open your PICT file in the program that created it, and add a small black box about ¼ of an inch below and to the right of the image. Save again as PICT, and when you reimport the image into QuarkXPress, it may simply content itself with lopping off your black mark, and not the picture itself.

The best solution, however, is to avoid the PICT format altogether. It's notoriously inconsistent and unreliable. The version of DeBabelizer on the disc in the back of the book can convert PICT files into TIFF files.

Crashes with FreeHand EPS with Large Graduated Fills

If XPress crashes while trying to display an Aldus FreeHand EPS that contains a very large (say, full letter size) graduated fill, the problem is with FreeHand, and specifically with a low-memory condition while exporting the EPS graphic.

The solution is simple: re-export the EPS from FreeHand after raising Free-Hand's memory allocation. Try to raise it to at least four megabytes, assuming you can afford it. Also, you might try changing the monitor colors setting to eight-bit color or less before exporting the EPS.

Downloadable Fonts turned on, you'll also get Courier. Yeah, this *is* bizarre. Usually, turning Unlimited Downloadable Fonts on would *solve* Courier substitution problems, not cause them. Strange but true. In this case, turn off Unlimited Downloadable Fonts (see "EPS Files and Unlimited Downloadable Fonts" in Chapter 8, *Printing*).

Exploding Text

Having unexplained troubles with your fonts? Does your text explode all over the place? (If you don't know what we're talking about, you don't have the problem.) Your trouble might be corruption in the kern/track tables of your XPress Preferences file.

1. Open the Kerning Table Editor with no open documents.

2. Export all the custom kern/track data by selecting each font and exporting the kerning data. (Note: if you've never made any special kerning pairs using the Kerning Table Editor, you can skip this step and step four.)

3. Remove the XPress Preferences file from your Quark-XPress folder, and copy a new XPress Preferences file from your installer disk (or, if you never use any of the fancy bitmapped frames, pull the XPress Preferences file out and let XPress build you a new one).

4. Import the custom kerning and tracking data that you saved into the new XPress Preferences file.

Although you'll have to recreate your preferences plus any custom frame and hyphenation data, with any luck your text will stop exploding.

When you open your old documents, XPress asks you if you want to use the new or old XPress Preferences; select Use XPress Preferences. The kern/track data you saved and reimported is used instead of the corrupted ones in the document.

Another potential reason for text exploding is duplicate font information. For example, you might have the same font open in more than one suitcase. This is a no-no, although both Suitcase and MasterJuggler should deal with it (MasterJuggler copes; Suitcase prompts).

Type Printing Too 'Fat'

If all the colored type in a text box is printing fatter, or bolder, than it should, you might be experiencing unwanted trapping. If the text box has a background color of "None", and it overlaps a picture box with an image in it or a background color (or even touches the box at all), the text might be spreading. Solutions?

▶ Turn off trapping in the Trap Preferences dialog box (under the Edit menu).

▶ Give the text box a white background (sometimes you can't do this, of course, if you need it to be transparent).

▶ Change the text's trapping to Overprint or Knockout in the Trapping Information palette.

COLOR SEPARATIONS

Big Ugly White Gaps Between Colors

You've output your four-color separations and sent the file off to your lithographer. A few days later your 12,000 final color proofs show up, and you see, much to your dismay, big white gaps appearing between each of the colors. What happened? You forgot about traps. It's easy to do, believe us. The remedy? Learn absolutely everything you can about traps (Aldus has a great little brochure that talks about trapping and why it's necessary), and how they're created in QuarkXPress.

COLOR SEPARATION

Registration Problems

Imagine the Rockettes kicking their legs to chorus line stardom in perfect synchronization. Then imagine the woman at one end having no sense of rhythm, kicking totally out of sync with the others. This is what happens when one color plate is misregistered with the others. When a sheet of paper is rushed through a printing press and four colors speedily applied to it, there is bound to be some misregistration—sometimes up to a point or two. However, you can help matters considerably by making sure that your film is as consistent as possible.

KICKER

Missing Fonts Can Cause Bombs

This is rather obscure, but could really wreck your day. You open an XPress document that's been created on another Mac, or you import a word-processing file that's been created elsewhere. QuarkXPress informs you that some of the fonts are missing. You attempt to scroll through the document, but QuarkXPress freezes when it appears to be trying to image one of the missing fonts. Since you can't display a problematic page without XPress freezing, how can you fix the trouble-causing fonts?

Go to the Font Usage dialog box, and replace all the fonts reported as missing with fonts that are available on your system. This should replace problem-causing fonts with more stable ones. Then save the document with a new file name, and salvage as much as you can.

Not Enough Space Between Pages

If your pages are printing too close together from a roll-fed printer, you may have to adjust the Page Gap value in the Page Setup dialog box. Note that Quark-XPress prints your document only as wide as it needs to. For example, if your page is four by four inches, QuarkXPress only tells the imagesetter to print four inches of film. This is a great saving for film or RC paper, but sometimes it's a hassle to handle the output.

Whenever we are told that a job printed great "except for one plate that was off register," we immediately ask if that plate was run at a different time than the others. The answer is almost always yes. We realize that it's expensive and time consuming to print four new plates every time you want to make a change to a page, but it is a fact of desktop life that you can almost never get proper registration when you reprint a single plate. Why? The weather, roll stretch, alignment of the stars . . . all sorts of reasons contribute to this massive hassle.

Enlarged Documents Print Off Page

You want an enlarged print of part of a page. You go to Page Setup and specify an enlargement. But when you print, the part of the page you were interested in has been enlarged right off the paper. The LaserWriter driver always enlarges from the top-left corner of any page; there's no way to tell it to enlarge from the center, or any other location. Here a few things you can try.

▶ Select Manual tiling in the Print dialog box. Move the origin to the upper-left corner of the area you want to see enlarged (see Figure 9-2). When you print with tiling on, this will be the upper-left corner of the area imaged on the first page out of the printer.

▶ Make your document smaller so that it just encompasses the size of the area you want to enlarge.

▶ Position the elements you want to have enlarged on the upper-left area of the page, so they're less likely to be cut off by the edge of the paper.

▶ Use the Print Area command from QuarkPrint (bundled with the Power Mac XPress CD-ROM) or an XTension such as PrintIt or PrintArea to specify the exact region of the page you want to print.

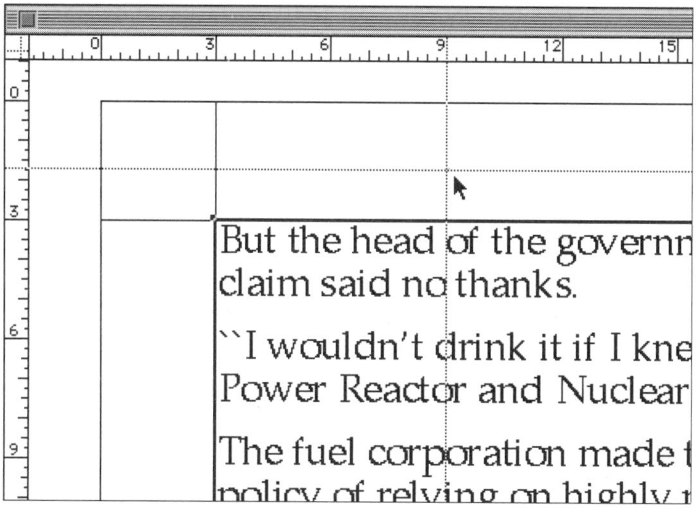

Figure 9-2
Manual tiling

But the head of the governn
claim said no thanks.

``I wouldn't drink it if I kne
Power Reactor and Nuclear

The fuel corporation made t
policy of relying on highly r

CRASHING

Unexpected Quits

There are all sorts of ways that XPress might unexpectedly quit on you: "random" quits (which happen for no apparent reason), document-specific quits (ones that happen while working on a specific document), quits that occur when you launch QuarkXPress or when you open a document, quits when saving a document, and quits when printing and faxing. No matter when one of these happens, this is what Quark's tech support says to do.

1. Don't attempt to relaunch XPress immediately. Your computer is quite unstable at this point.

2. Save all open files in any other open applications.

3. Restart your Mac.

4. Determine whether this was a random quit, by repeating the same thing you were doing when the quit happened. If XPress doesn't quit this time, it means you experienced a "random" quit previously; on the other hand, if it does quit again, then it was probably related to something specific.

QuarkXPress takes a large chunk of memory and works pretty closely with the system. If it quits unexpectedly, it can't give back its memory partition properly or finish other unsettled business. If the system tries to access this partition (which it now sees as available), bad things can happen. Shutting down and restarting require the system to reset itself, and then redistribute memory as applications are launched again after the restart.

If you get a lot of unexpected quits or Type 1 errors, no matter whether they're "random" or happen at specific times, you might try these following tips.

Avoiding Type 1 Errors

If QuarkXPress is crashing consistently or often (you can define "often" yourself; for us, it's more than once a day), try each of these before calling tech support or throwing your computer out the window.

▶ Set your disk cache to its lowest setting in the Memory control panel; it may be 32K or 96K depending on your machine. Programs that write a lot of data to disk at one time, like XPress or Photoshop, are slowed down by the disk cache, which tries to store frequently accessed data.

▶ Make sure your Adobe Type Manager (ATM) font cache is set high enough. A good rule of thumb is about 50K for each font that you're actually using (i.e., will need to be drawn on screen). If your Mac has enough RAM, we suggest you just give ATM about a megabyte (1,000K) and you'll almost certainly never have to worry about such things again.

▶ Give XPress itself at least 4,000K of RAM (select the Quark-XPress icon on the desktop and choose Get Info from the File menu). If your documents are particularly complex, or if you are running a large number of XTensions, you may need to allocate even more than this (certainly add another 1,000K if you're using EfiColor). Some say increasing the value to 8,000K can stop most crashes.

▶ If you're using Power Mac QuarkXPress, you can use the Power Mac virtual-memory scheme in the Apple system (Connectix's RAM Doubler 1.5 uses a similar approach). This can let XPress run with as little as 1,600K without Efi-Color or 3,001K with EfiColor.

▶ Make sure your Largest Unused Block of RAM is larger than the amount you've allocated to XPress in the previous step (you can find the block size by selecting About This Macintosh from the Apple menu when you're on the Finder desktop). If you don't have enough space, XPress won't have enough, no matter how much you allocate. If this suggestion seems contradictory with the previous one, it only means you need more RAM.

▶ Determine whether your XPress Preferences file is corrupt by temporarily moving it out of your QuarkXPress folder. Then launch XPress and see what happens. If your quits stop happening, throw away your old Preferences file and use the new one that XPress has created for you.

▶ If all else fails, reinstall the program from scratch (use your original install disks and install in a new folder).

▶ If that fails, reinstall your system. This can be tricky if you haven't done it before, and you should enlist some help to avoid trashing extensions, fonts, and other doodads.

XTENSIONS

XTension Loading Order

You can vary the order in which your XTensions load by changing their file-names. They load alphabetically. This can occasionally be useful in troubleshooting.

CRASHING

Quitting at Launchtime

Every now and again, people have a lot of trouble with crashes when launching QuarkXPress or opening a new document. Here's a little list that should solve many of those sorts of problems.

▶ If the quit happens while launching XPress from an alias, create a new alias (even those little alias files can get corrupted, it seems).

▶ If you quit while launching from a utility like HandOff or NowMenus, disable the utility; if that's successful, reinstall the utility. If you still have problems after reinstalling, then kill the utility (or kill QuarkXPress—whichever is least important to you).

▶ If you see the QuarkXPress menu bar before the quit occurs, there's a reasonable chance that the problem could be in your fonts. Try turning all your fonts off (this is easy if you use a font utility such as Suitcase, Font Minder, or MasterJuggler) and see if the quit happens again. You may need to do some trial-and-error experimenting to find out just which fonts are bad. Or the trouble could be that your copy of Suitcase or MasterJuggler is corrupted; the best choice then is to reinstall the utility.

Quit on Document Open

If QuarkXPress quits or crashes anytime you open a document, try all the same tips as were discussed in the last tip. If it's only with a specific document, then pay attention to what is happening when XPress crashes. If text is drawing, see "Font Problems," below. If it quits while a graphic is drawing, try "The Ol' Expanded Palette Trick" tip, also outlined below. If none of the methods in those two sections solves your problem, you're probably dealing with a hopelessly corrupted XPress file. The best you can probably hope to do in that event is to retrieve your text using Microsoft Word's Open Any File feature (Shift-Open or Shift-F6). The layout, and any graphics you drew using XPress's tools, are kaput.

▶ If you see the QuarkXPress splash screen (the one with the logo in it) just before the quit occurs, the problem could be with something in the QuarkXPress folder. You can determine this by dragging the program to the desktop and launching it from there. If it launches successfully, take a close look at the contents of your XPress folder; something must be corrupted or incompatible. This might be an XTension, an import/export filter, printer description file (PDF), or the XPress Preferences file (mentioned above). Try removing these and see if the error disappears.

▶ Try disabling system extension files by restarting your Mac with the Shift key down (hold down the Shift key until you see the "Extensions Off" message). If QuarkXPress stops quitting after that, the problem is probably a corrupted or incompatible system extension or control panel device (located in their respective folders in your System Folder). The only good way to troubleshoot this is by trial and error (removing all but one and restarting, removing all but two and restarting, and so on).

Crashing from Font Troubles

Fonts are mysterious, at best. They almost always work just fine, but they're software as much as anything else, and sometimes they break down and become corrupted. Or, sometimes the utilities that handle fonts can have troubles. Here are a few things to watch out for.

▶ Make sure ATM has enough RAM.

▶ Check what version of ATM you're using. If you're using a version earlier than 3.0, you're probably in trouble; preferably, you're using version 3.6.1 or later (3.8 or later if you have a Power Macintosh). Adobe charges for some of its updates, but ATM ships with all of its applications now.

▶ If you use a font utility such as MasterJuggler or Suitcase (you probably should be using one of these), check what version you're using. Every few months, try calling the company that makes your utility and ask them what the newest version is. ALSoft makes MasterJuggler, and they require you to pay from $5 to $20 for each upgrade. Suitcase is from Symantec/Fifth Generation, and their micro-upgrades are usually posted to online services and Internet ftp sites.

▶ Adobe Type Reunion (ATR) is notorious for incompatibilities with other programs; it's currently at version 1.1. This is always the first system extension that we disable to see if a problem goes away. In fact, Phil has stopped using it altogether, it was giving him so many troubles.

The Ol' Expanded Palette Trick

If you think a corrupt font or graphic is causing an unexpected quit or crash while opening a specific document, try this trick, which allows a document to open without actually being drawn on screen.

1. Launch QuarkXPress with no documents open.

2. Display either the Colors, Style Sheets, or Document Layout palette.

3. Move and resize the palette so it covers the entire screen (the resize box is in the lower-right corner of the palette).

4. Open the problem document. It opens behind the full-screen palette, making it unnecessary for XPress to draw the corrupted font or graphic.

5. If you think it's a font problem, use Font Usage to remove the suspect fonts or graphics.

6. If you think it's a picture problem, close your documents and select it in the Open dialog box. Hold down the Command key when pressing the Open button. That forces XPress to reimport the image. Otherwise, move the original graphics so that XPress thinks they're missing, then use Picture Usage to relink to a different picture.

7. Close or shrink the full-screen palette.

8. If the document doesn't quit at that point, do a Thumbnails-view drag to get all pages of this document into a new document. Reinstall the corrupt fonts, or resave the corrupt graphics from their creating application and re-import them into the new document.

Quits While Printing

One of the less frequent crashing errors in QuarkXPress is quitting when you print. However, just in case, here are a few little tips that might help.

▶ Determine whether you can print from any other application. If you can't, then the problem isn't related to XPress, but is probably related to printer drivers, memory, or system extension conflicts.

▶ If you're printing through a spooler or network queue, try bypassing it or turning it off. This includes local spoolers such as Apple's PrintMonitor (Background Printing options in the Chooser) and SuperLaserSpool. Also, remote spoolers such as those that often exist on AppleShare and NetWare servers. If the document prints while not being spooled, the spooler might not have enough memory. Try allocating more memory to it. Also, try selecting ASCII (rather than Binary) from the Format popup menu in the Page Setup dialog box.

▶ Some screen savers get in the way of printing in the background for some reason. If you turn off your screen saver, it might help.

▶ Try printing with system extensions turned off (hold down the Shift key while restarting).

Force Quit

When QuarkXPress freezes up your machine (we like to say that if XPress doesn't freeze up on you every now and again, you're just not trying hard enough), there's almost nothing you can do except restart your machine. Almost. You can try force quitting, by pressing Command-Option-Escape. This undocumented Macintosh feature works in any program, but we've found it really helpful every now and again for getting out of freezes.

If your machine isn't hopelessly frozen (i.e., the mouse pointer still moves), you may get a dialog box which says, "Force <application> to quit? Unsaved changes will be lost," and contains the Force Quit and Cancel buttons. Click the Force Quit button, and—if you're lucky—you'll be dropped into the Finder. You lose all changes made to any open files in XPress since the last save. Save your work in other applications and restart right away.

If you're not lucky, then the machine doesn't respond, displays the same dialog box again, or brings up a restart dialog box. In any of these cases, the only thing you can do is press the restart button on your computer; or use the power switch on the front of the computer if you don't have a restart button.

Note that it can be disastrous if you don't restart your computer after force-quitting and before starting XPress again.

SAVING

Can't Save, Resource Not Found

The "Can't Save, Resource Not Found" error message is typically evidence of a corrupted XPress Preferences file; it's possible that it didn't install correctly, or has gotten corrupted. This is especially likely on the 3.0-to-3.1 upgrade, where sometimes the old XPress Data file didn't convert correctly to an XPress Preferences file. The solution: either replace your XPress Preferences file with a backed-up copy (assuming you made one), or just throw away the file altogether (XPress makes you a new one next time you start the program—but you'll have to reset all your preferences).

SAVING

Trouble Saving? Try This

It's a very scary feeling when you suddenly can't save your document. Maybe XPress offers you some sort of lame error message when you select Save or Save As from the File menu (which leaves you in the unenviable position of having a document on your

---

CRASHING

Quits While Faxing

People try to do all sorts of wacky things with QuarkXPress, including trying to fax from it. Actually, that's not such a wacky thing at all. However, what you need to know is that faxing from within XPress can be problematic, at best. Nonetheless, Quark and software fax companies are beginning to work out the bugs.

Here are a couple things you should know, though. TelePort, Dove Fax, and Abaton Interfax are not compatible with XPress version 3.1; you need to upgrade to 3.11 or later. Telefax, from 3X France WYSIWYF, is not compatible with 3.2. The 3X France developers are aware of the problem and there should be a fix soonish (perhaps even by the time you read this).

Further, if you installed LaserWriter 8.0 (the very first release of it) and never updated to 8.1.1 or later, you'll probably have problems faxing from any software with any version of XPress.

Error -54 When Opening a File

You'll get a "File is locked (-54)" message when you try to open a file if the file is locked or is in use by someone else on your network. However, sometimes you can get the message even when neither of these things is happening. It's quite frustrating. If restarting your computer doesn't help, then just try to open the document. Sometimes it'll just open, on the third or fifth or seventh try or so. It's weird, but it works for some people.

screen that you can't save) or maybe Auto Save is acting up and giving you trouble. Either situation sucks raw eggs through coffee stir straws.

Instead of panicking or throwing your computer out a window, try simply closing your file, and then click Yes when XPress asks you if you want to save your changes. This may not work at all, but believe it or not, sometimes it does.

It Could Be an XTension

With all the possible things that could go wrong in XPress, it's amazing that you can get any work done at all with the program! Well here's one more trap to watch out for: if you're having any kind of trouble at all—from crashes to keystrokes not working to other oddities—alongside system problems, system extension conflicts, a corrupt XPress Preferences file, or a corrupt XPress itself, the problem could be a corrupt XTension. Try removing or otherwise turning off (if you have XTension Manager) all your XTensions and see if the problem goes away. If it does, then you need to figure out which XTension it was by turning them on and off one at a time.

Auto Save Saves the Day

If you have Auto Save turned on and your machine freezes up, there's a small chance that the function will still be working in the background. That means that if you wait for a little while instead of rebooting immediately, XPress might save all the work you've done since the last Auto Save. If Auto Save is set to save every five minutes, then wait five minutes after the freeze before rebooting. Then, when you open the document again, XPress might have saved your work.

Minor Repairs

If you get a message stating, "This document needs minor repairs" while opening a previous-version document in XPress, it's actually good news, believe it or not: XPress has found some inconsistencies, some anomalies, in the document, and it wants to fix them.

The problems aren't caused by the user doing something wrong; rather, they're all due to bugs in the program.

If you really want all the gory details, here are some of the conditions that can cause this message to come up, along with what remedy QuarkXPress takes.

▶ Invalid color in a document; any items colored with this are set to black.

▶ Text format specification (style, size, font, etc.) is bad (programmers use words like "invalid" and "bad" to describe all sorts of things, none of which are really relevant to us mere mortals); a valid type style is substituted.

▶ Paragraph format specification (indent, leading, etc.) is bad; a valid format is substituted.

▶ Two differing versions of the length of a story exist in the document; the longest one is used.

▶ An invalid H&J set is referenced; the reference is changed to a valid H&J.

▶ An invalid style sheet is referenced; the reference is changed to a valid style sheet.

If this is happening to many of your documents, it could be that they were all based on the same "bad" template or document; in that case, it would be a good idea to fix that template or document before any further files are created from it.

By the way, this all happens automatically; you're not given any options for or information about what's being fixed.

CRASHES
Deleting System Preferences

While this isn't strictly a QuarkXPress tip, it can save the day. If you're having repeated crashes when you run a certain application, look in the System Folder's Preferences folder. Find the preference file for the application that's causing you problems (or that you think is) and throw it away. Restart the machine or application. Often, you stop crashing.

LAUNCHING XPRESS
Serial Number Already in Use

Quark's copy protection won't let you run two copies of XPress with the same serial number on a network; you need to purchase a separate copy of the program for each machine you want to run it on. Every copy of XPress has a distinct serial number, so you

Power Mac Network Quit

We've found a problem with the newly released (at this writing) QuarkXPress 3.3 for Power Macintosh. On occasion, we get a message that XPress can't find the network. XPress lets you click the OK button on this message dialog box, and then dims most menu items and disables tools. You can save the file (or save it under another name), but you have to quit the program and launch it again. This message comes up even though you may have fileservers mounted, email going in the background, and experience no other problems. At the time of this writing, technical support is trying to find the cause; if you have this problem, get in touch with them for a solution (see "On-line Resources" and other information in Appendix B, *Resources*).

shouldn't get this error when running multiple registered copies on a network. This can be annoying for installation (if you own four copies, you don't necessarily want to keep track of four sets of disks), but Quark feels it's necessary to protect their license.

However, every now and then, someone finds themselves staring at a message saying that another version of XPress is running on your own computer, or on a computer that is *not* running XPress! It's very disconcerting. Often, restarting the machine helps. Occasionally, you may need to restart a server or another machine running XPress on the network to get this problem to go away.

Power Mac XPress *doesn't* warn you if another copy with the same serial number is in use. It just quits after loading XTensions with no message.

Bad F-Line Error

Some days it seems like just about everything goes wrong. When you start seeing "bad F-line" errors, you know it's time to think about lunch. Then, over your tofu hot dog and wheatgrass shake, think about what typically causes these problems.

- ▶ Faulty SCSI cables. Make sure your cables are the best you can get. You might get electrical interference through them otherwise. Good SCSI cables are hard to bend; bad ones are limp.

- ▶ System heap too small. Try increasing your system heap, using something like the NOW Utilities's Startup Manager. Set it to about 25 percent above the amount needed. This was more of a problem in System 6, but many people tell us that changing the heap helps programs with large memory requirements.

Import Crash Fix

Sometimes we'll export text from XPress or PageMaker in Word format, and open it in Word to make changes. When we save the file and try to import it into XPress, the application freezes up. Quark is constantly updating their Word import filter to solve nasty bits like this, so you may not experience it.

If you have this problem, the solution is simple. Open the file in Word. Create a new document. Select All (Command-A) in the first file, switch to the blank document, select Paste, and then save the file under a new name (like "Blahty-blah.fixed"). Import this new file. This usually works like a charm for us; it cleans up any weirdness in the XPress- or PageMaker-created Word export.

Font Headaches When You Open a Document

We hate getting the message, "This document was built with other versions of some fonts. It will be reflowed using this System's fonts." It could mean that a screen font used in your document has been changed since the document was last saved, or it could be one of a few other troubles.

► In the first few years of PostScript typefaces, type houses often made small tweaks to the metrics (character widths and kerning pairs) of their fonts. This led to a lot of confusion—for Adobe's release of Times, for instance, there have been several versions of the screen and printer fonts. In the last three or four years, this habit seems to have died away; however, you can still encounter this problem when working with service bureaus or people with older fonts. Even if you've just changed the kerning pair information using some sort of kerning utility, QuarkXPress generates the "other fonts" message and reflows the document. If reflowing is a problem, make sure that everyone who works on a document has the same versions of necessary screen fonts installed.

► You can also get this message if some of your screen fonts have become corrupted. Your fonts are particularly suspect if you frequently encounter this alert while you're typing. There aren't many utilities that will specifically check for a corrupted screen font. The latest version of Now Utilities' WYSIWYG Menus will alert you to corrupted fonts when you boot up. Aldus's installer program also checks for corrupted fonts on startup. If a screen font is corrupted, simply replacing it from the original manufacturer's disk should solve the problem.

MICROSOFT WORD

Don't Use Word's Fast Save

If incoming Microsoft Word files appear garbled, or seem to be responsible for freezing QuarkXPress, go to the Preferences command under the Tools menu in Word, click the Open and Save icon on the left, and turn off the Allow Fast Saves option. Then save the document again and try importing it.

Fast-saved Word documents can sometimes cause XPress problems. Saving Word documents with the old-fashioned "slow" options results in files that XPress can import with much less difficulty.

TEXT FLOW

Page-Dragging Crashes

We've heard reports that some people's machines crash when they drag an object or a page from an old document (pre-3.2) into a newer document (3.2 and later). The problem, it seems, has to do with a bug in the way that XPress handles text flow. The solution is to open the older document with the Option key held down (or Option-double-click on the document to open it from the desktop). This forces XPress to reflow the text and often clears up these sorts of problems.

▶ Occasionally you'll get this kind of trouble if you have both TrueType and PostScript versions of the same font. We heartily encourage you to get rid of all your TrueType fonts except the basic system fonts (Monaco, Geneva, New York, and Chicago).

▶ If the file was created in QuarkXPress 3.0, it could be a totally erroneous alert. Just ignore it, but do a Save As in your newer version of the program.

▶ This is kind of obscure, but if you save and close a document before XPress has internally had a chance to reflow all the text that's in it, the document is saved in what's called a reflow condition, so it has to reflow when you open the document again.

If the problem persists, try reducing your document to Fit in Window size, then scrolling though it, page by page. If you run into the "It will be reflowed using this System's fonts." message, click OK and continue scrolling until you get to the end of the document. Strangely enough, sometimes this seems to "flush out" whatever's causing the constant, irritating error messages.

FONT UTILITIES

Suitcase, MasterJuggler, and Corruption Crashes

Both Suitcase and MasterJuggler can make your life worth living (that is, if you care about type as much as we do). But Suitcase in particular, and sometimes MasterJuggler, can also cause some severe problems when they encounter corrupted font files.

After one of our colleagues sorted out the fonts on a friend's machine recently, he got a panicked call a few hours later when she restarted her machine. It turns out that one of the fonts he told Suitcase to load was corrupted, but instead of posting some sort of error message, Suitcase crashed the machine next time she restarted the computer.

The solution to this sort of problem is to hold down the Shift key at startup so system extensions don't load. Then find the corrupted font by either using the Aldus Installer utility or by investigating the bitmap fonts on your hard drive. If you double-click on suitcase files in the Finder, the ones that generate the "suitcase is damaged" error are the ones that are causing Suitcase to crash. Trash these fonts and reinstall clean copies from backups or the original disks. Then, when you restart the machine you can reopen the newly installed fonts with Suitcase. (Note that you can't just move the damaged fonts elsewhere on your machine; Suitcase still finds them.)

TYPE STYLE

Outline Style Doesn't Print as It Appears

If you apply the Outline style to type, be aware that these characters may not print as they appear on screen. This is due to limitations in Apple's QuickDraw routines (QuickDraw is also where that problematic file format, PICT, comes from).

In QuarkXPress, if the color of an Outline-styled character is white, its interior color should be the same as the background color of the text box. If the character isn't white, its interior should then be white regardless of the box's fill color.

What you see on screen is, however, sometimes different. Table 9-1 shows what we mean.

FONTS

Are My Fonts Damaged?

If you own any recent Aldus program, you can use the Aldus Installer Utility to check for damaged fonts (it's one of the functions available in the Installer's menu). Note that it only checks for common types of damage in bitmap suitcases, not outline fonts; but that's okay, because damaged suitcases are the ones that can bite you, and outline fonts (in our experience) almost never get corrupted.

Table 9-1

How Outline-styled text looks and prints

Type is . . .	Displays		Prints	
	Outline	Interior	Outline	Interior
Nonwhite, nonrotated	Character color	Box color	Character color	White
White, nonrotated	White	Box color	White	Box color
Nonwhite, rotated	Character color	White	Character color	White
White, rotated	White	White	White	Box color

Once you know what's happening, it won't surprise you when something that looks one way on the screen prints totally differently (our kingdoms for Display PostScript on the Macintosh!).

FONTS

TrueType No-Nos

We don't like TrueType. To us, it's just one more thing to worry about. TrueType fonts can drastically slow your output from a laser printer or imagesetter. There is one set of TrueType fonts we

Precise Page Sizes

If the work you're doing requires that a page size be within a point of precision ($\frac{1}{72}$ of an inch), you should be aware that the "BoundingBox" comment in both EPS and PostScript dumps are truncated values to the point. That is, if a page size is 436.7 points wide, the "BoundingBox" value only shows it as 436 points wide. This can make a difference (especially as it's not even rounding to the nearest point; just truncating to the smaller value), especially when transferring a PostScript file to a high-end system. There's not a lot you can do about it, other than going in and changing the "BoundingBox" comment in the PostScript code (which isn't hard if you have a text editor and a basic understanding of PostScript).

appreciate, though, and that's the system-font set included starting with System 7. No more onscreen jaggies for Geneva, Chicago, New York, and Monaco!

But just because you now have infinitely scalable TrueType versions of system fonts, that doesn't mean you should immediately trash the fixed-size screen font files for system fonts. QuarkXPress's menus and dialog boxes would immediately look strange, as no rasterizer, such as TrueType's, can automatically match the quality of a hand-tweaked bitmap optimized for a specific size. Also, since TrueType would have to be constantly rasterizing the type for menus and such, you'd suffer a drop in performance every time you accessed a menu or dialog box.

Here's an even bigger no-no: Don't *ever* have PostScript and TrueType versions of fonts with the same name active on your Mac at the same time. A classic example is the ever-popular Palatino. If you have the both versions of this font open on your system, you may end up applying the PostScript version of the font, rasterized by Adobe Type Manager, in your document, then downloading the TrueType version, and printing that.

Or suppose you want to use the TrueType version of a font, and don't even have the Adobe version on your Macintosh. Should be fine, and it is, except if a PostScript version of the same font, with the same name, resides in your laser printer's ROM or hard disk. The built-in fonts take precedence over the ones being sent from your Mac, so you may ask for a TrueType Times, say, and get an Adobe Times.

The best solution? We think it's to trash all TrueType fonts except for the system fonts mentioned above, and just stick with Type 1 PostScript fonts.

When 8.345" Isn't 8.345"

In 99 out of 100 instances, when you look in the Document Setup dialog box QuarkXPress shows you the real size of the document. But there's one case when the numbers you see won't reflect the actual document size. If you enter a page dimension for a custom page size that uses more than three decimal places, such as "8.0125"", QuarkXPress only displays "8.012"", but it actually remembers that last .0005. So, if you trustingly make a new document at what appears to be the old document's size according to the Document Setup dialog box, you won't be able to drag-copy pages, as the documents won't actually be the same size, even though their document setups insist that they are.

Unfortunately, there's no way to see if QuarkXPress is keeping track of page size information beyond the third decimal place. We recommend avoiding measurements that go to $\frac{1}{10000}$'s of an inch. If you must use them, write the measurements down on a piece of paper somewhere or make a note on the pasteboard in the file. You never know when it might come in handy.

KERNING
Lost Kerning Tables

Ah, what a delight! Since QuarkXPress 3.1, all the custom kerning you create in QuarkXPress is automatically included in both your XPress Preferences file and each document. (Kerning pairs are set globally, so changes you make with a document open apply to any future document you open.) This means that you never need to worry about your kerning pairs disappearing when you send a document to another QuarkXPress user. Well, hardly ever.

To really be safe, you need to know a little about how XPress reads and saves kerning pair information. The kerning pairs that you see when you use the kerning editor (by selecting Kerning Table Edit under the Utilities menu) can represent one of two things.

If you haven't defined (or imported) any custom kerning pairs for a typeface in QuarkXPress, then the kerning pairs you see displayed reside only in the "FOND" resource of the screen font (or TrueType font). This means that these pairs are not stored in your XPress Preferences file or the currently active document. In this case, the kerning editor is simply acting as a window into what's available on your fonts, specifically in their "FOND" resources.

However, as soon as you use QuarkXPress to modify or create a single pair, then QuarkXPress automatically saves *all* of the listed kerning pairs into XPress Preferences and your document.

Unfortunately, there's no way of knowing just by looking in the Kerning Values window whether what you're seeing represents information stored in your system's screen fonts, your XPress Preferences, or your document.

So, here's the problem. If you've invested in customized screen fonts for your Mac system, or you've used a kerning utility to tweak your system's fonts, your kerning pairs may be different than your colleague's. If that person opens your QuarkXPress document, the text gets reflowed using a different screen font

PICTURES
EPS Files and Blank Plate Printing

You've got black and two other spot colors in your QuarkXPress document. You have a few included EPS files, but you've made certain that they only use the same colors as in your QuarkXPress document. You go to print separations, and tell Quark-XPress to print all plates. Much to your chagrin—and that of your pocketbook, if you're going through a service bureau—you find QuarkXPress has printed blank plates for each process color, even though the only one you're using is black!

Your EPS files were probably created in FreeHand. For some reason, FreeHand EPS files cause every process plate to be printed, even when the color is not used in the EPS file. You really only have two solutions at this time: avoid selecting All Plates and print each plate you do want separately, one at a time, or dive into the PostScript (this is not a fun option).

Locked Libraries

If you have trouble opening a library, it may be that the library is locked or in use by someone else on the network. Sometimes the same things cause a library to appear totally empty when you do open it, even though there should be items in it.

(totally different line breaks, and so on).

One way to avoid the problem is to include your font suitcases with your documents, but there's a far easier way. Simply go into the Kerning Values dialog box for every typeface for which you have a customized screen font. Make a minor change to a single, seldom-used kerning pair, or add a new pair that's something you'd never encounter in the real world, such as "&&". When you save this pair, QuarkXPress writes the *entire* list of kerning pairs to XPress Preferences as well as to any open document which uses that typeface. This way, you can always be assured that your custom kerning pairs will follow your documents wherever they go.

Salvaging Damaged Documents

Yes, it does happen from time to time that QuarkXPress may corrupt a document. Sometimes, for example, what appears to be a perfectly good document won't print, giving you the infamous −8133 PostScript error. There are a few things you can try doing if you've got such a problem document.

First, try using the Save As command to save the document to a new file. This can sometimes help, since as you work on a document, it can become larger and more complicated as you edit text and arrange elements. Save As makes a "clean" copy of the file, without this information.

If you have a QuarkXPress document so badly corrupted that you can't even open it, you may be able to use CanOpener, from Abbott Systems, to pull out some of the text. A secondary approach would be to use Microsoft Word: hold down the Shift key and select Open to open the damaged QuarkXPress document. You'll be able to see all the text in the document, though it will appear garbled in places. Or you could use a utility like PrairieSoft's DiskTop to change the corrupted document's file type to "TEXT", then use the Get Text command to import it into a new QuarkXPress document. From there you can salvage at least some of the original document's text.

The next two tips show some more creative techniques (that can often save much more material).

Dragging Thumbnails to Resurrect Dead Docs

Another way to retrieve corrupted or weird files is to drag thumbnails around. It's a last resort method, but it can save your buttock.

1. Reduce your problem document to Thumbnails view.

2. Create a new document, with the same page dimensions as the problem one. Put it into Thumbnails view. (To shave a step off this procedure, hold down Shift and Option while selecting Tile Documents from the any document's title bar to resize all documents to Thumbnails view.)

3. Shift-click to select all the pages of the old document, and drag them to the new.

If you're lucky, the process of dragging from old to new will leave possible file corruption problems behind, and the new document will print correctly. Sometimes this actually works (Phil has had really good luck with this).

Bad File Format (70)

If you get the error "Bad File Format (70)" or "Unknown Error (-109)" while trying to open or save an XPress document, you're in big trouble. The file, as they say, is probably toast. However, try this if you have Norton Utilities:

In the Norton Disk Editor, open the file. If bytes nine through 12 have the following values:

FF FF FF FC *or* FF FF FF FD,

change them to the following:

00 3F 00 3F

It just might work. It's worth a try, anyway. Better than not opening the file at all. In fact, this sometimes works with other sorts of files that you can't open for one reason or another. We suggest editing a copy of the file rather than the file itself.

On the other hand, you should *only* try this if you're somewhat skilled and willing to take a risk. If you screw up in the Disk Editor, you could screw up your whole hard drive.

Can't Import TIFF

Contrary to popular opinion, not all TIFFs are created equal. Some scanner software creates TIFF images differently than others, and those are different from some applications' TIFF images. Sometimes QuarkXPress won't let you import a TIFF image because it doesn't recognize that particular flavor of TIFF. The solution is generally to open the TIFF in some other program and then resave it.

For example, if you can get Adobe Photoshop or DeskPaint to open a TIFF file that QuarkXPress can't read, you can save it from those programs and then XPress can probably read it. Also, DeBabelizer is an excellent solution for opening and resaving a whole mess o' files quickly.

Frame Editor Crashes

We don't like Frame Editor, but some folks use it nonetheless (who listens to us?). However, if you're having trouble with your Frame Editor crashing all the time, try the following:

▶ Don't run Frame Editor at the same time as QuarkXPress.

▶ Turn 32-bit addressing off in the Memory control panel and Restart the machine. (This isn't wise if you have more than eight megabytes of RAM, and it isn't possible if you have a Power Mac.)

Hope for Lost Icons

Sometimes QuarkXPress documents and libraries get confused and lose their desktop icons. Sometimes you might even have the file's type and creator scrambled. One side-effect of this is that you can't double-click on the icons to automatically open them. You can do three things to get around this.

▶ **Rebuild the desktop.** If you hold down the Option and Command keys while the Macintosh is starting up (after the Extensions have loaded and before the hard drives appear on the desktop), you'll be asked if you really want to rebuild the desktop. If you click OK, there's a good chance that your lost icons will appear again.

▶ **Drag and drop.** For a less complete solution, you can drag the icon onto the QuarkXPress program icon (or an alias of the program) using System 7's "drag-and-drop" ability. This opens the document or library. If the program's not running, the system launches it. Then you can Save As with the same or different name, which rebuilds the icon and its link to the application.

▶ **Rename as a Windows XPress file.** If your file's type and creator are scrambled, XPress doesn't know the document belongs to it. You can either use DiskTop, ResEdit, or another utility to fix these items, or you can use this goofy but excellent little hack. QuarkXPress can open any XPress file with the suffix ".QXD" (libraries are ".QXL", templates ".QXT"). If QuarkXPress is having difficulty opening the file with the techniques above, you can rename your file "filename.QXD", and then use the drag-and-drop tip above to open it.

KEYSTROKES

Keystrokes Conflicts

We'd love a utility that told us which modifier-key combinations were in use by QuicKeys, CEToolbox, the Apple system, Microsoft Word, and other keystroke-assigning programs. Such a utility doesn't exist. Because of this, there's a good chance that you'll end up with a keystroke or two that should work in XPress but doesn't.

For instance, depending on which version of system software you're running, some, many, or all of XPress's keystrokes that involve the Command and Option keys (simultaneously) just don't work when the Caps Lock key is down. The solution, of course, is to release the Caps Lock key.

A related problem is that Apple, when they released their WorldScript extensions for supporting multiple-language system software, seized the Command-spacebar and Command-Option-spacebar keystrokes. In XPress, you use these normally for different spaceband character. If you substitute the Control key for Command, you're back in business.

You might also encounter this if you have SCSIProbe installed. Its default "mount all volumes" keystroke is Command-spacebar. You can change it by selecting SCSIProbe from the Control Panels folder, clicking the Option button, and typing a new keystroke.

Finally, the default keystroke for pause sequence in QuicKeys is Command-Option-P—the same as the Page Setup dialog box in QuarkXPress. Bring up the QuicKeys dialog box and select Universal under its Sets menu. Click on the keystroke for Pause and press a new combination, like the F15 key (which has "pause" written all over it).

This is only a short list of the keystroke shortcuts you may find that don't work in XPress. Whenever you install new utilities or extensions, check their "hotkeys," "shortcuts," or "keystrokes" setup items to make sure they aren't overlapping.

MEMORY
Goofy Memory Problems

Sometimes QuarkXPress does something really goofy—such as not letting you type a word or character or not finding some text that you *know* is in your document somewhere. When it does this, it may mean that XPress is running out of memory. The solution? Quit the program and relaunch. That usually clears it up. If not, you may have to restart your computer.

macros
10
AND SCRIPTS

Any time you find yourself doing the same thing more than just a few times, you should be thinking, "why aren't I using a macro or a script for this?" If you select Colors from the Edit menu six times a day (or anything else, for that matter), why not save yourself the trouble and set a keystroke to do it for you. One tap on the keyboard is usually faster and easier than a long trip across the screen to a menu.

Or, better yet, you can set up macros to do sequences of events. For instance, we've made a macro that jumps to the beginning of a paragraph, adds a bullet followed by a tab, then formats the bullet to the desired font, size and baseline shift. It's *much* faster than trying to do it one paragraph at a time.

In this chapter, we cover macros and scripting—two ways to make your computer perform all those boring, repetitive, mind-numbing tasks for you. Remember: Computers are great at that stuff. Why suffer any more than you need to?

Using QuicKeys

Let's just get one thing perfectly clear: if you don't own and use a copy of CE Software's QuicKeys, you're not being efficient in your

The Control Key

Since most Mac programs don't use the Control key, it's a good modifier to use when defining custom keystrokes. XPress uses of the Control key as a shortcut to jump to View Percentage field (Control-V) and for the wordspacing controls (see "Adjusting Wordspacing" in Chapter 4, *Type and Typography*), and as alternatives to some keystrokes that already have a modified key shortcut. Add another modifier, like the Command or Option keys, and you can be certain any QuicKey you define won't conflict with something already in QuarkXPress.

work. QuicKeys lets you create macros to tell QuarkXPress—and any other program you use, including the Finder—what to do.

While QuarkXPress has scores of keyboard shortcuts, you can never really have enough of them. We like to use QuicKeys to devise even more ways to make our lives easier. Most of our QuicKeys for QuarkXPress let us do things right from the keyboard without having to grab the mouse and make menu selections. Others automate repetitive actions.

The best way to get the most out of QuicKeys (besides reading this chapter) is to drop everything and run out to the store and get *The QuicKeys 3 Book*, published by Addison Wesley. Don Sellers and Steve Roth, the book's authors, explain all the ins and outs of this deceptively simple program. (The fact that the authors share offices with David is *purely* coincidental and has nothing to do with this testimonial—it's a great book!)

But the most ingenious macros in the world won't help you if you don't have them set up for QuarkXPress. So, sometimes you have to go to a little extra trouble up front in order to be lazy later. Always ask yourself when you're using QuarkXPress, "Could I create a macro to do this for me? Will I need to do this often enough to justify creating a macro?" If the answer is yes, or even maybe, go ahead and do it!

Note that you can also use ResEdit to add or change keyboard shortcuts for any QuarkXPress menu command (see "ResEdit Keystrokes," later in this chapter), but QuicKeys lets you do much more than just that.

Conflict with Universal QuicKey Mousies

Here's another warning: QuarkXPress doesn't like Mousies very much. If you define a Universal QuicKey Mousie (a cutesy QuicKeys term that describes a category of shortcut that can perform tasks such as Page Up, Page Down, and so on), they will act up in XPress. For instance, Page Up, Page Down, Home, and End scroll any open palettes instead of the document window (which is what you *wanted* to be scrolled).

If you don't use those Mousies in other programs, just delete them from your Universal set (XPress has its own keystrokes to do all that). But if you really need them in your Universal Sets, define new Alias shortcuts in QuarkXPress's set that trigger the same keystrokes. For example, you can make an Alias QuicKey so that every time you press Page Up, it triggers the Page Up key. This effectively negates the Universal Mousie you may have made.

STEP AND REPEAT
Cloning an Object

QuarkXPress's Step and Repeat command is very handy for making multiple, offset copies of an object. But we frequently want to make a copy of an object right on top of the original, then drag the copy to a new position, as we can do in Aldus FreeHand using the Clone command. So we've used QuicKeys to do this for us.

If you've got QuicKeys, the easiest way to make a Clone key is to turn on Record Sequence, and then go ahead and invoke the Step and Repeat command, type "1", press Tab, "0", Tab, "0", and Return. You'll end up with a QuicKey sequence that selects the Step and Repeat menu item, then types "1" for the number of copies, "0" twice for the two offsets, and then presses the Return (see Figure 10-1). Simple, elegant, and it works. We've assigned Command-equals to this key, same as the Clone command in FreeHand.

STYLE SHEETS
Selecting Styles

XPress limits the keys you can use as shortcuts for styles to any combination of modifier keys (Command, Option, Control, Shift) with the 15 function keys (F1-15) and the numeric keypad. We find that's too limiting, and have defined alternate keystrokes for commonly used styles. Since XPress doesn't use the Control key for commands (except for the obscure wordspacing command available with the FeaturesPlus or Thing-a-ma-bob XTensions—see "Adjusting Wordspacing" in Chapter 4, *Type and Typography*—and Control-V, which jumps to the View Percentage field), using the Control and Command keys in combination with the first letter of the style gives you an easy-to-remember mnemonic.

QUICKEYS
Important QuicKeys Notice

If you're going to be using QuicKeys to select menu items in XPress, you should be aware that you must have the Search All Menus item selected in the QuicKeys Menu dialog box. Otherwise, QuicKeys won't be able to find some menu items (mainly hierarchical submenus).

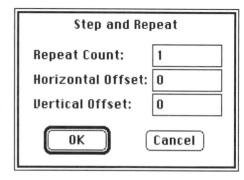

Figure 10-1
Cloning an object

KEYSTROKES
"No Style" and Edit Styles

Two essential QuicKeys select "No Style" from the Style menu (make sure that Search All Menus is turned on) and the Style Sheets item from the Edit menu. We often use Command-Control-N or Control-keypad-zero (QuicKeys distinguishes keypad keys from the main keyboard keys) for "No Style", and Command-Control-S to open the Style Sheets dialog box.

KEYSTROKES
Other Menu Commands

The Section command is also worth a keystroke. We use Command-Option-S. There's no key combination for the Make Fraction command available from the FeaturesPlus or Thing-a-ma-bob XTensions. We've assigned it to Command-Option-Control-1, but you can use any keystroke you like.

The only preset keystrokes for views are Command-zero for Fit In Window, and Command-1 for Actual Size. You can easily add others, such as Command-2 for 200% view and Command-5 for 50% view.

Command-2 normally inserts a previous page number token in text. You can fix the conflict by remapping this to Command-Option-2 using an Alias QuicKey. If you do this, Phil recommends that you also remap Command-3 and Command-4, adding Option to each, for the sake of consistency.

KEYSTROKES
Copying the Word Keypad

If you're used to the way Microsoft Word or Aldus PageMaker uses the numeric keypad for navigation and moving the cursor, you might like to redefine the keypad in QuarkXPress to work similarly. For example, you can redefine Command-keypad-6 to be Command-Right Arrow (move one word to the right), Command-keypad-3 to be Command-Option-Right Arrow, and Command-keypad-9 to be the Home key.

KEYSTROKES
Consistent QuicKeys Keystrokes

Try to assign the same keystrokes to QuicKey macros for similar functions in your different applications. It sure makes it easier to remember the keystrokes, especially if you use many different programs. For instance, Ray Robertson, king of QuicKey sets, uses the same key combinations for QuarkXPress, PageMaker, FreeHand, and Illustrator. As long as he's working on his machine, he can remember literally hundreds more keystrokes than he would have if he tried to remember the keystrokes built in to each program.

ResEdit Keystrokes

On the simpler side of macros, there's another way to create keystroke "macros" for selecting menu items: ResEdit. ResEdit is a program published by Apple, and available online and elsewhere, that lets you search through and edit a file's resource fork. Every application on the Macintosh has a resource fork that holds information about its menus, along with lots of other stuff.

Adding commands with ResEdit has an advantage over using QuicKeys: the key commands you create become an integral part of QuarkXPress, and not simply an add-on. They even appear next to the menu items for easy reference.

Let's say you want to add a keystroke that selects the Section feature from the Page menu.

1. Make a copy of QuarkXPress to work on (playing around with your only copy of any program is beyond foolish, because if you mess up you have to reinstall QuarkXPress from scratch).

2. Launch ResEdit.

3. In the ResEdit Open dialog box, choose and open the copy of the QuarkXPress application you just made. When it's open, you can see a list of every resource type (they all have four-letter names).

4. Double-click on the "MENU" resource type from the list.

5. From the View menu, select the "By MENU" item if it's not already selected. ResEdit then displays all of the "MENU" resources graphically. You can scroll around and see all of the menus that XPress uses (see Figure 10-2).

6. If you type in a resource number, ResEdit goes to that specific menu. So type 1007 and then double-click on the Page menu.

7. A window pops up for the resource showing each menu item, colors assigned to them (yes, you can assign colors to menu items but no one seems to do so yet), and keystroke assignments. Click once on any menu item name and the information for it shows up at the left (see Figure 10-3).

Other Handy Macros

Ever get tired of starting a new document, only to find that the values in the New Document dialog box for page size, margins, and so on, aren't at all what you want? Why not make macros that automatically create documents with the page size and margins you want? You could assign Control-N to a new letter-size document, Command-Control-N to legal-size, and Control-Option-N to tabloid. Or create keys to documents for any commonly-used custom-size papers.

We find the easiest way to create such macros is to use QuicKeys's Record Sequence command, go through the procedures we want to follow step by step, then edit the macro as necessary to fix the small problems that sometimes occur. The more you can accomplish in a dialog box using the keyboard instead of the mouse, the better. For instance, it's much better to tab to a text-entry field than to click in it, as tabs contained in macros play back more reliably and consistently than key clicks.

Figure 10-2

The "MENU" resource's graphical display

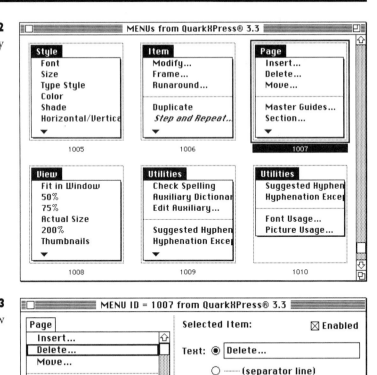

Figure 10-3

Menu item information window

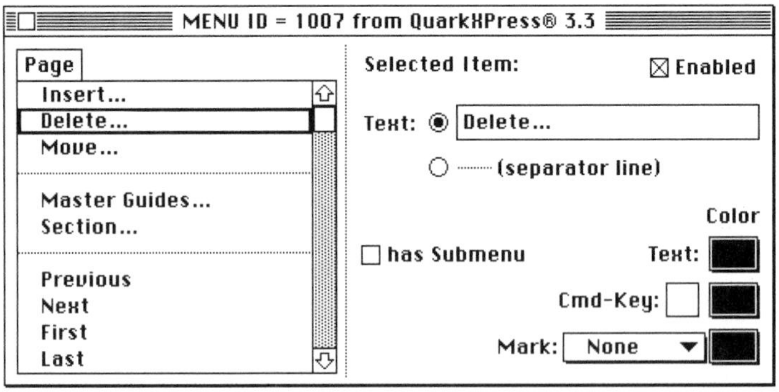

8. Click in the Cmd-Key field and type any character (don't hold down the Command key itself, though). For example, if you want Command-8 to open the Section dialog box, press the 8 key.

9. Quit ResEdit. If you are satisfied with your work, click OK when it asks you if you want to save the changes you have made. If you don't like what you've done, click No.

When you run the modified copy of QuarkXPress, you can see the new keystroke on the menu.

FRACTIONS

Making Fractions

Back in Chapter 4, *Type and Typography*, we explored several ways of making fractions. One of our favorite methods was explained in "Son of Fractions": use the subscript and superior styles together to create the denominator. This is preferable to Quark-XPress's Make Fraction command in that the size is not hard-coded, so it's easy to change the size of the text at any time. Here's the way our macro works (the cursor should be set before the first character in the fraction).

1. Shift-Right Arrow   *selects the numerator*

2. Command-Shift-V   *makes it superior*

3. Right Arrow   *positions cursor before slash*

4. Shift-Right Arrow   *selects the slash*

5. Option-Shift-1   *replaces slash with true virgule*

6. Shift-Right Arrow   *selects the denominator*

7. Command-Shift-V   *makes it superior*

8. Command-Shift-+   *makes it superscript*

9. Right Arrow   *positions cursor after the fraction*

10. Command-Shift-+   *toggles superscript off*

11. Command-Shift-V   *toggles superior off*

Depending on what font you use, you may have to adjust the superior and superscript styles in the Typographic Preferences dialog box before or after you run the macro.

This macro, as listed, only works with fractions that have one digit in the numerator and one in the denominator (such as ½ or ⅝); but, of course, it would be very easy to alter the macro to work with other numbers of digits.

KEYSTROKES
Assigning Keys to Tools

We think it's a major pain that there are no built-in keyboard shortcuts for selecting tools from the Tool palette. Plus, in earlier versions of QuicKeys and XPress, strange things happened when you tried to create conventional Click QuicKeys. However, with the newer versions of the programs, this isn't a problem: assign a keystroke (we've assigned Control-F1 through F4) to a Click. Make sure the click is relative to the window (the "Document" in QuicKeys), and the click will work even if you move the tool palette. (QuicKeys treats each palette in XPress like a window.)

TEXT
Changing the Case

Often, writers will think they're being helpful when they type words in uppercase letters. They're wrong. Here's a rough outline of a macro we sometimes use to solve the problem.

1. Cut the all caps text and paste it into Microsoft Word.

2. Select the text and choose Change Case from the Format menu. Choose the option you want, and press Return.

3. Switch back to XPress and press Command-Shift-H (to start the small caps type style).

4. Paste the text back into XPress.

The text that ends up pasted in shows up in the small caps style. The whole sequence takes much less time to run than it does to read this, and almost always less time than it usually takes to retype the word(s).

If you have a lot (we mean *a lot*) of all caps words to convert, you might take a look at "A Complex XPress Tags Example" in Chapter 5, *Copy Flow*. Note that the free ChangeCase XTension found on the disc bound into this book also does upper- to lowercase conversion and vice-versa.

SCRIPTING

The Power of Scripting

At the beginning of this chapter, we talked about using QuicKeys to build macros. There are two basic differences between macros and scripts. First, whereas macros automate particular tasks that you perform on a computer (like select that menu item, push that button, type such-and-such, and so on), scripts let you sneak in the back door of the program and control it from behind the scenes. Second, scripts have flow control and variables.

Flow control is a programming term that means you can set up decision trees and loops (you can do some conditional branching and looping with QuicKeys, but it's a pain). You can do much more complex and interesting things with scripting that you can with simple macros.

Note that scripting is usually done with either AppleScript or UserLand Frontier, but QuicKeys 3.0, HyperCard, and several other programs also support scripting. Also note that you must have System 7 with the AppleScript extension and related system materials installed in order to make this work (if you don't already have the AppleScript items, they're on the disc in the back of the book; AppleScript also ships as part of System 7.5).

The truth is that scripting is programming. However, it's not like any programming you've ever seen: it's easy! (Well, relatively easy.) To get more information about scripting, check out David's *The QuarkXPress Book* (starting with the fourth edition) and Danny Goodman's *Complete AppleScript Handbook*.

Most people who are scripting XPress these days are using AppleScript rather than UserLand Frontier. However, while Apple-Script is easier for people to learn at first, Frontier gives you much more power when you want to do really complex tasks, like creating a whole production workflow over a network. If you've only done a little scripting, stick with AppleScript. If you get excited by it, check out Frontier. In the meantime, all the tips in this book refer to AppleScript scripts.

UTILITIES
OSA Menu and ScriptIt

Once you have scripts to run (there are a bunch on the disc), how do you actually run them? Our favorite ways to run scripts from within QuarkXPress are OSA Menu, ScriptIT XTension, and QuicKeys. However, we'll cover QuicKeys in the next tip.

OSA Menu. OSA Menu is a free system extension (it's on the disc) that adds a menu item up near the Balloon Help icon (see Figure 10-4). You can place scripts in the menu and then trigger them at any time. Because this is a system extension rather than a Quark XTension, the menu is present in any program you're in (even on the desktop). Plus, the scripts in the menu change depending on what program you're in (while you're in XPress, you can see only XPress scripts and "universal" scripts).

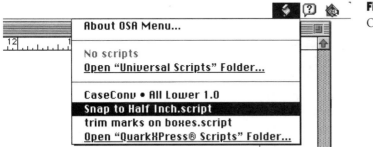

Figure 10-4
OSA Menu

ScriptIt. Paul Schmidt of "a lowly apprentice production" has come up with all sorts of cool XTensions (see Chapter 11, *XTensions*), including a must-have for anyone using scripts regularly in XPress: ScriptIt. This great XTension makes its appearance as a

Figure 10-5
ScriptIt XTension

floating palette in XPress (see Figure 10-5) from which you can run your scripts. You can add your scripts and combine the scripts into sets. Plus, you can run all the scripts in a set at the same time, consecutively.

QUICKEYS

Running Scripts with QuicKeys

As we noted earlier in this chapter, you should already have CE Software's QuicKeys; we think it should be standard issue with every Macintosh. And one of the many types of macros you can build with this utility is an AppleScript shortcut. That is, when you hit a keystroke, QuicKeys runs an AppleScript script.

To make QuicKeys run a script, you need to define a shortcut. Under the Define menu's Extension submenu you'll find the Scripting Extensions submenu. Select AppleScript from there (see Figure 10-6). In the AppleScript dialog box, you can choose whether the script is included in QuicKeys or on disk. While you'd think that a script would run faster if it were embedded in QuicKeys, unless the script is really small, it's usually faster to run it off the disk. The reason is that the script can be compiled once before it's saved to disk (using the Script Editor from Apple). If the script is typed within QuicKeys, the utility has to compile it every time it runs the script.

COMMANDS

Using Do Script

Where are those scripts being run? It's a boring programmer's question, but it turns out to be important if you want your scripts to run quickly. It turns out that a script can be run in AppleScript's "context" or in QuarkXPress's "context." If AppleScript is running it, it has to send instructions one at a time to QuarkXPress, and each time XPress receives an instruction, it carries it out. There's a lot of overhead involved in moving between the two programs.

On the other hand, you can make XPress run the entire script in its own context. In this scenario, AppleScript hands the entire script off to QuarkXPress at once and XPress follows all the

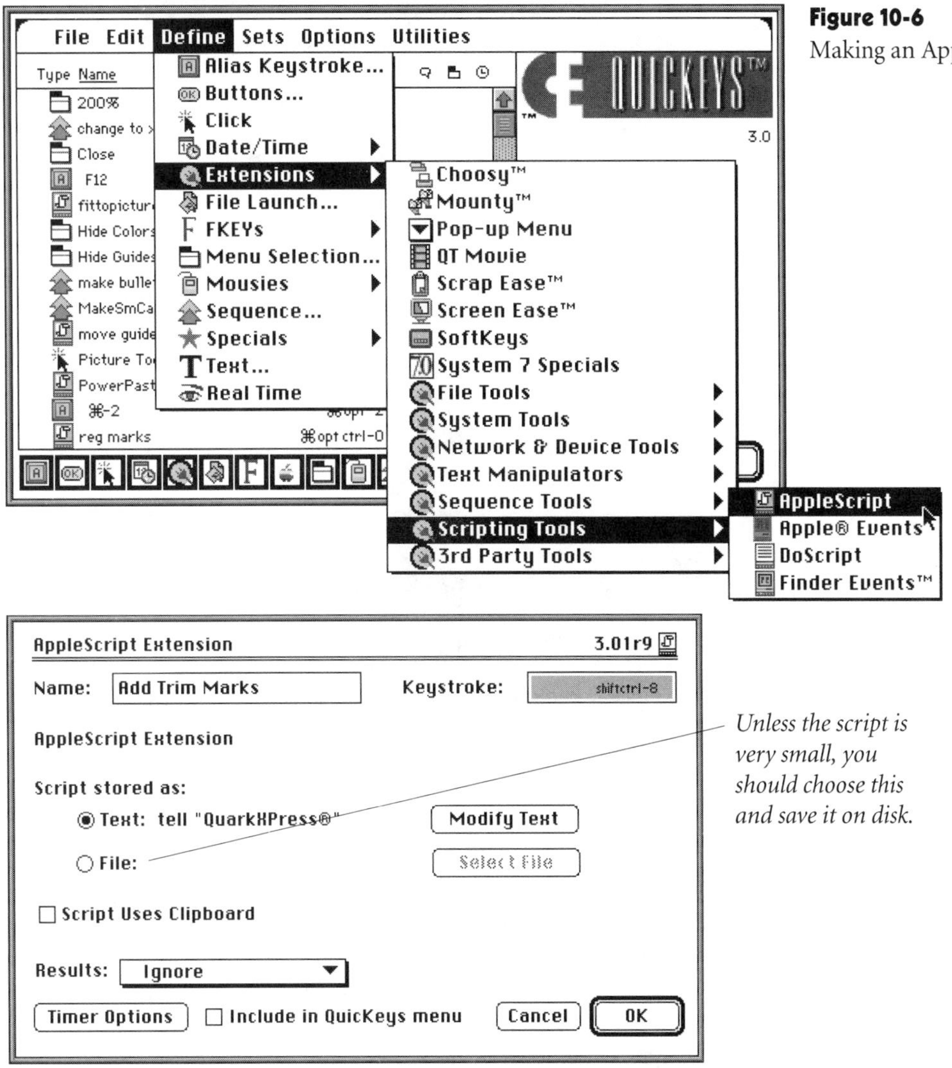

Figure 10-6
Making an AppleScript QuicKey

Unless the script is very small, you should choose this and save it on disk.

instructions by itself. This is much faster—sometimes as much as 10 times as fast. Plus, the entire script is run in the background and XPress won't redraw the screen until the script is done.

To make a script run inside another program's domain, you need to set up a script within a script using the "script" and "do script" commands. For example, here's a little script using these commands that fits the current spread in the window.

```
script FitSpread
tell application "QuarkXPress®"
    set curpage to current page of front document
    set oldwidth to pasteboard width
```

```
        set pasteboard width to 5
        set view scale of document 1 to fit spread in window
        set pasteboard width to oldwidth
        set current page of front document to curpage
        end tell
    end script

    tell application "QuarkXPress®"
        do script {FitSpread}
    end tell
```

First the script is defined within the "script" and "end script" commands. Then, the "do script" command tells XPress to perform that script. "Do script" hands the whole script over to XPress, and the program takes it from there.

QUICKEYS

Triggering QuicKeys within Scripts

The other side of using QuicKeys with AppleScript is to trigger QuicKeys from within a script. Typically, you wouldn't need to do this, but let's say you wanted to change to a different printer in the Chooser, select a menu item, or do something else that Quark's scripting commands can't accomplish. You can trigger a QuicKey by handing a message off to the QuicKeys Toolbox.

In this example, the script tells QuicKeys to run the keystroke named "NTX LW8", which is a Choosy shortcut that switches to the LaserWriter 8 driver and selects the LaserWriter IINTX on our network. (*Note:* For some reason, sometimes the name of the application is followed by a ™ and sometimes by ® ; change it to whatever your application is called.)

```
    tell application "QuarkXPress™"
        activate
        tell application "QuicKeys® Toolbox"
            PlayByName "NTX LW8"
        end tell
    end tell
```

You can control QuicKeys in other ways, too, including running its own internal AppleEvents scripting language. However, that's beyond the scope of this book.

Note that you have to have the QuicKeys Toolbox running in the background when you run this script. If you've installed Quic-Keys 3.0 or later, this "program" automatically starts up when you start your Mac (there's no customization of the installation). If you don't see QuicKeys Toolbox in your application menu (the little icon menu in the top right of your screen), go back and reinstall QuicKeys from scratch.

QUICKEYS

Use Macros When Scripting

As we said earlier in the chapter, QuicKeys can help take the monotony out of performing repetitive tasks. When we're scripting, we find ourselves typing some things over and over again. For example, we type

```
tell front document of application "QuarkXPress®"
```

at the beginning of almost every script we write. So we made a little QuicKey to type that for us whenever we press Control-F1 in the AppleScript Editor. It's simple, quick, and best of all, we don't have to get carpal tunnel syndrome from typing so much.

Other little text macros we've written include

```
end script
tell application "QuarkXPress®"
do script {XXXX}
end tell
```

Then we go back and change the "XXXX" to the name of the script.

PROGRAMMING

Debugging with Miniscripts

One of the strengths of Frontier and the weaknesses of the Apple Script Editor are its error-handling and debugging features. If you've typed your script wrong for some reason, you'll get an error when you run it; often, those error messages are pretty cryptic. One of the best ways to test the elements of your script (to see what's wrong) is to pull out pieces of the script—perhaps even only a few lines of code—and test them by themselves in another script. To do this, we often keep an "Untitled" script window open in the AppleScript Editor with

```
tell application "QuarkXPress®"
end tell
```

sitting there, ready to be used. Or, you could even create a little macro that opens a new untitled script and automatically types that code in it.

What is XPress XPecting?

As we noted back in Chapter 5, *Copy Flow*, one of the most useful tips for learning how to use XPress Tags is to format something the way you want it, then look at it in XPress Tags format. The same thing goes for learning scripting. One of the most useful functions of the Script Editor is the Result window. If you type "get x" at the end of a script, the variable "x" is displayed in the Result window.

Sometimes, while we're writing a script, we'll forget the name of a property, and we'll use this same technique to figure it out (of course, this is only marginally faster than looking it up in the manuals). For instance, we might open a new script and type the following.

```
tell application "QuarkXPress®"
    get properties of image 1 of picture box 1 of page 1 ¬
    of front document
end tell
```

This returns every property of that image, including how XPress expects us to type the values.

Minimize Crossing the Chasm

Earlier, in "Using Do Script," we recommended that you avoid moving back and forth between contexts as much as possible in order to speed up your scripts. In the same vein, you should try to avoid asking applications too many questions. That is, every time you ask for the bounds of a picture box or what the first word of a paragraph is, or whatever, it takes a little time. There's overhead in AppleScript asking XPress, XPress responding, and so on.

If you know you're going to be using the values of the top, left, width and bounds of a box a lot, save the bounds in a variable. Then pull the information from that variable instead of asking XPress again.

```
set thebounds to bounds of picture box 1
set leftpoint to item 1 of thebounds
```

This snippet by itself doesn't speed things up any. But if you use "thebounds" five or 10 times, then you'll notice a speed increase. (Our tests show that if you use a variable instead of polling XPress for the bounds 20 times, you cut your processing time in half.)

LITTLE GEM
Quickie Tips

Here's a quickie that took us weeks to figure out. AppleScript is smart enough to know that "return" means add a return. It also knows that the "tab" and "space"; and the "new line" character becomes ASCII 7 in AppleScript paralance. For instance, the following script adds a return and the current time and date at the end of "text box 1".

```
tell application "QuarkXPress®"
    tell page 1 of front document
        make text at end of text of text box 1 with data ¬
        (return & (current date as text))
    end tell
end tell
```

The ampersand (Shift-7) character lets you piece together (concatenate) two text strings. The ¬ character indicates to AppleScript that this isn't really the end of the line and that there's more text to come on the next line. You generate the symbol by pressing Option-L. In the AppleScript Editor, you can also press Option-Return.

TEXT
Changing Words

Some commands in AppleScript are incredibly easy to understand. It's this intuitive nature that attracted us to AppleScript to begin with. For instance, it's easy to make a global change with the following line.

```
set the color of every picture box to "Red"
```

However, we soon found out that there are syntaxes in scripting XPress that are much less intuitive. For instance, if you want to change every instance of the word "the" to "a", the easiest way to do it is with the following code.

```
tell story 1 of text box 1
    set every text where (it = "the") to "a"
end tell
```

Note that this script would find the "the" in "other," "theatre," and so on. Instead, you might want to use

```
set every word where (it = "the") to "a"
```

SCRIPTING

Acting on a Selection

Very often, we want a script to affect the text or page item we've selected. For instance, let's say we want to run a little script that reduces all the selected text by half a point. We select some text in a text box, and trigger this script.

```
tell front document of application "QuarkXPress®"
    try
    set the size of the selection to ((size of the selection ¬
    as real) - 0.5)
    on error
        beep
        display dialog "Error."
    end try
end tell
```

You could also copy the currently selected text from one document to another.

```
tell application "QuarkXPress®"
    copy the contents of the selection ¬
    to text box 1 of current page of document 2
end tell
```

In order for either of these to work, some text inside a text box has to be selected. If the Content tool is selected when you run a script with "selection" in it, the code refers to the selected word, picture, paragraph, or whatever. If the Item tool is selected, "selection" refers to the object itself (the picture or text box, or the line).

You can also act on the currently selected box or boxes by using the "current box" property. To tell whether a box is selected, you can say

```
if current box exists
```

Then you can do things to it. For instance, this script snaps the currently selected picture or text box horizontally to the nearest half inch.

```
tell front document of application "QuarkXPress®"
    if current box exists then
        set x to (left of bounds of current box) as inches
        set z to ((round ((x as real) * 2)) / 2) as inches
        set left of bounds of current box to z
    else
    display dialog "Please select a box."
    end if
end tell
```

Note that "current box" is the same as "selection" when the Item tool is selected. Also note that both "selection" and "current box" are elements of a document or the application. If you are inside a tell loop (if you're already talking to a page, or a box, or whatever), you'll get an error.

SCRIPTING

Coercing Numbers

One of the most powerful features in scripting is the ability to coerce one type of data into another. For example, you can say ""3p" as picas" and XPress changes the text string "3p" into a measurement. However, some coercions are more intuitive than others. It took us weeks to figure out that you can't change a number into a string in an XPress script. Rather, when scripting XPress, you have to change it into text. For instance, here's some code to display a dialog box with the page number of the currently selected box.

```
tell application "QuarkXPress®"
    display dialog (the page number of page 1 of current box ¬
    of document 1)
end tell
```

Check Syntax Quickly

Like any other program, after you use the AppleScript Script Editor for a while, you'll want to find keystroke equivalents to commonly-used features. Remember that you can press Command-R for Run, Command-period for Stop, and (here's the one that stumped us for the longest time) press Enter for Check Syntax.

Getting the page number is a little non-intuitive, but perhaps equally odd is that you can't simply say "display it". Rather, you have to coerce the number into a string of text like this:

```
display dialog (the page number of page 1 of current box ¬
    of document 1 as text)
```

Setting Tabs

The biggest problem with scripting QuarkXPress is not learning the scripting language, nor debugging the typos in your scripts. The biggest problem is that QuarkXPress's AppleScript functions are themselves somewhat buggy at times. If we knew where all the bugs were, they'd be easier to step around. However, as is, there are plenty of times when just basic things should work but don't.

A case in point is tabs. Until now, tabs have stumped scripters because they don't work as advertised. The key to adding tab stops is that each tab stop is a record within the "tab list". The best way to see what a tab list looks like is to add some tab stops to a paragraph on your page and then get the tab list from that paragraph, like this.

```
tell application "QuarkXPress®"
    get tab list of paragraph 1 of text box 1 of page 1 ¬
    of front document
end tell
```

The tab list is returned in the Return dialog box in the script editor and looks something like this.

```
{{justification:left, fill character:" ", position:"8p8"},
{justification:align on, align character:".", fill character:" ",
position:"14p4"}, {justification:right, fill character:" ",
position:"19p9"}}
```

If you want to add a tab stop to a paragraph, you can add a tab record to the tab list.

```
tell front document of application "QuarkXPress®"
    tell paragraph 1 of text box 1 of page 1
        set tab list to tab list & ¬
            {{justification:centered, fill character:"•", ¬
            position:(24 as points)}}
    end tell
end tell
```

Note that we're using the "&" to concatenate the original list with the new tab record. Since we're adding a record to a list, we need to surround it with two curly braces (the outer one signals the list, the inner one signals the record, in this case).

The problem with tabs is that although XPress displays their "justification" as "left", "right", "centered", and so on, you can't type them like this. Instead, you must use "left justified", "right justified", and "centered". (Thanks to Shane Stanley and Richard Pfeiffer on this and many other scripting tips.)

xtensions 11

Remember buying that first power drill? Your new tool opened new horizons of projects you could work on. However, you soon realized the sobering truth: some of the projects you wanted to do required drill bits that you'd have to buy separately.

QuarkXPress, of course, is just like that power drill. You can do so much with it, but at some point you find that you can do only so much. Fortunately, you can make a quick phone call and buy new drill bits, ratchets, or thingamabobs for XPress—and these extra tools let you extend the capabilities of your program. That's why they're called XTensions.

We've talked about XTensions throughout this book, but never focused on them directly. That's what we're going to do here. Most of these tips came from our friend and colleague Sal Soghoian, author of *The Quark XTensions Book* (published by Hayden) and frequent columnist for the *XChange Monthly* newsletter.

One more note: Where do you find these (and other) XTensions? Call the XChange. They've quickly become the central clearing house for almost every XTension developed around the world. You can reach them at the address and phone number located in Appendix B, *Resources*.

If you want to test-drive these XTensions, you'll find demo versions of many of them on the disc bound into this book plus a few free bonuses noted throughout the book. If you don't find the one you want on the disc, try calling the XChange (see Appendix B, *Resources*). See the disc for particulars.

Viewing the Stacking Order

Figure 11-1
ScriptIt can show layer order

The numbers indicate layer order

When working on complex pages, we constantly find ourselves wishing we knew what page items were above or below the others. You know that any element placed on a page in QuarkXPress assumes a position on the page's "stack." Think of the "stack" as a deck of cards. No two cards can be on the same level—they have to be either in front of or behind other cards. It's the same with objects on an XPress page. The problem is that it's difficult to figure out which level they're on. *Aha!*—But now there's ScriptIt.

ScriptIt is an XTension developed to run AppleEvent scripts from a palette in QuarkXPress. But it has another helpful feature: the ability to name any box or line. If you choose, ScriptIt will attach a small box to the bottom of any box or line containing the name and/or the stacking order of the object (see Figure 11-1). These little add-ons are nonprinting and can provide instant visual feedback as to which object is where. If you want to hide them, choose Hide Item Names from the View menu.

You can turn the names off (unless you're a scripter, you probably don't need them) and show just the numbers through the ScriptIt Preferences dialog box under the Edit menu.

Multiversion Layouts

One of the great things about desktop publishing is the ability to try out variations of design elements on your page. For instance, you might ask, "How would this heading look in Helvetica Condensed Bold Italic?" It would sure be nice to be able to easily toggle between the various combinations without tearing apart your design or creating duplicate page copies. Well, now you can.

Both LayerManager II and the Scitex Layers XTension let you selectively make items invisible or visible. Using this technique, you can have multiple variations of the same item in the document and easily toggle their visibility to see which one you like most.

Another use for this is creating a single document with multiple languages or office site information. For instance, you could have both an English and Spanish version of the same ad on the same page. Or, you could create a single piece of stationery with five different addresses on it (one for each of your national offices).

We often use this technique when presenting ideas to a client. We'll create three or four variations on the page and turn them off or on during the presentation. Never fails to impress the client.

MULTIPLE VERSIONS
Seeing the Invisible

If you use LayerManager II or the Layers XTension from Scitex, you know that you can make elements of a QuarkXPress page invisible by turning "off" that layer. Did you know, though, that you can still see the invisible elements and work around them without making them visible again?

Navigator 2.0 XTension or Co-Pilot (from the KitchenSink XTension) will let you peer into the "invisible dimension." If you want to see the invisible items in color, first make all items visible, then set the preview of either XTension to color, and refresh their redrawing of the thumbnail page proxy. In Navigator, click the R button; in Co-Pilot, click the fourth button from the left at the bottom of the palette.

Now make the items invisible again with whatever XTension you're using (either Layers or LayerManager II). As long as automatic update is turned off in the page proxy XTensions, the XTensions still show the invisible items.

Note that if you want active, updatable viewing of invisible objects, only Navigator has to the ability to see through walls: set Navigator to "wire-frame geometry" and the outline of every item on the page (invisible or otherwise) is always shown. You can place other objects on the page and still see how they relate positionally to the invisible items.

DROP SHADOWS
Creating a Drop Shadow over an Image

We all know how to create a drop shadow effect in QuarkXPress: simply duplicate a box behind itself and fill the duplicate with a 10- or 20-percent tint (also, see "Trapping Shadow Boxes" in Chapter 7, *Color*). But how do you create a drop shadow for an object that overlaps an existing image? With the Propagate feature of the PiXTrix XTension, it's easy (see Figure 11-2).

1. Duplicate the topmost image (the one that is casting the shadow) and place the duplicate behind the topmost image. Make sure the box is placed where you want the shadow to be.

2. Delete the image in the duplicate picture box, and make sure the box has no border (borders look really ugly on shadows).

Figure 11-2
PiXTrix can make better shadows

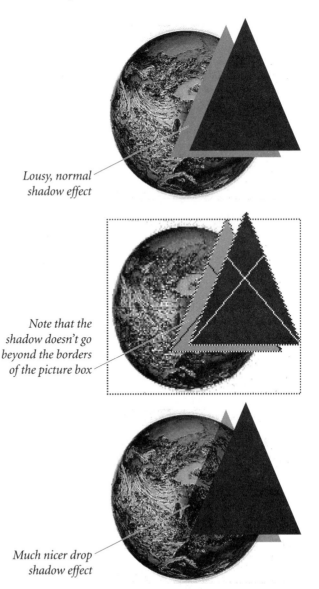

Lousy, normal shadow effect

Note that the shadow doesn't go beyond the borders of the picture box

Much nicer drop shadow effect

3. Select the background image (the one that has a shadow cast on it) and the empty duplicated box with the Item tool and choose Propagate from the PiXTrix submenu (under the Utilities menu). PiXTrix's Propagate feature pulls the background image into the duplicated box in the same position relative to the background image.

4. Select the duplicate box (the shadow box) with the Content tool and choose Other Contrast from the Style menu. Turn off the checkboxes for Hue and Saturation in the Picture Contrast Specifications dialog box, and leave only Brightness checked. Now you can make the shadow image darker by dragging the Input/Output graph to the bottom and right two or three tick marks. Note that if you Option-click the Apply button, you can preview the changes as you adjust the graph. When you've darkened the image to your liking, press OK.

5. Sometimes we add a thick white border to the topmost picture box, which adds to the contrast between images and enhances the overall effect.

Life gets a little more complex if the topmost image only partially overlaps the background image, because the propagated image looks totally wrong (see Figure 11-3). Instead, repeat the same process as above but add an empty duplicate box behind the background, and fill it with a shade (the shade should be similar

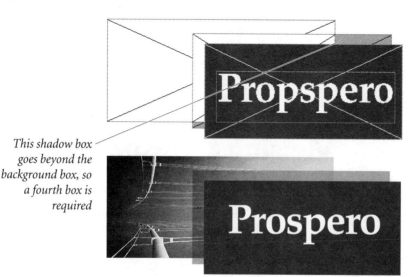

Figure 11-3
Partially overlapping shadow box

This shadow box goes beyond the background box, so a fourth box is required

in tone to the darker shadow image, of course). Also, remember to adjust the duplicate containing an image so that it doesn't bleed past the background image.

Centering a Document with Crop Marks

Say you want to print your five-by-seven-inch XPress document plus crop marks to an 8.5-by-11-inch piece of paper. You select US Letter in the Page Setup dialog box, and turn on Registration Marks (Centered or Off Center) in the Print dialog box. But when you print your document, the document page and crop marks are shifted to the upper-left corner of the printout! How can you center your document pages on your printed pages?

If you have the MarkIt XTension, it's easy. Create a new MarkIt style in your document and, in the upper-right corner of the MarkIt dialog box, enter a pasteboard size. Type in a horizontal measurement for the pasteboard equal to the printer's page minus the document page. In the example above, you'd type "3.5"" (8.5 minus five). Type that number followed by a slash character and the number two (3.5 inches divided by two; that is, half of 3.5 inches), then click OK. This evenly centers the document on the pasteboard.

Finally, print using the standard MarkIt procedures, and the document is centered just where you want it. Note that the maximum pasteboard available with MarkIt is 288 points (four inches), so this won't work if you have a really big sheet of paper and a really little document page size.

Viewing a Document Without Bleeds

Have you ever noticed that documents look different when they're printed than they do on the screen? Obviously, colors change. But there's more to it than that. They just don't have the same kind of impact. Perhaps this has to do with the fact that every XPress page is bordered on all sides by a bright white pasteboard. A more objective view might be to place the document against a neutral background.

We use the Co-Pilot from the KitchenSink XTension to make our special backgrounds (see Figure 11-4). Co-Pilot is a resizable page proxy for navigating XPress documents. Click anywhere on the palette's outline of the current page, and the corresponding part of the page jumps into view. There are other cool features of Co-Pilot, too, but a little known feature of this XTension is its ability as a full-page previewer. That is, it displays any document full-screen on any color background you choose. In fact, it even displays the document trimmed down without bleeds!

To see your page with a neutral background, open Co-Pilot and click its zoom box. Only the page is displayed—the pasteboard is masked out. If you're not fond of gray, you can set the color of the Co-Pilot's background by clicking the preferences button.

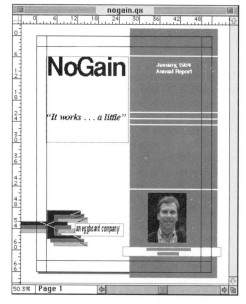

TEXT SELECTION
Selecting the Unselectable

Contiguous. You might remember that word from the fifth grade when Mrs. Carpenter embarrassed you to death by making you *sing* the names of the 48 contiguous states in front of class! (Well, that's what happened to some of us.) Its meaning is etched in our psyche: adjacent, next to, or bordering an object.

Using the built-in QuarkXPress Content tool, you can only select contiguous text. But suppose you have a series of numbered paragraphs and need to change the formatting of just the numbers. Is there a way to select them without selecting the text from their corresponding paragraphs? Or, what if you want to select all the text in one column of a table?

The StyleIt XTension provides a new selection tool and allows for the selection and styling of noncontiguous text (see Figure 11-5). Here's a simple example.

Click the StyleIt tool on the QuarkXPress Tool palette. The cursor changes to crosshairs. Using the crosshairs, drag a selection marquee around or touching the text you wish to style. The text can be in multiple text boxes or even on multiple pages on a spread, as long as it all fits inside the selection marquee. Then, in the StyleIt dialog box, you can pick any character attributes you want to apply, or use any or all of the attributes from an existing style sheet. Once you've made your choices, click OK and the chosen attributes are applied to the marqueed text.

Figure 11-4
Co-Pilot's page proxy

Figure 11-5

StyleIt XT

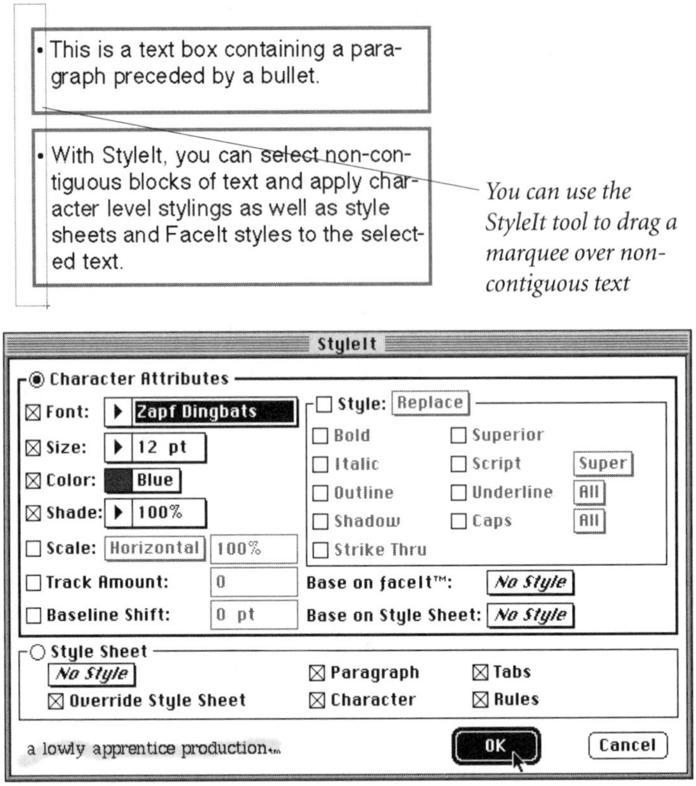

• This is a text box containing a paragraph preceded by a bullet.

• With StyleIt, you can select non-contiguous blocks of text and apply character level stylings as well as style sheets and FaceIt styles to the selected text.

You can use the StyleIt tool to drag a marquee over non-contiguous text

Plus, using StyleIt you can quickly copy character-formatting attributes from one group of text and apply those attributes to another group of text. And paragraph style sheets and FaceIt styles (see "Making Character Styles Unique," later in this chapter) can also be applied using this slick selection tool.

BAR CODES

Bar Codes Within QuarkXPress

Hey, it's the 90s—everyone needs a bar code sooner or later. A great solution for the creation of bar codes in QuarkXPress is the Azalea Bar Code XTension. Choose Azalea UPC-EAN Bar Codes from the Utilities menu, and fill in the appropriate information in the accompanying dialog (see Figure 11-6). The XTension creates an EPS image, saves it to your disk, and automatically imports it into any selected picture box.

Figure 11-6
Barcodes

Jerry Whiting of Azalea, king of PostScript bar codes, has created almost every kind of barcode you'd ever need, including UPC-A, UPC-E, EAN-8, EAN-13, and Bookland ISBN. If you need something this doesn't do, we bet he'd even customize the XTension for you.

TEXT EFFECTS

Stencil Text with SXetchPad

You've seen examples of this: an image peeking through the letters of a word. It's a cool effect, but sometimes it's a drag to switch to an illustration program to create it. We've found a couple ways of accomplishing this without leaving the ol' XPress homeland.

The SXetchPad XTension brings to XPress a full-featured drawing program similar to Illustrator or FreeHand—in fact, the new version of SXetchPad even imports many Illustrator files into XPress in a format that you can edit on the page. Using this XTension, it's easy to create a stencil effect (see Figure 11-7).

(*Note:* For those not familiar with SXetchPad, the illustration tools only work inside a special SXetchPad box that you can draw anywhere on the QuarkXPress page. The box can be moved and sized like any other XPress box, but you can manipulate the contents of this box only with SXetchPad's set of tools.)

The SXetchPad palette

The stencil sitting on top of an image

The final image (note: we've left the image peeking out from the top and side on purpose)

1. Create a new SXetchPad box, select the Type tool, and type the words you want to stencil.

2. Choose Convert to Curve from the Item menu.

3. Draw a big rectangular box and place it behind the letters you've converted.

4. Select the letters and choose Split from the Item menu.

5. Select the letters *and* the background box (press Command-A for Select All) and choose Join from the Item menu. The elements are fused into a single group.

6. Because the new group picks up the color of the letters (probably black), it's necessary to change the color of this new composite object to "White". Select the new item and choose "White" from the SXetchPad Color menu. (The SXetchPad box will now appear to be empty since everything it contains is now "White", but *trust us*—the stencil is still there.)

7. With the SXetchPad box selected, choose Modify from the Item menu and set the box's background color to "None".

8. Finally, import an image into a picture box the way you always would, and place this picture behind the SXetchPad box. The image appears through the lettershapes! To adjust the positioning of the image, just move either the SXetchPad box or the picture box below it.

When you add other elements to your page, remember to keep the SXetchPad box behind the other elements. Note that the stencil color in the example above was white; if your page is colored, then the stencil should be colored the same. Another cool thing about this tip is that this stenciled image prints faster than one made in an illustration program using Paste Inside or a masking path. The reason is that no clipping needs to happen; rather, you're simply putting a big white box with cutout letters on top of an image.

TEXT EFFECTS

Stencil Text with PiXTrix

Once again, PiXTrix demonstrates its versatility: besides being able to propagate images into other picture boxes (see "Creating a Drop Shadow Over an Image" earlier in this chapter), PiXTrix can convert type into XPress picture boxes. This is perfect for the stencil effect we're examining here.

Figure 11-8
Stencils made with PiXTrix

PiXTrix converted these letters into polygonal picture boxes.

1. Create a text box containing the word to stencil (be sure to size and stretch the type first; it's hard to change later).

2. Select the text to convert and choose Convert Type to Pictures from the PiXTrix submenu of the Utilities menu (see Figure 11-8).

3. Once the type has been converted to picture boxes, select the first letter-cum-picture-box on the left with the Content tool and import a picture into it.

4. Shift-select the remaining letters (don't deselect the first one) and choose Propagate from the PiXTrix submenu. The stencil image is imported into each of the other selected letters automatically.

If you want to adjust the picture's position inside the letter-shaped picture boxes, select all the letters and choose Position Picture from the PiXTrix submenu.

A couple of things to note. The letters are standard Quark-XPress polygons, and as such they can be edited, framed, and

OPENING

Open Documents Quickly

If you're sick and tired of the message "Some settings saved with this document are different from those in the XPress Preferences file" when you open a file, and you wish you could have it use the document preferences all the time, then get QuickOpen. It's a free XTension (found on the disc in the back of the book) from "a lowly apprentice production" that makes XPress open documents as if you'd clicked Use Document Preferences—and it bypasses that annoying dialog. You'll still see the missing and modified picture and fonts dialog boxes, though.

Figure 11-9

The LinkIt palette

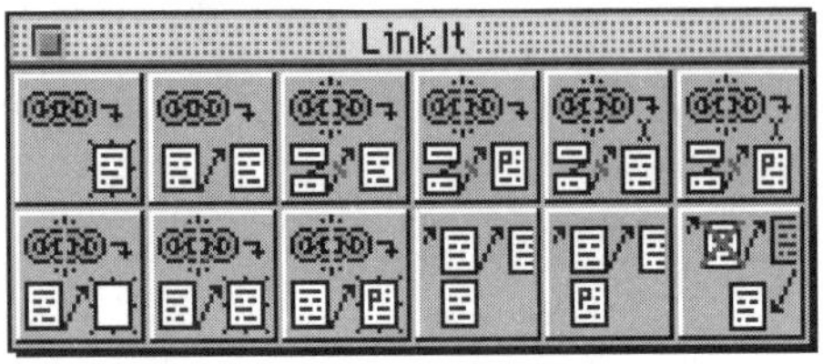

filled. However, because the current version of QuarkXPress doesn't support bezièr curves, these shapes are built like normal polygons. Because of this, you might notice some chunkiness in the curves of some of the letters—especially when they're printed at high resolution.

Also note that unlike the SXetchPad example, these shapes are not transparent. The hole or counterform in an "R" won't show what's behind it. To accomplish this illusion, fill the center of the "R" with whatever shade or color is behind it. If the "R" is over a photograph, use the Propagate feature of PiXTrix to import the image into the counterform of the "R." This gives the illusion of the "R" being transparent.

TEXT LINKING

Linking Text Boxes

If you live to link, or love to link, or maybe you just think n' link, then this tip's for you. Wouldn't it be nice to have the option of linking two existing text chains together; or, perhaps, duplicate only a single text box and its contents without copying the whole story chain? How about deleting a text box and its contents from a chain without disturbing the rest of the text? When it comes to text and linking in QuarkXPress, the wish list is a long one. LinkIt delivers answers to many of those wishes (see Figure 11-9).

Besides linking two existing text chains and duplicating a text box and its contents, LinkIt can do the following things.

▶ Link a text box or chain to the next selected text box.

▶ Link a text box or chain to the next selected chain.

▶ Split a text chain at the selected text box.

▶ Split a text chain at the selected box using a feature that retains the look of the text before the chain was broken (the Smart Paragraphs feature).

▶ Unlink all text boxes, while retaining all the text in the first text box.

▶ Unlink all boxes while retaining the text in each text box using the Smart Paragraphs feature.

▶ Duplicate or delete a text box and its contents (and only its contents).

Opening 3.3 Files in 3.2

That's right, you didn't read that title wrong! A new XTension from Markzware called MarkzTools can convert your 3.3 documents to either 3.2 or 3.1 documents. With this XTension, you can be compatible with everyone—even those QuarkXPress recalcitrants we all know and work with.

Another feature of this XTension is the ability to compress a file and decompress it automatically when you select it in the Open dialog box.

You must have MarkzTools installed in the XTensions folder (or QuarkXPress folder) of both the copy of XPress 3.3 you save from and the copy of 3.2 or 3.1 that you open the document with. To prevent confusion, MarkzTools places a small version box in the upper left of the document title bar and posts a warning when you save into another version.

See Spot Bark.
Bark, Spot, Bark!

We've noted a couple of Easter Eggs in XPress (little hidden features that don't make you more productive, but are sort of fun). Well, the XTension world is not without these little treats.

If you're using the KitchenSink XTension (and who isn't?), click the Spot icon on the command pad (the icon of a dog's face) and the Spot Color Change dialog box appears (or, if you don't use the Command Pad, select Spot from the Edit menu). Spot is a very useful tool: you can change any color (or all colors) in your document from spot color to process color and vice versa. Phil thinks this is one of his most useful production tools.

At the top of the Spot Color Change dialog box is a picture of our favorite Quark pooch. Give him a click and he's likely to yelp with joy at being paid some attention to.

Drawing Prelinked Text Boxes

If you've got a whole mess o' text boxes to draw, and each of them must be linked to the next, you'll want to find any shortcut you can to shave steps off the process. You can use the LinkIt XTension for drawing prelinked text boxes, too.

When you have the LinkIt XTension loaded, you can open the LinkIt palette. Hold down the Option key and click the Text Box tool in the QuarkXPress Tool palette (this locks the Text Box tool as the current tool until another tool is selected). Draw the first text box, then click the first icon on the LinkIt palette—this is the Link to Next Box tool. Then draw another text box and click the same LinkIt icon again. Continue this procedure (clicking the LinkIt icon between the drawing of each text box), and when you're finished drawing the text boxes, they're all linked and ready to import a story.

Slide Shows and Previews

Sometimes it's difficult to get a good overview of your work on screen before printing all those pages out. If you work on long documents, such as books, and would like an unencumbered, easy way to review your work, try the QuarkPresents XTension. This often-overlooked XTension is part of the "Red, Hot, and Publish" disk available from the XChange (the money raised from this disk goes to AIDS research; see Appendix B, *Resources*). With a single menu selection, it turns XPress and your document into a slideshow.

You can choose to have XPress flip from one page to another automatically, or only when you click your mouse. Plus, there's a popup page Go To menu available at any time by holding down the Command key and clicking on the screen. But what's really great about QuarkPresents is that all the palettes and menus are turned off so you can view the document's pages, shown without bleeds, centered on the screen.

Making Character Styles Unique

Until QuarkXPress develops character-level style sheets, the FaceIt XTension is the best way we know of to create and use character-level styles (see Figure 11-10). However, FaceIt uses no hidden text characters; instead, it relies on the uniqueness of each FaceIt style to "recognize" a particular character style. For instance, you can create a new FaceIt character style called "Head3" and spec it as 14-point Futura Book. Then, every piece of text you apply this style to is changed to this formatting. When you change the FaceIt style, all the text tagged with "Head3" gets changed, too.

But there's a catch: if you've formatted some other text in your document to 14-point Futura Book, FaceIt changes *that*, too (because it's looking for unique formatting).

One way we've found to ensure that FaceIt's styles are unique is to duplicate the color Black and name the duplicate color "FaceItBlack". When you use FaceItBlack for your FaceIt style sheets, you can rest assured that you won't get any surprises when changing or applying FaceIt attributes. Note that unless you specifically make this new black color a process color (set it to CMYK and turn Process Separation on in the Edit Color dialog box), your FaceIt-styled text may appear on the wrong plate when you make color separations.

TableWorks Plus

Sooner or later, every graphic designer or desktop-publishing wizard confronts the daunting task of creating tables in QuarkXPress. What at first looks easy soon can become a quagmire of cutting and pasting and painful menial formatting. We can't even count the times we've gotten that panic midnight call from the designer down the street, stuck and looking for a way out of the table muck.

▶ How can I edit and style the table and yet keep items precisely aligned?

▶ How can I link the data to outside programs?

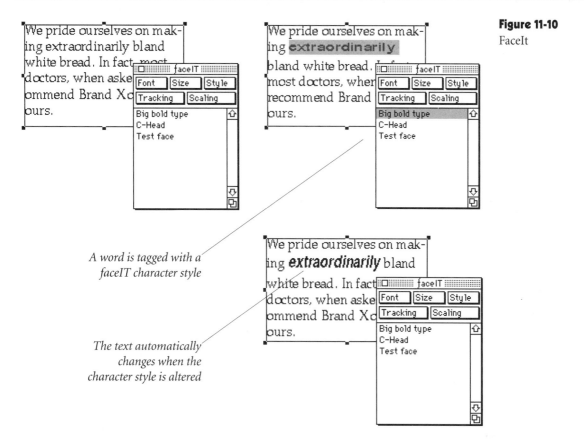

A word is tagged with a faceIT character style

The text automatically changes when the character style is altered

Figure 11-10
FaceIt

▶ How can I create multiline table cells with text wrapping within the cells?

▶ How can I add to or remove data without messing up the entire table?

Our standard answer is, "TableWorks Plus." This XTension is *the* answer for creating tables in QuarkXPress—ranging from the simple to the formidable.

Because TableWorks Plus uses standard XPress text and picture boxes and lines to create its tables, each cell in the table is fully editable using the standard XPress tools; plus, colors in the table print and trap like any other color in your document.

When you create a table using TableWorks Plus, you can import data into it from databases or spreadsheets such as Excel or FileMaker Pro. Plus, editing the table is a snap (see Figure 11-11). Want to move a row or column? Just drag it to where you want it or cut the selection and paste it in someplace else (even into another table). Best of all, TableWorks, when used with its partner TextLinker, can create dynamically updating tables linked to your database or spreadsheet with Publish and Subscribe. That way, when you change some data in your spreadsheet, the changes appear automatically in your XPress layout.

Need multipage tables? TableWorks Plus can do that, too. The XTension can update the tables and headers on each following page. If you need to convert those klunky tables you've already created by hand, TableWorks Plus can make a table from a loose collection of text boxes placed close together.

Note that TableWorks Plus isn't the only XTension that can make tables (and it's certainly not the least expensive of the bunch). Two other XTensions you might want to look into are Xtable and ProTabs XT. You can call the XChange for more information (see Appendix B, *Resources*).

Figure 11-11
Complex tables
in TableWorks Plus

Active tables have selection buttons around the table to make selecting rows and columns of data easy.

Mineral	Specific Gravity	Conductivity	Pricing		Relative Abundance
			Raw	Refined	
Flourite	4.35	32.7	$4.30	$32.43	9
Blorchenite	2.54	56.3	7.89	89.32	8
Jasper	8.21	48.6	.23	5.21	1
Rhobundium	24.30	3.4	56.89	264.56	12
Flubber	32.60	0.2	423.34	645.32	23
Migdalite	0.32	412.2	45.31	785.96	314
Feldspar	36.50	2.6	1.28	5.64	3

CROP MARKS ○

Automatic Crop Marks

Every now and again, we find ourselves trying to build our own crop and registration marks on our pages instead of using XPress's built-in marks. Let's see . . . first you drag guides around the box, then you select the Line tool and draw the small lines around the box snapped to the guides . . . Wait a minute, are the guides really touching the box, and which side of the line is on the guide? And what do I do for color bars? Aaaaugh!

Frustrate yourself no more. The Crop&RegIt XTension places crop marks, registration targets, and gray and color bars around any selected box or group (you can set all sorts of preferences for what you want or don't want). Select any box or group and choose Create Crop and Reg Marks from the Item menu (see Figure 11-12).

On the other hand, if you want to customize the crop and registration marks for your document, use the MarkIt XTension instead. Besides offering complete control of marks, it can also import custom marks and logos, as well as print the pasteboard area that surrounds a document.

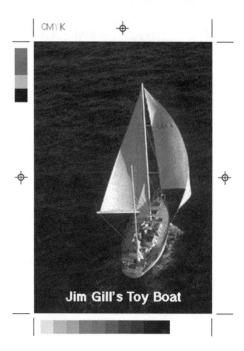

Figure 11-12
Crop and Reg Marks additional marks

IMPOSITION

Printer Spreads

Back in "Saddle-Stitch Imposition," in Chapter 8, *Printing*, we told you one kind of kludgy way to make your own printer spreads, but we told you there were certainly better ways of going about it. One of those ways is the INposition XTension or the significantly more affordable INposition Lite (the former is for service bureaus and large production facilities; the latter, about $1,000 cheaper, is for the rest of us).

Unlike other XTensions, INposition Lite does not reorder or alter the document; all the work is done at print time. After choosing Print Signatures from the File menu, a specialized version of the Print dialog box appears (see Figure 11-13). Here you can choose to use crop and bleed marks, fold marks, targets, and color and gray bars. Layouts can be printed two-up or four-up, and you can specify your binding as perfect bound or saddle stitched. There's even a preview dialog that displays your document re-ordered as printer's spreads (see Figure 11-14).

Figure 11-13

INposition Lite's Print dialog box

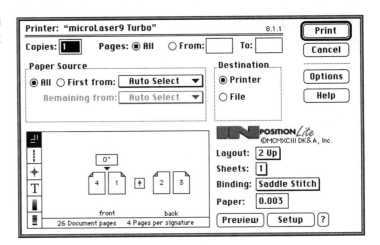

Figure 11-14

The Preview and Help screens
in INposition Lite

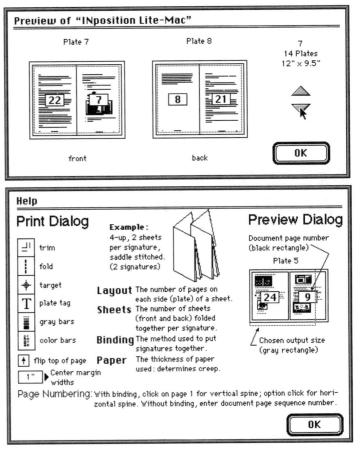

Retrieving Embedded Captions in TIFF Images

Let's say you work for a sports magazine, and your photographers hand off their photographs to the art department to be scanned and prepared for print along with their caption notes (who the image is of, the photographer's name, and so on). However, once that information has gone through the art department, it has to somehow get to you so you can use it on the page layout. Hey, this is the 90s! We don't need no stinkin' pieces of paper cluttering up our lives. Let's do the handoff electronically.

As it turns out, besides being your favorite image format, TIFF files can also carry other data inside them, including captions and other notes. Try it yourself: Open a TIFF image in Photoshop and choose Page Setup from the File menu. Then click the Caption button and type in a caption pertaining to the photo you have open. Now that caption is saved as part of the TIFF image file. "Great!" you say, "But how do I access or view the caption while in XPress?" That's where the XTension world comes in.

WhatzIt. WhatzIt is an XTension that gives you information and controls for any picture on your XPress page. When WhatzIt is installed and activated (via the View menu), it displays a small gold triangle at the top left of each image-filled picture box (see Figure 11-15). When you click on this triangle, a popup palette appears, displaying information about the image, including the file path and name, resolution, bit-depth, and file type (if the image is an object-oriented EPS file, it also displays fonts and colors used). Any embedded captions are displayed as well. These captions can be copied to the clipboard as regular text.

TIFFormation. Another XTension useful for reading captions contained in TIFFs is TIFFormation. TIFFormation uses a floating palette to display pertinent file and caption information (see Figure 11-16), which you can also copy to the Clipboard (very handy for getting the caption and credit text onto the page). Similar to WhatzIt, TIFFormation displays information about resolution, size, and file type of the selected image. It even has another palette that checks the images contained in the document for proper scaling versus resolution ratios to ensure correct print quality.

Note that besides Photoshop captions, TIFFormation also displays caption data from AP and Leaf Systems software.

SETUP

Pre-Fab Page Sizes

Why isn't there a button in the New Document or Document Setup dialog boxes for page orientation? You know: Portrait or

Figure 11-15
WhatzIt XTension

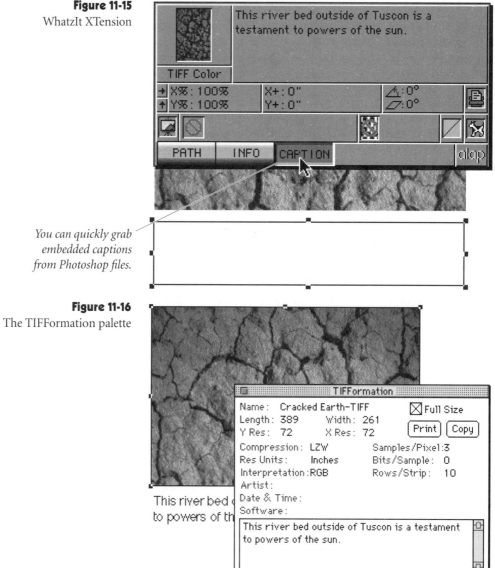

You can quickly grab embedded captions from Photoshop files.

Figure 11-16
The TIFFormation palette

Landscape. Every time we want a letter-size page set to horizontal, we have to type new numbers into the Width and Height fields. But no more: now we use the Page Sets feature of the KitchenSink XTension (see Figure 11-17).

KitchenSink adds a popup Page Sets menu to the New Document dialog box which lets you choose from page sizes that you've defined and saved. Creating a new page setup is simple: set the dialog box the way you want it and choose Add from the Page Sets popup menu. Next time you need that particular page setup, select your setting from the list.

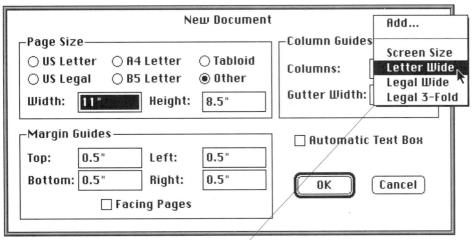

Figure 11-17
Page Sets from
Kitchen Sink

Kitchen Sink adds this customizable popup menu

PRINTING

Estimating Printing Time Accurately

"Eye of newt . . . Shorts from frog . . . Eat a Fig Newton . . . Kiss a dog!"

Nope, it don't work. We can never remember the proper incantation for calculating the amount of time required to print a document on an imagesetter. No matter how hard we try, we can never seem to get it right. Fortunately for us, there's a new XTension that takes the guesswork and hocus pocus out of the print process—it's called PStiMate-X.

PStiMate-X works like this: first, you run some PStiMate-X-generated timing tests on your PostScript printer's RIP. The tests only need be run once for each image resolution on each RIP. Once you've created your library of tests, PStiMate-X accesses them whenever you want to check a file for estimated print time.

To get an estimate of how long a document will take to print, open the file and choose PStiMate-X Time Estimation from the Utilities menu. Using the results from previously stored tests, PStiMate-X scans the file and related images to determine about how long it'll sit in your printer's RIP before a page pops out.

If you need to plan the work flow for your imagesetters, this XTension can be invaluable for getting the most out of your time and for knowing when to go to lunch!

SCALING

Scaling Images and Callouts Together

Real Life XPress Quiz No. 105: After working for two days, you've just completed that full-page map in QuarkXPress (why you did this in XPress, we'll never know). It's loaded with illustrations, arrows, and callouts. Suddenly you're told that it has to be scaled to 66 percent of its current size! What can you do, other than spend two days reworking it?

If you have to scale anything—and we mean *anything*—in XPress, you should turn to the ScaleIt XTension. It scales any object or group of objects to any available size or measurement. This includes text, pictures, lines, text attributes, gutters, and so on. You can specify scale size by percentage or any measurement system (picas, inches, etc.), and the vertical scale percentage can even be different than the horizontal percentage.

But what most people don't know is that ScaleIt (version 1.1.1 and later) has the option to try to maintain every scaled item in the same relative position, which is exactly what is needed when scaling objects with callouts (see Figure 11-18).

This option is not guaranteed to work every time (hence the word "Try" in the ScaleIt dialog box), but it can really be a lifesaver.

Note that ScaleIt is not the only XTension that provides this kind of functionality. Another cool scaling XTension is ResizeXT.

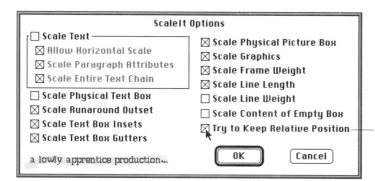

Figure 11-18
Scale It XTension dialog box

ScaleIt can keep items in their relative position

Kill Runts with SeXT

The Line Check feature in Quark's FeaturesPlus and Thing-a-ma-bob XTensions finds widows and orphans in a document. That's nice, but it doesn't find short lines at the end of a paragraph (what we call "runts"). Besides, what do you do with them when you've found them? Shortline Eliminator (SeXT) from Kytek provides an easy solution by automatically eliminating widows and orphans.

You can define your parameters in the SeXT dialog (see Figure 11-19) and SeXT does the rest: it searches your document and automatically adjusts the letter- and wordspacing of shortlined paragraphs until the problem is resolved. It also provides a report that lists every paragraph changed. Parameters include the number of characters that signal a short line, the maximum loosening and tightening values the XTension will use, and whether to use looser or tighter tracking in the event that both methods fail to eliminate the short line.

Figure 11-19
Shortline Eliminator

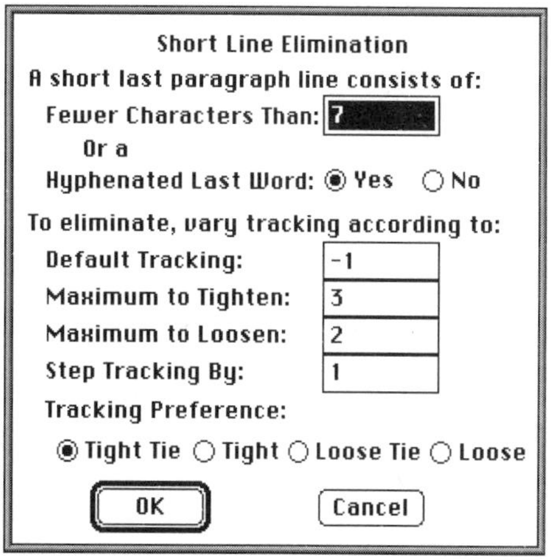

Publish and Subscribe with Text

With all the commotion about interconnectivity and database publishing, many of us overlook a very powerful data-linking tool we all have access to: Publish and Subscribe. The problem is that XPress normally only lets you subscribe to pictures from other programs. However, with the TextLinker XTension, QuarkXPress can also publish and subscribe to text. This lets you link data in your documents to other sources and programs, including Excel, Microsoft Word, FileMaker Pro, and even other QuarkXPress documents.

TextLinker adds a Publisher submenu to the Edit menu, which lets you publish or subscribe to any text edition. To subscribe to an edition, place the text cursor in the text box and choose Subscribe To (see Figure 11-20). If you're publishing a story from XPress, select the text to publish and choose Create Publisher. The Publisher Options dialog box appears, and you can choose to update the edition file each time you save your XPress document or only when you click the Send Edition Now button in the dialog box (see Figure 11-21).

As with all Publish and Subscribe data in System 7, links can be canceled at any time and still retain the current data in your layout. Note that text formatting—such as italic, bold, and so on—is often lost when subscribing to text from other programs. However, once you've applied a style sheet to the data in XPress, it retains its look when updated. Character-level adjustments will be lost, though, when the edition is updated, since an update is the same as a reimport.

FORMATTING DATA

Power Formatting with Xdata

As we said at the beginning of this chapter, XTensions are like extra drill bits for your QuarkXPress power tool. Well, if most XTensions are little drill bits that let you turn XPress into a specialized screwdriver or wrench, then Xdata turns XPress into one of those giant Caterpillar earth-movers used to make mountains into smooth highways! It shapes and formats mounds of data from spreadsheets or databases (or any other program that spits out loads o' repetitively formatted data) into beautifully styled text and images.

Xdata lets you create an example of the way you'd like each record to be formatted and then applies that formatting to every record in your imported data. You can use Xdata for anything from interoffice phone books to classified ads to catalogs.

The steps to using Xdata are simple.

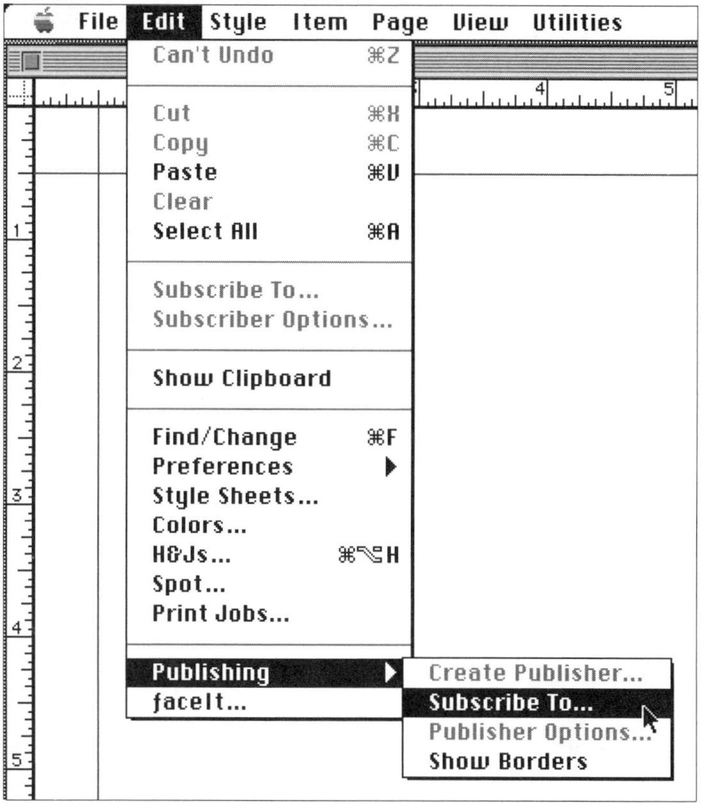

Figure 11-20
TextLinker lets you publish and subscribe text

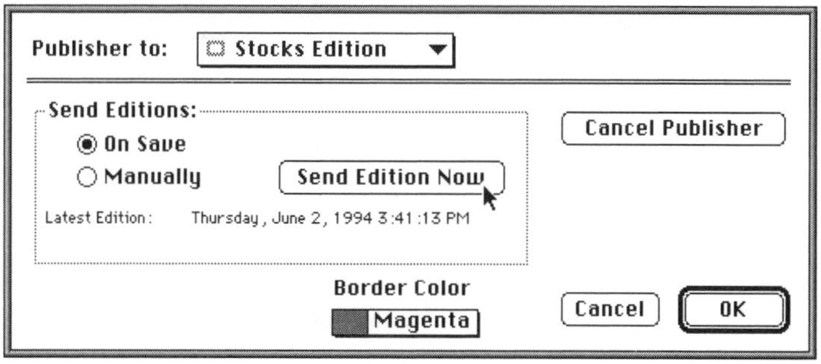

Figure 11-21
Updating an edition

1. Export the data from the spreadsheet or database.

2. Create a fully formatted prototype (example) in XPress.

3. Import the data into XPress using the Xdata menu.

Let's say the data for our real-estate publication is stored in a FileMaker Pro database (see Figure 11-22), and each record of the database contains fields containing the company, address, price, agent, headline, description, and MLS number for each house.

Figure 11-22

Data stored in a
FileMaker Pro
database

Figure 11-22

Data stored in a
FileMaker Pro
database

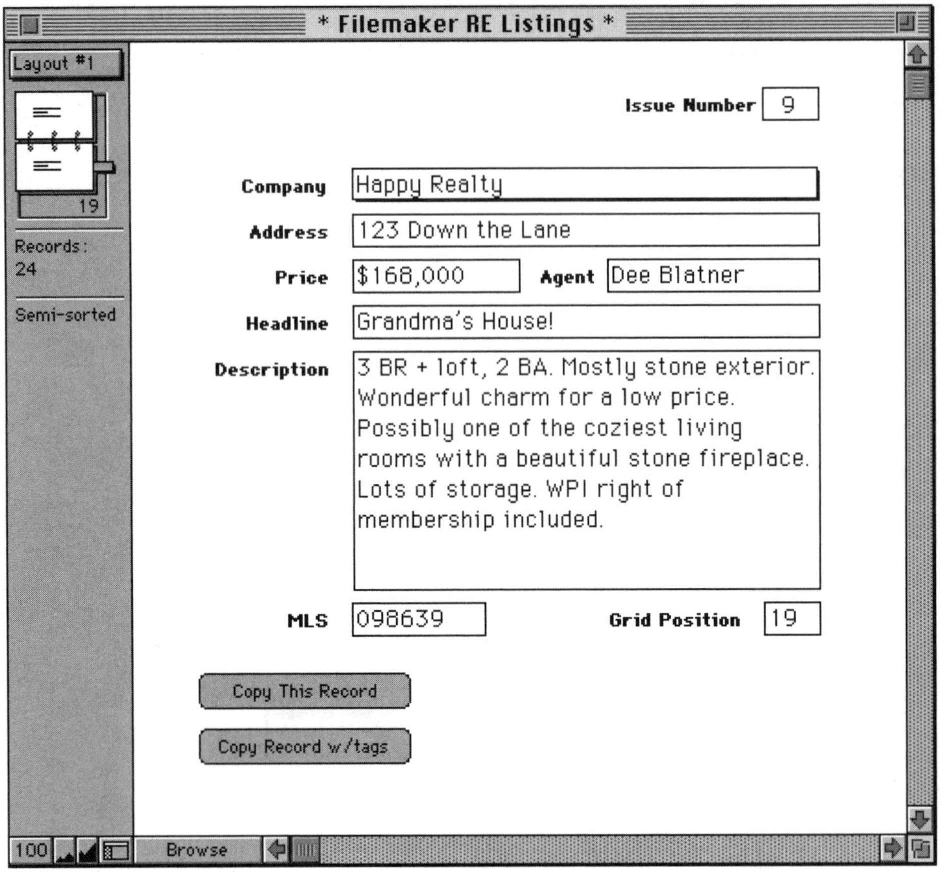

When the data in the file is exported from FileMaker Pro as comma-delimited text (Xdata recognizes most data formats, including this one), each record looks like the following.

"123 Down the Lane","$168,000","3 BR + loft, 2 BA. Mostly stone exterior. Wonderful charm for a low price. Possibly one of the coziest living rooms with a beautiful stone fireplace. Lots of storage. WPI right of membership included.","Grandma's House!","098639"

Note that we told FileMaker Pro to export only the fields we needed, and in a specific order.

The next step is to create our prototype. The first line of the prototype tells Xdata what fields to expect; the following lines show Xdata how to format the rest of the data. Note that the prototype can include fields of information in any order and can be formatted any way you want (See Figure 11-23).

PROTOTYPE FOR LEFT SIDE OF PAGE

«fields address,price,description,headline,mls
«set fn of pic 1 to mls

«**HEADLINE**» «Description» «Price» «MLS»

Figure 11-23
Xdata prototype formatting

You can format your prototype using any XPress feature, including anchored graphics.

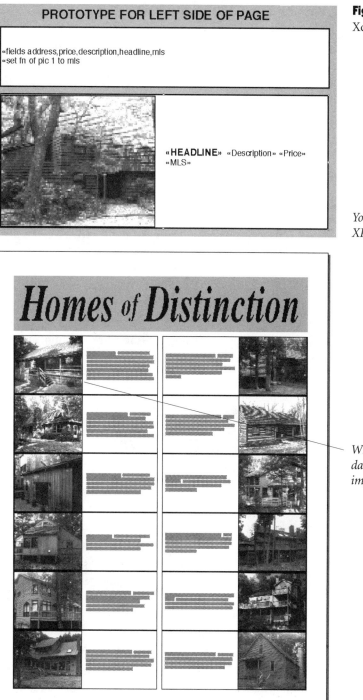

When you import the data from your database, Xdata formats the text and imports the graphics.

Delinking Xdata's Chains

After Xdata has flowed and formatted your data, all your text from the database is still in one long linked chain. If you'd like to be able to rearrange, delete, or resize some of the listings, sometimes it's best to break the linked chain into separate boxes, each retaining the data that's in it. You can use the LinkIt XTension to do this automatically for you.

Select the chain and click the third button from the bottom left on the LinkIt palette, and the chain is broken into individual text boxes. This is great for those publications that are composed of many listings with photos and descriptions, such as real estate tabloids and car ad magazines.

The final step is importing the data using the Xdata menu. The speed at which Xdata imports the information is determined by how complex the page layout is and what kind of prototype you've written. Prototypes can be very complex, including conditionals ("If there's no telephone number, then don't include this line"; or, "If the first letter of the name field is 'K' then place a star after the name") and running heads ("Put the first item tagged with 'Title' in the running head on this page"). You can even automatically import graphics; the key is to name the graphic files on disk the same as some item in your database.

Xdata from the Clipboard

Sometimes you don't want to format 100 or 1,000 records at a time with Xdata; you just want one or two. That's where the Clipboard comes in handy. People sometimes don't notice that you don't have to pull your data in from a file; rather, Xdata can read it right from the Clipboard using the Import from Clipboard item in the Xdata menu. This is also an excellent method for updating a single record.

XTend Your Styles

There's no doubt that you should keep one eye on the Measurements palette while working with text; it displays and lets you edit the current font, size, and formatting style, not to mention alignment and leading. However, to check your indents and interparagraph spacing, you still have to take a detour to the Paragraph Formats dialog box. And if someone was kind enough to apply a baseline shift to half the text in your document, you can tear your hair out trying to figure out why your baselines won't align before you think to check the Style menu (that's the only place that shows whether you've got Baseline Shift applied). Wouldn't it be great to have *all* that information in one palette?

Xstyle fits the bill, picking up where the Measurements palette leaves off: it shows you every piece of relevant information about the text you're working with, including style sheets, paragraph formatting, and character formatting, and the color, shade, scaling, and baseline shift of your type. You can edit all these fields, too, avoiding the menus and dialog boxes (see Figure 11-24).

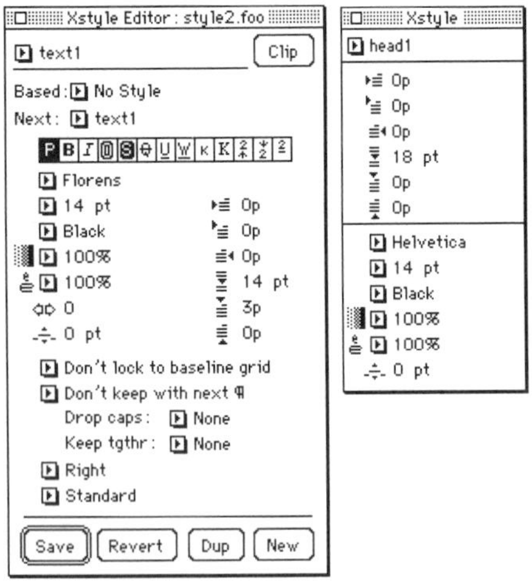

Figure 11-24
Xstyle's palettes

Xstyle's Editor palette lets you edit style sheets quickly without forcing you to go to the klunky Edit Style Sheet dialog box. About the only things you *can't* edit in this palette are the style's name, tabs, Rule Above, and Rule Below.

Get Precise with CursorPos

Some folks are clickers-and-draggers, zoom-in, and align-it-by-eye people. Other folks feel more secure if they stick to the numbers: typing in tab settings, text-box widths, and screen magnifications. If you fall into the latter category, you'll love the three-decimal-place accuracy you get with the CursorPos XTension.

CursorPos has only one purpose in life: it displays the x and y coordinates of your cursor relative to the edge of the page, the edge of the text box, or the margin (see Figure 11-25). The vertical measurement can be set so CursorPos snaps to text baseline measurements. Even if you're used to positioning things by eye, you can use this information to speed up your work and improve your pages. Here are three ways that we've used it.

Aligning baselines. Let's say you've got facing book pages that contain a number of different leading values, Space Before or Space After, maybe even extracts with varying amounts of space around them, and so on. Your art director wants every column of text to align, so you've got to play with interparagraph spacing. Typically, to do this, you pull out guides and pay attention to the rulers, zooming in and out to be as accurate as possible. Of course, when you go to the next spread you have to start all over again.

On the other hand, if you use CursorPos, you can speed up the process by staying at Fit in Window view. Position the cursor on the last line of each page, and CursorPos tells you where the baseline of each line is, so you can add space between paragraphs without doing any zooming at all. No matter how fast your machine is, the less screen redraw you do the better.

Baseline to baseline. Page designs are frequently expressed in distances from baseline to baseline. For example, "the baseline of text should be 18 points from the baseline of the head above." If the text is in one text block, you can figure this out easily. But it's not so easy when they head is in a separate text box. Of course, you could

Figure 11-25
The CursorPos palette and its popup menus

eyeball it (maybe your art director won't notice). Or you could position the text boxes at a glance with the CursorPos palette.

Text alignment. Lastly, we often find ourselves needing to find a coordinate on the page in order to format our text. For instance, in the closing of a formal letter, you want the closing, name, and title all aligned left with each other, but the longest of the three lines set at the right margin (see Figure 11-26). Instead of playing with paragraph indents or tabs through trial and error, you can try this.

1. Highlight all the closing lines and set them flush right.

2. Position your cursor at the beginning of the longest line. Note the distance from the left side of the box in the CursorPos palette (unfortunately, you may have to write it down because there's no way to copy it to the Clipboard).

3. Set the lines back to flush left and set their left indent to the number you got from CursorPos. (Note that because of some weird rounding errors, in some fonts you may have to round down the CursorPos value to the nearest hundredth of a point.)

Figure 11-26
Aligning text with CursorPos

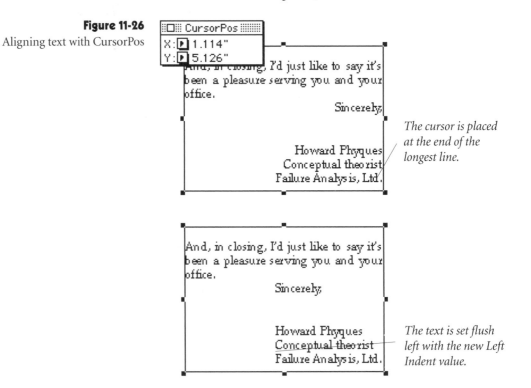

The cursor is placed at the end of the longest line.

The text is set flush left with the new Left Indent value.

older 12
VERSIONS

When software companies announce an upgraded version of a product, some people send in their money as soon as they get the news. Some people upgrade their software months after the new version is released, just to be sure that it's stable enough to use reliably. Some people, when they find software that works just the way they like, even let years go by. Other people lose the upgrade notice and are only later dragged, kicking and screaming, into taking the upgrade plunge. Even then, they complain that they were forced into it.

For whatever reason, you may be using earlier versions of QuarkXPress, or the Macintosh system software. If so, this chapter is for you.

UPGRADING
System Software

We're born proselytizers here, so we just can't help wanting to convert you to the true faith: The faith of System 7. If you're not running System 7, but you have at least five megabytes of RAM and an 80 Mb hard drive, it's time to upgrade.

Both System 7.0.1 and 7.1 have reached their final plateau of stability, so you can upgrade to either version without worrying about whether or not they're stable. (System 7.5 was in beta when

CRASHING

Make Sure You're Zapped

If you haven't made the move to version 3.1 yet, at least make sure that your version of 3.0 has been properly zapped. The first version of QuarkXPress 3.0 that came out had a bug that caused many memory problems in printing. Quark released an XTension called Zapper 2.0A which fixed the bug in a jiffy—all you need to do is drop the Zapper into your QuarkXPress folder, then launch QuarkXPress. Zapper 2.0A sets QuarkXPress to subversion (also known as a *patch level*) 3. Hold down the Option key while selecting About Quark-XPress from the File menu to see what subversion you've got.

Note that this only applies in the US. German XPress 3.0, for instance, had five zaps. Since version 3.1—and even more so since 3.3—the international and US versions have been more in sync.

we wrote this, and while it looks neat-o, we can't yet recommend that you upgrade to it, since we haven't tested the final release).

System 7.0.1 is still free to anyone with eWorld, AppleLink, or Internet ftp access, or who can find someone with the correct set of disks (see "Online Resources" in Appendix B, *Resources*). You also need the System 7 Tune-Up package.

System 7.1 was the first system software that Apple charged for, but if you belong to a user group, you can usually get a discount. It should cost less than $50. The latest—and last—release of 7.1 is version 7.1.2 with the System Update 3.0 (note that you only need the ".2" version if you have a Power Mac).

There's one thing to make sure you don't miss if you upgrade: Your existing hard disks need new disk drivers (this is software) to work properly. Your hard drive manufacturer should supply you with software to update the disks with these drivers, or you can buy it from a third party like FWB, which makes Hard Disk Toolkit. Apple's HD SC Setup software only works with Apple-branded drives, but it has the necessary driver update in it; it takes just a few seconds to upgrade your drives. Fixing the drivers typically doesn't require totally reformatting the disk (which is a real pain). Either way, you'll be sorry if you don't do it: you can have strange, unexplained crashes, and even directory damage where you actually lose files.

FILE MANAGEMENT

Too Many Files Open

The early Macintosh systems (pre-System 7) only let you have a limited number of files open at one time. This number was determined for the original Finder, and—for some obscure reason—was never raised when MultiFinder was created. Obviously, the more applications you have running at a time, the more files you have open. This is especially true because many applications open "invisible" files that you don't ordinarily know about. For example, QuarkXPress opens one file for each XTension you have available in your QuarkXPress folder, plus a file for the XPress Dictionary, XPress Hyphenation, and so on.

When you run two or more applications at a time under System 6.0.x, you may find yourself staring at warning dialog boxes that say you can't open another file, and listening to mysterious beeps when you try to open anything from the Apple menu. You can use a utility such as Fedit, Bootman, or Suitcase II (the old version, not Suitcase 2, which mysteriously dropped the feature) to increase Apple's limit. Any utility that lets you alter the boot blocks of your system should work fine. This is a very easy process. David sets his to 80. Eric and Phil, who don't believe in doing things by halves, prefer 99.

CRASHING

Mystery IIfx Bombs!

If you use a Mac IIfx and QuarkXPress 3.0, and you often have strange bombs, you might try these three tricks.

► Turn off AppleTalk.

► Make sure you're running system 6.0.7 or 6.0.8.

► Make sure that the video board is in a slot other than Slot D (they're labeled on the circuit board if you look carefully).

QuarkXPress 3.1 doesn't seem to have these problems, but you never know…

XPRESS PREFERENCES

Wordspacing or Custom Frames Are Wrong

In version 3.0, you lose all of your custom kerning pairs, frames, and other settings when you open an XPress document on another machine (say, at your service bureau) without bringing your own XPress Data file with you. Without access to the custom information in the XPress Data file, the copy of QuarkXPress that you open the document with uses its own values, which are almost certain not the same as those with which your document was created.

If you're still using QuarkXPress 3.0, make certain you include a copy of your XPress Data file when you send your documents to be imaged. Of course, if you send PostScript dumps rather than the document itself, you'll never have to worry about this, as the document contains all the information necessary to correctly print the document (except, perhaps, the fonts you need).

UPGRADING

Patching Version 3.1

Some people are still working with the first release of XPress 3.1. But Quark released some bug fixes in a minor upgrade to version 3.11. How do you know which you're using? Check the Environments dialog box (see "Your Environment" in Chapter 9, *Problems and Solutions*). This upgrader patch is on the disc. All of your files will still be readable by 3.1 versions of XPress.

CRASHING

Stop Quitting When Printing

Many service bureaus have reported problems when printing a document in XPress 3.0 and 3.1 under System 7. Many of these difficulties seem to be caused by quitting the application (XPress, in this case) before the PrintMonitor has finished printing and cleared the screen (when printing in the background).

Memory-Allocation Basics

Remember that you should increase the amount of memory allocated to XPress by selecting the program in the Finder and selecting Get Info from the file menu (or press Command-I). In fact, the only time you *don't* have to concern yourself with allocating your RAM is if you're running System 6.0.x and not running Multi-Finder: under that scenario, you can only run one program at a time, and the program that's running has all your computer's RAM available to it. However, if you're not in System 7 yet, you've got more problems that just this!

This problem was fixed in version 3.1, when the XPress Preferences file was created to replace XPress Data. Now, all those preferences, frames, hyphenation exceptions, kerning pairs, and so on are stored in individual documents (if no documents are open when you change a preference, the change gets stored in the XPress Preferences file and is applied to all subsequent new documents).

LAUNCHING
Turnkey XPress on Old Systems

In the tip "Turnkey XPress" in Chapter 1, QuarkXPress Basics, we showed how to make XPress start up automatically when you start up your Macintosh. You can do this in older systems, too, but in a slightly different way. In System 6 with MultiFinder installed, while QuarkXPress is already open and running, go to the Finder and choose Set Startup under the Special menu. Click the Opened Applications and DA's button. Every program that is open when you do this is automatically launched every time you restart your Mac. To disable this, open the applications you want automatically launched and do the above process again.

STYLE SHEETS
You Can't Replace Styles, But . . .

Whether you import styles along with text from a Microsoft Word document with the Include Style Sheets option selected, or bring them in from another QuarkXPress document by clicking the Append button in the Style Sheets dialog box, the pre-3.2 version of QuarkXPress stubbornly refuses to import styles if you've already got a style with the same name in your document. Suppose you want to replace existing styles with styles from another document? In those versions, there's no way to force QuarkXPress to replace existing settings, unless you get clever.

1. Use the Save Text item on the File menu to save your text in the XPress Tags format.

2. In the QuarkXPress document, delete all the text that you just saved.

3. Delete all the styles in the QuarkXPress document that have the same names as those you want to import or append from another document.

4. Import or append the styles from the other document. Since you've deleted all styles with duplicate names, all the styles should come in.

5. Import the text you saved in XPress Tags format back into the target document, making sure to check Include Style Sheets.

That's all there is to it. Since you saved with XPress Tags, you don't lose any local formatting with this technique. One word of warning, though. As you can never delete the "Normal" style, the only way to change "Normal" is the old-fashioned way: using the Edit Style Sheet dialog box. (This is just another reason not to use the "Normal" style.)

PRINTERS

Editing the Printer Types List

You know that long popup menu in the Page Setup dialog box that lists all the printer types that XPress knows about? Don't you find it somewhat annoying to have to scroll though all those different printers you've never heard of? Fortunately, you can delete printers from the list. If you're using version 3.3, see "Is it a PPD or PDF?" in Chapter 8, *Printing*.

However, if you're still using an earlier version, you can fake this same thing using ResEdit. The trick is to open a copy of XPress (don't work on the original) and delete the appropriate entries in the "LASR" resource. You also need to delete the *same* entries in the "LASR" resource in the XPress Preferences file.

Note that you will *corrupt* your list (and possibly QuarkXPress itself) if you later open a document that was set up to use one of the printers you deleted, so be careful with this technique. This is one of those ResEdit tips that we can't fully recommend; Quark doesn't want you modifying XPress, and you can mess up your program and your documents pretty badly so you have to re-install (but who are we to stop you?).

FILE MANAGEMENT

Opening Old Documents in New Versions

When upgrading from QuarkXPress 3.1 to 3.2 or from 3.2 to 3.3, double-clicking on a previous-version document will launch the version of XPress you just upgraded to—whether you've removed the old version of the program or not.

However, this does not work when going from QuarkXPress 3.0 to 3.1. There, you'll have to launch 3.1 manually, and use the Open command. Of course, once you make any changes and save the document in the newer version, the document then "belongs" to the newer version forevermore; you can't go back.

XPRESS TAGS

Baseline Shift Changes

If you're working with XPress Tags files created in versions of XPress prior to version 3.1, you should know that the XPress Tags filter had the baseline shift values work backwards: negative values shifted up and positive values shifted down. This has been corrected as of QuarkXPress 3.1 and the XPress Tags filter version 1.5.

Tagged text files exported from XPress using the Tags filter have the version number at the beginning. This version number tells XPress which way to push the baseline shift. Also, Mark My Words (a great utility written by Greg Swann; it's on the disc) inserts whatever version number you specify at the beginning of files it creates.

PUBLISH & SUBSCRIBE
Editions and System 6

System 6 doesn't know from edition files, which are a part of the Publish and Subscribe feature of System 7. If you have a document created in System 7 using editions, and you have to print the document from a System 6 machine, only the low-res screen preview is printed. You could replace the edition with a regular EPS graphic, but it sort of defeats the purpose of using the editions in the first place. The three morals of this story are: Plan ahead carefully and thoroughly; don't use Publish and Subscribe unless you need to; and, finally, don't use System 6 any more!

RULE BELOW/ABOVE

Trapping Text on a Paragraph Rule

If you have a paragraph rule behind some text, XPress traps text to the rule differently in version 3.0 and later versions.

In 3.0, text doesn't trap directly to a rule it's on top of. You can trap the text to the background color, but not to the rule directly.

In 3.1 and later, you *can* do this and it works fine.

TRAPPING

Same Color, Different Trap

In version 3.1, Quark introduced the Trap Information palette, which lets you set object-by-object trapping. But if you're still using QuarkXPress 3.0 and you need to set different objects of the same color to different trapping values, simply make two or more duplicate colors with different names and different trapping pair values. Black is a good example of this. You can create an overprinting black (regular black will always overprint) and a non-overprinting black. Both print on the black plate when you create color separations, but trap with other colors differently.

TRAPPING

Out-of-House Trapping Gotcha

Until version 3.2, XPress didn't save any of your automatic trapping preferences with your document. The result? If you adjusted the Trapping Preferences dialog box in version 3.0 or 3.1, and then sent that document to a service bureau, your settings were lost. If you must use one of these older versions, there are two options.

▶ Instruct your service bureau how you want trap preferences to be set.

▶ Use Quark's free Trap Preferences XTension, and make sure your service bureau does, too.

Again, this is only relevant for earlier versions of XPress (in fact, note that the Trap Preferences XTension should definitely *not* be used with version 3.2 or later). Since 3.2, this problem has been fixed and the settings are saved in the document itself.

On the other hand, no matter what version you have, all the trapping information you spec, such as trapping pairs, object-level trapping, and so on, *is* saved with the document, so you never need to worry about that.

When Your Palette Arrives in Chicago

We'll make a prediction here (Nostradamus, look out). If the font in your Measurements palette has changed to the unreadable Chicago typeface when you're working in System 7, we predict that you're not only using QuarkXPress version 3.0, but you're also using a Mac based on a 68000 chip (a PowerBook 100, Mac Plus, Classic, or SE). The solutions? Upgrade to a newer version of XPress; upgrade to a II, Centris, Performa, Quadra, or Power Mac; or use a different System.

The Death of a Server File

We all know there are bugs in every piece of software. Here's one that has caused some major problems in the past with versions of 3.0 and 3.1 of XPress.

The problem arises if you are working on a QuarkXPress file that is saved on a central file server. If that server goes down, you lose connection, or you change network drivers in the control panel, you are prevented from saving your document anywhere; you're stuck with just restarting the machine and losing your work.

There have also been reports that this sort of thing can corrupt a QuarkXPress document so badly that you can't even open it again. The moral of the story? If you use documents that are resident on a server somewhere, make sure that you're working with a newer version of the software. Or, better yet, copy the file to your own hard drive, work on it, and then copy it back to the server.

Saving Problems

If you're using version 3.1 and are crashing every now and again when you save a document, note that there's a bug in that version (it's fixed in 3.11 and later versions) that crashes XPress if you have more than one master-page item selected at the time you save. It's odd, it's uncommon, and it's fixed in all later versions.

Can't Access XPress Temporary File

An error message to the effect that you can't access the XPress Temporary file probably means that you're very low on hard disk space, although it could also mean you're running into the number-of-open-files barrier mentioned in another tip in "Too Many Open Files," earlier in this chapter.

windows
& QUARKXPRESS

It's a rare office these days that can claim a pure system environment. We have a lot of Macintoshes in our offices, but we can't ignore the Windows-based PCs that sit in dusty corners. Many of our clients work with PCs, and it's crucial that we have at least rudimentary skill with them. While almost every XPress-specific tip in this book can be applied to QuarkXPress for Windows, in this chapter we discuss how you can more easily work with Macintoshes and PCs together.

If you want more specific information about using Windows QuarkXPress itself, check out David and his co-author Bob Weibel's book, *The QuarkXPress Book, Second Edition for Windows*, which covers XPress for Windows in great detail.

FILE MANAGEMENT
Translations Versus Universal File Formats

While you can now move QuarkXPress files between Macs and PCs, there's still no such thing as a "universal" QuarkXPress document format that's identical on both platforms. Each time QuarkXPress opens a document saved on the opposite platform, it must translate the file. The file name doesn't change, but—as

Previewing DOS Names on a Macintosh

If you're using PC Exchange (included as part of System 7.5) or another PC disk mounter, you can see how a document name is going to look when it gets to the PC. First, copy it to a PC disk. Then select it in the Finder and choose Get Info from the File menu (Command-I). At the top of the dialog box, you can see the name of the file. Click on it and it switches to the eight-dot-three PC name. Click on it again and it switches back.

one Quark tech-support person puts it—"the dirty bit is on," so you should immediately save the file. And since some information gets lost (as we'll describe) or needs to be fixed when you translate files, we'd recommend you keep your cross-platform transfers to the minimum necessary to finish a job. Remember: Fewer translations equals less clean-up.

Careful with Your Naming

The file naming conventions used by the Macintosh and the PC are so different that, for some people, they become the central issue in cross-platform compatibility. Macintoshes use 31-character names, while PCs use eight characters plus three extension characters after a period (eight-dot-three). The two most dangerous traps in file naming are name size and characters within the name.

▶ **Name size.** When you move a document from the Macintosh to the PC and the name of that document is longer than eight letters or numbers (alphanumerics), the operating system (or the transfer software) generates a new name in eight-dot-three form. For instance, if you use Apple's PC Exchange software on the Macintosh, and move a document called "David's Document" to a PC floppy disk, the name comes across as "!DAVID'S.DOC".

   If you open this file in QuarkXPress for Windows and then save it again with the same name, chances are the file will return to the Macintosh with its full name. That's because PC Exchange (and other similar utilities) stores the full name inside a directory called "RESOURCE.FRK". However, if you either move the file to a disk without moving "RESOURCE.FRK" or save the file with a different name, the full name is lost.

▶ **Characters.** The only character you can't use in a Macintosh file name is a colon. That's because the Macintosh operating system uses colons internally to keep track of file paths (what files are within what folders). DOS-based systems, however, use lots of these "internal" characters for all sorts of stuff. That means you can't use spaces, question marks, asterisks, slashes, backslashes, equal signs, plus signs, or angle brackets in DOS filenames.

Because of these limitations, we reluctantly recommend that—if you have to move your files around a lot—you use the lowest common denominator for all your graphics and document names. That means only PC filenames (if you can stand it).

LIBRARIES

Transferring Libraries

We love it when the folks at Quark say things like, "You can't do that." We take it as a personal challenge. For example, Quark said, clear as a Texas sky in June, that you can't move libraries from the Macintosh to the PC. After some intense thought, sweat, and caffeine, we found that Quark really should have said, "You cannot move libraries from the Macintosh to the PC *easily*."

If you have a library that you absolutely must take from one platform to another, you can. However, it's what we call a kludge—pronounced "kloodge." (Our friend Steve Broback recently came up with the best definition of "kludge" we've heard: "It's Yiddish for 'duct tape.'" It's something you use at the last moment to fix a problem, but for which you hope there'll be a better solution soon.) The trick is in understanding what libraries really are.

A QuarkXPress library is simply an XPress document with some additional preview and labeling information. That means that you can actually open a XPress library within QuarkXPress for Windows as a document. If you move a Macintosh library to the PC, open it by either selecting "All Types *.*" in the Open dialog box or by changing the file name extension to ".QXD".

What you see is each library entry on a separate page of a big QuarkXPress document. Each page is the maximum size allowable—48 by 48 inches. If you don't see the library entry, look in the upper-left corner of the page. Now you can open a new library in QuarkXPress for Windows and use the Item tool to drag the old page items into the library, one page at a time. Of course, this is not only a pain in the lower back, but you also lose all your labels.

MENUS

Moving the View Menu

We move back and forth between the Macintosh and the PC quite a bit. And although our little brains can handle many of the differences between the two platforms, there's only so much we can take.

So whenever possible, we like to simplify our life. Here's something you can do to help in a small way: Move the View menu from where it normally is on the PC to where it is on the Macintosh.

All you have to do is use a text editor to open the "QUARK. INI" file (it's in your Windows subdirectory) and add the line "MacMenuOrder=1" somewhere in the file. Make sure it's on a line by itself, typed just like that. And make sure you do this when QuarkXPress isn't running. Then, next time you start the program, the menu order is changed.

KEYSTROKES

Macintosh Keystrokes

In the last tip we described making XPress for Window's menus more like the Macintosh version's. Here's one more modification you might want to make. If you type "MacKBCommands=1" on a line by itself (no quotes) in the "QUARK.INI" file on the PC, XPress uses Control-L to check the spelling of a word and Control-W to close the frontmost document (just like the Macintosh).

KICKER

Don't Remap Symbol Fonts

The Macintosh uses different character encoding (mapping) than Windows. However, the characters in some symbol and dingbat fonts are encoded similarly for both Macintosh and Windows. Obviously, QuarkXPress's internal character set translator only succeeds in scrambling these sorts of fonts in its attempt to map between the character sets. However, you can tell QuarkXPress for Windows not to try to remap certain fonts by adding a short bit of text to the "QUARK.INI" file in your Windows subdirectory.

Add the line, "DoNotTranslate=" followed by the names of the font(s), separated by commas with no spaces. For example: "DoNotTranslate=Carta,Sonata,ZapfDingbats" (no quotes, of course, and this would be on a line by itself).

xpress tags

Character Formats

Style	Code[1]
Plain	<P>
Bold	<B>
Italic	<I>
Outline	<O>
Shadow	<S>
Underline	<U>
Word underline	<W>
Strikethrough	</>
All caps	<K>
Small caps	<H>
Superscript	<+>
Subscript	<->
Superior	<V>
Type style of current style sheet	<$>

[1] *These codes act as toggle switches; the first time they're encountered, the format is activated. The second time, the format is deactivated. Note the similarity to formatting keystrokes.*

Style/Attribute	Code[2]	Value type or units
Typeface	<f"name">	Name of font
Size	<z#>	Points
Color	<c"name">	Name of color (the four process colors and white can be specified by C, M, Y, K, and W, without quotes, as in <cY>)
Shade	<s#>	Percentage
Horizontal scale	<h#>	Percentage
Kern next 2 characters	<k#>	¹⁄₂₀₀ em
Track	<t#>	¹⁄₂₀₀ em
Baseline shift	<b#>	Points

Paragraph Formats

Attribute	Code[3]	Value type or units
Left-align	<*L>	None
Center-align	<*C>	None
Right-align	<*R>	None
Justify	<*J>	None
Paragraph formats	<*p(#,#,#,#,#,G or g)>	Left Indent, First Line, Right Indent, Leading, Space Before, Space After, Lock to Baseline Grid (G=lock, g=don't lock)
Drop cap	<*d(chars,lines)>	Character Count and Line Count

[2] In these codes, "#" should be replaced with a number. This number can be set to the same precision as QuarkXPress's measurements (tenths, hundredths, or thousandths of a unit). The measurement units used are shown. If you replace "#" or any other code value with a dollar sign ($), QuarkXPress uses the formatting of the current style sheet.

[3] In these codes, "#" should be replaced with a measurement in points. If you replace "#" or any other code value with a dollar sign ($), XPress uses the formatting of the current style sheet. If the code requires multiple values, every value must be present and delineated by a comma.

Attribute	Code	Value type or units
Keep With Next ¶	<*kn1> or <*kn0>	1=keep with next, 0=don't keep with next
Keep Lines Together	<*kt(A)> or <*kt(start,end)>	"A"=all; start and end are number of lines
Set Tab Stops	<*t(#,#,"character")>	Position, Alignment (0=left, 1=center, 2=right, 4=decimal, 5= comma), Fill character[4]
H&J	<*h"name">	Name of H&J specification
Rule Above	<*ra(#,#,"name",#,#,#,#)>	See "Rule Below"
Rule Below	<*rb(#,#,"name",#,#,#,#)>	Width, Style (from 1–11), Name of color, Shade (percent), From Left, From Right, Offset (if you specify Offset as a percentage place a percent sign after the number)

Special Characters

Character	Code
Soft return	<\n>
Discretionary return	<\d>
Discretionary hyphen	<\h>
Indent Here	<\i>
Previous text box page #	<\2>
Current text box page #	<\3>
Next text box page #	<\4>
New column	<\c>

[4]*Align on is specified by replacing the alignment number by the character contained within quotation marks. QuarkXPress 3.3 allows two-character tab leaders.*

Character	Code
New box	`<\b>`
@	`<\@>`
<	`<\<>`
\	`<\\>`
ASCII character	`<\#decimal value>`[5]
Standard space	`<\s>`[6]
en space	`<\f>`[6]
Flex space	`<\q>`[6]
Punctuation space	`<\p>`[6]
En dash	`<\#208>`[7]
Em dash	`<\#209>`[7]
Return (new paragraph)	`<\#13>`[7]
Tab	`<\#9>`[7]
Right-aligned tab	`<\t>`

Style Sheets

Description	Code	Values
Define style sheet	@name=	Name of style sheet; follow the equal sign with definition
Use "Normal"	@$:	
Use "No Style"	@:	
Apply style sheet	@name:	Name of style sheet
Based on/ next style	@name=[S"based-on_name","next style name"] Name of based-on style sheet followed by definition	

General Codes

Code	Means . . .
`<v#>`	XPress Tags filter version number. XPress 3.2's filter is 1.60; XPress 3.3 is version 1.70.
`<e#>`	Platform number: 0=Mac, 1=Windows.

[5] Note that the number sign must precede the ASCII character value.
[6] Precede these codes with an exclamation point to make them nonbreaking. For example, `<\!s>`.
[7] You can also type type the character itself on the Macintosh.

resources

General Addresses

QuarkXPress
Quark Publishing System (QPS)
Quark Passport
QuarkLibraries
Quark Multi-Paks and Lab-Paks
Quark Inc.
1800 Grant St.
Denver, CO 80203
303/894-8888; Product Information Line: 800/788-7835

XTension of the Month Club
XPress XPerts XChange (X³)
The XChange
PO Box 270578
Fort Collins, CO 80527
800/788-7557 or 303/229-0620
Fax 303/229-9773
CompuServe: 75300,2337
America OnLine: XChange

Online Resources

We're online all of the time; between CompuServe, America Online, Prodigy (bleah!), MCIMail, and the Internet, we almost never unplug ourselves. Quark offers reasonable support through some of these services, and excellent support on others. Although Quark has their own forum on America Online, the most active XPress discussions are typically on CompuServe (even founder and vice president of R&D Tim Gill often posts to the DTP Forum). Here's where you can find them on-line.

▶ CompuServe: in the DTPForum ("Go DTPFORUM"); their email is 75140,1137 (Macintosh) or 70414,2101 (Windows).

▶ America Online: Quark forum (keyword: QUARK); e-mail to quarktech

▶ Internet: Although Quark says they don't offer support on the Internet, you can e-mail them at quarktech@aol.com.

More Internet Access

You can also find lots of material out on the Internet. However, to get at it, you have to have either an Internet account that allows "ftp" (file-transfer protocol), or a SLIP or PPP setup. (If you don't know what any of this means, you probably don't have the capability and can skip the next few paragraphs.)

Macintosh shareware and freeware, and free updates of commercialware, is found via anonymous ftp at the Internet archive *sumex-aim.stanford.edu.*. In fact, much of the shareware and freeware found on the disc bundled with this book was retrieved initially from this archive. Although the sumex-aim archive is usually totally overwhelmed (so it runs really slowly, or you can't get in) you can often find identical copies of the software on "mirror" sites that contain identical copies of the software. Our favorite is *ftp.hawaii.edu,* but you should try to find the site closest geographically to your provider or location. You can also try *mac.archive. umich.edu,* which has a slightly different set of software.

Plus, note that Apple finally put all of their software on AppleLink and eWorld (two relatively pricey services) out on the Internet. Try to ftp anonymously to get to *ftp.support.apple.com,* and transfer away!

Software

FontDownloader
Illustrator
Photoshop
Adobe Dimensions
Adobe Type Manager (ATM)
Adobe Type Reunion (ATR)
Adobe Systems Inc.*
1585 Charleston Road
PO Box 7900
Mountain View, CA 94039-7900
415/961-4400

StuffIt Deluxe
Aladdin Systems, Inc.
Deer Park Center, Suite 23A-171
Aptos, CA 95003
408/685-9175

FreeHand
PageMaker
PrePrint
TrapWise
Aldus Corporation*
411 First Avenue S., Suite 200
Seattle, WA 98104
206/622-5500

MasterJuggler
ALSoft Inc.
PO Box 927
Spring, TX 77383-0927
713/353-4090

Fontographer
Altsys Corporation
269 W. Renner Road
Richardson, TX 75080
214/680-2060

LaserWriter Font Utility
ResEdit
Apple Computer, Inc.
1 Infinite Loop
Cupertino, CA 95104
408/996-1010

Bitstream Fonts
Bitstream, Inc.
215 First Street
Cambridge, MA 02142-1270
617/497-6222

Bullets and Boxes
Caseys' Page Mill
6528 S. Oneida Court
Englewood, CO 80111
303/220-1463

Lightning Textures
Blue Sky Research
800/622-8398 or 503/222-9571

QuicKeys
CE Software
801 73rd Street
Des Moines, IA 50312
515/224-1995

ParaFont
MathType
Design Science
6475B E. Pacific Coast Highway
Suite 392
Long Beach, CA 90803
213/433-0685

We went to press before the reorganization of Aldus and Adobe was finalized.

EfiColor profiles
EfiColor Works
EfiColor Cachet
Electronics for Imaging
2855 Campus Drive
San Mateo, CA 94403
415/286-8600

Epilogue
Total Integration, Inc.
334 E. Colfax Street
Suite A
Palantine, IL 60067

Fraction Fonts
EmDash
PO Box 8256
Northfield, IL 60093
708/441-6699

DeBabelizer (full version, Lite, and Lite LE)
Equilibrium Software
475 Gate Five Road, Suite 225
Sausalito, CA 94965
415/332-4343; fax 415/332-4433

Display Typeface Collection
FontBank
2620 Central Street
Evanston, IL 60201
708/328-7370

Hard Disk Toolkit
FWB
2040 Polk St., Suite 215
San Francisco, CA 94109
415/474-8055; fax 415/474-0956

PlateMaker
In Software
2403 Conway Drive
Escondido, CA 92026
619/743-7502

Precision Imagesetter Linearization Software
Kodak Electronic Printing Systems, Inc.
164 Lexington Road
Billerica, MA 01821-3984
508/667-5550

Foreign-language fonts
Linguist's Software
206/775-2063

FontStudio
Letraset USA
40 Eisenhower Drive
Paramus, NJ 07653
201/845-6100

Enhance
Micro Frontier
7650 Hickman Road
Des Moines, IA 50322
515/270-8109

Microsoft Word
Microsoft Excel
Microsoft
1 Microsoft Way
Redmond, WA 98052-6399
206/882-8080

Super Boomerang
(part of Now Utilities)
Now Software
319 SW Washington St., 11th Floor
Portland, OR 97204
503/274-2800

Mac-in-DOS
Pacific Micro
201 San Antonio Circle, C250
Mountain View, CA 94040

Color Access
Pixel Craft
PO Box 14467
Oakland, CA 94614
800/933-0330 or 510/562-2480

DiskTop
LaserStatus
PrairieSoft
1650 Fuller Rd.
PO Box 65820
West Des Moines, IA 50265
515/225-3720

Exposure Pro
McSink
Vantage
Preferred Software, Inc.
5100 Poplar Avenue, Suite 706
Memphis, TN 38137
800/446-6393

Electronic Border Tape
EBT Frame Mover
ShadeTree Marketing
5515 N. 7th St. Suite 5144
Phoenix, AZ 85014
800/678-8848

SUM Toolbox
Suitcase (formerly from Fifth Generation)
Symantec
10201 Torre Avenue
Cupertino, CA 95014-2132
408/253-9600

LaserCheck
Advanced PostScript Error Handler
Systems of Merritt, Inc.
2551 Old Dobbin Drive East
Mobile, AL 36695
205/660-1240

Color Calibration Software
Technical Publishing Services, Inc.
2205 Sacramento
San Francisco, CA 94115
415/921-8509

Impostrip
Ultimate Technographics, Inc.
4980 Buchan St., Suite 403
Montreal, Quebec PQ H4P 1S8 Canada
514/733-1188

DeskPaint
Zedcor
4500 East Speedway, Suite 22
Tucson, AZ 86712
800/482-4567

Images with Impact
3G Graphics
114 2nd Ave. S, Suite 104
Edmonds, WA 98020
800/456-0234

User Groups

X³ (X-cubed)
The XChange
PO Box 270578
Fort Collins, CO 80527
800/788-7557 or 303/229-0620
Fax 303/229-9773
CompuServe: 75300,2337
America OnLine: XChange

QuarkXPress Users International
PO Box 170
1 Stiles Road, Suite 106
Salem, NH 03079
603/898-2822 or Fax 603/898-3393

Color-Matching Systems

Pantone
55 Knickerbock Rd.
Moonachie, NJ 07074
201/935-5500

TruMatch
25 West 43rd St., Suite 802
New York, NY 10036
212/302-9100

ANPA
Newspaper Association of America
11600 Sunrise Valley Drive
Reston, VA 22091
703/648-1367

Focoltone
Springwater House
Taffs Well, Cardiff
CF4 7QR, United Kingdom
44/222-810-962

Toyo Ink Manufacturing Co. Ltd.
3-13, 2-chome Kyobashi
Chuo-ku, Tokyo 104
81/3-2722-5721

Magazines and Publications

PostScript Language Reference Manual
PostScript Language Program Design
PostScript Language Tutorial
   and Cookbook
(also known as the Red, Green,
and Blue books)
Addison-Wesley Publishing
6 Jacob Way
Reading, MA 01867
617/944-3700

Digital Prepress Book
Agfa Compugraphic
200 Ballardvale Street
Wilmington, MA 01887
508/658-5600

MacWeek
Coastal Associates Publishing Company
PO Box 5821
Cherry Hill, NJ 08034
609/461-2100

Design Tools Monthly
2111–30th St., Suite H
Boulder, CO 80301
303/444-6876, fax 303/440-3641

Step-By-Step Electronic Design
Dynamic Graphics
6000 N. Forest Park Drive
Peoria, IL 61614-3592
309/688-8800

The Form of the Book
Hartley & Marks, Inc.
79 Tyee Drive
Point Roberts, WA 98281

U&lc
International Typeface Corporation
2 Hammarskjold Plaza
New York, NY 10017
212/371-0699

Macworld
Macworld Communications, Inc.
501 Second Street
San Francisco, CA 94107
800/234-1038

Before and After
PageLab
331 J Street, Suite 150
Sacramento, CA 95814-9671

How To Boss Your Fonts Around
Learning PostScript
The Little Mac Book (also for PCs)
The Mac is not a typewriter (also for Windows)
The Photoshop Wow! Book (Mac and Windows)
The QuarkXPress Book (Mac and Windows)
QuarkXPress Visual Quickstart Guide
Real World FreeHand 4
Real World Scanning and Halftones
. . . and many, many more
Peachpit Press
2414 Sixth St.
Berkeley, CA 94710
800/283-9444 or 510/548-4393; Fax: 510/548-5991
Internet: orders@peachpit.com or info@peachpit.com

Publish!
501 Second Street
San Francisco, CA 94107
800/274-5116

QuarkXPress Unleashed
Random House Electronic Publishing
400 Hahn Road
Westminster, MD 21157

Seybold Report on Desktop Publishing
Seybold Publications
PO Box 644
Media, PA 19063
215/565-2480

MacUser
Ziff-Davis Publishing Company
950 Tower Lane, 18th Floor
Foster City, CA 94404

index

The Future is Now

We hear it all the time: "Hey! Where do you come up with all those cool tips?"

As we said back in the preface, we cull tips from all over the place, but the most valuable source for tips is you. If you have great tips, tricks, or techniques that make your life with XPress better, let us know. We'll act as a filtering conduit, gathering tips from all over the world, and passing the *crème de la crème* back to you.

If you have tips, comments on the book (we're always trying to make it better), or you've found something wrong (yes, we admit to imperfection), you can reach David Blatner at the following addresses. We look forward to hearing from you!

1619 Eighth Avenue N
Seattle, WA 98109-3007
Fax 206/285-0308
CompuServe: 72647,3302
America Online and AppleLink: Parallax1
Internet: parallax1@aol.com *or* david@moo.com

Colophon

Text and Typing

We entered the text in Microsoft Word, and tagged it using styles exported from QuarkXPress (see "Exporting Styles to Word" in Chapter 5, *Copy Flow*). However, because the typefaces the design called for aren't the easiest to see on the screen, we re-defined the Microsoft Word styles entirely differently (see "Don't Worry About Word Styles" in Chapter 5, *Copy Flow*).

Finally, we created the table of contents using the VisionContents XTension from Vision's Edge Software, and generated the index painstakingly by hand.

Artwork and Pages

We created all the artwork in QuarkXPress, Adobe Illustrator, Adobe Photoshop, and Aldus FreeHand. For screen shots, we used Baseline's Exposure Pro and then converted the file to the TIFF format with Zedcor's DeskPaint or Adobe Photoshop. To be efficient, we saved and labeled each figure in a library (one library per chapter).

Body text is set in Adobe Minion and Minion Italic. Heads are ITC Kabel Black and Adobe Minion Black. Chapter numbers are set in Brian Wu's rendition of Neuland.

Equipment

We used a variety of equipment in producing this book, including a Macintosh Quadra 650, Power Mac 6100, and Macintosh IIcx, and an Apple LaserWriter IINTX and Pro 630. David uses a Super-Mac SuperMatch 17•T monitor with a Thunder II card. He also uses Hewlett-Packard IIc and IIcx scanners. Color pages were proofed on a SuperMac ProofPositive printer.

Output

We sent the pages as PostScript dumps to be output as imposed film to Consolidated Printers of Berkeley, California; they also printed this book. The color pages and CD-ROM art were output to film at Seattle Imagesetting on a Linotronic 330 using HQS screening. The book is printed on 50# Claris Opaque. The CD-ROM was premastered at 21st Century Media, and duplicated and silkscreened at Technicolor.

More from Peachpit Press

Camera Ready with QuarkXPress
Cyndie Kopfenstein

A practical guide with a template disk for creating direct-to-press documents using XPress. The disk of QuarkXPress templates makes it easy for you to create postcards, brochures and other common documents. $35.00 *(206 pages)*

Everyone's Guide to Successful Publications
Elizabeth Adler

This comprehensive reference book pulls together all the information essential to developing and producing printed materials that will get your message across. Packed with ideas, practical advice, examples, and hundreds of photographs and illustrations, it discusses planning the printed piece, writing, design, desktop publishing, preparation for printing, and distribution. $28.00 *(412 pages)*

Desktop Publisher's Survival Kit
David Blatner

Here is a book that provides insights into desktop publishing on the Macintosh: troubleshooting print jobs, working with color, scanning, and selecting fonts. A disk containing 12 top desktop publishing utilities, 400K of clip art, and two fonts is included. $22.95 *(176 pages)*

Four Colors/One Image
Mattias Nyman

Find step-by-step procedures and detailed explanations on how to reproduce and manipulate color images using Photoshop, QuarkXPress and Cachet. A terrific, invaluable resource for those who need high-quality color output. Winner of the 1994 Benjamin Franklin Award (computer book category). $18.00 *(84 pages)*

How to Boss Your Fonts Around
Robin Williams

This book will answer all your Macintosh font questions. What is a screen font, an outline font, a resident font, a down–loadable font? What is ATM? How do you install fonts, use Suitcase or MasterJuggler, avoid font ID conflicts and make sure your fonts print at a service bureau? Written in a friendly style by the author of the bestselling *The Little Mac Book*. $12.95 *(120 pages)*

The Illustrator 5.0/5.5 Book
Deke McClelland

Experienced Illustrator users and novices alike will learn many helpful tips and techniques about this high-powered graphics program. You'll find information that will help you make best use of the new features of Illustrator 5.5. $29.95 *(660 pages)*

Illustrator Illuminated, 2nd edition
Clay Andres

Illustrator Illuminated uses full-color graphics to show how professional artists use Illustrator to create a variety of styles and effects. Each chapter shows the creation of a specific illustration from concept through completion. Additionally, it covers using Illustrator in conjunction with Adobe Streamline and Photoshop. Covers the latest features of Illustrator 5.5. $27.95 *(200 pages)*

Jargon: An Informal Dictionary of Computer Terms
Robin Williams with Steve Cummings

Finally! A book that explains over 1,200 of the most useful computer terms in a way that readers can understand. This book is a straightforward guide that not only defines computer-related terms but also explains how and why they are used. Covers the Mac and PC worlds. $22.00 *(688 pages)*

The Little QuicKeys Book
Steve Roth and Don Sellers

This handy guide to CE Software's QuicKeys 2.0 explores the QuicKeys key-sets and the different libraries QuicKeys creates for each application; shows how to link together functions and extensions; and provides lots of useful macros. $18.95 *(288 pages)*

The Macintosh Bible, 5th Edition
Edited by Darcy DiNucci

This classic reference book for the Macintosh, is now completely updated. *The Macintosh Bible, 5th Edition* is crammed with tips, tricks, and shortcuts that cover the most current software and hardware. It has been redesigned and edited to make *The Macintosh Bible, 5th Edition* the most comprehensive overview of the Macintosh ever published. New chapters cover multimedia, children's software, PowerPCs, GX fonts and more. $30.00 *(1,165 pages)*

The Macintosh Bible CD-ROM
Edited by Jeremy Judson

A dazzling array of special goodies, featuring more than 600 MB of utilities, games, sounds, video clips, digitized photos, clip art, fonts, and demos. Also includes selections from Peachpit books in Acrobat format. $25.00 *(CD-ROM)*

The Macintosh Bible/CD-ROM Combo
Save when you buy *The Macintosh Bible* and *The Macintosh Bible CD-ROM* bundle. $42.00 *(book and CD-ROM)*

The Macintosh Bible "What Do I Do Now?" Book, 3rd Edition
Charles Rubin

Completely updated, this bestseller covers just about every sort of basic problem a Mac user can encounter. The book shows the error message exactly as it appears on screen, explains the problem (or problems) that can produce the message, and discusses what to do. For beginners and experienced users. $22.00 *(352 pages)*

The Non-Designer's Design Book
Robin Williams

This book is for anyone who needs to design, but who has no background or formal training in the field. Follow these basic principles and your work will look more professional. This highly popular book is full of practical design exercises. $14.95 *(144 pages)*

PageMaker 5: Visual QuickStart Guide
Webster and Associates

Here's an ideal book for new users and for those who want to use the latest features of PageMaker 5. Learn the powerful innovations through an easy, right-brained approach that shows you how to get the most out of PageMaker. $13.95 *(234 pages)*

Peachpit's PageMaker 5 Companion
Robin Williams
with Vicki Calkins and Barbara Sikora

Find out why this innovative, comprehensive reference book is a "must-have" for both novice and experienced desktop publishers. You'll discover quick and concise answers to any PageMaker question with numerous sidebars, quotes, and real-life wisdom from bestselling author Robin Williams. $34.95 *(964 pages)*

Photoshop 3: Visual QuickStart Guide
Elaine Weinmann and Peter Lourekas

The author of our award-winning *QuarkXPress 3.2: Visual QuickStart Guide* does it again. This is an indispensable guide for Mac users who want to get started in Photoshop but don't like to read long explanations. The QuickStart way focuses on illustrated, step-by-step examples that cover how to use masks, filters, colors, the new features of Photoshop 3, and more. $18.00 *(264 pages)*

 For a complete list of Peachpit Press titles call 1-800-283-9444 and request our latest catalog.

The Photoshop Wow! Book (Mac Edition)
Linnea Dayton and Jack Davis

This book is really two books in one: an easy-to-follow, step-by-step tutorial of Photoshop fundamentals and over 150 pages of tips and techniques for getting the most out of Photoshop version 2.5. Full color throughout, *The Photoshop Wow! Book* shows how professional artists make the best use of Photoshop. Includes a disk containing Photoshop filters and utilities. $35.00 *(208 pages, includes disk)*

Protect Your Macintosh
Bruce Schneier

A hands-on guide that discusses all aspects of Macintosh security: backups, viruses, data protection, encryption, network security, and physical security. You'll find product reviews that can help you avert or recover from disaster. $23.95 *(350 pages)*

The QuarkXPress Book, 4th Edition (Mac)
David Blatner and Eric Taub

This is the highest rated, most comprehensive, and best-selling QuarkXPress book ever published. Now totally updated to cover the newest version, this book is made for easy access, including a handy tear-out keystroke shortcut card. You'll find valuable information on XTensions, Efi color, AppleEvent scripting and more. Winner of the 1991 Benjamin Franklin Award (computer book category). $29.95 *(784 pages)*

QuarkXPress 3.3:
Visual QuickStart Guide (Mac Edition)
Elaine Weinmann

Winner of the 1992 Benjamin Franklin Award, this book is a terrific way to get introduced to QuarkXPress in just a couple of hours. Lots of illustrations and screen shots make each feature of the program absolutely clear. This book is helpful to both beginners and intermediate QuarkXPress users. $15.95 *(240 pages)*

Real World FreeHand 4
Olav Martin Kvern

The ultimate insider's guide to FreeHand, this authoritative and entertaining book first lays out the basics, then concentrates on advanced techniques and the new features of FreeHand 4. $29.95 *(632 pages)*

Real World Scanning and Halftones
David Blatner and Steve Roth

Master the digital halftone process—from scanning images to tweaking them on your Mac to imagesetting them. Learn about optical character recognition, gamma control, sharpening, PostScript halftones, Photo CD and image-manipulating applications like Photoshop and PhotoStyler. $24.95 *(296 pages)*

Silicon Mirage
Steve Aukstakalnis and David Blatner

Silicon Mirage provides an easily understandable explanation of the "virtual senses" already possible, the broad array of fields where virtual reality is having an impact, and the breathtaking horizons yet to be discovered. $15.00 *(300 pages)*

ZAP! How your computer can hurt you—and what you can do about it
Don Sellers

At last, a book that tackles the critical issues of computer-related health from A to Z. This unusual book suggest hundreds of remedies and resources to help you cope with the information age. There's information on everything from eyestrain to pregnancy to carpal tunnel and back problems. *ZAP!* helps you work smarter—and healthier. $12.95 *(150 pages)*

UPS Ground orders arrive within 10 days on the West Coast and within three weeks on the East Coast. UPS Blue orders arrive within two working days anywhere in the U.S., provided we receive a fax or a phone call by 11 a.m. Pacific Time

Order Form

to order, call:
(800) 283-9444 or (510) 548-4393 or (510) 548-5991 (fax)

Qty	Title	Price	Total

Shipping	First Item	Each Additional		
			Subtotal	
UPS Ground	$ 4	$ 1	8.25% Tax (CA only)	
UPS Blue	$ 8	$ 2		
Canada	$ 6	$ 4	Shipping	
Overseas	$14	$14	**T O T A L**	

Name

Company

Address

City   State   Zip

Phone   Fax

❑ Check enclosed   ❑ Visa   ❑ MasterCard   ❑ AMEX

Company purchase order #

Credit card   Exp. Date

What other books would you like us to publish?

Please tell us what you thought of this book:

Peachpit Press • 2414 Sixth Street • Berkeley, CA • 94710

Demo XTensions on disc

AdTracker™ 1.0.1 demo
Assassin 1.0.2 demo
AutoLib 1.1 demo
AutoXTract™ 1.0.1 demo
Azalea Barcode demo
Batch Print™ demo
BoxStyles™ demo
CapSize 1.0 demo
Catavert demo
Color Usage 2.0 demo
ColorChange 1.0.3 demo
Copy & Apply 1.0 demo
CopySet™ 1.0.5 demo
CopyStyle demo
Crop&RegIt demo
Crops XT demo
Doug demo
EDGAR Filter demo
Exposé 1.0.1 demo
FaceIt demo
fcsPress 1.0.3 demo
fcsPrint 3.1.5 demo
fcsTableMaker 2.0.2 demo
FlexScale 1.0.5 demo
Fontasy 1.0 demo
Footnote demo
Grid Master 1.0 demo
Guide Master 1.0 demo
HyphenSet 1.0 demo
Image Editor demo
IndeXTension 3.1.5 demo
INposition demo
INpositionLite demo
ItemStyles demo
JobSlug 1.0 demo
KerningPalette demo
KitchenSink™ demo

Layer It! demo
LayerManager™ II demo
LineCount QXP demo
LinkIt demo
Man Ed XT 3.2 (Gatherer) demo
MarkIt demo
MarkzTools1.2demo
MasterMenus™ 1.0.5 demo
Missing Link 1.0.4 demo
MS Word Dos import demo
Navigator XT 2.0.1 demo
Nouveau II demo
OverMatter QXP (3.2)
OverrideSeps 1.0 demo
PageCopy 1.0 demo
PageShot 1.1 demo
PartialPrints™ 1.0 demo
Picture Dæmon 1.0 demo
Picture Tools 1.1.1 demo
PictureMaster™ 2.0 demo
PlaceMat demo
Polygons demo
PressMarks™ 1.0.6k demo
Preview Editor 2.0.1 demo
Pricer XT 1.0 demo
Printer's Spreads demo XT
PrintIt™ demo
PrintMaster demo
Puzzlemaker demo
RedLining QXP
RefleXTion 1.0 demo
Resize XT 2.0.3 demo
ScaleIt™ demo
Scanning Parameters QXP
ScriptIt™ demo
Shadow Master 1.0 demo
Short Line Elimination demo

StoryEditor QXP for 3.2
Style™ demo
Stylin' 1.0.1 demo
SXetch Pad™ (PPC) demo
SXetch Pad™ demo
Tab Grabber™ demo
Tableworks Plus demo
Tableworks® SC (3.2) demo
TeXT Tools 2.0.1 demo
Text Grabber™ demo
TextLinker XT
TeXTractor 1.0.7 demo
TheGrabberXT™
Thesaurus reX 1.0.2 demo
TIFFormation 1.0 demo
TimeKeeper demo
TimeStamp 1.1 demo
Touch™ 1.0 demo
Verbaytum 1.0.1 demo
Vertical Justification Demo
Vision Contents 1.0.1 demo
Vision Utilities 1.0.1 demo
WhatzIt™ demo
WordPerfect Dos Import demo
Xdata 2.5 demo
XFlow demo
XNotes™ 1.0.1 demo
XPreview demo
XReference 1.0 demo
XState2.2 demo
Xstyle 1.5 demo
Xtags 1.1 demos
XTend demo
ƒaceIt™ demo
ΔDemoRescue

Free XTensions
!Son of Bob (3.1)
Bob (3.1)
Bobzilla Facelift
Bobzilla XT*
Bring'em Back
Calibration XT v3.25
ChangeCase
ChangeCase Pro QXP
ChangeIt
Click XT*
Color Tables
ColorPick 1.0.2
ColorPrefs
ColorSpy 1.0.1
CopyDesk XTLite
Default settings updater
DocStamp™ 1.01
Easel 1.0
fcsAngles
FeaturesPlus (3.1)
GuideLiner 1.0
LaserSelect (3.2 & earlier)
Lepton BoxSwitch™
Macintosh XTLite
MarxWare
More Boxes
Notes XT
Nudger™
PasteIt
PiXize XT
PM Import filter
Power Macintosh XTLite
Prepare for Service Bureau (3.1)
Protab
ProTag
PS Printing Patch (3.3) folder
QuarkXPress® 3.2 Patcher
QuickFont 1.0.1
QuickOpen
freshIt

Save/Stamp (3.1)
Scale Text (3.1)
ScaleLock 1.0.1
Scaling Clicks XT
ScriptMenu XT
Sounds 1.3.1 (3.0/3.1)
SpeedOpen 1.2
Spot 1.0.2
Stars&Stripes™ 1.0
Story Stats
StoryChaser 1.1.2
StoryLock
Superior to Super 1.0b1 XTen
SXetch Pad Viewer
Thing-a-ma-Bob™ 1.01
Trap Preferences (3.1)
Typesetting Marks XT
UngroupAll
Yomueigo XT (3.1J)
Zoom XT

Shareware/ Freeware
Add/Strip
Cat o' Seven Tails
Clip 'n' Save
Compact Pro 1.50
Disinfectant 3.5
DPI Calculator
Graphic Nerd-DPI/LPI
Mark My Words 1.0 demo
MungeImage
Pairing Knife 1.0
PixelFlipper
PixPex
PM2LIN
PopChar
QX tags to RTF
Sep102
Shane the Plane 1.0.3
Shane the Plane demo

ShawBerry
SmartKeys 2.1
Swan Stuff
theTypeBook v3.26
Torquemada the Inquisitor 1.1.0
Torquemada's Ghost
USPS Postal Modern Art
WindowShade 1.2
Keywords & Annotation
PicturePlacer Utility
Schizo!
Unity
McSink V7.0

Commercial Software
Adobe Acrobat full installer
Adobe Type Manager
Adobe Type Reunion
AppleScript 1.1 system
AppleScript Editor
DeBabelizer Lite LE

Demo Software
TRUMATCH™ ColorPrinter demo
Quark Publishing System demo
QuarkXPress for Macintosh demo
Demo XTensions
FaceIt*
IndeXTension
INpositionLite
Kitchen Sink*
LayerManager II*
ScaleIt*
SXetchPad
TableWorks Plus
VisionContents
Xdata
Xstyle

...and 99 more!
See previous page for list

s Applescripts, QuickTime movies, Clip art from 3G Graphics, Artbeats, and T/Maker!

ish magazine's 10 most valuable XTensions